DATE DUE

			PRINTED IN U.S.A.

SOMETHING ABOUT THE AUTHOR®

Something about
the Author *was named
an "Outstanding
Reference Source"
the highest honor given
by the American
Library Association
Reference and Adult
Services Division.*

ISSN 0276-816X

something ABOUT THE AUTHOR®

Facts and Pictures about Authors
and Illustrators of Books for Young People

EDITED BY
DIANE TELGEN

VOLUME 71

Gale Research Inc. • DETROIT • WASHINGTON, D.C. • LONDON

STAFF

Editor: Diane Telgen

Associate Editor: Elizabeth A. Des Chenes

Senior Editor: James G. Lesniak

Sketchwriters: Sonia Benson, Kathleen J. Edgar, Marie Ellavich, David M. Galens, James F. Kamp, Denise E. Kasinec, Thomas Kozikowski, Margaret Mazurkiewicz, Mark F. Mikula, Michelle M. Motowski, Tom Pendergast, Mary K. Ruby, Pamela L. Shelton, Kenneth R. Shepherd, Deborah A. Stanley, and Polly A. Vedder

Research Manager: Victoria B. Cariappa

Research Supervisor: Mary Rose Bonk

Editorial Associates: Reginald A. Carlton, Clare Collins, Andrew Guy Malonis, and Norma Sawaya

Editorial Assistants: Mike Avolio, Patricia Bowen, Rachel A. Dixon, Shirley Gates, Sharon McGilvray, and Devra M. Sladics

Production Director: Mary Beth Trimper

External Production Assistant: Mary Kelley

Art Director: Cynthia Baldwin

Keyliners: Nick Jakubiak and C. J. Jonik

 This book is printed on acid-free paper that meets the minimum requirements of American National Standard for Information Sciences—Permanence Paper for Printed Library Materials, ANSI Z39.48-1984.

Library of Congress Catalog Card Number 72-27107

ISBN 0-8103-2281-1 ISSN 0276-816X

Printed in the United States of America.

Published simultaneously in the United Kingdom by Gale Research International Limited
(An affiliated company of Gale Research Inc.)

10 9 8 7 6 5 4 3 2 1

Contents

Introduction

Something about the Author (*SATA*) is an ongoing reference series that deals with the lives and works of authors and illustrators of children's books. *SATA* includes not only well-known authors and illustrators whose books are widely read, but also those less prominent people whose works are just coming to be recognized. This series is often the only readily available information source on emerging writers or artists. You'll find *SATA* informative and entertaining whether you are a student, a librarian, an English teacher, a parent, or simply an adult who enjoys children's literature for its own sake.

What's Inside SATA

SATA provides detailed information about authors and illustrators who span the full time range of children's literature, from early figures like John Newbery and L. Frank Baum to contemporary figures like Judy Blume and Richard Peck. Authors in the series represent primarily English-speaking countries, particularly the United States, Canada, and the United Kingdom. Also included, however, are authors from around the world whose works are available in English translation. The writings represented in *SATA* include those created intentionally for children and young adults as well as those written for a general audience and known to interest younger readers. These writings cover the entire spectrum of children's literature, including picture books, humor, folk and fairy tales, animal stories, mystery and adventure, science fiction and fantasy, historical fiction, poetry and nonsense verse, drama, biography, and nonfiction.

Obituaries are also included in *SATA* and are intended not only as death notices but as concise views of people's lives and work. Additionally, each edition features newly revised and updated entries for a selection of *SATA* listees who remain of interest to today's readers and who have been active enough to require extensive revision of their earlier biographies.

Two Convenient Indexes

In response to suggestions from librarians, *SATA* indexes no longer appear in each volume, but are included in alternate (odd-numbered) volumes of the series, beginning with Volume 57.

SATA continues to include two indexes that cumulate with each alternate volume: the Illustrations Index, arranged by the name of the illustrator, gives the number of the volume and page where the illustrator's work appears in the current volume as well as all preceding volumes in the series; the Author Index gives the number of the volume in which a person's Biographical Sketch or Obituary appears in the current volume as well as all preceding volumes in the series.

The Author Index also includes references to authors and illustrators who appear in Gale's *Yesterday's Authors of Books for Children, Children's Literature Review,* and the *Something about the Author Autobiography Series.*

Easy-to-Use Entry Format

Whether you're already familiar with the *SATA* series or just getting acquainted, you will want to be aware of the kind of information that an entry provides. In every *SATA* entry the editors attempt to give as complete a picture of the person's life and work as possible. A typical entry in *SATA* includes the following clearly labeled information sections:

- *PERSONAL:* date and place of birth and death, parents' names and occupations, name of spouse, date of marriage, and names of children, educational institutions attended, degrees received, religious and political affiliations, hobbies and other interests.

- *ADDRESSES:* complete home, office, and agent's address.

- *CAREER:* name of employer, position, and dates for each career post; military service.

- *MEMBER:* memberships and offices held in professional and civic organizations.

- *AWARDS, HONORS:* literary and professional awards received.

- *WRITINGS:* title-by-title chronological bibliography of books written and/or illustrated, listed by genre when known; lists of other notable publications, such as plays, screenplays, and periodical contributions.

- *ADAPTATIONS:* a list of films, television programs, plays, and other media which have been adapted from the author's work.

- *WORK IN PROGRESS:* description of projects in progress.

- *SIDELIGHTS:* a biographical portrait of the author's development, either directly from the person—and often written specifically for the *SATA* entry—or gathered from diaries, letters, interviews, or other published sources.

- *FOR MORE INFORMATION SEE:* references for further reading.

- *EXTENSIVE ILLUSTRATIONS:* photographs, movie stills, manuscript samples, book covers, and other interesting visual materials supplement the text.

How a SATA Entry Is Compiled

A *SATA* entry progresses through a series of steps. If the biographee is living, the *SATA* editors try to secure information directly from him or her through a questionnaire. From the information that the biographee supplies, the editors prepare an entry, filling in any essential missing details with research and/or telephone interviews. When necessary, the author or illustrator is sent a copy of the entry to check for accuracy and completeness.

If the biographee is deceased or cannot be reached by questionnaire, the *SATA* editors examine a wide variety of published sources to gather information for an entry. Biographical and bibliographic sources are consulted, as are book reviews, feature articles, published interviews, and material sometimes obtained from the biographee's family, publishers, agent, or other associates. Entries compiled entirely from secondary sources are marked with an asterisk (*).

We Welcome Your Suggestions

We invite you to examine the entire *SATA* series, starting with this volume. Please write and tell us if we can make *SATA* even more helpful to you. Send comments and suggestions to: The Editor, *Something about the Author,* Gale Research Inc., 835 Penobscot Bldg., Detroit, Michigan 48226.

Acknowledgments

Grateful acknowledgment is made to the following publishers, authors, and artists whose works appear in this volume.

CAROL ADORJAN. Cover of *The Cat Sitter Mystery,* by Carol Adorjan. Copyright © 1973 by Carol Adorjan. Reprinted by permission of Avon Books, New York./ Cover of *That's What Friends Are For,* by Carol Adorjan. Reprinted by permission of Scholastic, Inc./ Photograph by William Dormin, courtesy of Carol Adorjan.

SANDY ASHER. Cover of *Daughters of the Law,* by Sandy Asher. Copyright © 1980 by Sandy Fenichel Asher. Cover illustration by Michael Garland. Reprinted by permission of Beaufort Books, Inc./ Jacket of *Everything Is Not Enough,* by Sandy Asher. Copyright © 1987 by Sandy Asher. Used by permission of Delacorte Press, a division of Bantam Doubleday Dell Publishing Group, Inc./ Illustration from *Teddy Teabury's Peanutty Problems,* by Sandy Asher. Dell, 1989. Text copyright © 1989 by Sandy Asher. Illustrations copyright © 1989 by Bob Jones. Reprinted by permission of Dell Publishing, a division of Bantam Doubleday Dell Publishing Group, Inc./ Photograph courtesy of Sandy Asher.

AVI. Cover of *Captain Grey,* by Avi. Copyright © 1977 by Avi Wortis. Cover illustration by George Gaadt. Reprinted by permission of Pantheon Book, a division of Random House, Inc./ Cover of *Night Journeys,* by Avi. Copyright © 1979 by Avi Wortis. Cover illustration by Ted Hanke. Reprinted by permission of Pantheon Books, a division of Random House, Inc./ Cover of *S.O.R. Losers,* by Avi. Avon Books, 1986. Copyright © 1984 by Avi Wortis. Cover illustration by Tom Newsom. Reprinted by permission of Avon Books, New York./ Cover of *The Fighting Ground,* by Avi. Harper Trophy, 1987. Copyright © 1984 by Avi. Cover art copyright © 1987 by Michael Garland. Cover copyright © 1987 by Harper & Row, Publishers, Inc. Reprinted by permission of HarperCollins Publishers./ Jacket of *The Man Who Was Poe,* by Avi. Copyright © 1989 by Avi. Jacket painting copyright © 1989 by Ted Lewin. Reprinted by permission of Orchard Books, New York./ Cover of *Nothing But the Truth,* by Avi. Copyright © 1991 by Avi. Reprinted by permission of Orchard Books, New York./ Photograph by David Gullette.

JUDY BAER. Cover of *Lost And Found,* by Judy Baer./ Photograph courtesy of Judy Baer.

ANNE BAILEY. Jacket of *Scars,* by Anne Bailey. Jacket illustration by John Raynes. Reprinted by permission of Faber and Faber Ltd./ Photograph courtesy of Anne Bailey.

JOHN D. BAINES. Photograph courtesy of John D. Baines.

BARBARA BEIRNE. Photograph courtesy of Barbara Beirne.

NEAL BERNARDS. Photograph courtesy of Neal Bernards.

DON BOLOGNESE. Illustration by Don Bolognese from *All Upon a Stone,* by Jean Craighead George. Copyright © 1971 by Jean Craighead George. Illustrations copyright © 1971 by Don Bolognese. Reprinted by permission of HarperCollins Publishers./ Illustration by Don Bolognese and Elaine Raphael from *Letters to Horseface,* by F.N. Monjo. Text copyright © 1975 by Ferdinand Monjo & Louise L. Monjo. Illustrations copyright © 1975 by Don Bolognese and Elaine Raphael. Used by permission of Viking Penguin, a division of Penguin Books USA Inc.

MARC BRANDEL. Jacket of *The Mine of Lost Days,* by Marc Brandel. Copyright © 1974 by Marc Brandel. Jacket illustration by John Verling. Reprinted by permission of HarperCollins Publishers./ Cover of *The Three Investigators in the Mystery of the Rogues' Reunion,* by Marc Brandel. Copyright © 1985 by Random House, Inc. Cover art by Bob Adragna. Reprinted by permission of Random House, Inc.

JAN BRETT. Illustration by Jan Brett from her *Fritz and the Beautiful Horses.* Copyright © 1981 by Jan Brett. Reprinted by permission of Houghton Mifflin Company. All Rights Reserved./ Illustration by Jan Brett from her *The Wild Christmas Reindeer.* G.P. Putnam's Sons, 1990. Copyright © 1990 by Jan Brett. Reprinted by permission of G.P. Putnam's Sons./ Photograph by Susie Cushner, courtesy of Jan Brett.

LAURENT DE BRUNHOFF. Illustrations by Laurent de Brunhoff from his *L'anniversaire de Babar.* Copyright © 1970 by Random House, Inc. Copyright © 1972 by Librairie Hachette. Reprinted by permission of Random House, Inc./ Illustration from *Babar's Mystery,* by Laurent de Brunhoff. Random House, 1978. Copyright © 1978 by Laurent de Brunhoff. Reprinted by permission of Alfred A. Knopf, Inc./ Illustration titled 'Beach Blanket Babar,' from *Mirabella Magazine,* August 1989. Courtesy of Laurent de Brunhoff./ Photograph by Anne de Brunhoff.

something about the author

ADAMS, Edith
See SHINE, Deborah

* * *

ADORJAN, Carol 1934-

PERSONAL: Surname is pronounced "a-dor-i-an"; born August 17, 1934, in Chicago, IL; daughter of Roland Aloysius (in sales) and Marie F. (a housewife; maiden name, Toomey) Madden; married William W. Adorjan, August 17, 1957; children: Elizabeth Marie, John Martin, Katherine Therese, Matthew Christian. *Education:* Mundelein College, B.A. (magna cum laude), 1956. *Politics:* Independent. *Religion:* Roman Catholic.

ADDRESSES: Home and office—1667 Winnetka Rd., Glenview, IL 60025. *Agent*— c/o Publicity Director, Albert Whitman and Company, 6340 Oakton, Morton Grove, IL 60053.

CAREER: Writer, 1956—. Taught high school English, history, and anthropology; instructor at writing workshops. Writer-in-residence, National Radio Theater of Chicago, 1980, Illinois Arts Council, 1981-82, and Iowa Arts Council, 1983; guest author, Illinois Young Writers' Conference, 1986, 1990.

MEMBER: International PEN, Midland Society of Authors, Children's Reading Roundtable, Dramatists' Guild.

AWARDS, HONORS: Josephine Lusk Award, Mundelein College, 1955; Earplay Award, University of Wisconsin, 1972, for *The Telephone;* Fellowship, Midwest

CAROL ADORJAN

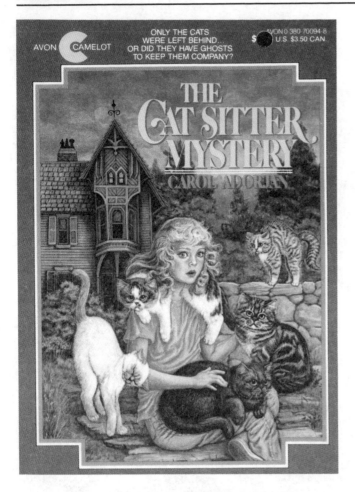

This mystery involving a noisy old mansion and a cat-sitting job was based on the experiences of Adorjan's daughter Beth.

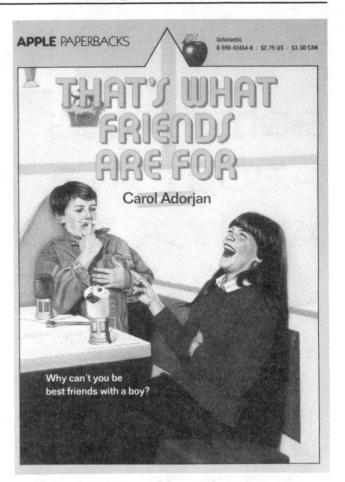

Sixth grade and growing up complicate a girl's friendship with a boy in *That's What Friends Are For*.

Playwrights' Laboratory, 1977; Society-National Playwriting Contest (first award), University of Dubuque, 1978, for *The Magic Box;* O'Neill National Playwright's Conference (finalist), 1979; Ohio State Award, 1981, for *The Sea Wolf;* Jacksonville University Playwriting Contest (first prize), 1988, for *Bridges.*

WRITINGS:

JUVENILE

Someone I Know, Random House, 1968, revised edition published as *I Can! Can You?,* Albert Whitman, 1990.
Jonathan Bloom's Room, J. Philip O'Hara, 1973.
The Cat Sitter Mystery (also see below), J. Philip O'Hara, 1973.
The Electric Man, Children's Press, 1981.
Pig Party, Children's Press, 1981.
(Adaptor) Frances Hodgson Burnett, *A Little Princess,* Troll Associates, 1988.
(With Yuri Rasovsky) *Easy Radio Plays,* Albert Whitman, 1988.
The Copy Cat Mystery, Avon, 1990.
That's What Friends Are For, Scholastic, 1990.
The Campout Mystery, Scholastic, 1992.

"JUNIOR HIGH" SERIES

Eighth Grade to the Rescue, Scholastic, 1987.
Those Crazy Eighth Grade Pictures, Scholastic, 1987.
The Big Date, Scholastic, 1988.
The Revolt of the Eighth Grade, Scholastic, 1988.

PLAYS

How America Lives, produced at University of Wisconsin, 1977.
The Magic Box, produced at University of Dubuque, 1978.
The Cat Sitter Mystery (adapted from book of same title), produced by Children's Theater of Winnetka, 1978.

RADIO PLAYS

Friends, WFMT (Chicago), 1976.
A Safe Place, WFMT, 1976.
All Things Even Frisky, WMBI, 1977.
The Outcasts of Poker Flat, WFMT, 1978.
The Sea Wolf, WFMT, 1980.

Also author of short fiction and articles for numerous periodicals, including *Redbook, Today,* and *North American Review.*

SIDELIGHTS: Carol Adorjan told *SATA:* "I have always written. I remember my first story about a small, noisy dog, written in the second grade after my class had learned cursive. There was something about that new skill, the flow of it perhaps, that unleashed an enthusiastic desire to write.... I knew that I would always write—it was necessary like breathing—but, since it was so natural to me, I never considered it a career option."

Adorjan's family and teachers supported her early writing efforts. A great lover of books, Adorjan spent many hours in the local library with her friends, reading and working on new tales. By the time she was a high school senior, Adorjan had begun sending stories to teen magazines, but "they always came back," she noted. Adorjan worked on the college literary magazine and was greatly influenced by the publication's moderator, who also taught writing and literature courses. After graduation, Adorjan became an English teacher; eventually, however, the demands of a new marriage, teaching, and writing became too much. "I knew that I could not be married, teach, and write," Adorjan noted. "I quit teaching except as an occasional substitute and began concentrating on my writing."

Adorjan's first three books were based on the experiences of her daughter Beth. "Most of my books have been the direct result of my own experience or the experiences of people in my life," Adorjan related. "Even when the ideas have come from outside this circle of experience, I have borrowed elements from neighbors and friends to give my work authenticity.... My advice to the aspiring writer: Nothing is ever lost; Never give up; Enjoy!"

*   *   *

ASHER, Sandy (Fenichel) 1942-

PERSONAL: Full name, Sandra Fenichel Asher; born October 16, 1942, in Philadelphia, PA; daughter of Benjamin (a doctor) and Fanny (Weiner) Fenichel; married Harvey Asher (a professor), January 31, 1965; children: Benjamin, Emily. *Education:* Attended University of Pennsylvania, 1960-62; Indiana University, B.A., 1964; graduate study at University of Connecticut, 1973; Drury College, elementary education certificate, 1974.

ADDRESSES: Home—721 South Weller Ave., Springfield, MO 65802. *Office*—Department of Literature, Drury College, 900 North Benston, Springfield, MO 65802. *Agent*—Harold Ober Associates, Inc., 425 Madison Ave., New York, NY 10017.

CAREER: WFIU-Radio, Bloomington, IN, scriptwriter, 1963-64; Ball Associates (advertising agency), Philadelphia, PA, copywriter, 1964; *Spectator,* Bloomington, drama critic, 1966-67; Drury College, Springfield, MO, instructor in creative writing, 1978-85, writer in residence, 1985—. Instructor, Institute of Children's Literature, 1986—. Instructor in creative writing for children's summer programs, Summerscape, 1981-82, and

Artworks, 1982. Frequent guest speaker at conferences, workshops, and schools.

MEMBER: ASSITEJ—The International Association of Theatre for Children and Young People (member of Board of Directors, 1989—), Dramatists Guild, National Council of Teachers of English Assembly on Literature for Adolescents, Society of Children's Book Writers (Missouri advisor, 1986-1989; member of Board of Directors, 1989—), Children's Reading Round Table of Chicago, Phi Beta Kappa.

AWARDS, HONORS: Honorable mention from *Envoi* magazine, 1970, for poem, "Emancipation"; award of excellence from Festival of Missouri Women in the Arts, 1974, for *Come Join the Circus;* creative writing fellowship grant in playwriting from National Endowment for the Arts, 1978, for *God and a Woman;* first prize in one-act play contest from Little Theatre of Alexandria, 1983, and Street Players Theatre, 1989, for *The Grand Canyon;* first prize from Children's Musical Theater of Mobile contest and Dubuque Fine Arts Players contest, both 1984, both for *East of the Sun/West of the Moon;* University of Iowa Outstanding Books for Young Adults Award and Child Study Association Best Books Award, both 1985, both for *Missing Pieces; Little Old Ladies in Tennis Shoes* was named best new play of the season by Maxwell Anderson Playwriting Series, 1985-86, and was a finalist for the 1988 Ellis Memorial Award, Theatre

SANDY ASHER

Americana; *God and a Woman* won Center Stage New Horizons contest in 1986, Mercyhurst College National Playwrights Showcase, 1986-87, and the Unpublished Play Project of the American Alliance for Theatre in Education, 1987-88; *Things Are Seldom What They Seem* was nominated for Iowa Teen Award and Young Hoosier Award, both 1986-87; Children's Theatre Indianapolis Children's Theatre Symposium playwriting awards, from Indiana University/Purdue University, 1987, for *Prince Alexis and the Silver Saucer,* and 1989, for *A Woman Called Truth;* Joseph Campbell Memorial Fund Award from the Open Eye, 1991-92, for *A Woman Called Truth;* New Play Festival Award from the Actors' Guild of Lexington, Inc., 1992, for *Sunday, Sunday.*

WRITINGS:

PLAYS; UNDER NAME SANDRA FENICHEL ASHER

Come Join the Circus (one-act), produced in Springfield, MO, at Springfield Little Theatre, December, 1973.
Afterthoughts in Eden (one-act), first produced in Los Angeles, CA, at Los Angeles Feminist Theatre, February, 1975.
A Song of Sixpence (one-act), Encore Performance Publishing, 1976.
The Ballad of Two Who Flew (one-act), *Plays,* March, 1976.
How I Nearly Changed the World, but Didn't (one-act), produced in Springfield, MO, at National Organization for Women Herstory Women's Fair, November, 1977.
Witling and the Stone Princess, Plays, 1979.
The Insulting Princess (one-act; first produced in Interlochen, MI, at Interlochen Arts Academy, May, 1979) Encore Performance Publishing, 1988.
Food Is Love (one-act), first produced in Springfield at Drury College, January, 1979.
The Mermaid's Tale (one-act; first produced in Interlochen at Interlochen Arts Academy, May, 1979), Encore Performance Publishing, 1988.
Dover's Domain, Pioneer Drama Service, 1980.
The Golden Cow of Chelm (one-act; produced in Springfield at United Hebrew Congregation, December, 1980), *Plays,* 1980.
Sunday, Sunday (two-act), first produced in Lafayette, IN, at Purdue University, March, 1981.
The Grand Canyon (one-act), first produced in the Little Theatre of Alexandria, Virginia, 1983.
Little Old Ladies in Tennis Shoes (two-act; first produced in Philadelphia, PA, at the Society Hill Playhouse, 1985), Dramatic Publishing Co., 1989.
East of the Sun/West of the Moon (one-act), first produced in the Children's Musical Theatre of Mobile, AL, 1985.
God and a Woman (two-act), first produced in Erie, PA, at the National Playwrights Showcase, 1987.
Prince Alexis and the Silver Saucer (one-act), first produced in Springfield, MO, at Drury College, 1987.
A Woman Called Truth (one-act; first produced in Houston, TX, at the Main Street Theatre, 1989), Dramatic Publishing Co., 1989.

The Wise Men of Chelm (one-act; first produced in Louisville, KY, at the Jewish Community Center, 1991) Dramatic Publishing Co., 1992.
Blind Dating (one-act), first produced in New York City at TADA!, 1992.
Perfect (one-act), first produced in New York City at The Open Eye: New Stagings, 1992.
Where Do You Get Your Ideas? (adapted for stage from book of same title), first production New York City at Open Eye: New Stagings for Youth, 1992.

NOVELS FOR CHILDREN, EXCEPT AS NOTED; UNDER NAME SANDY ASHER

Summer Begins, Elsevier-Nelson, 1980, published as *Summer Smith Begins,* Bantam, 1986.
Daughters of the Law, Beaufort Books, 1980, published in England as *Friends and Sisters,* Gollancz, 1982.
Just Like Jenny (Junior Literary Guild selection), Delacorte, 1982.
Things Are Seldom What They Seem (Junior Literary Guild selection), Delacorte, 1983.
Missing Pieces, Delacorte, 1984.
Teddy Teabury's Fabulous Fact, Dell, 1985.
Everything Is Not Enough (Junior Literary Guild selection), Delacorte, 1987.
Teddy Teabury's Peanutty Problems, Dell, 1987.
Princess Bee and the Royal Good-night Story (picture book), illustrated by Cat Bowman Smith, A. Whitman, 1990.
Out of Here: A Senior Class Yearbook, Dutton/Lodestar, in press.

"BALLET ONE" SERIES

Best Friends Get Better, Scholastic, 1989.
Mary-in-the-Middle, Scholastic, 1990.
Pat's Promise, Scholastic, 1990.
Can David Do It?, Scholastic, 1991.

NONFICTION

(Under name Sandra Fenichel Asher) *The Great American Peanut Book,* illustrated by Jo Anne Metsch Bonnell, Tempo, 1977.
Where Do You Get Your Ideas? Helping Young Writers Begin, illustrated by Susan Hellard, Walker & Co., 1987.
Wild Words! How to Train Them to Tell Stories, illustrated by Dennis Kendrick, Walker & Co., 1989.

Contributor of plays to anthologies, including *Center Stage,* Harper, 1990. Contributor of stories and articles to books, including *Visions,* edited by Don Gallo, Delacorte/Dell, 1987; *Speaking for Ourselves,* edited by D. Gallo, NCTE, 1990; *Writers in the Classroom,* edited by Ruth Nathan, Christopher-Gordon, 1991; *Performing the Text: Reading, Writing, and Teaching the Young Adult Novel,* edited by Virginia Monseau and Gary Salvner, Heinemann-Boynton/Cook, 1992; *Authors' Perspectives: Turning Teenagers into Readers and Writers,* edited by Donald Gallo, Heinemann-Boynton/Cook, 1992. Contributor of stories and articles to magazines, including *Highlights for Children, Humpty Dumpty's Magazine, Parents Magazine,* and *Writers Digest.*

WORK IN PROGRESS: (tentative titles): *Blue Perry,* a novel with an upper elementary school setting; *Princess Bee and the Royal Birthday Party,* a picture book; and *Wolf Quest,* a play commissioned by the Emmy Gifford Children's Theatre, Omaha, Nebraska.

SIDELIGHTS: Sandra Fenichel Asher, a playwright and children's author who is probably best known for her young adult novels written under the name Sandy Asher, gets many of the ideas and characters for her writings from her childhood memories. She grew up in Philadelphia, Pennsylvania, where the abundant sights and sounds and varieties of people in her neighborhood delighted the active and observant child. But while young, Asher also learned to be alone even when there were lots of people around. She explained in an essay for *Something about the Author Autobiography Series (SAAS)* that, while living with her older brother, parents, aunt, uncle, cousin, and grandparents in a large row house that also served as office space for her father's medical practice, "I learned early that inner space is

A boy's collection of peanut trivia makes for humorous situations in Asher's lighthearted novel *Teddy Teabury's Peanutty Problems.* (Illustration by Bob Jones.)

worth exploring and that even when alone, you can find yourself in fascinating company. Much of the time was spent in a fantasy world where I grew up to be the people I saw in movies and read about in books: a dancer, actor, circus juggler, magician, world traveler, puppeteer..."

As she grew up, Asher recalls that the difference between the social world and her own private "inner space" became increasingly pronounced, as it became more and more difficult to communicate her dreams and insecurities to those around her. Although she aspired to be a professional writer from an early age, her efforts at writing were "considered amusing by my family, but certainly not significant," she wrote in *SAAS.* Looking back, Asher understands why her parents were not more encouraging. "I can't blame them for the way they saw me. They were products of their time. They were good, decent people trying to raise a good, decent female child." Since they believed that for a woman marriage was the only key to a secure future, they viewed her interests in writing, drama, and dance as harmless pastimes or hobbies. As a young woman, Asher had to learn to separate her own sense of identity from her parents' perception of her.

Asher's relationships with friends at school also became strained in early adolescence. Although she was an excellent student, the author recalled in *SAAS* that secondary school was "like a forced visit to a strange planet." Growing increasingly shy in a social environment she did not always understand, she responded to her peers with "a sarcastic sense of humor" and "a sharp tongue." Realizing later that other young people around her were probably as insecure as she was, Asher perceived that adolescents are often socially isolated at just the time they are developing their deepest concerns about identity. A young child, she once observed in *Something about the Author (SATA),* can take his or her questions to a parent, an older adolescent can talk to a boyfriend or girlfriend, an adult confides in a spouse, close friend, or psychiatrist. But friendships in early adolescence are often tenuous. "So you're alone with your fears and confusions at the very point in life when frightening and confusing changes are happening to you every day," she said in *SATA.* "You tell no one the truth about how you feel, no one tells you, and everyone ends up thinking, 'I am the only person this crazy in the whole world.'"

However uncomfortably, Asher thrived in her adolescence, pursuing youthful dreams into challenging experiences in ballet, the theater, and finally into writing—professionally. She credits teachers and role models from books (Jo March of Louisa May Alcott's *Little Women* in particular), for her perseverance in the things she loved. But she also believes that adolescence is not just a difficult time, it is a "time of hope," she told *SATA.* "You *can* solve problems. You *can* learn how to live well. No one can tell children that life is not worth living. They just got here and they're rarin' to go."

Asher's first attempt at writing a novel, *Daughters of the Law,* remained in the revision stage for ten years. (Cover illustration by Michael Garland.)

After an eventful high school and college career that included performing in plays with La Salle College Masque and Indiana University Theatre, musicals on the traveling showboat, the Majestic, and ballet with the Philadelphia Civic Ballet Company, Asher graduated from Indiana University and married her husband, Harvey. Within a span of several years her parents and her grandparents died, and her husband's job necessitated a move to Missouri. During these years she worked as a scriptwriter for a radio station, a copywriter in advertising, and a drama critic for an alternative newspaper before having her two children and beginning graduate studies in child development. "My twenties, in short," Asher said in *SAAS,* "were a decade of turmoil, and I had to learn how to deal with it, how to sort it all out and survive it, far from old friends and what little was left of my family."

In 1969, a year after the birth of her second child, she began to write her first novel, *Daughters of the Law,* a story about a young girl trying to understand her Jewish heritage in light of her mother's unexpressed but painful memories as a survivor of the Holocaust of World War II. The novel would be revised many times over the next ten years before its publication, as Asher became more familiar with her genre. During these years she also began to write plays that have been produced throughout the country, winning numerous awards.

Before she finalized *Daughters of the Law,* Asher wrote and published *Summer Begins,* a novel about an eighth-grade girl named Summer who submits an article to her school newspaper suggesting that the holiday celebrations at her school should include Buddhist and Jewish traditions along with the exclusively Christian ones currently observed. Summer finds herself the unwilling center of attention when the principal demands that she retract her article, and her teacher resigns in protest of this violation to Summer's civil rights. *Summer Begins* raises important issues of censorship and religious freedom, but many critics noted that the book's strength lies in its focus on Summer's development toward maturity, related in invitingly human and often humorous terms. A *Washington Post Book World* reviewer commented that "Summer is a winningly self-aware 13-year-old and her reluctance to take on the heroine's role is often very funny."

In her 1982 novel, *Just Like Jenny,* Asher explores the friendship between Stephie and Jenny, two talented young dancers. When they are both asked to audition for a semi-professional dance group, Stephie, who is under pressure from her parents and envious of Jenny's classic skills, decides that she is not good enough to try out. The resolution of Stephie's loss of nerve, according to Judith S. Baughman in her *Dictionary of Literary Biography Yearbook: 1983* essay, entails lessons in "the nature of real friendship and the motivation underlying commitment to hard but fulfilling goals." A *Times Literary Supplement* reviewer of *Just Like Jenny,* although criticizing the story for "relying on inevitable disappointments and triumphs," commended Asher for her knowledge of teenagers. "Sandy Asher knows about the dreams and aspirations of young people.... She understands also the stubborn crises of confidence which afflict adolescents who do not know how they compare in ability and maturity with others."

In later novels, Asher continued to raise social issues while focusing on her adolescent characters' development of identity. In her award-winning 1983 book, *Things Are Not Always What They Seem,* she examines the effect a teacher's sexual abuse—and the silence of the adult world about what he has done—has on some of his students. Baughman noted that the significant focus in this story is "how these complexly developed fourteen- and fifteen-year-olds deal with their discovery that things are seldom what they seem, that deceptions or misperceptions do undermine relationships." Asher's 1987 novel, *Everything Is Not Enough,* the story of a seventeen-year-old boy's move toward independence, tackles the theme of violence against women in a similar manner. In this story a supportive friendship arises between a young man and a female coworker at a restaurant when, together, they confront the fact that a friend is being beaten by her alcoholic boyfriend.

Asher says that writing, for her, has been a means to "take control, puzzle things through, and work them

A relationship develops between a young man and a coworker when they realize that a friend is being beaten by her boyfriend in Asher's *Everything Is Not Enough*.

out." In her novels she continues to reflect on what happened to her in her own early years. She wrote in *SAAS,* "In a word, what happened was 'adolescence,' but there don't seem to be enough words in the world to illuminate that murky tunnel. To reach adulthood, a child must become more like his or her parents. To establish an individual identity, that same child must become *less* like his or her parents. It's a difficult passage, hard on parents and young people alike. Slowly but surely, as I write my books and plays, I find I've repaired broken bridges to my past and laid old sorrows to rest. I hope I also show readers that this does happen, that it can be done in their own lives. It takes time and understanding, and a willingness to forgive—oneself and others—and move on. A sense of humor also comes in handy."

WORKS CITED:

Asher, Sandy, article in *Something about the Author Autobiography Series,* Volume 13, Gale, 1991, pp. 1-16.
Baughman, Judith S., article on Sandy Asher, *Dictionary of Literary Biography Yearbook: 1983,* Gale, 1984, pp. 179-186.

Review of *Just Like Jenny, Times Literary Supplement,* September 7, 1984, p. 1006.
Something about the Author, Volume 36, Gale, 1984, pp. 27-30.
Review of *Summer Begins, Washington Post Book World,* July 11, 1982, p. 12.

FOR MORE INFORMATION SEE:

PERIODICALS

Bulletin of the Center for Children's Books, September, 1982; June, 1984; December, 1987.
Horn Book, December 1982, p. 654.
School Library Journal, October, 1980, p. 164; August, 1987, p. 88-89; September, 1987, p. 184-85; March, 1990, p. 184.
Times Literary Supplement, September 17, 1982.
Voice of Youth Advocates, June, 1987, p. 74.

—*Sketch by Sonia Benson*

*   *   *

AVI 1937-

PERSONAL: Full name is Avi Wortis; given name is pronounced "Ah-vee"; born December 23, 1937, in New York, NY; son of Joseph (a psychiatrist) and Helen (a social worker; maiden name Zunser) Wortis; married Joan Gabriner (a weaver), November 1, 1963 (divorced); married Coppelia Kahn (a professor of English); children: Shaun Wortis, Kevin Wortis; Gabriel Kahn (stepson). *Education:* Attended Antioch University; University of Wisconsin—Madison, B.A., 1959, M.A., 1962; Columbia University, M.S.L.S., 1964.

ADDRESSES: Home—15 Sheldon St., Providence, RI 02906. *Agent*—Dorothy Markinko, McIntosh & Otis, Inc., 475 Fifth Ave., New York, NY 10017.

CAREER: Writer, 1960—. New York Public Library, New York City, librarian in Performing Arts Research Center, 1962-70; Lambeth Public Library, London, England, exhange program librarian, 1968; Trenton State College, Trenton, NJ, assistant professor and humanities librarian, 1970-86. Visiting writer in schools across the United States.

MEMBER: PEN, Authors Guild, Authors League of America.

AWARDS, HONORS: Snail Tale: The Adventures of a Rather Small Snail was named one of the best books of the year by the British Book Council, 1973; Grants from New Jersey State Council on the Arts, 1974, 1976, and 1978; Mystery Writers of America Special Award, 1975, for *No More Magic,* 1979, for *Emily Upham's Revenge,* and 1983, for *Shadrach's Crossing;* Christopher Book Award, 1980, for *Encounter at Easton;* Children's Choice Award, International Reading Association, 1980, for *Man from the Sky,* and 1988, for *Romeo and Juliet, Together (and Alive) at Last; School Library Journal* best books of the year citations for *Night Journeys,* 1980; Scott O'Dell Award for historical fic-

AVI

tion, *Bulletin of the Center for Children's Books,* and American Library Association (ALA) best books for young adults citation, both 1984, both for *The Fighting Ground;* ALA best books for young adults citation, 1986, *School Library Journal* best book of the year citation, 1987, and Virginia Young Readers' Award, 1990, all for *Wolf Rider: A Tale of Terror;* Library of Congress best books of the year citations for *Something Upstairs,* 1989, and *The Man Who Was Poe,* 1990; Newbery Honor Book, ALA, Golden Kite Award, Society of Children's Book Writers, ALA notable book citation, and *School Library Journal* best books of the year citation, all 1990, and *Horn Book-Boston Globe* Award, and Judy Lopez Memorial Award, both 1991, all for *The True Confessions of Charlotte Doyle;* Volunteer State Award, 1991-92, for *Something Upstairs: A Tale of Ghosts;* Newbery Honor Book, and *Boston Globe/Horn Book* honor book, both 1992, both for *Nothing but the Truth.*

WRITINGS:

Things That Sometimes Happen, illustrated by Jodi Robbin, Doubleday, 1970.
Snail Tale: The Adventures of a Rather Small Snail, illustrated by Tom Kindron, Pantheon, 1972.
No More Magic, Pantheon, 1975.
Captain Grey, illustrated by Charles Mikolaycak, Pantheon, 1977.
Emily Upham's Revenge; or, How Deadwood Dick Saved the Banker's Niece: A Massachusetts Adventure, illustrated by Paul O. Zelinsky, Pantheon, 1978.
Night Journeys, Pantheon, 1979.
Encounter at Easton (sequel to *Night Journeys),* Pantheon, 1980.
Man from the Sky, illustrated by David Weisner, Knopf, 1980.

History of Helpless Harry: To Which Is Added a Variety of Amusing and Entertaining Adventures, illustrated by Zelinsky, Pantheon, 1980.
A Place Called Ugly, Pantheon, 1981.
Who Stole the Wizard of Oz?, illustrated by Derek James, Knopf, 1981.
Sometimes I Think I Hear My Name, Pantheon, 1982.
Shadrach's Crossing, Pantheon, 1983.
The Fighting Ground, Lippincott, 1984.
S.O.R. Losers, Bradbury, 1984.
Devil's Race, Lippincott, 1984.
Bright Shadow, Bradbury, 1985.
Wolf Rider: A Tale of Terror, Bradbury, 1986.
Devil's Race, Avon, 1987.
Romeo & Juliet—Together (& Alive) at Last (sequel to *S.O.R. Losers),* Avon, 1988.
Something Upstairs: A Tale of Ghosts, Orchard Books, 1988.
The Man Who Was Poe, Orchard Books, 1989.
The True Confessions of Charlotte Doyle, Orchard Books, 1990.
Windcatcher, Bradbury, 1991.
Nothing but the Truth, Orchard Books, 1991.
"Who Was That Masked Man, Anyway?", Orchard Books, 1992.
Blue Heron, Bradbury, 1992.
Judy and Punch, Bradbury, in press.
City of Light/City of Dark, Orchard Books, in press.

Also author of numerous plays. Contributor to books, including *Performing Arts Resources, 1974,* edited by Ted Perry, Drama Book Publishers, 1975. Contributor to periodicals, including *New York Public Library Bulletin, Top of the News, Children's Literature in Education, Horn Book,* and *Writer.* Book reviewer for *Library Journal, School Library Journal,* and *Perviews,* 1965-73.

Translations of Avi's books have been published in Germany, Austria, Denmark, Norway, Spain, Italy, and Japan.

ADAPTATIONS: A recording of *The Fighting Ground* was produced by Listening Library; *Emily Upham's Revenge, Shadrach's Crossing, Something Upstairs, The Fighting Ground,* and *The True Confessions of Charlotte Doyle,* were produced on the radio programs "Read to Me," Maine Public Radio, and "Books Aloud," WWON-Rhode Island.

SIDELIGHTS: Avi is known to critics, teachers, parents, and particularly to young readers for his invitably readable novels. His award-winning books include mystery, adventure, historical, supernatural, coming-of-age, and comic novels—and many that are a bit of all of these categories. While captivating even reluctant readers with fast-paced, imaginative plots and plenty of action, Avi's books also offer complex, thought-provoking, and sometimes disturbingly realistic reflections of American culture to adolescents. The author summed up his goals as a young adult novelist in *Twentieth-Century Children's Writers:* "I try to write about complex issues—young people in an adult world—full of irony and contradiction, in a narrative style that relies heavily on suspense with a texture rich in emotion and imagery. I take a great deal of satisfaction in using popular forms—the adventure, the mystery, the thriller—so as to hold my reader with the sheer pleasure of a good story. At the same time I try to resolve my books with an ambiguity that compels engagement. In short, I want my readers to feel, to think, sometimes to laugh. But most of all I want them to enjoy a good read."

Born in Manhattan in 1937, raised in Brooklyn, Avi grew up in an artistic environment. His great-grandparents and a grandmother were writers, so was an aunt. Two uncles were painters, one a composer. Both parents wrote. Today his twin sister is a writer and many members of his close, if extended, family, are active in music, the arts, theatre, film, and television. Avi's family was also quite politically active in ways considered radical, actively working against racism, for women's rights and labor— concerns emanating from the Great Depression of the 1930s. The author explained in an interview with *Something about the Author (SATA)* that his extended family comprised "a very strong art community and what this meant for me as a child was that there was always a kind of uproarious sense of debate. It was all a very affectionate sharing of ideas— arguing, but not arguing in anger, arguing about ideas."

This early stimulation at home may have prepared Avi for challenges to come in his education. Although he was an avid reader as a child, difficulties in writing eventually caused him to flunk out of one school. He later learned that he has a dysfunction known as dysgraphia, a marginal impairment in his writing abilities that causes him to reverse letters or misspell words. "One of my aunts said I could spell a four letter word wrong five ways," he told *SATA.* "In a school environment, I was perceived as being sloppy and erratic, and not paying attention." Despite constant criticism at school, Avi kept writing and he credits his family's emphasis on books for his perseverance. When papers came back to him covered in his teachers' red ink, he simply saved them, corrections and all. "I think there was so much criticism, I became immune to it," he told *SATA.* "I wasn't even paying attention to it. I liked what I wrote."

Like many teens, Avi felt like an outsider in many social circles. His family's political views gave him early knowledge of what it meant to be in a minority. "You always assumed that your point of view was quirky or different," Avi told *SATA.* At school, aside from writing difficulties, he had some typical teenage insecurities. "When I was sixteen or seventeen I looked like I was twelve or thirteen. At that time that means a lot to you. It's hardly anyone's fault but you blame it on everybody, right?" Avi reflected: "I've led a very ordinary life in most respects. I think my adolescence was unhappy in the way that many adolescents' lives are unhappy."

Avi says that the first step on his course to writing professionally was reading. He learned more from reading—everything from comic books and science magazines to histories, plays, and novels—than he learned in school. Despite the skepticism of his teachers,

he determined while still in high school to make a career of writing. Avi once commented, "After my junior year in high school, my parents were informed that I was in desperate need of a tutor, for somehow I had never taken the time to learn to write or to spell. That summer I met every day with a wonderful teacher who not only taught me writing basics, but also instilled in me the conviction that I wanted to be a writer myself. Perhaps it was stubbornness. It was generally agreed that was one thing I could not possibly do." Avi told *SATA* that he still has the diary entry from his senior year of high school in which he logged his decision to be a writer, adding "I can't wait! I've made up my mind."

At Antioch University, Avi avoided English but enrolled in playwriting classes. "That's where I really started to write seriously," he told *SATA.* "The first playwriting instructor that I had would say, 'this is the way you do it.' You didn't have much choice in it, you had to do it in a very specific way. He even had charts for you to fill out. And I think I learned how to organize a story

The first of several novels to be set in colonial America, Avi's *Captain Grey* follows a young boy's attempts to escape from the pirate that murdered his father. (Cover illustration by George Gaadt.)

according to this man's precepts. It didn't even matter what [his system] was except that I absorbed it. I think, although I'm not sure of this, that that is still the structure I use when I write." One of the plays Avi wrote in college won a contest and was published in a magazine. The author said that during that time he wrote "a trunkful of plays but I would say ninety-nine per cent of them weren't very good."

After working at a variety of jobs, Avi took a job in the theater collection of the New York Public library. Enrolling in night school to study librarianship, he began a twenty-five year career as a librarian. But his determination to be a writer never flagged. He had written nearly 800 pages of his "great American novel," when, through an odd series of events, he turned to children's literature. It all began with telling stories to his two sons, Avi told *SATA*. "My oldest would tell me what the story should be about—he would invent stuff, a story about a glass of water and so forth. It became a game, and here I had a writing background so I was telling some fairly sophisticated stories."

Along with telling stories, Avi was a doodler, drawing pictures for fun. A friend who was writing a children's book, having seen his drawings, wanted Avi to provide illustrations. When the friend took the book with Avi's illustrations to a publisher, although the book was rejected, Avi was asked to illustrate other children's books. Arguing with the publisher that he was a writer and not an artist, Avi agreed to illustrate if he could also write the book. "Two weeks after this conversation, I was supposed to go to England on a library exchange thing, so I took a week off of work. Some neighbors were gone and I used their apartment. I put down all the stories that I had told my son and drew the pictures, all within one week. So this gets submitted to the publisher and of course she turned everything down. But—seven publishers down the road—Doubleday accepted it."

Avi's first children's book, *Things That Sometimes Happen,* was published—although without his art-work—in 1970. His agent called one day and asked what name he wanted on the book. "That's an odd question to ask," Avi remarked to *SATA*. "It was never an issue, but I thought about it, and I said, 'Oh well, just put Avi down,' and that was the decision. Just like that." *Things That Sometimes Happen,* a collection of "Very Short Stories for Very Young Readers," was designed with Avi's very young sons in mind. For several years he continued to write children's books geared to his sons' advancing reading levels, but he told *SATA,* "At a certain point they kept growing and I didn't. I hit a fallow period, and then I wrote *No More Magic.* Suddenly I felt 'This is right! I'm writing novels and I love it.' From then on I was committed to writing novels."

Avi has written many different forms of the novel. Since several of his early works, including *Captain Grey, Night Journeys,* and *Encounter at Easton,* are set in colonial America, he quickly earned a reputation as a historical novelist. Avi's 1984 novel *The Fighting Ground,* winner

In order to recover his only possession, a horse, an orphaned boy must decide whether to turn in a runaway servant. (Cover illustration by Ted Hanke.)

of the Scott O'Dell Award for historical fiction for children, presents one event-filled day in the life of Jonathan, a thirteen-year-old boy caught up in the Revolutionary War. The novel begins as Jonathan slips away from his family's New Jersey farm one morning in order to take part in a skirmish with the Hessians (German mercenary soldiers hired by the English). Jonathan sets out full of unquestioned hatred for the Hessians, the British, and for Americans who were loyal to the British—the Tories—and full of hope for a chance to take part in the glory of battle. "O Lord, he said to himself, make it be a battle. With armies, big ones, and cannons and flags and drums and dress parades! Oh, he could, *would* fight. Good as his older brother. Maybe good as his pa. Better, maybe. O Lord, he said to himself, make it something *grand!*"

Avi portrays no grandeur in the war. Jonathan can barely carry his six-foot long musket, and has a worse time trying to understand the talk among the men with whom he marches. The small voluntary group's leader is a crude man who lies to the men and is said to be "overfond of killing." After a bloody and confusing skirmish, Jonathan is captured by three Hessians, and briefly comes to understand them as individual human beings. Later, when he is called upon to be the brave soldier he had yearned to be, Jonathan's harrowing experience reveals the delusion behind his wish. At the close of the novel the reader, along with Jonathan, is brought to an understanding of what war means in human terms. *The Fighting Ground* was widely praised by critics, many of whom expressed sentiments similar to a reviewer for the *Bulletin of the Center for Children's Books* who, describing *The Fighting Ground* as "a small stunner," summarized that the novel "makes the war personal and immediate: not history or event, but experience; near and within oneself, and horrible."

Avi says he is more interested in finding a way to tell a good story and to provide a means of imagining and understanding the past than he is in teaching a specific historical fact. "The historical novel is a curious construction," he told *SATA*. "It represents history but it's not truly accurate. It's a style." He elaborated in an interview with Jim Roginski in *Behind the Covers:* "Somewhere along the line, I can't explain where, I

Winner of the Scott O'Dell Award for historical fiction, *The Fighting Ground* harrowingly details a young soldier's discovery of the realities of combat. (Cover illustration by Michael Garland.)

developed an understanding of history not as fact but as story. That you could look at a field and, with only a slight shift of your imagination, suddenly watch the battle that took place there.... You have to have a willingness to look beyond *things....* Take the Battle of Bunker Hill during the Revolution. The leader of the American troops was Dr. Warren, who was killed during the battle. His body had been so dismembered and disemboweled, the only way he could be identified was by the nature of his teeth. And it was Paul Revere who did it. When you tell the story of war that way, a much stronger statement about how ghastly war really is, is made."

In *Something Upstairs: A Tale of Ghosts,* Avi's 1988 combination of historical novel, ghost story, and science fiction, a young man discovers the ghost of a murdered slave in the historic house his family recently moved into in Providence, Rhode Island. He travels back in time to the days of slave trading, where he learns about the murder and, perhaps more importantly, about the manner in which American history is collectively remembered. Although Avi was praised for his historical representation in this work, the author told *SATA* that "the irony is that in those Providence books there is nothing historical at all; it's a kind of fantasy of my neighborhood." Like his narrator in *Something Upstairs,* Avi moved from Los Angeles to Providence; in fact, he moved into the historic house featured in this novel. He told *SATA* that in his neighborhood, just walking down the street can inspire a story. The move to Providence "was truly like going back in history."

The Man Who Was Poe, Avi's fictionalized portrait of nineteenth-century writer Edgar Allan Poe, intertwines fiction and history on several levels. Historically, Poe went through a period of severe depression and poverty, aggravated by alcoholism during the two years preceding his death in 1849. Avi, whose novel focuses on this period, said he became fascinated with Poe because he was so extraordinary and yet such "a horrible man." In the novel, a young boy, Edmund, has recently immigrated to Providence from England with his aunt and twin sister in order to look for his missing mother. When both aunt and sister disappear, the penniless boy must elicit help from a stranger—who happens to be Edgar Allen Poe. Poe, noticing similarities in Edmund's story to his own life and detecting material for his writing, agrees to help the boy. Between maddening bouts of drunkeness, Poe ingeniously finds a trail of clues. Edmund, who has been taught to defer to adults, alternates between awe of the great man's perceptive powers and despair at his madness.

Vividly reflecting the macabre tone of Poe's fiction, Avi portrays the old port city of Providence as a bleak and chaotic world in which compassion and moral order seem to have given way to violence and greed. The character Poe, with his morbid imagination, makes an apt detective in this realm until it becomes clear that he wants the "story" of Edmund's family to end tragically. Edmund's plight is a harsh one, relying on Poe as the only adult who can help him, while at the same time

The Man Who Was Poe

A NOVEL BY AVI

Nineteenth-century writer Edgar Allan Poe, whose works of horror often reflected his own mental turmoil, plays a pivotal role in Avi's thriller about a young boy's search for his missing relatives. (Cover illustration by Ted Lewin.)

attempting to ensure that Poe's vision does not become a reality. A reviewer for the *Bulletin of the Center for Children's Books,* describing the novel as "a complex, atmospheric thriller," remarked that "Avi recreates the gloom of 1840s Baltimore (sic) with a storyteller's ease, blending drama, history, and mystery without a hint of pastiche or calculation. And, as in the best mystery stories, readers will be left in the end with both the comfort of puzzles solved and the unease of mysteries remaining."

In another unique twist on the convention of historical novels, Avi's 1990 *The True Confessions of Charlotte Doyle* presents the unlikely story of a very proper thirteen-year-old girl who, as the sole passenger and only female on a trans-Atlantic ship in 1832, becomes involved in a mutiny at sea. Holding her family's aristocratic views on social class and demeanor, Charlotte begins her voyage trusting only Captain Jaggery, whose fine manners and authoritative command remind her of her father. She is thus shocked to find that Jaggery is a viciously brutal shipmaster. This discovery, along with her growing fondness for members of the ship's crew, gradually leads Charlotte to question—and discard—the values of her priviledged background. As she exchanges her finishing school wardrobe for a common

sailor's garb and joins the crew in its work, she reveals the strength of her character, initially masked by her restrictive upbringing.

In the adventures that follow, including a mysterious murder, a storm, and a mutiny, Charlotte's reeducation and emancipation provide a new version of the conventionally male story of rugged individualism at sea. The multi-award-winning novel has received accolades from critics for its suspense, its evocation of life at sea, and particularly for the rich and believable narrative of its protagonist as she undergoes a tremendous change in outlook. The impact of Charlotte's liberation from social bonds and gender restrictions in *The True Confessions of Charlotte Doyle* has a powerful emotional effect on many of its readers. Avi told *SATA* that "many people, mostly girls, and even adults, have told me of bursting into tears" at the book's ending—tears of relief that Charlotte finds the freedom to realize herself as she chooses. In his *Boston Globe-Horn Book* Award acceptance speech, referring to the words of a critic who spoke of the "improbable but deeply satisfying conclusion" of the novel, Avi commented: "I am deeply grateful for the award you have given me today. But I hope you will understand me when I tell you that if the 'improbable' life I wrote lives in someone's heart as a life *possible,* then I have already been given the greatest gift a writer can receive: a reader who takes my story and endows it with life by the grace of their own desire."

Avi, although an enthusiastic reader of history, is by no means tied to the historical novel and delights in finding new ways to structure his stories. He told *SATA:* "People constantly ask 'How come you keep changing styles?' I think that's a misquestion. Put it this way, 'What makes you so fascinated with technique?' You know that there are a lot of ways to tell a story. To me that's just fun." With his extensive background in theater, it is no surprise that many of Avi's novels have roots in drama.

In 1984, Avi published *S.O.R. Losers,* a funny contemporary novel about a group of unathletic boys forced by their school (which is based on Avi's high school in New York City) to form a soccer team. Opposing the time-honored school ethic that triumph in sports is the American way, the boys form their own opinions about winning at something that means little to them. In a team meeting, they take stock of who they are and why it's so important to everyone *else* that they should win their games. The narrator, who is the team's captain, sums it up: "Every one of us is good at something. Right? Maybe more than one thing. The point is *other* things.... But I don't like sports. I'm not good at it. I don't enjoy it. So I say, so what? I mean if Saltz here writes a stinko poem—and he does all the time—do they yell at him? When was the last time Mr. Tillman came around and said, 'Saltz, I *believe* in your being a poet!'"

Avi makes a clear statement with his humor in *S.O.R. Losers.* He told *SATA* that he sees an irony in the American attitude toward education. "On the one hand,

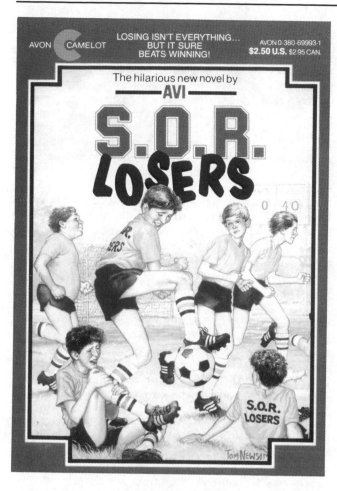

The author pokes fun at the American obsession with sports and winning in *S.O.R. Losers,* about a group of boys who are forced to form a school soccer team. (Cover illustration by Tom Newsom.)

our culture likes to give a lot of lip service to support for kids, but on the other hand, I don't think the culture as a whole likes kids. And kids are caught in this contradiction. I ask teachers at conferences 'How many of you have athletic trophies displayed in your schools?' You know how many raise their hands. And I ask, 'How many of you have trophy displays for the best reader or writer?' Nobody raises their hands. And I say 'What is it therefore that stands as the essential achievement in your school?' With test scores falling, we need to make kids better readers, but instead we're interested in a minority of kids, mostly males, whose primary focus is sports."

But with its narrator's deadpan reporting of the fiascos involved in being consistent losers in sports, *S.O.R. Losers* does more than make a point. *Horn Book* contributor Mary M. Burns, who called the novel "one of the funniest and most original sports sagas on record," particularly praised Avi's skill with comedic form. "Short, pithy chapters highlighting key events maintain the pace necessary for successful comedy. As in a Charlie Chaplin movie, emphasis is on individual episode—each distinct, yet organically related to an overall idea." Avi has written several other comic

novels, including his sequel to *S.O.R. Losers, Romeo and Juliet, Together (and Alive) At Last,* and two well-received spoofs on nineteenth-century melodrama, *Emily Upham's Revenge* and *The History of Helpless Harry.*

Avi has also written several acclaimed contemporary coming-of-age novels, including *A Place Called Ugly* and *Sometimes I Think I Hear My Name.* His 1992 Newbery honor book, *Nothing but the Truth* is the story of Philip Malloy and his battle with an English teacher, Miss Narwin. With bad grades in English keeping him off the track team, Philip repeatedly breaks school rules by humming the national anthem along with the public address system in Miss Narwin's home room. Eventually, the principal suspends Philip from school. Because the school happens to be in the midst of elections, various self-interested members of the community exploit this story of a boy being suspended for his patriotism. Much to everyone's surprise, the incident in home room snowballs into a national media event that, in its frenzied patriotic rhetoric, thoroughly overshadows the true story about a good teacher's inability to reach a student, a young man's alienation, a community's disinterest in its children's needs, and a school system's hypocrisy.

Nothing but the Truth is a book without a narrator, relating its story through school memos, diary entries, letters, dialogues, newspaper articles, and radio talk show scripts. Presented thus, without narrative bias, the story takes into account the differing points of view surrounding the incident, allowing the reader to root out the real problems leading to the incident. Avi told *SATA* that he got the idea for the structure of this novel from a form of theater that arose in the 1930s called "Living Newspapers"—dramatizations of issues and problems confronting American society presented through a "hodge podge" of document readings and dialogues.

Avi displays his sympathy to the "outsider" position of adolescence with his character, Philip Malloy. In all the national attention Philip receives as a patriotic hero, no one asks him what he feels or thinks, and no one seems to notice that he changes from a fairly happy and enthusiastic youth to a depressed and alienated adolescent. Philip's interest in *The Outsiders,* S. E. Hinton's novel about rival gangs of teenagers (written when Hinton was only seventeen years old herself), reveals that Philip would like to read about a world that looks like his own, with people experiencing problems like his. The Shakespeare plays assigned in school do not reach him. Avi explained to *SATA:* "It's not an accident that in the last decades the book most read by young people is *The Outsiders.* I wish Stephen King's novels were taught in the schools, so that kids could respond to them and talk about them." Avi does not hesitate to set complexities and harsh truths before his readers because, he said to *SATA,* these truths are already well-known to children. "I think writers like myself say to kids like this, 'We affirm your sense of reality.' We help frame it and give it recognition."

NOTHING BUT THE TRUTH
a documentary novel by
AVI

Told through articles, diary entries, memos, letters, and other documents, Avi's Newbery Honor Book tells the story of how an alienated teenager's act of rebellion becomes a national media event.

Although now writing on a full-time basis, Avi maintains regular interaction with children by traveling around the country, talking in schools about his writing. "I think it's very important for me to keep these kids in front of my eyes. They're wonderfully interesting and they hold me to the reality of who they are." Avi told *SATA* that children are passionate and honest readers who will either "swallow a book whole" if they like it, or drop it "like a hot potato" if they don't. In an article in *School Library Journal,* he provides a telling anecdote about his approach to children: "Being dysgraphic, with the standard history of frustration and anguish, I always ask to speak to the learning-disabled kids. They come in slowly, waiting for yet another pep talk, more instructions. Eyes cast down, they won't even look at me. Their anger glows. I don't say a thing. I lay out pages of my copy-edited manuscripts, which are covered with red marks. 'Look here,' I say, 'see that spelling mistake. There, another spelling mistake. Looks like I forgot to put a capital letter there. Oops! Letter reversal.' Their eyes lift. They are listening. And I am among friends."

With his success as a professional writer, Avi has proved his childhood critics—his teachers—wrong about his abilities. But he reacts to the surge of critical attention

he is now getting in the same skeptical way he responded to the red ink of his teachers many years ago. "I feel awkward about all of this. It's a kind of craziness," he told *SATA.* "I know it's all nonsense. You know, one magazine had a review of a new book of mine and referred to my 'uncanny' insight into character. I mean, the best thing you can say about that line is it's great in a family argument. My wife may say, 'You didn't wash those dishes very well,' and I can say 'Yeah, but I've got an uncanny insight.'" Avi maintains his own perspective on the merits of his work. Although he loves to write and is never at a loss for ideas, he says he never feels secure that his next book will be as successful as the last. This uncertainty, he told *SATA,* keeps him striving to do his best. "The minute you sit back and say 'this is good, this is right,' you've had it."

Avi describes himself as a committed skeptic, yet reveals an idealistic center when he discusses children and their role in American culture. He believes that children have a different outlook than most adults. Avi remarked to *SATA:* "When do you become an adult? Sometimes I think the difference is that psychological shift when you start to accept that tomorrow is going to be the same as today. When you're a kid, there are still options, major options. For a writer like myself, a child is a kind of metaphor for a return to idealism and passionate concern: a metaphor for the ability to change or react, to be honest about all those things that as adults we tend to slide over as we make compromises to obligations and necessities." In an article for *Horn Book* he contrasts children's literature, which generally espouses values such as "sharing, nonviolence, cooperation, and the ability to love," to the adult world where power and self-interest seem to rule. "More than anything else," Avi asserted in *Horn Book,* "children's literature is about the place and role of the child in society.... If we—in the world of children's literature—can help the young stand straight for a moment longer than they have done in the past, help them maintain their ideals and values, those with which you and I identify ourselves, help them demand—and win—justice, we've added something good to the world."

WORKS CITED:

Avi, "All That Glitters," *Horn Book,* September-October, 1987, pp. 569-576.

Avi, *The Fighting Ground,* Lippincott, 1984.

Avi, *Boston Globe-Horn Book* Award acceptance speech, *Horn Book,* January-February, 1992, p. 24-27.

Avi (with Betty Miles), "School Visits: The Author's Viewpoint," *School Library Journal,* January, 1987, p. 21.

Avi, telephone interview with Sonia Benson for *Something about the Author,* conducted March 16, 1992.

Avi, *S.O.R. Losers,* Bradbury, 1984.

Avi, autobiographical statement in *Twentieth-Century Children's Writers,* St. Martin's, 1989, pp. 45-46.

Burns, Mary M., review of *S.O.R. Losers, Horn Book,* January-February, 1985, p. 49.

Review of *The Fighting Ground, Bulletin of the Center for Children's Books,* June, 1984, p. 180.

Review of *The Man Who Was Poe, Bulletin of the Center for Children's Books,* October, 1989, p. 27.
Review of *Nothing but the Truth, Publishers Weekly,* September 6, 1991, p. 105.
Roginski, Jim, *Behind the Covers: Interviews with Authors and Illustrators of Books for Children and Young Adults,* Libraries Unlimited, 1985, pp. 33-41.

FOR MORE INFORMATION SEE:

PERIODICALS

Best Sellers, August, 1979, pp. 165-66; June, 1981, pp. 118-19; May, 1982, p. 76.
Bulletin of the Center for Children's Books, July, 1978, p. 170; July-August, 1980, p. 206; June, 1983; December, 1986, p. 61; February, 1986, p. 102; October, 1987, p. 21; September, 1988, p. 2.
English Journal, November, 1981, p. 94.
Five Owls, January, 1991, p. 56.
Horn Book, August, 1979, p. 410; April, 1980, pp. 169-70; October, 1980, pp. 517-18; April, 1981, p. 136; June, 1981, pp. 297-98; August, 1983, p.439; June, 1984, p. 325; January-February, 1989, p. 65.
Language Arts, October, 1979, p. 822; November-December, 1983, p. 1017; March, 1985, p. 283.
New York Times Book Review, September 11, 1977; March 1, 1981, p. 24.
Publishers Weekly, April 17, 1978, p. 78; December 5, 1980; January 30, 1981, p. 75; November 16, 1984, p. 65; December 26, 1986, p. 61; August 28, 1987, p. 81; September 14, 1990, p. 128; September 6, 1991, p. 105.
School Library Journal, March, 1978, p. 124; May, 1980, p. 64; November, 1980, p. 68; September, 1984, p. 125; October, 1984, p. 164; December, 1986, pp. 111-12; October, 1987, p. 124.
Voice of Youth Advocates (VOYA), August, 1981, pp. 23-24; August, 1982, p. 27; December, 1984, pp. 261-62; February, 1985, p. 321; February, 1989, p. 293.

—Sketch by Sonia Benson

B

BAER, Judy 1951-
(Judy Kaye)

PERSONAL: Born January 18, 1951, in Rugby, SD; daughter of Nels (a farmer) and Hazel (Fox) Fosen; married Larry Baer (an attorney), June 3, 1972; children: Adrienne, Jennifer. *Education:* Concordia College, Moorhead, MN, B.A. (summa cum laude), 1972. *Religion:* Lutheran.

ADDRESSES: Office—Box 807, Cando, ND 58324.

CAREER: Writer, 1983—. *Woman's Day,* stringer, 1985-89; *Minot Daily News,* Minot, ND, regional correspondent, 1987-91.

MEMBER: Society of Children's Book Writers, Romance Writers of America, Mystery Writers of America, Western Writers of America, National Federation of Press Women, American Film Institute, North Central Romance Writers of America, Northlight Writers' Association, Prairie Writers' Guild, North Dakota Professional Communicators (director of northeast district, 1987-89), Minnesota Published Writers' Network.

AWARDS, HONORS: First place, young-adult fiction, North Dakota Press Women and National Federation of Press Women, both 1986, for *Paige;* first place, fiction, North Dakota Press Women communications contest, 1987, for *Dakota Dream;* first place, young-adult fiction, North Dakota Press Women, first place National Award, National Federation of Press Women, both 1988, for *Adrienne;* first place award, news reporting, *Minot Daily News.*

WRITINGS:

NOVELS

Love's Perfect Image, Zondervan, 1984.
The Girl Inside, Silhouette, 1984.
Tender Adversary, Zondervan, 1985.
Shadows along the Ice, Zondervan, 1985.
Dakota Dream, Thomas Nelson, 1986.
Paige, Bethany House, 1986.

JUDY BAER

Moonglow, Zondervan, 1986.
Bid for My Heart, Ballantine, 1987.
Adrienne, Bethany House, 1987.
Riddles of Love, Bantam, 1988.
Spring Break, Lynx, 1989.
Working at Love, Bantam, 1989.
My Perfect Valentine, Bantam, 1989.
My Mutant Stepbrothers, Willowisp Press, 1990.
No Place to Live, Willowisp, 1990.
Camp Pine Tree Pals, Willowisp Press, 1991.
(Under pseudonym Judy Kaye) *Ariana's Magic,* Harlequin, 1992.

Also author of *London Quarter,* Lynx.

*"CEDAR RIVER DAYDREAMS" SERIES; YOUNG-ADULT
NOVELS*

New Girl in Town, Bethany House, 1988.
Trouble with a Capital "T", Bethany House, 1988.
Jennifer's Secret, Bethany House, 1989.
Journey to Nowhere, Bethany House, 1989.
Broken Promises, Bethany House, 1989.
The Intruder, Bethany House, 1989.
Silent Tears No More, Bethany House, 1990.
Fill My Empty Heart, Bethany House, 1990.
Yesterday's Dream, Bethany House, 1991.
Tomorrow's Promise, Bethany House, 1991.
Something Old, Something New, Bethany House, 1991.
Vanishing Star, Bethany House, 1991.
No Turning Back, Bethany House, 1991.
Second Chance, Bethany House, 1991.
Lost and Found, Bethany House, 1992.
Unheard Voices, Bethany House, 1992.

**Baer's "consuming" project, her "Cedar River
Daydreams" series features the trials and tribulations
of a group of teenage friends.**

OTHER

Contributor to periodicals, including *Faith 'n' Stuff,
Guideposts, REC, Romance Writer's Report,* and *Type-
Hi.*

ADAPTATIONS: Journey to Nowhere and *The Intruder*
were adapted as musicals by Dayspring, Phoenix, AZ.

SIDELIGHTS: Judy Baer told *SATA:* "Though born
and reared in rural North Dakota, I made a valiant
effort to 'leave home.' I attended college in Minnesota
and married a man from Montana, yet I still reside only
seventeen miles from the farm on which I grew up.

"Born an only child to middle-aged parents, I was quiet
and introspective and given to entertaining myself with
books. I also dabbled in writing them. My first publishing effort produced a family newsletter—no easy task,
since I was not only in charge of writing, illustration,
production, and sales but also generating the news. My
second effort—a fiction piece—sold to an unlikely trade
magazine, *The Dakota Farmer,* for the sum of ten
dollars. I did not try to submit for publication again for
several years. Instead, I graduated as valedictorian of
my high school, received English and education majors
and a religion minor from Concordia College, and
graduated summa cum laude. It was not until after I'd
become a mother—twice—and put my husband
through law school that I decided it was time to revive
my writing career.

"It was my lifelong dream to write a book. I decided that
if I were going to do it, I'd better start. My first effort—
still packed in a closet—was my 'freshman year in the
college of writing.' I learned a great deal about how to
finish a project and how to construct a novel from that
as-yet-unsold piece. My second and third works sold
immediately, and I was on my way.

"Though I write for both adults and children, I've
discovered that I have an aptitude for speaking to
teenagers. Something else quite amazing has happened
over the years—the older I get, the younger the age I
choose to write for. If this trend continues, in my dotage
I will be writing picture books for infants!

"One of my consuming projects has been my own series
for Bethany House Publishers, called the 'Cedar River
Daydreams' ('CRD'). An ensemble cast of continuing
characters populate the 'Daydreams' books, and I've
grown to know and love them over the course of the
books. Those characters are now my friends—lovable,
irritating, funny, and all the other things that friends can
be.

"In addition to the 'CRD' books, I have written middle-
grade fiction including *My Mutant Stepbrothers* and
Camp Pine Tree Pals for Willowisp Press. When I write
for the eight- to twelve-year-old reader I find myself
telling the story in first person rather than third. It's the
odd but effective way my mind keeps my 'voices'
straight.

"Someday I would love to do a picture book and see my characters come to life through an artist's vision of them."

FOR MORE INFORMATION SEE:

PERIODICALS

Christian Writer, March, 1986.
School Library Journal, January, 1989, p. 103.
Voice of Youth Advocates, June, 1989, p. 112; December, 1990, p. 276; April, 1991, p. 25.

*   *   *

BAILEY, Anne 1958-

PERSONAL: Born October 3, 1958, in St. Johns, Woking, Surrey, England; daughter of Anthony Bailey (a civil engineer) and Margaret Juliet Weddell (maiden name, Westbrook). *Education:* Attended secondary school in West Byfleet County, England, 1969-73. *Politics:* Labour. *Religion:* Church of England. *Hobbies and other interests:* Reading, knitting.

ADDRESSES: Home—120 Mead Lane Caravan Park, Mead Lane, Chertsey, Surrey KT16 8NT, England. *Office*—Tiltwood, Hogs Hill Lane, Cobham, Surrey, England. *Agent*—Laurence Pollinger, 18 Maddox St., Mayfair, London W1R 0EU, England.

CAREER: Ashley Cook's Dry Cleaners, Woking, Surrey, England, presser, 1973-76; Crater Controls (hair dryer factory), Knaphill, Surrey, assembler, 1976-77; W. R. Bennett Ltd., Pyrford, Surrey, farm hand, 1977-81; Sottley Clean (dry cleaners), Addlestone, Surrey, presser, 1983-87; Tiltwood (senior citizen home), Cobham, Surrey, part-time domestic, 1989—; writer. Special constable, 1982-84.

WRITINGS:

Scars (young adult novel), Faber, 1987.
Burn Up, Faber, 1988.
Rhythm and Blues, Faber, 1990.
Israel's Babe (young adult novel), Faber, 1991.
Breaking Point (young adult novel), Faber & Faber, in press.

SIDELIGHTS: Anne Bailey told *SATA:* "I was never interested in working hard while I was at school. I spent most of my time looking out the window and daydreaming. I used to fantasize about people I knew, and I realize now these fantasies were how I worked out ideas for books and new story lines. I never used to have dreams about becoming a writer, though. I used to dream about being a tennis player or other athlete. I was not much good at these sports, but it didn't stop me from dreaming. I guess writing just came naturally to me, though. I was always, from a young age, writing stories and poems in a notebook. There is something special to me about a shiny new exercise book and ink pen. I love going into stationers and always have to buy something just for the sake of it.

"From a young age I always loved to read. I much preferred to sit indoors and read quietly by myself than go out to play with friends. When I did play outside, it was usually on my own with many imaginary characters. Some such characters stayed with me for many years of my childhood. I seemed to glean more satisfaction from having pretend rather than real friends—perhaps because I could always get them to do what I wanted. I loved to lose myself in books, though. I think I got that trait from my father, who has always been an avid reader. Neither of my parents are in the literary field. Neither are any relations, although my great-grandfather used to love to write and had excellent handwriting. He also loved to read. So maybe some of my talent originated from there.

"For my first book, *Scars,* I drew a lot from my own experiences. After suffering a couple of breakdowns I could understand something about psychological trauma, and that was how I came to write the book. I hope that in *Scars* I went some way to distinguish the stigma attached to mental illness, especially for teenagers. As the main character went through a breakdown I hope the reader could understand her problems and then, perhaps, understand those people in life who have suffered breakdowns.

"*Scars* was published when I was twenty-seven, although I wrote my first book when I was seventeen. I was writing ten years before getting a break. But in a way I was learning my trade in that time. I was greatly helped by my agent. I just learned through making mistakes and trying again, hopefully without the same mistakes. Luckily, it worked. *Scars* was in fact about the tenth book I'd written.

"I have always been very interested in father-daughter relationships. This is why in my first three books there's

ANNE BAILEY

SCARS

Anne Bailey

The story of a teenager who suffers a mental breakdown, *Scars* is based in part on the author's own experiences. (Cover illustration by John Raynes.)

always a strong father figure. I'm not sure why I stray toward this side of things, but perhaps it's because through my teens and twenties I had a number of father figures in my life who were very important to me.

"In *Burn Up* I drew a lot from my experiences from helping out at a youth club. At this club there were many difficult teenagers with slightly violent tendencies. I used to talk with them a lot and got to understand some of their problems. *Burn Up* is a slightly violent book, but I think this only tends to reflect society as it is. In my adolescence I experienced some of that rebellion against authority and my parents. Indeed, writing about them helped me control these emotions. I was lucky to be able to use writing to channel all my aggressive, angry, and vivid emotions. It sometimes came as a great relief to put thoughts to paper, although I had the actual art of constructing a book to learn.

"I used to find it very difficult to control my ideas before I put them down on paper, especially when I worked full time. I would become very frustrated that I could only write in the evenings. This is why I walked out on a few jobs—which wasn't a very sensible thing to do and which gave my mother nightmares. But I just

couldn't stand the thought of not being able to write when I needed to. Now I work part-time and therefore can spend more time writing, so I don't become frustrated. Writing is still almost like an obsession with me, though. I soon get fed up if I haven't written for a few days, which is why I'm almost constantly working on a book.

"I believe *Israel's Babe* is my best book to date, although, oddly enough, I wrote that without inspiration. I had to completely rewrite my first draft of the book, which was worth it in the end but not at the time. I had been to live on a kibbutz in Israel when I was in my twenties, which I used for the book. I had never written anything like a romantic book before, so I thought it would be a pleasant change to do so. It all worked very well, and I hope the main character experienced some emotions and problems that teenagers will be able to relate to. My sister had just had her second baby, so I could question her about pregnancy and so forth to hopefully get all my facts right.

"I always like my books to have somewhat of a happy ending. I like the main characters to be able to go through some sort of trauma in their lives and, no matter what, come out winning in the end. For this, I think, is very much like life. No matter how bad the problem seems at the time, if you take it day by day and keep plodding on, you will finally get through that dark tunnel and find the light. I hope my books inspire people to come through problems and not to give up on life. I have found of my own experience that you have to plod on through life, no matter how hard. But finally everything turns out all right and perhaps you can see why it happened. If my writing is able to help people get through life then I can only think of it as being worthwhile."

*   *   *

BAINES, John (David) 1943-

PERSONAL: Born November 12, 1943, in Walsall, West Midlands, England; son of James (an accountant) and Edna (a nurse; maiden name, Scott) Baines; children: Joanna, Justin. *Education:* Durham University, B.A. (honors), 1965; Newcastle University, diploma in education, 1966. *Politics:* Liberal. *Religion:* "Broadly Christian values."

ADDRESSES: Home—"Seaview", Lower Rd., Chorleywood, Hertfordshire WD3 5LB, England.

CAREER: Teacher in Tanga, Tanzania, 1966-68, Bradford, England, 1968-71, and Rickmansworth, England, 1971-75; Commonwealth Institute, London, England, editor and education officer, 1975-78; Council for Environmental Education, Reading, England, director, 1978-89; writer and consultant, 1989—. Institution of Environmental Sciences, member of council and education committee, 1979—; Pictorial Charts Educational Trust, chairman, 1980—; World Conservation Union Commission on Education and Training, secretary of North West Europe Committee, 1985—; International

JOHN D. BAINES

Centre for Conservation Education, chairman of education advisory group, 1990—.

MEMBER: National Association for Environmental Education, Geographical Association.

AWARDS, HONORS: Member, Order of the British Empire, 1989; high commendation, Sir Peter Kent Conservation Book Award, 1992, for *This Fragile Earth.*

WRITINGS:

The Environment, Batsford, 1973.
Acid Rain, Wayland, 1989.
Conserving the Atmosphere, Wayland, 1989.
Protecting the Oceans, Wayland, 1990.
(With Barbara James) *This Fragile Earth,* Simon & Schuster Young Books, 1990.
(With James) *World Resources,* Simon & Schuster Young Books, 1990.
Conservation and Development, Hobsons, 1990.
Up the Chimney, Wayland, 1991.
On the Road, Wayland, 1991.
Water, Wayland, 1991.
Human Influences on the Earth, Wayland, 1991.
(With James) *Bellamy Rides Again* (booklet), British Broadcasting Corporation Education, 1991.
Japan, Simon & Schuster, 1992.
U.S.A., Simon & Schuster, 1992.
Global Concerns, Pearson, 1992.

Consultant editor for "Conserving Our World" series, Wayland, 1989—.

WORK IN PROGRESS: "Education packs on the Earth Summit 1992 and an introduction to appropriate technology."

SIDELIGHTS: John Baines told *SATA:* "It is a great privilege to be an author of education books. I am able to write about the relationship between people and the environment, something that interests me and that I care about very much. But it is also a great responsibility. It would be very easy to try to persuade people to think like me, but I believe it is important to let people make up their own minds about such important issues as the environment.

"My books provide information to help young people understand the ways human activities damage the environment and suggest solutions. I point out that solving the problems is not easy, but I believe we should not be overwhelmed or depressed by them. We have some difficult choices to make about how we live our lives, but the problems can be solved. I always try to show that there are things that each one of us can do to help solve some of the environmental problems. I do not like those books that predict very gloomy futures, because they can upset children and make them feel there is no point in trying to do anything to improve things. I do not believe they are necessarily accurate; we have seen that when people make up their minds to do something they can change the world. For example, who would have thought a few years ago that we would see an end to the Cold War?

"I often wonder why some people and not others are interested in the environment. Although I did not realize it until much later, one of the earliest influences on my own interest was my training as a member of the Scouts. We were taught how to live in and off the environment without damaging it. We were only allowed to take wood that had fallen on the ground. Turf had to be removed from the area where a fire was to be made. The turf had to be kept properly so it could be replaced at the end of the camp. All rubbish was burned and the ash buried. Deep pit latrines were dug away from the site, and so forth. When we left a site, all traces of our visit would soon disappear.

"At school we were all 'taught' to care for our environment. If we did not, we were punished. This applied to anyone caught dropping litter or doing any act of vandalism to buildings or plants. The teachers generally set a good example. In fact, throughout my life, caring for the environment, albeit in rather simple ways, has been a way of life.

"During the 1960s and 1970s there was a lot of interest in the environment, and it was then that I wrote my first book. It was called simply *The Environment.* It described how in Britain people had been changing the environment for hundreds of years, and each century had left its own mark on the landscape. Some of these marks were pretty terrible, such as the spread of towns over the countryside and damage to wild animals and plants from pollution and chemical sprays and dumping waste dangerously. However, while it made me depressed, it did not make any fundamental difference to the way I ran my life. Even when I went to work in environmental education as director of the Council for

Environmental Education, at first I cannot say I set a particularly good example. It was all saying what 'they' should do.

"However, the latest wave of environmentalism has made a much bigger impact on me, and I am now trying to live more environmentally without becoming too much of a freak. There are now many more people who think like me and are trying to live more environmentally friendly lives. I feel much better informed now about the environment, and I think the people who read my books already know a lot and think a lot about the environment before they even open my books. I think it is very important for me to set a good example to young people and adults. How else can I believe in what I write about? Although I have a car, I try to use it as infrequently as possible, whenever possible using my bike or going by public transport. In the home we save all our paper, bottles, cans, and aluminum foil and take it to be recycled. We have learned to live in a cooler house so we use less energy and now hate going into hot offices. There is a lot more that I still want to do, but I have learned to feel good about the things I am doing for the environment rather than bad about all the things I am not doing to help protect the environment. I believe that by protecting the environment I am in fact protecting myself, because without the environment to provide me with food, air, water, and all the other resources that I need, I would not be alive.

"I left the Council on Environmental Education to give more time to writing. As well as writing books about the environment I am now running courses for people to help them find ways of living lives that are more in harmony with nature. Many of the people who attend are teachers and are able to carry some of the ideas back to the children they teach. I feel very lucky to do what I do, and it is always nice to hear what young people think of my books."

*   *   *

BEIRNE, Barbara 1933-

PERSONAL: Surname is pronounced "burn"; born August 4, 1933, in Newark, NJ; daughter of Edward W. (in sales) and Gladys (a homemaker; maiden name, Cross) Treacy; married John J. Beirne, Jr. (a medical doctor), June 7, 1958; children: John Beirne III, Treacy Beirne Gaffney, Chris, Mike. *Education:* Marymount College, B.A., 1955; Pratt Institute, M.F.A., 1988. *Hobbies and other interests:* Tennis, hiking, skiing.

ADDRESSES: Home and office—20 Gaston Rd., Morristown, NJ 07960.

CAREER: Free-lance photographer, 1980—; County College of Morris, Randolph, NJ, adjunct professor of photography, 1991-92.

MEMBER: American Society of Magazine Photographers.

WRITINGS:

Under the Lights: A Child Model at Work, illustrated with own photographs, Carolrhoda, 1988.
A Pianist's Debut: Preparing for the Concert Stage, illustrated with own photographs, Carolrhoda, 1990.
Riders Up!, Carolrhoda, 1992.
Siobhan's Journey, Carolrhoda, 1992.

ILLUSTRATOR

(Photographer) Penny Pollock, *Water Is Wet,* Putnam, 1985.
(Photographer) Kathleen Dwyer, *What Do You Mean I Have a Learning Disability?,* Walker, 1991.

WORK IN PROGRESS: The Children of Ecuador; The Children of Northern Ireland.

SIDELIGHTS: Barbara Beirne told *SATA:* "I am a freelance photographer specializing in portraits of both children and adults. I am also particularly interested in documentary photography. One of my projects is documenting the religious and political conflicts in Northern

BARBARA BEIRNE

Ireland, with special emphasis on how these conflicts affect the children of Northern Ireland."

*   *   *

BERNARDS, Neal 1963-

PERSONAL: Born June 18, 1963, in Minneapolis, MN; son of Wallace (a high school principal) and Elaine (a real estate agent and homemaker; maiden name, Nelson) Bernards. *Education:* Bethel College, B.A. (magna cum laude), 1985. *Politics:* "Evolving." *Religion:* Protestant. *Hobbies and other interests:* "Travel, reading books on spy agencies and modern Middle Eastern politics, basketball, exploring fine malted beverages."

ADDRESSES: Home—1869 Golden Gate Ave., San Francisco, CA 94115.

CAREER: Camfel Productions, Monrovia, CA, media technician, 1985-86; Greenhaven Press, St. Paul, MN, editor, 1986-87; free-lance writer and editor, 1987-91; America West Airlines, San Francisco, CA, customer service representative, 1990-91. Kibbutz Kfar Hachoresh, Israel, volunteer, 1988.

WRITINGS:

FOR YOUNG ADULTS; PUBLISHED BY GREENHAVEN PRESS, EXCEPT AS NOTED

Living in Space: Opposing Viewpoints, 1990.
The Palestinian Conflict: Identifying Propaganda Techniques, 1990.
(With Bonnie Szumski) *Prisons: Detecting Bias,* 1990.
Nuclear Power: Examining Cause and Effect Relationships, 1990.
Advertising: Distinguishing between Fact and Opinion, 1991.
The War on Drugs: Examining Cause and Effect Relationships, 1991.
Gun Control: An Overview, Lucent Books, 1991.
Population: Detecting Bias, 1992.
America's Elections: Locating the Author's Main Idea, 1992.

EDITOR; FOR YOUNG ADULTS; PUBLISHED BY GREENHAVEN PRESS

(With others) *Soviet Union: Opposing Viewpoints,* 1987.
(With Lynn Hall) *American Foreign Policy: Opposing Viewpoints,* 1987.
The Mass Media: Opposing Viewpoints, 1988.
(With others) *Teenage Sexuality: Opposing Viewpoints,* 1988.
Euthanasia: Opposing Viewpoints, 1989.
(With Terry O'Neill) *Male-Female Roles: Opposing Viewpoints,* 1989.
The War on Drugs: Opposing Viewpoints, 1990.
The Environmental Crisis: Opposing Viewpoints, 1991.

OTHER

Contributor to periodicals, including *San Francisco Chronicle.*

NEAL BERNARDS

WORK IN PROGRESS: "Pursuing more creative essay-writing projects with intent on becoming a regular columnist."

SIDELIGHTS: Neal Bernards told *SATA:* "Though I have no science background, I found writing *Living in Space* immensely pleasurable because the topic interested me. It is important to remember that one need not be an expert in a given area to write about the topic; one needs only the ability to do thorough research and to make complicated ideas simple. In my experience, the single greatest skill to have is the knowledge of how to effectively use libraries and institutions as research tools. Also, the most important class I've ever taken to help my writing career was typing in the tenth grade. No English class or creative writing workshop has ever helped me as much as the ability to type quickly. Being able to compose at the keyboard is an essential skill to writing lengthy manuscripts. But in the era of children growing up with computers, I imagine that this is dated advice.

"My other bit of advice is to write about topics and ideas that really, really thrill you. Otherwise, the laborious, painful process of writing will become too much to handle, and you will abandon the project. My experience in writing *Gun Control* in 1991 bore this out. Though I had initially thought the subject matter held some interest for me due to my interest both in hunting and in nonviolence, I quickly discovered that the burden of researching and writing about gun control quickly outstripped my enthusiasm for it. The six-month process of writing and rewriting and reworking made me vow never to tackle another book whose topic I did not care deeply about.

"The rewards of writing are certainly worth the effort. In moments of depression I go to the library to look up the books I've had published to remind me of why I'm researching and writing and rewriting. The feeling of accomplishment and personal satisfaction is greater in writing than in any other occupation."

*   *   *

BOLOGNESE, Don(ald Alan) 1934-

PERSONAL: Surname is pronounced "bo-lo-*nay*-see"; born January 6, 1934, in New York, NY; married Elaine Raphael Chionchio (a writer and illustrator), 1954; children: two daughters. *Education:* Graduated from Cooper Union Art School, 1954.

ADDRESSES: Home—New York and Vermont. *Office*—c/o Franklin Watts Inc., 387 Park Ave. S., New York, NY 10016.

CAREER: Free-lance illustrator, 1954—; Pratt Institute, Brooklyn, NY, instructor in lettering and calligraphy, 1960—. Has also taught at Cooper Union Art School, New York University, and the Metropolitan Museum of Art's medieval museum, The Cloisters; calligrapher.

AWARDS, HONORS: The Colt from the Dark Forest by Anna Belle Loken received the Children's Spring Book Festival Middle Honor Award in 1959; *Plays and How to Put Them On* by Moyne Rice Smith was featured in the American Institute of Graphic Arts Children's Book Show in 1962; *All upon a Stone* by Jean Craighead George received the Children's Spring Book Festival Picture Book Award in 1971 and was named an American Library Association Notable Book; *Me, Myself and I* by Gladys Yessayan Cretan was included in the Society of Illustrators Show in 1971; *The Black Mustanger* by Richard Edward Wormser was named a Western Heritage honor book in 1972; *Fireflies* by Joanne Ryder was honored by the New Jersey Institute of Technology in 1978.

WRITINGS:

SELF-ILLUSTRATED

The Miracles of Christ (woodcuts and calligraphy from the exhibit at the Vatican Pavilion at the New York World's Fair), Centurion, 1964.
Once upon a Mountain, Lippincott, 1967.
A New Day, Delacorte, 1970.
Squeak Parker, Scholastic Book Services, 1977.
Drawing Horses and Foals, F. Watts, 1977.
Drawing Dinosaurs and Other Prehistoric Animals (part of the "How to Draw" series), F. Watts, 1982.
Drawing Spaceships and Other Spacecraft (part of the "How to Draw" series), F. Watts, 1982.
(With Robert Thorton) *Drawing and Painting with the Computer*, F. Watts, 1983.
Mastering the Computer for Design and Illustration, Watson-Guptill Publications, 1988.

Also contributor of articles to magazines, including *Jubilee*.

WITH WIFE, ELAINE RAPHAEL

The Sleepy Watchdog, Lothrop, 1964.
Sam Baker, Gone West, Viking, 1977.
Donkey and Carlo, Harper, 1978.
Turnabout, Viking, 1980.
Donkey It's Snowing, Harper, 1981.
Drawing Fashions: Figures, Faces, and Techniques, F. Watts, 1985.
Pen and Ink, F. Watts, 1986.
Pencil, F. Watts, 1986.
Charcoal and Pastel, F. Watts, 1986.
Printmaking, F. Watts, 1987.
Drawing History: Ancient Greece, F. Watts, 1989.
Drawing History: Ancient Egypt, F. Watts, 1989.
Drawing History: Ancient Rome, F. Watts, 1990.

ILLUSTRATOR

Anna Belle Loken, *The Colt from the Dark Forest*, Lothrop, 1959.
Moyne Rice Smith, *Plays and How to Put Them On*, Walck, 1961.
Aurora Dias Jorgensen, *Four Legs and a Tail*, Lothrop, 1962.
Edward W. Dolch and Marguerite P. Dolch, *Stories from Spain*, Garrard Press, 1962.
Maryhale Woolsey, *The Keys and the Candle*, Abingdon, 1963.
Joan M. Lexau, *Jose's Christmas Secret*, Dial, 1963.
Lexau, *Benjie*, Dial, 1964.
William Faulkner, *The Wishing Tree* (text in Japanese), Fuzambo (Tokyo), 1964, English-language edition, Random House, 1967.
Gaylord Johnson, *The Story of Animals: Mammals around the World*, second edition, Harvey House, 1965.
Jean Ritchie, *Apple Seeds and Soda Straws: Some Love Charms and Legends*, Walck, 1965.
Walter Rollin Brooks, *Jimmy Takes Vanishing Lessons*, Knopf, 1965.
Barbara Walker, *Just Say Hic!*, Follett, 1965.
Elizabeth Jane Coatsworth, *The Secret*, Macmillan, 1965.
Roger L. Green, *Tales the Muses Told*, Walck, 1965.
Robert Louis Stevenson, *Treasure Island*, Whitman Publishing, 1965.
Robin Palmer, *Dragons, Unicorns, and Other Magical Beasts*, Walck, 1966.
William Jay Smith, *If I Had a Boat*, Macmillan, 1966.
Lexau, *More Beautiful Than Flowers*, Lippincott, 1966.
Beth Greiner Hoffman, *Red Is for Apples*, Random House, 1966.
Irene Hunt, *Up a Road Slowly*, Follett, 1966.
Claire H. Bishop, *Yeshu, Called Jesus*, Farrar, Strauss, 1966.
Frederick James Moffitt, *The Best Burro*, Silver Burdett, 1967.
William Roscoe, *The Butterfly's Ball and the Grasshopper's Feast*, McGraw, 1967.
Beman Lord, *A Monster's Visit*, Walck, 1967.
Lucy Pennell and Jackie M. Smith, *Our Church at Work in the World*, John Knox, 1967.

Don Bolognese and his wife Elaine visited Italy to research their drawings for F. N. Monjo's book about young Mozart, *Letters to Horseface.*

Clyde Robert Bulla, *Washington's Birthday,* Crowell, 1967.

Michael Mason, *The Book that Jason Wrote,* Funk, 1968.

(With Betty Fraser and Kely Oechsli) *Favorite Stories: A Collection of the Best-loved Tales of Childhood,* designed by Walter Brooks, Whitman Publishing, 1968.

Bulla, *The Ghost of Windy Hill,* Crowell, 1968.

W. J. Smith, *Mr. Smith and Other Nonsense,* Delacorte, 1968.

M. R. Smith, *Seven Plays and How to Produce Them,* Walck, 1968.

Thea Heinemann, *Stories of Jesus,* Whitman Publishing, 1968.

Hunt, *Trail of Apple Blossoms,* Follett, 1968.

Richard Edward Wormser, *The Kidnapped Circus,* Morrow, 1968.

Mary Chase, *The Wicked Pigeon Ladies in the Garden,* Knopf, 1968.

Palmer, *Centaurs, Sirens, and Other Classical Creatures,* Walck, 1969.

Mary O'Neill, *Fingers Are Always Bringing Me News,* Doubleday, 1969.

Eva-Lis Wuorio, *The Happiness Flower,* World Publishing, 1969.

Jane Hyatt Yolen, *It All Depends,* Funk, 1969.

Just One More, compiled and retold by Jeanne B. Hardendorff, Lippincott, 1969.

Gladys Yessayan Cretan, *Me, Myself, and I,* Morrow, 1969.

Lexau, *Benjie on His Own,* Dial, 1970.

Wormser, *Gone to Texas,* Morrow, 1970.

Barbara Rinkoff, *Headed for Trouble,* Knopf, 1970.

Jean Craighead George, *All upon a Stone,* Crowell, 1971.

Wormser, *The Black Mustanger,* Morrow, 1971.

Philip Balestrino, *Hot as an Ice Cube,* Crowell, 1971.

Eric Mowbray Knight, *Lassie Come Home,* revised edition, Holt, 1971.

Ernest J. Gaines, *A Long Day in November,* Dial, 1971.

Balestrino, *The Skeleton Inside You,* Crowell, 1971.

Ruth Belov Gross, *What Do Animals Eat?,* Four Winds, 1971.

(With wife, Elaine Raphael) W. J. Smith, *Poems from Italy,* Crowell, 1972.

Doris Gates, *The Warrior Goddess: Athena,* Viking, 1972.

Lexau, *The Christmas Secret,* Scholastic Book Services, 1973.

George, *All upon a Sidewalk,* Dutton, 1974.

(With Raphael) F. N. Monjo, *Letters to Horseface: Being the Story of Wolfgang Amadeus Mozart's Journey to Italy 1769-1770 When He Was A Boy of Fourteen,* Viking, 1975.

(With Raphael) Margaret Hodges, *Knight Prisoner: The Tale of Sir Thomas Malory and His King Arthur,* Farrar, Straus, 1976.

Nathaniel Benchley, *Snorri and the Strangers,* Harper, 1976.

Ann Himler, *Waiting for Cherries,* Harper, 1976.

Joanne Ryder, *Fireflies,* Harper, 1977.

Benchley, *George, The Drummer Boy,* Harper, 1977.

Betty F. Horvath, *Jasper and the Hero Business,* F. Watts, 1977.

Barbara Brenner, *Wagon Wheels,* Harper, 1978.

(With Raphael) Robert Penn Warren, *Selected Poems, 1923-1975,* Franklin Library, 1981.

James Preller, *Maxx Trax II: Monster Truck Adventure,* Scholastic Inc., 1988.

Also contributing illustrator for various publications, including the *New York Herald Tribune.*

ADAPTATIONS: All upon a Stone was adapted as a filmstrip with cassette by Miller-Brody Productions in 1976.

SIDELIGHTS: Don Bolognese is an author and illustrator who has designed the graphics for some ninety children's books. Often collaborating with his wife, artist and writer Elaine Raphael, Bolognese has penned and designed popular stories like *The Sleepy Watchdog* and *Sam Baker, Gone West,* has produced books describing various artistic mediums, and has created volumes explaining the art of ancient cultures and how to draw it. Bolognese's solo and joint efforts have been recognized by critics who applaud his work for its attractive and vivid presentation. For example, Mary B. Mason in a review for *School Library Journal* asserted that Bolognese's pictures in Gladys Yessayan Cretan's award-winning book *Me, Myself, and I* "create a beautiful kaleidoscopic effect appropriate to the theme."

Bolognese was born and raised in New York City. Pursuing an interest in design, he attended Cooper Union Art School, graduating in 1954. That same year he married fellow student Raphael, an artist he had worked with during his studies. In an autobiographical sketch for the *Fourth Book of Junior Authors,* Bolognese described his school experience, recalling that the couple learned "the value of artists working together" as well as the need to expose their work to their peers and each other. "And while it is not always easy living with your most perceptive critic," he added, "it is instructive and enriching."

Beginning his career as a free-lance illustrator in 1954, Bolognese first saw his artwork published in book form in Anna Belle Loken's *The Colt from the Dark Forest* in 1959. More design work for other authors' stories followed before he teamed with Raphael to write and illustrate *The Sleepy Watchdog* in 1964. Also published that year was a volume containing reproductions of the woodcuts and calligraphic text that the artist had prepared for "The Miracles of Christ" exhibit for the Vatican Pavilion at the New York World's Fair. His

first solo, self-illustrated children's book, *Once upon a Mountain,* appeared in 1967.

In this work, Bolognese tells the story of a young shepherd boy who mischievously yells for help one day, only to receive the taunting reply "he haw haw" from someone on a nearby mountain. Angered, he informs his king of the insulting rebuttal, and the ruler declares war on the people of the neighboring peak. But when the monarch's army invades the foreign land, the soldiers find their adversaries to be nothing more than an old hermit and a loud-braying donkey. Bolognese's illustrations for the book were deemed inventive and interesting by some reviewers. Noting that the artist used an array of paper colors, *Library Journal* contributor Della Thomas asserted that Bolognese's "scratchy drawings ... swarm with activity."

Bolognese has also received critical recognition for his artistic contributions to award-winning books such as Jean Craighead George's *All upon a Stone,* which describes the adventures of a young mole cricket who climbs from beneath a rock one day. The illustrator's design work with Raphael has also met positive reviews. Their work in F. N. Monjo's *Letters to Horseface: Being the Story of Wolfgang Amadeus Mozart's Journey to Italy 1769-1770 When He Was a Boy of Fourteen,* for example, was deemed "elegantly and imaginatively designed," by a *Horn Book* magazine contributor. The critic also pointed out that the couple had visited Italy in order to conduct research for their sketch work.

Bolognese recreated the world of a young mole cricket in his illustrations for Jean Craighead George's *All upon a Stone.*

In recent years Bolognese has concentrated on preparing a variety of "how-to-illustrate" books, many with Raphael. The works have ranged from describing the techniques involved in drawing horses, dinosaurs, and spacecraft, to designing and painting with computers, to learning to create figures and faces. Among these volumes are the couple's *Pen and Ink, Pencil,* and *Drawing Fashions: Figures, Faces, and Techniques.* The first two books, according to a *Bulletin of the Center for Children's Books* reviewer, feature "unusually articulate discussion[s] of the materials, techniques, practice, and vision" needed to succeed in these mediums. While some critics were quick to note the duo's effective use of illustration to present a concept or describe an effect, other commentators thought the books showed readers how to appreciate art as well as its creation. *Drawing Fashions* received similar praise. Eleanor K. MacDonald in a review for *School Library Journal* called the volume "well-written, the advice sound and the sketches attractive."

During the course of his career, Bolognese has self-illustrated some eight books, has collaborated with Raphael on some thirteen more, and has illustrated the texts of nearly seventy other stories. An instructor of lettering and calligraphy at Brooklyn's Pratt Institute, he has also served as an educator at Cooper Union Art School, New York University, and the Metropolitan Museum of Art, sometimes teaching in conjunction with Raphael. In the late 1980s, Bolognese and his wife began a series of books explaining the history of ancient cultures through art as well as how to draw in said styles. Titled *Drawing History,* the series has focused on ancient Greece, Egypt, and Rome.

WORKS CITED:

Bolognese, Dan, essay in *Fourth Book of Junior Authors and Illustrators,* edited by Doris De Montreville and Elizabeth D. Crawford, Wilson, 1978.
Review of *Letters to Horseface: Being the Story of Wolfgang Amadeus Mozart's Journey to Italy 1769-1770 When He Was a Boy of Fourteen, Horn Book,* February, 1976, pp. 51-52.
MacDonald, Eleanor K., review of *Drawing Fashions: Figures, Faces, and Techniques, School Library Journal,* April, 1986, p. 96.
Mason, Mary B., review of *Me, Myself, and I, School Library Journal,* January, 1970, p. 48.
Review of *Pen and Ink* and *Pencil, Bulletin of the Center for Children's Books,* July, 1986.
Thomas, Della, review of *Once upon a Mountain, Library Journal,* November 15, 1967, p. 4241.

FOR MORE INFORMATION SEE:

PERIODICALS

Bulletin of the Center for Children's Books, May, 1970, p. 142; April, 1971, p. 118; February, 1988.
Horn Book, April, 1971, p. 163.
Kirkus Reviews, September 15, 1967, p. 1129.
Library Journal, May 15, 1971, p. 1795.

School Library Journal, October, 1986; January, 1987, p. 71.*

—*Sketch by Kathleen J. Edgar*

* * *

**BOWLER, Jan Brett
See BRETT, Jan (Churchill)**

* * *

BRANDEL, Marc 1919-

PERSONAL: Name originally Marcus Beresford; name legally changed during 1960s; born March 28, 1919, in London, England; son of John Davis Beresford (a writer) and Beatrice Roskams; married Ruda Podemska, September, 1956; children: Antonia, Vanessa Tara, Shaena. *Education:* Attended St. Catharine's College, Cambridge, 1937-38, and Westminster College, 1939-40. *Politics:* Liberal. *Religion:* None. *Hobbies and other interests:* Sailing, the movies, and living in other coutries, such as Mexico, France, and Ireland.

ADDRESSES: Home—1228 Euclid St., No. 10, Santa Monica, CA 90404. *Agent*—William Morris Agency, 1350 Avenue of the Americas, New York, NY 10019.

CAREER: Writer. Dover Film Productions, Inc., director, 1960-64; Grenada Television, England, writer/producer, 1964-69. *Military service:* Served in merchant marine during World War II.

MEMBER: PEN, Writers Guild of America West.

WRITINGS:

NOVELS FOR YOUNG PEOPLE

The Mine of Lost Days, illustrated by John Verling, Lippincott, 1974.
The Mystery of the Kidnapped Whale, Random House, 1983.
The Mystery of the Two-Toed Pigeon, Random House, 1984.
The Mystery of the Rogues' Reunion, Random House, 1985.
An Ear for Danger, Random House, 1989.

NOVELS FOR ADULTS

Rain before Seven, Harper, 1945.
The Rod and the Staff, Harper, 1947.
The Barriers Between, Dial, 1949.
The Choice, Dial, 1950.
The Time of the Fire, Random House, 1954.
The Man Who Liked Women, Simon & Schuster, 1972.
Survivor, Simon & Schuster, 1976.
The Lizard's Tail, Simon & Schuster, 1979.
Murder in the Family, Avon, 1985.
A Life of Her Own, Houghton, 1985.

PLAYS AND SCREENPLAYS

Captive City (screenplay), [Rome], 1962.

The Mine of Lost Days
Marc Brandel

After working in television for over fifteen years, Marc Brandel turned to writing fiction for a young audience with *The Mine of Lost Days*. (Cover illustration by John Verling.)

The Man Who Let It Rain (play), first produced in London at Theatre Royal, 1964.
Double Trouble (screenplay), MGM, 1967.

Contributor to numerous television series, including *Kraft Theater, Playhouse 90, Amos Burke, Barnaby Jones, Alfred Hitchcock Hour,* and *Fantasy Island.*

OTHER

Contributor of short stories to periodicals, including *Colliers, Cosmopolitan,* and *Atlantic Monthly.*

ADAPTATIONS: The Lizard's Tail was adapted for the film *The Hand,* Orion Pictures, 1981.

WORK IN PROGRESS: The Hope, a novel of suspense; *Murder in a Nudist Colony,* a "whodunit" set in the Republic of Belize.

SIDELIGHTS: Marc Brandel told *SATA:* "My father was a professional writer, author of some fifty novels, and a staff reviewer for the *Times Literary Supplement.* I grew up surrounded by books. Talk of publishers, agents, reprints, and foreign rights are among my first memories. At the age of about five, my brother and I used to play a game called 'manuscript reader.' We would pretend to leaf through a typescript and then decide whether to publish it or not. Usually not.

"Perhaps because of this early influence, I decided at the age of eleven to become a painter. For the next seven or eight years I looked at everything visually, in terms of line, color, and perspective. The unfortunate teachers who tried to educate me at a series of Dickensian English boarding schools existed for me as little more than canvases, perpetually enclosed in imaginary frames. I was keenly aware of the highlights on their noses and foreheads, but only rarely of what they were saying to me.

"I left school at sixteen to become a painter. I had miraculously graduated with special credits in eight subjects, but my only real interest was in colored reproductions of the works of Francisco Jose de Goya, Diego Velazquez, Rembrandt van Rijn, and El Greco. If I went into a library it was to learn all I could about these masters.

"A year at a provincial art school taught me that I had absolutely no talent.

"For the next two years I drifted uneasily between the desire to be a movie director and an advertising executive. I had a series of menial jobs in movie studios and advertising agencies. I learned, among other things, that the actual craft of making motion pictures was the most boring manufacturing process in the world. Except the recording of radio commercials. I spent a year at Cambridge University. After two years of earning my own living in the outside world, I was too old to enjoy and too young to appreciate student life.

"I decided to emigrate to the United States. By the time I landed in New York I had made up my mind to be a writer. I kept this ambition to myself. I never talked about it. But during the next couple of years, as I worked at even more menial jobs, dishwasher, busboy, stock clerk, student-teacher at a college in Missouri, I wrote three novels, abandoning each one at around page 140. I have no idea what they were like, probably dreadful. But at least they were not autobiographical. They were stories. I was gradually learning something about writing. I would read a few pages by some writer I admired, Graham Greene, Somerset Maugham, *never* Ernest Hemingway, close the book and try to reproduce the passage in my own words. I believe many other writers have tried this same learning method.

"At the time of Pearl Harbor [the Japanese attack that prompted the U.S. entry into World War II] I was about forty pages into a fourth novel. I spent the next three years as a merchant seaman. My only relevant memory of that time is of standing watch in the Indian Ocean one night on one of those interminable convoy voyages. It suddenly popped into my head that I was never going to make a living as a writer. A moment later the realization also popped into my head that I might as well jump into the Indian Ocean if I couldn't. I didn't jump.

"I was released from the merchant marine around Christmas, 1944. I immediately went back to those forty pages. I cannot explain this, but it was as though those three intervening years had never existed. I simply picked up the story where I had left off without changing a word of the original manuscript. I finished it in six weeks. *Rain before Seven* was published by Harper in September, 1945, and was moderately successful. It went into two editions and was translated into several foreign languages. It was also sold to the movies, but never produced.

"I published four more novels during the next nine years. The first three of them were dreadful. I cannot look at them to this day without wincing. They should never have been written and they should never have been published. The fourth, *The Time of the Fire,* an allegory on McCarthyism published by Random House in 1954, still seems to me a reasonably good book. During those nine years I also learned to write accept-able short stories for *Colliers, Cosmopolitan, Atlantic Monthly,* and others.

"By the early 1950s, the 'Golden Age of Television' was flourishing in New York. Such programs as *Studio One, The Philco-Goodyear Playhouse, Kraft Theater,* and *Playhouse 90* were bringing a whole new generation of serious and talented playwrights to the attention of the public. Some of their plays even wound up on Broadway. The networks began to buy the rights to my published short stories. My agent persuaded me that I should adapt them for television myself.

"I did not write another novel for sixteen years. Instead I wrote somewhere around a hundred and fifty television scripts. I lost count of them after a hundred. By the late 1950s the 'Golden Age' was over. The television play had been replaced by the series. Originality had been swamped by repetition and imitation. The need for scripts seemed insatiable. Over one five-year period I did not spend a single day without having some future script deadline to be met. But—and I think this is true of most television writers, even those who churn out the soaps—I never deliberately wrote junk. I wrote to rigid specifications, but I was never aware of myself as a hack. I approached each assignment with the hope of making the script as well constructed and as entertaining as I could. I was also lucky because I spent many of those years in Europe. I worked a lot for the British Broadcast-ing Corporation and the other English companies who were having a 'Golden Age' of their own. For four years, I also produced my own television plays for Grenada Television. Six to eight of them a year.

"By the early 1970s I felt it was time to get back to writing novels. I wasn't bored with the actual writing of scripts, but I was bored with actors, directors, produc-ers, and, most of all, network executives who insisted on 'contributing' to what I wrote. I wanted to work on my own. Since then I have published four more novels and

Brandel has written several mysteries for younger readers, including *The Mystery of the Rogues' Reunion,* featuring The Three Investigators.

five books for younger readers. I have just finished another novel.

"I have never thought of myself as a success. Only as a 'small winner.' Since 1945 I have earned my living entirely as a writer. I'm glad I didn't jump into the Indian Ocean that night. My only practical regret is that I wasted that year in art school. I could have spent it learning shorthand and touch-typing. Both would have been invaluable to me as a writer. Bernard Shaw wrote all his plays in shorthand. It was the only way his words could keep pace with his thoughts.

"But on the other hand I guess I had to find out for myself that I couldn't paint."

FOR MORE INFORMATION SEE:

PERIODICALS

Booklist, October 15, 1974, p. 241; September 15, 1983, p. 164; March 1, 1984, p. 966; September 15, 1985, p. 126.
Kirkus Reviews, August 15, 1974, p. 876.
Publishers Weekly, October 28, 1974, p. 49.

School Library Journal, December, 1983, p. 80; May, 1984, p. 101.

*   *   *

BRETT, Jan (Churchill) 1949-
(Jan Brett Bowler)

PERSONAL: Born December 1, 1949, in Hingham, MA; daughter of George (a sales engineer) and Jean (a teacher; maiden name, Thaxter) Brett; married Daniel Bowler, February 27, 1970 (divorced, 1979); married Joseph Hearne (a musician), August 18, 1980; children: (first marriage) Lia. *Education:* Attended Colby Junior College (now Colby-Sawyer College), 1968-69, and Boston Museum of Fine Arts School, 1970. *Hobbies and other interests:* Horses, gliding.

ADDRESSES: Home—132 Pleasant St., Norwell, MA 02061.

CAREER: Painter; author and illustrator of children's books. *Exhibitions:* Master Eagle Gallery, New York City, 1981; Gallery on the Green, Lexington, MA, 1985; Main Street Gallery, Nantucket, MA, 1987; Society of Illustration show, New York City, 1991.

AWARDS, HONORS: Parents' Choice award, Parents' Choice Foundation, 1981, for *Fritz and the Beautiful Horses,* 1988, for *Mother's Day Mice; In the Castle of Cats* and *Fritz and the Beautiful Horses* were chosen as "Children's Choices" by the International Reading Association, 1982; Ambassador of Honor Book, English-Speaking Union of the United States, 1983, for *Some Birds Have Funny Names;* Best of the Year Award, Critic Gene Shalit of National Broadcasting Company, Inc. (NBC-TV), 1983 and 1984, for Sunrise Publication calendar; children's book award, University of Nebraska, 1984, for *Fritz and the Beautiful Horses;* Outstanding Science Trade Book for Children, National Science Teachers Association, 1984, for *Some Plants Have Funny Names;* top ten children's books of the year, *Redbook* magazine, 1985, for *Annie and the Wild Animals; Booklist* magazine editor's choice, American Library Association (ALA), 1986, for *The Twelve Days of Christmas,* 1987, for *Goldilocks and the Three Bears;* best of the year award, *Parent's* magazine, 1988, for *Mother's Day Mice,* 1991, for *The Owl and the Pussycat.*

First prize juvenile book, New York Book Show, 1987, for *Mother's Day Mice;* best of the year award, *Newsweek* magazine, 1987, for *Goldilocks and the Three Bears,* 1991, for *Berlioz the Bear; The Enchanted Book* received a certificate of merit from the Bookbuilders West Book Show in 1987; Pick of the Lists, American Bookseller, 1988, for *The First Dog,* 1989, for *The Mitten,* 1990, for *The Wild Christmas Reindeer,* 1991, for *The Owl and the Pussycat* and *Berlioz the Bear;* Best Children's Books citation, *New Yorker* magazine, 1988, for *The First Dog,* 1989, for *The Mitten,* 1990, for *The Wild Christmas Reindeer,* 1991, for *Berlioz the Bear; The Mitten* was named a *Booklist* best children's book of the 1980s in 1989; artist award, New England Booksellers' Association, 1990; *School Library Journal* best

book of the year citation, Waldenbooks' best children's book honor award, and ALA notable book citation, all 1991, for *The Owl and the Pussycat.*

MEMBER: Society of Children's Book Writers.

WRITINGS:

SELF-ILLUSTRATED CHILDREN'S BOOKS

Fritz and the Beautiful Horses, Houghton, 1981.
Good Luck Sneakers, Houghton, 1981.
Annie and the Wild Animals, Houghton, 1985.
The First Dog, Harcourt, 1988.
The Wild Christmas Reindeer, Putnam, 1990.
Berlioz the Bear, Putnam, 1991.
The Trouble with Trolls, Putnam, 1992.

RETELLER AND ILLUSTRATOR; FOR CHILDREN

Goldilocks and the Three Bears (adapted from the Andrew Lang version), Dodd, 1987.
The Mitten: A Ukrainian Folktale, Putnam, 1989.
Beauty and the Beast, Clarion Books, 1989.

ILLUSTRATOR; ALL FOR CHILDREN

(Under name Jan Brett Bowler) Stephen Krensky, *Woodland Crossings,* Atheneum, 1978.
Mary Louise Cuneo, *Inside a Sand Castle and Other Secrets,* Houghton, 1979.
Simon Seymour, *The Secret Clocks: Time Senses of Living Things,* Viking, 1979.
Eve Bunting, *St. Patrick's Day in the Morning,* Clarion Books, 1980.
Mark Taylor, *Young Melvin and Bulger,* Doubleday, 1981.

JAN BRETT

Betty Boegehold, *In the Castle of the Cats,* Dutton, 1981.

Diana Harding Cross, *Some Birds Have Funny Names,* Crown, 1981.

Ruth Krauss, *I Can Fly,* Golden Press, 1981.

Jeanette L. Groth, *Prayer: Learning How to Talk to God,* Concordia, 1983.

Bunting, *The Valentine Bears,* Clarion Books, 1983.

Cross, *Some Plants Have Funny Names,* Crown, 1983.

Taylor, *The Great Rescue* (part of the "Cabbage Patch Kids" series), Parker Brothers, 1984.

Jennifer Perryman, *Where Are All the Kittens?,* Random House, 1984.

Annetta Dellinger, *You Are Special to Jesus,* Concordia, 1984.

Dorothy Van Woerkom, *Old Devil Is Waiting: Three Folktales* (part of the "Let Me Read" series), Harcourt, 1985.

The Wizard of Oz: A Story to Color, Random House, 1985.

Bunting, *The Mother's Day Mice,* Clarion Books, 1986.

The Twelve Days of Christmas, Dodd, 1986.

Pamela Jane, *Noelle of the Nutcracker,* Houghton, 1986.

Bunting, *Scary, Scary Halloween,* Clarion Books, 1986.

Janina Porazinska, *The Enchanted Book: A Tale from Krakow,* translated by Bozena Smith, Harcourt, 1987.

Bunting, *Happy Birthday, Dear Duck,* Clarion Books, 1988.

Edward Lear, *The Owl and the Pussycat,* Putnam, 1991.

Also illustrator of a calendar for Sunrise Publications.

ADAPTATIONS: The Great Rescue was adapted for audiocassette by Parker Brothers in 1984.

SIDELIGHTS: When Massachusetts-born Jan Brett rendered the drawings for Stephen Krensky's 1978 work of fables, *Woodland Crossings,* she began to realize her childhood dream of becoming a professional illustrator of children's books. As Brett developed her career, she continued to provide art for the texts of others, adapted classic fairy tales such as *Goldilocks and the Three Bears,* and illustrated her own stories, including the critically acclaimed *Fritz and the Beautiful Horses.* Brett's work, which frequently concerns animals and nature, has often incorporated Old World folklore and motifs. Her books have received attention from critics who are quick to applaud her effective use of illustration to further the meaning, symbolism, and moral of a story. Her inclusion of detailed borders and side panels to graphically reveal additional aspects not presented in the main story line and pictures has, in fact, become her trademark. Such ornamental peripherals offer "a story around a story, so that the reader instantly becomes an insider," pointed out *New York Times Book Review* contributor Pat Ross in a critique of Brett's illustrations for *Annie and the Wild Animals.* Praising the artist's work on *Beauty and the Beast* as "a brilliant marriage of artwork and text," a *Publishers Weekly* reviewer judged Brett "a contemporary illustrator of consummate skill."

Daughter of a sales engineer and a teacher, Brett attended the Boston Museum of Fine Arts School in 1970 to refine her artistic skills. She credits her keen ability to create fantasy through pictures and words to her mother, who encouraged her to be imaginative, and to her own penchant for becoming part of the stories she read in her childhood. "I remember the special quiet of rainy days when I felt that I could enter the pages of my beautiful picture books," she once told *Something about the Author (SATA).* "Now I try to recreate that feeling of believing that the imaginary place I'm drawing really exists." To elicit such an authentic air, Brett often uses real-life people, settings, and occurrences as the basis for her work. She feels the beauty and tranquility of her summer home in the mountains, near where her husband plays with the Boston Symphony Orchestra, provides a source of inspiration and new ideas. Brett's stories and illustrations are also influenced by images she has stored in her memory.

For example, the artist's childhood love of horses infiltrated her 1981 children's story *Fritz and the Beautiful Horses*—her first published book to feature her talents as both writer and illustrator. Centering around the theme that one's inner beauty is more important than one's outer appearance, the volume describes how a shy, lanky pony named Fritz wins the hearts of townspeople through kindness and good deeds, despite his lack of grandeur and physical presence. Featuring Eastern European motifs and settings, Brett's book was widely lauded by critics, many of whom claimed her art evoked the enchantment of a distant era. Many reviewers assessed the book's paintings as special and magnificent. A *Publishers Weekly* commentator, for instance, described the text of *Fritz and the Beautiful Horses* as "simple but engaging," adding that Brett's drawings showcase "the beauty of equines as few pictures do."

Brett continued to win critical approval with subsequent self-illustrated storybooks like 1985's *Annie and the Wild Animals* and 1990's *The Wild Christmas Reindeer.* In the former title, Brett draws from her daughter Lia's fascination with undomesticated critters to show what happens when a little girl's pet kitty disappears one winter and she searches for new friends in the untamed forest. Sad and lonely, the child leaves corn cakes in the snow to attract potential playmates and eventually meets a moose, wildcat, bear, and other beasts. However, she discovers each to be an unacceptable replacement for her beloved cat as they are either too ferocious, ornery, or unruly. Annie's desperation is short-lived, however, as she is reunited in the spring with her favorite feline. In the end, as foreshadowed in the border art of earlier pages, the tabby returns with three kittens in tow. A number of commentators remarked on the style of clothing and backdrops used in *Annie and the Wild Animals,* pointing out that both were greatly detailed and featured a Scandinavian design. The book's art utilizes a "treasury of motifs taken from the universal tradition of folk art and crafts," asserted Ross in the *New York Times Book Review.* Brett's depiction of animals was also praised. A *Horn Book* reviewer found

In *Fritz and the Beautiful Horses,* author/illustrator Brett evokes motifs and settings of a distant era in Eastern Europe.

the work's creatures "rendered with ... humor," and praised the artist's "elaborate illustrations" for adeptly conveying the change from winter to spring.

Like *Annie and the Wild Animals,* Brett's *Wild Christmas Reindeer* features a young female protagonist and the lessons she learns from her experiences with a group of disobedient beasts. Charting the frustrations of the youngster who trains Santa Claus's reindeer for their infamous journey on Christmas Eve, Brett shows how uncooperative the feisty reindeer become when scolded by the girl following a poor practice session. After the child realizes the ineffectiveness of her harsh instruction and subsequently offers kind words of encouragement to her pupils, the rambunctious creatures respond earnestly and the trainer succeeds in readying the group for its important flight. Brett again uses borders and side panels to disclose additional action. The peripheral illustrations feature gift-making elves at work, while the borders contain other holiday paraphernalia. A hit with many critics, *Wild Christmas Reindeer* was deemed a

"sweet Christmas fantasy that shows Brett at her best," in *Publishers Weekly.*

In addition to her self-illustrated children's books, Brett has won acclaim for her art for other authors' texts, particularly works like Eve Bunting's *St. Patrick's Day in the Morning* and *Valentine Bears,* Diana Harding Cross's *Some Birds Have Funny Names* and *Some Plants Have Funny Names,* and Betty Boegehold's *In the Castle of the Cats.* Brett's retelling and picture work for classic fairy tales such as *Goldilocks and the Three Bears* and *Beauty and the Beast* has also met positive critical response. These books again demonstrate Brett's artistic vision as she furthers the main story lines through ornate pictures. In the latter title, for example, the book's moral—that appearances can be deceiving—is graphically presented in the tapestries that adorn the walls within the principal illustrations. In these wall hangings, the beast's servants, who appear in animal form in the primary story, are depicted as they truly exist in human form. "Brett shows real finesse in drafting various animals," observed a reviewer of *Beau-*

A young girl learns an important lesson while training Santa's reindeer for their Christmas flight in Brett's self-illustrated *The Wild Christmas Reindeer.*

ty and the Beast in the *Bulletin for the Center of Children's Books.* Calling the book "lovely, carefully made," a *Kirkus Review* contributor deemed it a "simple, yet graceful retelling." The artwork for *Goldilocks* received equal praise. Brett's illustrations "burst with action," noted *Horn Book*'s Ellen Fader, adding that the volume "infuses the old nursery tale with new life."

Jan Brett told *SATA:* "My imagination has always run away with me. As a child, this was entertaining but confusing. As an adult, I can direct my ideas toward children's books. Often I put borders in my books to contain the overflow of thoughts."

WORKS CITED:

Review of *Annie and the Wild Animals, Horn Book,* July, 1985, p. 434.
Review of *Beauty and the Beast, Bulletin of the Center for Children's Books,* December, 1989, p. 79.
Review of *Beauty and the Beast, Kirkus Reviews,* August 15, 1989, p. 1242.
Review of *Beauty and the Beast, Publishers Weekly,* September 8, 1989, p. 69.
Fader, Ellen, review of *Goldilocks and the Three Bears, Horn Book,* February, 1988, p. 75.
Review of *Fritz and the Beautiful Horses, Publishers Weekly,* January 9, 1981, p. 76.
Ross, Pat, review of *Annie and the Wild Animals, New York Times Book Review,* August 25, 1985, p. 25.
Something about the Author, Volume 42, Gale, 1986.
Review of *The Wild Christmas Reindeer, Publishers Weekly,* August 10, 1990, p. 443.

FOR MORE INFORMATION SEE:

PERIODICALS

Bulletin of the Center for Children's Books, December, 1986.
Kirkus Reviews, May 15, 1981, p. 1.
New York Times Book Review, April 30, 1978, p. 46.
Publishers Weekly, March 14, 1980, p. 75; December 4, 1981, p. 50; August 12, 1988, pp. 456, 458.
School Library Journal, May, 1978, p. 69; May, 1980, p. 51; April, 1981, pp. 109-110; April, 1985, p. 75; December, 1987, p. 70; November, 1988, p. 83; October, 1990, p. 34.

*   *   *

BRIGHT, Sarah
See SHINE, Deborah

*   *   *

BROWN, Fornan 1901-
(Richard Meeker)

PERSONAL: Born January 8, 1901, in Otsego, MI; daughter of George Richard Brown (an editor-publisher) and Pet Forman (a homemaker). *Education:* University of Michigan, B.A., 1922, M.A., 1923.

ADDRESSES: Home and office—1141 North El Centro Ave., Los Angeles, CA 90038.

CAREER: University of Michigan, Ann Arbor, MI, instructor in English, 1924; North Carolina College for Women (now University of North Carolina at Greensboro), Greensboro, assistant professor of English, 1925-27; Yale Puppeteers, Teatro Torito, Los Angeles, CA, cofounder and writer, 1929-31; affiliated with The Puppet Show, New York City, 1933; Turnabout Theatre, Los Angeles, emcee, accompanist, and writer, 1941-56.

AWARDS, HONORS: Award from Los Angeles Drama Critics Circle, 1989, for distinguished work in theater.

WRITINGS:

Walls (poems), [privately printed], 1925.
Spider Kin (poems), R. Packard (Chicago), 1929.
The Pie-Eyed Piper, and Other Impertinent Puppet Plays, Greenberg (New York), 1933.
(Under name Richard Meeker) *Better Angel,* Greenberg, 1933, Alyson, 1989.
Punch's Progress, Macmillan, 1936.
Small Wonder, Scarecrow, 1980.
A Gamut of Girls, Capra, 1988.
The Generous Jefferson Bartleby Jones, Alysonwonderland, 1991.

Also author of plays, songs, and sketches for puppet theater, including the Yale Puppeteers, Los Angeles, CA; author of lyrics for productions of Los Angeles Civic Light Opera, including *The Merry Widow;* author of plays, sketches, and songs for Turnabout Theatre, Los Angeles.

SIDELIGHTS: Fornan Brown told *SATA:* "I began writing verse in high school, and poetry later in Ann Arbor, Michigan, where I met and became friends with Robert Frost, who was poet in residence at the University of Michigan in the early 1920s. I remember his warning me to watch out for my facility, and it is amusing and ironic that without this facility I should probably have starved, for all my life has been connected with the theater, both in original writing and rewriting. Starting out with writing plays, songs, and sketches for puppets and marionettes, over the years I have written all the material used by the Yale Puppeteers (of which I was, along with Harry Burnett and Richard Brandon, cofounder). I also rewrote and brought up to date lyrics of a dozen productions of the Los Angeles Civic Light Opera— including a completely new set of lyrics for *The Merry Widow,* the production that opened the Lincoln Center Theater in New York City in the 1950s. At our Los Angeles theater, Turnabout Theatre, from 1941 to 1956, I not only acted as accompanist and emcee, but wrote all the plays, sketches, and songs performed there. This included over fifty songs for our guest star, Elsa Lanchester, and material for all the rest of the company—a task where my 'facility' was my bread and butter.

"I am now ninety years old, and I regret that my later years have been relatively unproductive, though I am thankful that at this age I can still spin a rhyme or two. Writing *The Generous Jefferson Bartleby Jones* was fun, but I think the most rewarding thing that has happened to me has been the rediscovery of *Better Angel,* and the realization that its message of hope, or the possibility of hope, is still pertinent and as warming as it proved sixty years ago."

*   *   *

BRUNHOFF, Laurent de 1925-

PERSONAL: Surname is pronounced "*Broon*-off"; born August 30, 1925, in Paris, France; son of Jean (an author and illustrator) and Cecile (a pianist; maiden name, Sabouraud) de Brunhoff; married Marie-Claude Bloch, 1951 (divorced, 1987); married Phyllis Rose (a writer), 1989; children: (first marriage) Anne, Antoine. *Education:* Attended Lycee Pasteur and Academie de la Grande Chaumiere. *Hobbies and other interests:* Gardening, yoga.

ADDRESSES: Home—74 Wyllys Ave., Middletown, CT 06457. *Office*—122 East 82nd St., New York, NY 10028.

CAREER: Author and illustrator of children's books. Began to work seriously at painting c. 1945; at the same time he became involved in continuing the "Babar" picture book series his father had originated.

EXHIBITIONS: Brunhoff's paintings in the 1950s were displayed at the Galeire Maeght and the Salon de Mai.

Exhibitions of watercolors from his books include: "Original Watercolors by Jean and Laurent de Brunhoff," International Exhibitions Foundation, 1983-84; "Babar and Watercolors of Laurent de Brunhoff," Mary Ryan Gallery, New York, 1987 and 1990; Art Services International, 1989-91; "Fifty Years of Babar," 1990-92; and "The Art of Babar," a display featured in different museums in the U.S., 1991—. Works have been displayed at various museums in the United States, including the National Academy of Design, New York City.

AWARDS, HONORS: New York Times "Best Illustrated Books of the Year," 1956, for *Babar's Fair;* Officier des Arts et Lettres, 1984; "Walter" award, Parson's School of Design, 1988, for work with educational illustration; Chevalier of the Legion of Honor (France), 1992.

WRITINGS:

"BABAR THE ELEPHANT" SERIES; SELF-ILLUSTRATED

Babar's Cousin: That Rascal Arthur, translated by Merle Haas, Random House, 1948 (published in French as *Babar et ce coquin d'Arthur,* Hachette, 1947).

Babar's Picnic, translated by Haas, Random House, 1949 (published in French as *Pique-Nique chez Babar,* Hachette, 1949).

Babar's Visit to Bird Island, translated by Haas, Random House, 1952 (published in French as *Babar dans l'ile aux oiseaux,* Hachette, 1951).

Babar's Fair, translated by Haas, Random House, 1954 (published in French as *La Fete de Celesteville,* Hachette, 1954).

LAURENT de BRUNHOFF

Babar and the Professor, translated by Haas, Random House, 1957 (published in French as *Babar et le Professeur Grifaton,* Hachette, 1956).

Babar's Castle, translated by Haas, Random House, 1962 (published in French as *Le Chateau de Babar,* Hachette, 1961).

Babar's French Lessons, Random House, 1963 (published in French as *Je parle Anglais avec Babar*).

Babar's Spanish Lessons (Spanish words by Roberto Eyzaguirre), Random House, 1965 (published in French as *Je parle Espanol avec Babar*).

Babar Comes to America, translated by M. Jean Craig, Random House, 1965 (published in French as *Babar a New York* and *Babar en Amerique,* Hachette, 1966).

Babar Loses His Crown, Random House, 1967.

Babar's Games (pop-up book), Random House, 1968.

Babar's Moon Trip (pop-up book), Random House, 1969.

Tele-Babar (based on the French television series), Hachette, 1969.

(Reteller) Jean de Brunhoff, *Babar aux sports d'hiver,* 7th edition, Hachette, 1969.

Babar's Birthday Surprise (also see below), Random House, 1970 (published in French as *L'Anniversaire de Babar,* Hachette, 1970).

Babar Visits Another Planet (also see below), translated by Haas, Random House, 1972 (published in French as *Babar sur la planete molle,* Hachette, 1972).

Meet Babar and His Family (also see below), Random House, 1973.

Babar and the Wully-Wully (also see below), Random House, 1975 (published in French as *Babar et le Wouly Wouly,* Hachette).

Babar Saves the Day, Random House, 1976.

Babar's Mystery (also see below), Random House, 1978 (published in French as *Babar et les quartre voleurs,* Hachette).

Babar Learns to Cook, Random House, 1978.

Babar the Magician (shape book; also see below), Random House, 1980.

Babar and the Ghost (also see below), Random House, 1981 (published in French as *Babar et le fantome,* Hachette).

(Illustrated with father, Jean de Brunhoff) *Fifty Years of Babar* (exhibition catalogue), introduction by Maurice Sendak, International Exhibitions Foundation (Washington, DC), 1983.

Babar's ABC, Random House, 1983.

Babar's Book of Color, Random House, 1984 (published in French as *Babar, le livre des couleurs,* Hachette).

Babar's Counting Book, Random House, 1986 (published in French as *Babar, le livre des chiffres,* Hachette).

Babar's Little Girl (also see below), Random House, 1987 (published in French as *Babar et sa fille Isabelle,* Hachette).

Babar's Little Circus Star, Random House, 1988.

(Illustrator with Jean de Brunhoff) *The Art of Babar: Drawings and Watercolors by Jean and Laurent de Brunhoff* (catalogue), Art Services International (Alexandria, VA), 1989.

Babar's Busy Year: A Book about Seasons, Random House, 1989.

Babar's Colors and Shape, Random House, 1989.

Babar's Number Fun, Random House, 1989.

Babar's Paint, Random House, 1989.

Babar's Busy Week, Random House, 1990.

Isabelle's New Friend, Random House, 1990.

Hello, Babar!, Random House, 1991.

Babar's Battle, Random House, 1992 (published in French as *La Victoire de Babar,* Hachette).

Also author of *Babar in the Snow* and *Je parle Italien avec Babar,* both for Hachette. Portions of the "Babar" series have been translated into eighteen languages. All "Babar" books have been published in England by Methuen.

"BABAR" BOXED SETS; SELF-ILLUSTRATED

Babar's Trunk (includes *Babar Goes on a Picnic, Babar at the Seashore, Babar the Gardener,* and *Babar Goes Skiing*), translated by Haas, Random House, 1969 (published in French as *Babar en promenade, Babar a la mer, Babar jardinier,* and *Babar fait du ski,* Hachette, 1966).

Babar's Other Trunk (includes *Babar the Camper, Babar the Athlete, Babar and the Doctor,* and *Babar the Painter*), Random House, 1971 (published in French as *Babar campeur, Babar fait du sport, Babar et le docteur* [6th edition], and *Babar artiste peintre,* Hachette, 1969).

Babar's Bookmobile (includes *Babar Bakes a Cake, Babar's Concert, Babar to the Rescue,* and *Babar's Christmas Tree*), Random House, 1974 (published in French as *Babar patissier, Babar musicien, Babar aviateur,* and *Babar et l'arbre de Noel,* Hachette, 1970).

Babar Box (includes stories *About Water, About Fire, About Air,* and *About Earth*), Diogenes Verlag (Switzerland), published in the United States as *Babar's Little Library,* Random House, 1980.

(With Jean de Brunhoff) *Babar's Anniversary Album: Six Favorite Stories* (includes Jean de Brunhoff's *The Story of Babar, The Travels of Babar,* and *Babar the King,* and Laurent de Brunhoff's *Babar's Birthday Surprise, Babar's Mystery,* and *Babar and the Wully-Wully*), introduction by Sendak, Random House, 1981.

Babar's Family Album: Five Favorite Stories (includes *Meet Babar and His Family, Babar and the Ghost, Babar the Magician, Babar Visits Another Planet,* and *Babar's Little Girl*), Random House, 1991.

OTHER CHILDREN'S BOOKS; SELF-ILLUSTRATED

Serafina the Giraffe, World Publishing, 1961 (published in French as *Serafina le Girafe,* Editions du Pont Royal, 1960).

Serafina's Lucky Find, World Publishing, 1962.

Captain Serafina, World Publishing, 1963.

Anatole and His Donkey, translated from the French by Richard Howard, Macmillan, 1963.

Bonhomme, translated from the French by Howard, Pantheon, 1965.

Gregory and Lady Turtle in the Valley of the Music Trees, translated by Howard, Pantheon, 1971 (published in French as *Gregory et Dame Tortue,* Ecole Loisirs, 1971).

Bonhomme and the Huge Beast, translated by Howard, Pantheon, 1974 (published in French as *Bonhomme et la grosse bete qui avait des escailles sur le dos,* Grasset, 1974).

The One Pig with Horns, translated from the French by Howard, Pantheon, 1979.

OTHER

(With Jean de Brunhoff) *Albums roses "Babar,"* Volume VI, Hachette, 1951-53.

(Editor) Jean de Brunhoff, *Les Adventures de Babar* (textbook), Hachette, 1959.

(Illustrator) Auro Roselli, *The Cats of the Eiffel Tower,* Dial, 1967.

ADAPTATIONS: Babar Comes to America (along with Jean de Brunhoff's *The Story of Babar*) was adapted for an animated television film, narrated by Peter Ustinov, by Lee Mendelson/Bill Melendez Productions in 1971. *Babar Comes to America* and *Babar's Birthday Surprise* were reworked for a sound recording, read by Louis Jordan, with music composed and conducted by Don Heckman, by Caedmon in 1977. *Babar's Mystery* and *Babar and the Wully-Wully* were issued on disc and cassette, read by the author, by Caedmon. The characters and situations created by Jean and Laurent de Brunhoff were adapted for the animated film *Babar: The Movie,* with voices by Gordon Pinsent and Sarah Polley, by Nelvana Entertainment in 1989. The Babar stories were also adapted by Nelvana for a television series, broadcast by Home Box Office (HBO).

SIDELIGHTS: Laurent de Brunhoff is a French author and illustrator of some thirty hardcover and more than a dozen mini books for children. He achieved widespread fame for his efforts to continue the adventures of popular elephant king Babar—a character first appearing in 1931's *Story of Babar,* written and illustrated by Brunhoff's father Jean, who died in 1937 after completing only seven "Babar" books. Brunhoff's diligent efforts to craft the pachyderm and its tales in his late father's style have proved successful with children and with some critics, although a few reviewers have asserted that Babar lost part of his distinctiveness and spirit in the transition between father and son. Due to the work of both Brunhoffs, however, Babar has become a classic figure in children's literature and a favorite with readers. The younger Brunhoff is also credited with keeping the situations and activities of Babar contemporary. Since publishing his first "Babar" story in 1946, the artist has taken Babar on visits to other countries and planets and has engaged the animal in a number of hobbies, such as camping, cooking, painting, and gardening. Under Brunhoff's guidance, the Babar series has expanded to provide readers with an educational experience as the character helps children learn the alphabet, numbers, colors, and other languages. The author has also ventured from Babar's kingdom to create a realm of original animal protagonists in books like *Serafina the*

Giraffe and *Bonhomme.* These stories have provided Brunhoff with the opportunity to showcase his own talents for art and storytelling.

Born on August 30, 1925, in Paris, France, Brunhoff is the eldest of three sons born to Jean, a post-impressionist painter, and Cecile, a pianist. During his childhood, Brunhoff was introduced to the character of Babar by his mother. In an interview with Emma Fisher in *Pied Pipers,* Brunhoff described the beginnings of the amiable pachyderm: "[My father] never had it in mind to write a book for children. He was a painter, and it just happened one day that my mother narrated a story about a little elephant to us, my brother and me. We were five and four. We liked this story of the little elephant and we told my father about it. He simply had the idea of making some drawings for us. Then he became very excited about it and made a whole book, and that was the first one."

Focusing on the early years of the future king of elephantland, that book, *The Story of Babar,* established the situations and characters upon which the originator's son would later expand. Commenting on the humanlike traits that the Brunhoffs have given Babar, Edmund Leach described the animal and his kingdom in an article for *New Society.* "Babar himself is a thoroughly civilized elephant who sleeps in a bed, reads the newspaper, drives a car, and so on," the critic assessed. "To wear no clothes is a mark of savagery. . . . Elephant society is strictly on par with that of men, and intermingles with it directly without evoking astonishment on the part of either the elephants or the humans. This land of elephants is merely a different country, as England is to France. . . . The Old Lady, the only 'real' human [shown in many of the books], has no name."

Laurent de Brunhoff has continued the character created by his father Jean in stories such as *Babar's Mystery.* (Illustration by Laurent de Brunhoff.)

The King of the Elephants and his Queen, Celeste, mingle with their subjects in Brunhoff's self-illustrated *Babar's Birthday Surprise.*

Babar became an important part of Brunhoff's childhood. Brunhoff often experimented with drawing the pachyderm, mimicking his father's creations. He was only twelve when Jean died in 1937. In all, Jean completed seven Babar stories before his death. Many readers and critics mourned the loss of Babar's genius, not anticipating further tales. But as he grew older, young Brunhoff opted to pursue his father's profession and began to paint in earnest toward the end of World War II. During this time he prepared to continue his father's legacy. "Babar was a friend to me," Brunhoff told *Publishers Weekly* in 1961. "I had lived with him for years. It occurred to me that I could follow a tradition that had been cut off too early."

Brunhoff's first attempt was *Babar's Cousin: That Rascal Arthur,* published in 1947. The book presents the childlike antics of the king's young cousin as he stows away on an airplane and must be rescued by the monarch. Carrying the inscription "dedicated to the memory of my father," the work was warmly received by some critics. In *Three Centuries of Children's Books in Europe,* Bettina Huerlimann recalled, "We scarcely dared believe our eyes when ... from a hungry Paris there appeared a new Babar book." While she admits that "it was obvious that there would be indications of weakness in the work of the twenty-year-old son of the painter," Huerlimann noted that children were not concerned by the transition. "Laurent the son gave them much pleasure in continuing his father's work with so much of his own fancy." Other reviewers expressed their delight at the expansion of the series. The *New York Times*'s Alice Fedder deemed that Brunhoff had continued to create the spirit conveyed in his father's earlier books "to a marked degree." A. M. Jordan of *Horn Book* magazine wrote that the new Babar story makes one feel like the pachyderm's "adventures had never been interrupted."

As Brunhoff produced more tales about the famed elephant, critical response was mixed. Some reviewers voiced enthusiasm when seeing Babar in new situations; others reported that the unique essence of Babar was missing. Several professed that the son, however, had succeeded in copying his father's style. "At first I found it very hard to get exactly the same elephant design as my father," remarked Brunhoff to *Publishers Weekly* in 1968, "but after a while I got it pretty well, although *I* can still see the difference." Like his father, the artist used real-life experiences in his stories, often presenting situations common to his son and daughter. In *More Junior Authors* Brunhoff explained that his children "were quite pleased to recognize themselves [in the story lines] and regard it as perfectly normal that they should be in the book along with Babar."

Composing his work in pen and watercolor, Brunhoff has taken Babar to new places in books like *Babar Comes to America,* has used the character to help children learn in volumes such as *Je parle Espanol avec Babar* and *Babar's Counting Book,* and has shown the pachyderm's experiences with fatherhood in stories like *Babar's Little Girl.* A number of critics have lauded Brunhoff's artistry as he incorporates subtle hints of elephantland into his drawings. For example, when the king travels into space in *Babar Visits Another Planet,* the aliens are presented with pachydermish shapes. Brunhoff's illustration work has also been honored. In 1956, *Babar's Fair* was named one of the *New York Times* "Best Illustrated Books of the Year."

Babar's popularity on the printed page has made the character a hot merchandizing item for retailers. The pachyderm's image has appeared on an assortment of toys, including stuffed likenesses, as well as t-shirts and a range of other items. Brunhoff's Babar has also been featured on television in a series of sixty-five episodes.

A motion picture, *Babar: The Movie,* was released in 1989, based on the characters of the books, not the works themselves. Amid his successes with Babar, Brunhoff has found time to create original stories featuring animal protagonists. These include books such as *Serafina the Giraffe* and *Bonhomme,* two series begun in the 1960s, *Gregory and Lady Turtle in the Valley of the Music Trees* in 1971, and *The One Pig with Horns,* in 1979. In a review of *Serfina the Giraffe, New York Herald Tribune* contributor Margaret Sherwood Libby assessed, "we are delighted to have him branch out for himself."

Brunhoff summed up his feelings about children and his books to Fisher: "I love children; they are always ready to follow you into a dream. For them there is no border between dream and reality." He added, "If you dream, you escape; but at the same time there are things in my books which are essential in life, even today, and which are not at all an escape—I mean friendship and love, the search for harmony and refusal of violence. And I believe that these traits are common both in my father's books and in my own."

WORKS CITED:

"Authors and Editors," *Publishers Weekly,* October 28, 1968.

"Babar: The de Brunhoff Books for Children," *Publishers Weekly,* November 20, 1961.

Brunhoff, Laurent de, *Babar's Cousin: That Rascal Arthur,* Random House, 1948.

Fedder, Alice, review of *Babar's Cousin: That Rascal Arthur, New York Times,* November 14, 1948, p. 3.

Huerlimann, Bettina, *Three Centuries of Children's Books in Europe,* translated and edited by Brian W. Alderson, Oxford University Press, 1967, pp. 195-200.

Jordan, Alice M., "New Books for Christmas: 'Babar's Cousin,'" *Horn Book,* November-December, 1948, p. 452.

Leach, Edmund, "Babar's Civilization Analysed," *New Society,* December 20, 1962, pp. 16-17.

Libby, Margaret Sherwood, review of *Serafina the Giraffe, New York Herald Tribune Lively Arts and Book Review,* March 5, 1961, p. 35.

More Junior Authors, edited by Muriel Fuller, H. W. Wilson Co., 1963, p. 33.

Wintle, Justin, and Emma Fisher, *The Pied Pipers: Interviews with the Influential Creators of Children's Literature,* Paddington Press, 1974, pp. 77-86.

Brunhoff's portraits of Babar the elephant have been the focus of museum retrospectives and have been featured in magazines, including this piece, "Beach Blanket Babar."

FOR MORE INFORMATION SEE:

BOOKS

Children's Literature Review, Volume 4, Gale, 1982, pp. 19-40.

Doyle, Brian, *The Who's Who of Children's Literature,* Schocken Books, 1968.

Fisher, Marjorie, *Who's Who in Children's Books: A Treasury of Familiar Characters of Childhood,* Holt, 1975, pp. 33-35.

Hildebrand, Ann Meizen, *Jean and Laurent de Brunhoff: The Legacy of Babar,* Twayne, 1992.

Kingman, Lee, and others, compilers, *Illustrators of Children's Books, 1957-1966,* Horn Book, 1968.

Kingman, Lee, and others, compilers, *Illustrators of Children's Books, 1967-1976,* Horn Book, 1978.

Miller, B. M., and others, compilers, *Illustrators of Children's Books, 1946-1956,* Horn Book, 1958.

Something about the Author, Volume 24, Gale, 1981, pp. 59-62.

Weber, Nicholas Fox, *The Art of Babar,* with color illustrations, Abrams, 1989.

PERIODICALS

Bulletin of the Center for Children's Books, February, 1984, p. 103; June, 1986, p. 182; June, 1987.

Chicago Sunday Tribune, November 11, 1956, p. 10; May 14, 1961, sect. 2, p. 3.

Entertainment Weekly, May 4, 1990, p. 115.

Growing Point, November, 1965, p. 604; May, 1984, p. 4269.

Horn Book, January-December, 1948; August, 1978.

Junior Bookshelf, December, 1948, p. 178; November, 1950, pp. 194-195; August, 1979, p. 194.

Kirkus Reviews, September 1, 1948, p. 434; January 15, 1961, p. 53; October 1, 1972, p. 1139.

Library Journal, November 15, 1948, p. 1672.

Life, November 26, 1965.

New Republic, December 6, 1948, p. 33.

New Statesman, November 9, 1962, p. 670; November 3, 1967, pp. 603-604.

New York Herald Tribune Book Review, November 14, 1948, p. 6; November 25, 1956, p. 12; November 17, 1957, p. 4.

New York Review of Books, December 9, 1965, p. 38.

New York Times, November 13, 1949, p. 12; November 2, 1952, p. 24; October 7, 1956, p. 38.

New York Times Book Review, April 29, 1979, p. 29.

People, March 26, 1984.

San Francisco Chronicle, November 14, 1948, p. 14.

Saturday Review, December 22, 1956, p. 37.

Saturday Review of Education, March 10, 1973, pp. 67-68.

School Library Journal, February, 1984, p. 57; February, 1985, p. 62; September, 1987, p. 162.

Spectator, November 12, 1965, p. 627.

Time, December 21, 1970.

Times Literary Supplement, December 9, 1965, p. 1154; June 26, 1969, p. 695.

Variety, July 21, 1989, pp. 2, 12.

Wilson Library Bulletin, December, 1987, p. 64.

—Sketch by Kathleen J. Edgar

BUFFIE, Margaret 1945-

PERSONAL: Born March 29, 1945, in Winnipeg, Manitoba, Canada; daughter of Ernest William John (a lithographer) and Evelyn Elizabeth (Leach) Buffie; married James Macfarlane (a teacher), August 9, 1968; children: Christine Anne. *Education:* University of Manitoba, received degree, 1967, certificate in education, 1976.

ADDRESSES: Home and office—165 Grandview St., Winnipeg, Manitoba, Canada R2G 0L4.

CAREER: Hudson's Bay Co., Winnipeg, Manitoba, illustrator, 1968-70; Winnipeg Art Gallery, Winnipeg, painting instructor, 1974-75; River East School Division, Winnipeg, high school art teacher, 1976-77; freelance illustrator and painter, 1977-84; writer, 1984—.

MEMBER: Writers' Union of Canada, Canadian Authors Association, Canadian Society of Children's Authors, Illustrators, and Performers.

AWARDS, HONORS: Young Adult Canadian Book Award, 1987-88; Ontario Arts Council grants, 1987 and 1989. Works placed on Notable Canadian Young Adult Fiction List, Canadian Children's Book Centre Our

MARGARET BUFFIE

Choice List, Canadian Library Association Notable Canadian Fiction List, and American Library Association Best Books for Young Adults List.

WRITINGS:

Who Is Frances Rain?, Kids Can Press (Toronto), 1987, published in United States as *The Haunting of Frances Rain,* Scholastic Inc., 1989.

The Guardian Circle, Kids Can Press, 1989, published in United States as *The Warnings,* Scholastic Inc., 1991.

WORK IN PROGRESS: "Another young adult novel with a supernatural twist," tentatively titled *My Mother's Ghost.*

SIDELIGHTS: Margaret Buffie told *CA:* "I was born, raised, and continue to live in Winnipeg, Manitoba, a city full of the history of the Canadian fur trade and, later, the gateway to the settlement of western Canada. I love the Manitoba prairies to the south and the lakes and tundra to the north. East of Winnipeg, just over the border of Ontario, is a small lake called Long Pine. In 1919, my grandfather built a log cabin there as a summer home for his family. My mother and father built another log house on their own property across the bay in 1943. My sisters and I have, in turn, built cottages all around this log cabin and on any given summer day you will find someone sunning on the docks or picking blueberries on the pine-covered, rocky hills that surround Long Pine. That wonderful place has wound its spell around three generations of my family and is now onto its fourth.

"As a very young child, I loved the long summers spent at my grandpa's log cabin. But I had a secret I kept from everyone else. You see, I knew that the big, swaybacked log cabin breathed quietly—watching and waiting and listening. Oh, its beds were comfortable and the smell of varnished logs and woodsmoke hung in the air, but I knew that for the cabin, there was another world beyond my family's—a world that went on when we weren't there, or perhaps even while we slept—a world that belonged to the shadowy places in the deep woods surrounding us.

"Even the inside of the cabin made of spruce logs seemed to belong to that other world. High above were the rafters spun with cobwebs, and down below were the hidden entrances for nocturnal mice to slide through and raid the kitchen. I never could find their private doors into the night.

"It was those secret places that I wanted to capture in *Who Is Frances Rain?* [published in the United States as *The Haunting of Frances Rain*]. When Lizzie McGill digs through an old cabin site and discovers a pair of spectacles, she puts them on and finds herself looking at the flickering shadows of a time past—a time that the cabin remembers and shares with her in order that she can help a restless spirit find peace on the other side.

"My second novel, *The Guardian Circle* [published in the United States as *The Warnings*], takes place in an old house in Winnipeg. The central character, fifteen-year-old Rachel MacCaw, abandoned by her parents, arrives at 135 Cambric Street one drizzly fall day. She describes the place as a crumbling pile of bricks the color of raw beef liver, set in a yard of tangled yellowing weeds and wild hedges. Leafless vines like licorice whips crawl all over the outside, and Rachel decides that they are probably the only things holding the building together. When Rachel enters 135 Cambric, she is acted upon by the magic within it. How she deals with the old people in the house and how she deals with the ghostly magic make up the story in *The Warnings.*

"I knew when I sat down with my notebooks and pencils to begin a first draft that I would have to draw on what poet Archibald MacLeish called 'the brain's ghostly house'—to walk through its darkened rooms, perhaps hear a door slam behind me or the creak of a secret stair tread. Slowly, I began to create a world that Rachel and other characters such as Luther Dubbles and Gladys Snodgrass and Dunstan Gregor could live in. A world that was made up of bright sunshine one minute and darkened hallways the next. A world of reality, but a world, also, where magic could happen at the flick of a cat's shadow."

C

CALDWELL, Doreen (Mary) 1942-

PERSONAL: Born December 13, 1942, in Leeds, Yorkshire, England; daughter of Alfred Harrison (a physician) and Joan (a teacher; maiden name, Eddy) Hollings; married Robin Caldwell (a managing director), April 27, 1963; children: James Benedict, Bridget Jane. *Education:* Attended Slade School of Fine Art, 1960-63; Manchester College of Education, teacher's certificate, 1972; Manchester Polytechnic, B.A.Hons., 1975. *Hobbies and other interests:* "My family and yoga."

ADDRESSES: Home—Cheshire, England

CAREER: Illustrator.

MEMBER: Association of Illustrators.

WRITINGS:

And All Was Revealed: Ladies' Underwear, 1907-1980, St. Martin's, 1981.

ILLUSTRATOR

Adele Geras, *Tea at Mrs. Manderby's,* Hamish Hamilton, 1976.
Geraldine Kaye, *A Different Sort of Christmas,* Kaye & Ward, 1976.
Frances Eagar, *The Rabbit Hunt,* Hamish Hamilton, 1977.
Geras, *Apricots at Midnight, and Other Stories from a Patchwork Quilt,* Hamish Hamilton, 1977, Atheneum, 1982.
Denise Hill, *No Friends for Simon,* Hamish Hamilton, 1977.
Elizabeth Beresford, *Toby's Luck,* Methuen, 1978.
Richard Dennant, *Riverboat Summer,* Hamish Hamilton, 1978.
Edith Nesbit, *The Fiery Dragon,* Kaye & Ward, 1978.
Mary Cockett, *The Birthday,* Hodder & Stoughton, 1979.
Dennant, *The Trouble with Kuri,* Hamish Hamilton, 1979.
Geras, *The Painted Garden,* Hamish Hamilton, 1979.

DOREEN CALDWELL

Eric Houghton, *Steps out of Time,* Methuen, 1979.
Leonard Clark, *The Singing Time,* Hodder & Stoughton, 1980.
Mary Stewart, *A Walk in Wolf Wood,* Hodder & Stoughton, 1980.
Hill, *The Wrong Side of the Bed,* Hamish Hamilton, 1981.
Moira Miller, *Oh, Abigail!,* Methuen, 1981.
Cockett, *The Cat and the Castle,* Hodder & Stoughton, 1982.
Joan Smith, *The Great Cube Race,* Hamish Hamilton, 1982.
Geras, *The Christmas Cat,* Hamish Hamilton, 1983.
Miller, *Just Like Abigail!,* Methuen, 1983.
Allen Saddler, *Mr. Wizz,* Abelard, 1983.
Miller, *What Size Is Andy?,* Methuen, 1984.
Gwyneth Vacher, *The Road to Merion,* Hodder & Stoughton, 1984.

Mabel Esther Allan, *The Flash Children in Winter,* Hodder & Stoughton, 1985.
Cockett, *Zoo Ticket,* Hodder & Stoughton, 1985.
Cockett, *Birthday Blues,* Hodder & Stoughton, 1986.
Cockett, *The Day of the Squirrels,* Hodder & Stoughton, 1987.
Miller, *Merry-Ma-Tanzie: The Playbook Treasury,* Oxford University Press (New York), 1987.
Miller, *Where Does Andy Go?,* Methuen, 1987.
Miller, *It's Abigail Again!,* Methuen, 1988.
Sally Grindley, *Sardines,* Hamish Hamilton, 1989.
Miller, *What Does Andy Do?,* Methuen, 1990.

Also illustrator of book covers and jackets for Dent and R. Hale.

SIDELIGHTS: Doreen Caldwell told *SATA:* "One of my earliest memories is of drawing a face. It was a beautiful face. I took it to my mother, who said, 'Lovely! Now draw the body!' I couldn't—it just wouldn't go right. In a fine fury I scribbled over everything. 'I'm too little to do bodies,' I screamed. 'You shouldn't have asked me. I will do them, but not now. I AM TOO LITTLE.' It was this incident that started my passionate involvement with drawing and made me vow never to forget what it was like to be a child.

"All through my childhood I drew and drew. I tried to copy the real world, but perhaps more importantly I drew the pictures that grew in my head, conjured by stories. At seventeen I went to the Slade School of Fine Art where Patrick George, Andrew Forge, and John Aldridge taught me how to make my hand obey my eyes. It was difficult and frustrating because I still wanted to put down the pictures that came from words. However, their persistence and patience established my knowledge of anatomy and draftsmanship.

"Eight years, a husband, and two children later I started to draw again at teacher training college. I was there because I wanted to work with or for children. I thought I could achieve this through teaching; I couldn't—my drawing was more important. After qualifying as a teacher I went to the school of graphic design at Manchester Polytechnic to study illustration. The tutors there gave me the freedom and confidence to build up and develop what abilities I had.

"Now I am an illustrator and consider it a duty to be able to draw anything and everything. This frequently demands careful research, which can prove enjoyable. I particularly like studying historical costume and have even drawn a brief history of ladies' underwear in the twentieth century. But essentially I am an illustrator of children's books. My drawings are for children, but I also hope to please the authors, whose words are the inspiration for my pictures. My job is to get under the skin of these words, to make them more imaginatively immediate. I strive continuously to create a living, breathing emotional space for the child to wander in. Lack of technical skill has often hampered this aim.

Caldwell attempts to bring emotional immediacy as well as accurate detail to her illustrations, such as this one from Adele Geras's *Tea at Mrs. Manderby's.*

"Pen and ink is a fiendishly difficult medium to master. Moreover, it took ages to discover that I worked best on a very smooth, hard-surfaced paper with an extremely fine, flexible nib. Early drawings, like those that appear in *Apricots at Midnight,* were drawn with a child's mapping pen on knobbly watercolor paper. They were torture to execute.

"During these technical flounderings, it was hard to remember that the most important thing was to hold on to the picture in one's head and have the courage to put it down on paper. Without daring to take that risk, without being able to overcome the fear of failure, one cannot do one's job properly. Finally, while working, I think of the children for whom I am drawing, because it is they who initiate the fun in illustrating."*

*   *   *

CARPENTER, Angelica Shirley 1945-

PERSONAL: Born March 28, 1945, in St. Louis, MO; daughter of James (a salesman) and Jean (a writer) Shirley; married Richard Carpenter (a psychologist), June 22, 1968; children: Carey Anne. *Education:* University of Illinois, A.B., 1967, M.Ed., 1974, M.S. in Lib.Sci., 1977.

ANGELICA CARPENTER

ADDRESSES: Home—Palm Springs, FL. *Office*—Palm Springs Library, 217 Cypress Ln., Palm Springs, FL 33461.

CAREER: University of Guelph, Guelph, Ontario, interviewer and test administrator, 1975-76; Southwest Missouri State University, Springfield, audiovisual cataloger, 1977-78; Burrell Community Mental Health Center, Springfield, librarian, 1978-79; Kearney Branch Library, Springfield, manager, 1979-82; Palm Springs Library, Palm Springs, director, 1982—. Bookfest of the Palm Beaches, executive director, 1990—.

MEMBER: American Library Association, Florida Public Library Association (secretary, 1987-88), Palm Beach County Library Association (president, 1990-91), Springfield Area Librarians Association (president, 1981), International Wizard of Oz Club, Society of Children's Book Writers, National Organization for Women.

WRITINGS:

(With mother, Jean Shirley) *Frances Hodgson Burnett,* Lerner Publications, 1990.
(With Shirley) *L. Frank Baum,* Lerner Publications, 1992.

Also author of television scripts for affiliate of Columbia Broadcasting System (CBS-TV) in Springfield, MO. Editor of newsletter for Florida Public Library Association, 1988—.

SIDELIGHTS: Angelica Shirley Carpenter told *SATA:* "My mother, Jean Shirley, is my inspiration and my coauthor. She moved to Florida to be near me after I took the job as Palm Springs Library director. It is our great pleasure to write books together. We are both lifelong fans of L. Frank Baum's 'Oz' books and also

both loved Frances Hodgson Burnett's *Secret Garden* as children, so we are especially happy to write about these authors. Mother has been writing all my life, but I am new to this business."

*   *   *

CARRIER, Lark 1947-

PERSONAL: Born March 27, 1947, in Whitefish, MT; daughter of Karl M. (a carpenter) and Fern May (a nurse; maiden name, Stolte) Kemppainen; married Ron Carrier, August 4, 1967 (divorced, 1977). *Education:* Received honors degree from Parsons School of Design, 1971; attended writing courses at Radcliffe College and Harvard University. *Politics:* Independent.

ADDRESSES: Home and office—325 Tremont St., Duxbury, MA 02332.

CAREER: Graphic designer, 1971-85; illustrator and author of children's books, 1985—.

AWARDS, HONORS: There Was a Hill . . . received a Gold Medal Award from the New York Art Directors' Annual Show, 1986; *Do Not Touch* received a Special Mention Award from the Bologna International Children's Book Fair, 1989.

WRITINGS:

SELF-ILLUSTRATED

There Was a Hill . . . , Picture Book Studio, 1985.
A Christmas Promise, Picture Book Studio, 1986.
Scout and Cody, Picture Book Studio, 1987.
Do Not Touch, Picture Book Studio, 1988.
The Snowy Path: A Christmas Journey, Picture Book Studio, 1989.
A Perfect Spring, Picture Book Studio, 1990.

LARK CARRIER

Mr. and Mrs. Seabird bring a foundling turtle egg home to complete their nest in Carrier's self-illustrated *A Perfect Spring*.

WORK IN PROGRESS: A Tree's Tale, for Dial Press, publication expected in 1994.

SIDELIGHTS: Lark Carrier told *SATA:* "Some cultures believe the place you were born on earth is your mother. Montana still nourishes me even though I moved to Seattle when I was eleven years old. Montana was a perfect place to be a part of nature. There was the excitement of waking up and rushing outdoors to a big blue sky, or standing in a hollowed tree stump surrounded by a field of two-foot-high dandelions. My pockets were always full of found treasures. Even the long winters were a wonderland of snow castles.

"At age eight I discovered the power of drawing. I wanted a toy stuffed monkey for Christmas—his name was Charlie. To make sure my mother would find him in the store I drew his picture, and to my amazement it looked like Charlie. I still have him, and he lives in my studio.

"My first book, *There Was a Hill...,* appeared in my mind while sitting in the woods. Since my background was in graphic design, not illustration, it took seven years before it was made into a book. Through experimenting with materials, I found pastels and handmade paper worked best for my style of drawing. Now I also use watercolors.

"*A Christmas Promise* was inspired by a place I lived in upstate New York: a hundred-year-old house that stood alone on the bank of the Canestio River. Its name was Lonesome Lodge, but after living in Manhattan for nine years I called it paradise. *Do Not Touch* brought out the graphic designer in me. I love wordplay and puzzles. Being a designer is problem solving and reducing ideas to communicate quickly.

"After the wordless book *The Snowy Path,* I wanted to write at length. Taking some writing courses at Radcliffe and Harvard taught me the power of drawing with words. Now I'm enjoying another way of expressing. It makes me think that the act of creating is like being an archaeologist. While an archaeologist digs into the earth, the creator searches within, but in the end they both weave a story from found fragments."

FOR MORE INFORMATION SEE:

PERIODICALS

Booklist, September 15, 1985, p. 130; November, 1986, p. 406; November 1, 1987, p. 472; April 1, 1989, p. 1379.
Publishers Weekly, September 26, 1986, p. 75; February 10, 1989, p. 70.
School Library Journal, October, 1985, p. 149; October, 1986, p. 109; May, 1989, p. 78; April, 1991, p. 90.
Wilson Library Bulletin, November, 1985, p. 44.

*   *   *

CASTANEDA, Omar S. 1954-

PERSONAL: Surname is pronounced "kah-stah-nye-dah"; born September 6, 1954, in Guatemala City, Guatemala; son of Hector-Neri (a philosopher) and Miriam Blanca (Mendez) Castaneda. *Education:* Indiana University, B.A., 1980, M.F.A., 1983. *Politics:* "In constant dialogue." *Religion:* None.

ADDRESSES: Office—Western Washington University, English Department, Bellingham, WA 98225. *Agent*—Jim Trupin, JET Literary Association, 124 East 84th St., Suite 4A, New York, NY 10028.

CAREER: Beijing Teachers College, Beijing, China, foreign expert, 1983-84; Rollins College, Winter Park, FL, visiting assistant professor, 1985-88; Western Washington University, Bellingham, visiting assistant professor, 1989-90, assistant professor, 1990—. *Military service:* U.S. Air Force, 1972-76; became E-5 sergeant.

MEMBER: Modern Language Association, Associated Writing Programs, Society of Children's Book Writers.

AWARDS, HONORS: Writers Conference Workshop awards, 1980 and 1983; Critchfield Research Award, 1987; Florida Arts Council Individual Artists Grant, 1988-89; Fulbright Senior Central America Research Award, 1989-90.

WRITINGS:

Cunuman (novel), Pineapple Press (Sarasota, FL), 1987.
(Editor with Chris Blackwell and Jonathan Harrington, and contributor) *New Visions: Fiction by Florida Writers,* Arbiter Press (Orlando, FL), 1989.
Among the Volcanoes (young adult novel), Dutton, 1991.
Esperanza's Weave (for children), Lee & Low, 1992.

OMAR S. CASTANEDA

Also author of the novels *The Voice of the Mat* and *White Sand* and the short story collections *On the Way Out* and *Faint Maps of Strange Countries.*

Free-lance writer for school department of Harcourt, 1987-88. Contributor of short stories to numerous periodicals, including *Americas Review, Blue Light/Red Light, Brushing, Calapooya Collage, Caliban, Five Fingers Review, George Washington Review, Imagine, Kenyon Review, Latin American Literary Review, Mid-American Review, Nuestro, Oxford Magazine, Painted Hills Review, Pencil Press Quarterly, Seattle Review,* and *Special Report: Fiction.* Contributor of articles and poems to additional periodicals. *Chiricu,* co-founding editor, 1979-82; *Five Fingers Review,* corresponding editor, 1991—.

WORK IN PROGRESS: A sequel to *Among the Volcanoes,* tentatively titled *Where the Sky Settles to Earth,* for Dutton; *The Fortuitous Madness of Encanta Walker-Mendez,* a novel; associate writer for *La ecologia guatemalteca,* a television documentary on the sociopolitical roots of Guatemalan ecology.

SIDELIGHTS: Omar S. Castaneda told *SATA:* "If there is anything overridingly important to my writing it is my bicultural background. My most important themes include the clash of cultures, how people create their identity out of the turmoil when traditions and new worldviews collide. I think of myself as active in bringing to light the struggles of ethnic and minority issues within American and global society. I count myself a feminist, an activist for those who are struggling to break the sometimes oppressive weight of history and find just a little space for themselves where they might have dignity and voice.

"I am mostly an adult fiction writer, but I see children's literature as vitally important and as a rich area. We too often think of children's literature as a 'talking down' or as a place to perpetuate the traditional, but I like to think that children are sometimes the most open and flexible readers. I can see young people able to entertain ideas and a newness that too often frightens adults because it might threaten their vision of normalcy. Young readers haven't yet created such rigid world-views.

"Moreover, my theme of creating identity is particularly relevant to children and young adults. It is the essence of their lives: trying to judge what of their 'traditions' are worth keeping and yet trying to formulate for themselves something quite new. This is tremendously exciting to me!"

FOR MORE INFORMATION SEE:

PERIODICALS

Horn Book, May, 1991, p. 335.
Kirkus Reviews, February 15, 1991, p. 245.
Publishers Weekly, December 21, 1990, p. 57.
School Library Journal, March, 1991, p. 211.

* * *

CHANG, Margaret (Scrogin) 1941-

PERSONAL: Born July 12, 1941, in Portola, CA; daughter of Frank Piety (a lumber salesman) and Hope (a secretary; maiden name, Millar) Scrogin; married Raymond Chang (a college professor), August 3, 1968; children: Elizabeth Hope. *Education:* Scripps College, B.A., 1963; Rutgers University, M.L.S., 1965; Simmons College, M.A., 1988. *Politics:* Democrat. *Religion:* Liberal Protestant.

ADDRESSES: Home—146 Forest Rd., Williamstown, MA 01267. *Office*—North Adams State College, North Adams, MA 01247.

CAREER: Joseph Estabrook School, Lexington, MA, librarian, 1965-67; New York Public Library, New York City, children's librarian, 1967-68; Mount Greylock Regional High School, Williamstown, MA, librarian, 1968-72; Williams College, Williamstown, part-time reference librarian, 1979-89; Buxton School, Williamstown, librarian, 1985—; North Adams State College, North Adams, MA, instructor in literature for children and young adults, 1989—; writer.

MEMBER: American Library Association, Society of Children's Book Writers.

WRITINGS:

Discovering Your Library, Creative Teaching Press, 1976.
(With husband, Raymond Chang) *Speaking of Chinese,* Norton, 1978, revised edition published by Deutsch (London), 1980.
(With Chang) *In the Eye of War,* Margaret K. McElderry Books, 1990.

MARGARET CHANG

Also author of the play *The Great Man's Wife,* produced locally; frequent contributor to *School Library Journal.*

SIDELIGHTS: Margaret Chang told *SATA:* "I was born in California's High Sierra and grew up in postwar [World War II] Los Angeles, where I savored the multicultural flavor of my surroundings. My two abiding interests as a child were reading and observing the marine life in the tide pools and on the beaches of southern California. I earned a library degree, specializing in service to children and young adults and have worked in public, school, and academic libraries. My marriage to Raymond Chang took me to Williamstown, where I have lived ever since. Since moving to Williamstown, I have been a high school librarian, mother, community volunteer, playwright, student and teacher of children's literature, and 'constant scribbler.'"

*   *   *

CHANG, Raymond

PERSONAL: Born in Hong Kong; married Margaret Scrogin (a teacher, librarian, and writer), August 3, 1968; children: Elizabeth Hope. *Education:* University of London, B.S. (with first class honours), 1962; Yale University, Ph.D., 1966. *Politics:* Independent. *Hobbies and other interests:* Gardening, tennis, playing the violin.

ADDRESSES: Home—146 Forest Rd., Williamstown, MA 01267. *Office*—Department of Chemistry, Williams College, Williamstown, MA 01267.

CAREER: Williams College, Williamstown, MA, professor of chemistry, 1968—.

MEMBER: American Chemical Society.

WRITINGS:

WITH WIFE, MARGARET CHANG

Speaking of Chinese, Norton, 1978, revised edition published by Deutsch (London), 1980.
In the Eye of War, Margaret K. McElderry Books, 1990.

OTHER

Basic Principles of Spectroscopy, McGraw, 1971.
Physical Chemistry with Applications to Biological Systems, second edition, Macmillan, 1981.
General Chemistry, Random House, 1986.
(With W. Tikkanen) *The Top Fifty Industrial Chemicals,* Random House, 1988.
Chemistry, fourth edition, McGraw, 1991.

SIDELIGHTS: Raymond Chang told *SATA:* "Although I was born in Hong Kong, my family moved to Shanghai when I was a baby, and I lived there during the 1940s, from Japanese occupation through the Communist regime. Then I moved back to Hong Kong, and from there to London, where I studied chemistry at the University of London. I came to America to earn my Ph.D. at Yale University. After brief stints as a postdoctoral researcher in St. Louis and as a teacher at Hunter

RAYMOND CHANG

College, I became a teacher of chemistry at Williams College in Williamstown, where I have lived since 1968."

[Information for sketch provided by wife, Margaret Chang.]

*   *   *

COLE, William (Rossa) 1919-

PERSONAL: Given name, William Harrison Cole; born November 20, 1919, in Staten Island, NY; son of William Harrison (in business) and Margaret (a nurse and writer; maiden name, O'Donovan-Rossa) Cole; married Peggy Bennett (a writer), May, 1947 (divorced); married Galen Williams (a cultural administrator), July 10, 1967 (marriage ended); children: (first marriage) Cambria Bennett, Jeremy Rossa (daughters); (second marriage) Williams, Rossa (sons). *Education:* High school graduate. *Politics:* Socialist. *Religion:* None.

ADDRESSES: Home and office—201 West 54th St., New York, NY 10019.

CAREER: Writer. Worked as a clerk in a deli and a bookstore in Rye, NY, in the 1930s; Alfred A. Knopf, Inc., New York City, publicity director, 1946-58; Simon & Schuster, Inc., New York City, publicity director and editor, 1958-61. Co-publisher, with Viking Press, of William Cole Books. Member of National Book Award Committee, beginning in 1950. *Military service:* U.S. Army, 1940-45; served in infantry in Europe; became sergeant; received Purple Heart.

WILLIAM COLE

MEMBER: International PEN (vice-president, American Center, 1955-56; executive board member, 1956—), American PEN, Poetry Society of America (member of governing board, 1979-81), Authors Guild, Poets and Writers (member of executive board, 1970—).

AWARDS, HONORS: I Went to the Animal Fair: A Book of Animal Poems appeared on the American Library Association (ALA) list of notable children's books, 1940-59, and was named an ALA notable book, 1958; *Beastly Boys and Ghastly Girls: Poems* was named an ALA notable book, 1964; *The Birds and the Beasts Were There: Animal Poems* was named an ALA notable book.

WRITINGS:

FOR CHILDREN

Frances Face-Maker: A Going-to-Bed Book, illustrated by Tomi Ungerer, World Publishing, 1963.
What's Good for a Six-Year-Old?, illustrated by Ingrid Fetz, Holt, 1965.
What's Good for a Four-Year-Old?, illustrated by Ungerer, Holt, 1967.
What's Good for a Five-Year-Old?, illustrated by Edward Sorel, Holt, 1969.
Aunt Bella's Umbrella, illustrated by Jacqueline Chwast, Doubleday, 1970.
That Pest, Jonathan, illustrated by Ungerer, Harper, 1970.
What's Good for a Three-Year-Old?, illustrated by Lillian Hoban, Holt, 1974.
Knock Knocks: The Most Ever, illustrated by Mike Thaler, F. Watts, 1976.
A Boy Named Mary Jane, and Other Silly Verse, illustrated by George MacClain, F. Watts, 1977.
Knock Knocks You've Never Heard Before, illustrated by Thaler, F. Watts, 1977.
Give Up? Cartoon Riddle Rhymers, illustrated by Thaler, F. Watts, 1978.
New Knock Knocks, illustrated by Thaler, Granada, 1981.
(With Thaler) *Monster Knock Knocks,* illustrated by Thaler, Pocket Books, 1982.
Have I Got Dogs!, Viking, in press.

Contributor to *Cricket's Choice,* Open Court, c. 1974; also contributor of introduction to *Nonsense Literature for Children: Aesop to Seuss,* by Celia C. Anderson, Shoe String Press, 1989.

FOR ADULTS

(With Ungerer) *A Cat-Hater's Handbook; or, The Ailurophobe's Delight,* Dial, 1963.
Uncoupled Couplets: A Game of Rhymes, Taplinger, 1966.

Author of column, "Trade Winds," *Saturday Review,* 1974-79; author of book review column for *Endless Vacation,* c. 1990—; book reviewer for *Prime Time.* Also contributor to *Atlantic, Harper's, New York Times Book Review,* and *New Yorker.*

EDITOR; ANTHOLOGIES FOR CHILDREN

Humorous Poetry for Children, illustrated by Ervine Metzl, World Publishing, 1955.

Story Poems, New and Old, illustrated by Walter Buehr, World Publishing, 1957.

I Went to the Animal Fair: A Book of Animal Poems, illustrated by Colette Rosselli, World Publishing, 1958.

Poems of Magic and Spells, illustrated by Peggy Bacon, World Publishing, 1960.

(With Julia Colmore) *The Poetry-Drawing Book,* Simon & Schuster, 1960.

Poems for Seasons and Celebrations, illustrated by Johannes Troyer, World Publishing, 1961.

(With Colmore) *The Second Poetry-Drawing Book,* Simon & Schuster, 1962.

The Birds and the Beasts Were There: Animal Poems, illustrated by Helen Siegl, World Publishing, 1963.

Beastly Boys and Ghastly Girls: Poems, illustrated by Ungerer, World Publishing, 1964.

Oh, What Nonsense! Poems, illustrated by Ungerer, Viking, 1966.

The Sea, Ships, and Sailors: Poems, Songs, and Shanties, illustrated by Robin Jacques, Viking, 1967.

D. H. Lawrence: Poems Selected for Young People, illustrated by Ellen Raskin, Viking, 1967.

W. S. Gilbert, *Poems,* illustrated by W. S. Gilbert, Crowell, 1967.

A Case of the Giggles (contains the two volumes *Limerick Giggles, Joke Giggles* and *Rhyme Giggles, Nonsense Giggles*), illustrated by Ungerer, World Publishing, 1967, published in England as *Limerick Giggles, Joke Giggles,* Bodley Head, 1969.

Man's Funniest Friend: The Dog in Stories, Reminiscences, Poems and Cartoons, World Publishing, 1967.

Poems of Thomas Hood, illustrated by Sam Fischer, Crowell, 1968.

A Book of Nature Poems, illustrated by Robert Andrew Parker, Viking, 1969.

Rough Men, Tough Men: Poems of Action and Adventure, illustrated by Enrico Arno, Viking, 1969.

Oh, How Silly! Poems, illustrated by Ungerer, Viking, 1970.

The Book of Giggles, illustrated by Ungerer, World Publishing, 1970.

The Poet's Tales: A New Book of Story Poems, illustrated by Charles Keeping, World Publishing, 1971.

Oh, That's Ridiculous! Poems, illustrated by Ungerer, Viking, 1972.

Pick Me Up: A Book of Short, Short Poems, Macmillan, 1972.

Poems from Ireland, illustrated by William Stobbs, Crowell, 1972.

A Book of Animal Poems, illustrated by Parker, Viking, 1973.

Making Fun! A Book of Verse, F. Watts, 1976.

An Arkful of Animals, illustrated by Lynn Munsinger, Houghton, 1978.

I'm Mad at You! Verses, illustrated by MacClain, Collins, 1978.

Oh, Such Foolishness! Poems, illustrated by Tomie de Paola, Lippincott, 1978.

Dinosaurs and Beasts of Yore: Poems, illustrated by Susanna Natti, Collins, 1979.

The Poetry of Horses, illustrated by Ruth Sanderson, Scribner, 1979.

Good Dog Poems, illustrated by Sanderson, Scribner, 1981.

Poem Stew, illustrated by Karen Ann Weinhaus, Lippincott, 1981.

A Zooful of Animals, illustrated by Munsinger, Houghton, 1990.

Also editor of *The Square Bears and Other Riddle Rhymers,* c. 1977.

EDITOR; CARTOON ANTHOLOGIES

(With Marvin Rosenberg) *The Best Cartoons from Punch: Collected for Americans from England's Famous Humorous Weekly,* Simon & Schuster, 1952.

(With Dougles McKee) *French Cartoons,* Dell, 1954.

(With McKee) *More French Cartoons,* Dell, 1955.

(With Florett Robinson) *Women Are Wonderful! A History in Cartoons of a Hundred Years with America's Most Controversial Figure,* Houghton, 1956.

(With McKee) *Touche: French Cartoons,* Dell, 1961.

(With McKee) *You Damn Men Are All Alike: French Cartoons,* Gold Medal, 1962.

(With Thaler) *The Classic Cartoons,* World Publishing, 1966.

The Punch Line: Presenting Today's Top Twenty-five Cartoon Artists from England's Famous Humor Magazine, Simon & Schuster, 1969.

EDITOR; POETRY ANTHOLOGIES FOR ADULTS

The Fireside Book of Humorous Poetry, Simon & Schuster, 1959.

Erotic Poetry: The Lyrics, Ballads, Idyls, and Epics of Love, Classical to Contemporary, foreword by Stephen Spender, decorations by Warren Chappell, Random House, 1963.

A Book of Love Poems, illustrated by Lars Bo, Viking, 1965.

Eight Lines and Under: An Anthology of Short, Short Poems, Macmillan, 1967.

Pith and Vinegar: An Anthology of Short Humorous Poetry, Simon & Schuster, 1969.

Poetry Brief: An Anthology of Short, Short Poems, Macmillan, 1971.

Half Serious: An Anthology of Short, Short Poems, Eyre Methuen, 1973.

Poems: One Line and Longer, Grossman, 1973.

EDITOR; OTHER ANTHOLOGIES

The Best Humor from Punch, illustrated by Sprod, World Publishing, 1953.

Folk Songs of England, Ireland, Scotland, and Wales, illustrated by Edward Ardizonne, Doubleday, 1961.

(With Colmore) *New York in Photographs,* Simon & Schuster, 1961.

The Most of A. J. Liebling (essays), Simon & Schuster, 1963.

A Big Bowl of Punch: A Heady Potpourri of Cartoons, Prose, and Verse from England's Famous Humorous Weekly, Simon & Schuster, 1964.

. . . And Be Merry! A Feast of Light Verse and a Soupcon of Prose about the Joy of Eating, Grossman, 1972.

(With Louis Phillips) *Sex: The Most Fun You Can Have without Laughing and Other Quotations,* St. Martin's, 1990.

Bah Humbug! A Book Against Christmas, St. Martin's, 1992.

New York: A Literary Companion, Pushcart, 1992.

Also editor, with Phillips, of *Oh, What an Awful Thing to Say!,* 1992.

SIDELIGHTS: William Cole is primarily known for his more than fifty anthologies for children and adults, including the collection of children's poetry *Beastly Boys and Ghastly Girls: Poems.* His anthologies vary in subject matter, reflecting his enthusiasm for poetry, humor, and folk songs. A *Horn Book* contributor, in a review of *Man's Funniest Friend: The Dog in Stories,*

They said
"Naughty boy!"
To their
Uncle
Fred,
And boxed
His ears
And sent him
To bed.

Cole's "pack rat" tendencies provide him with the material for his many anthologies of poetry. (Illustration by Tomi Ungerer from *Beastly Boys and Ghastly Girls,* edited by Cole.)

Reminiscences, Poems and Cartoons, described Cole as "an enthusiastic anthologist" who creates his collections with "gusto." Cole is committed to organizing distinctive books which spark children's interest in poetry and reading, stating in *Something about the Author Autobiography Series* (*SAAS*) that "any anthology, to serve its full purpose, should lead the reader to further books." Cole is also an author of several children's books of poetry and humor, including *What's Good for a Six-Year-Old?* and *A Boy Named Mary Jane, and Other Silly Verse.*

Born in Staten Island, New York, in 1919, Cole was educated in Catholic schools in various suburbs of New York City. In his early teens, he suffered a major illness and was required to take a year off from school. In his essay for *SAAS,* Cole discussed how he spent this time developing a life-long passion for books: "The year away from school was good in that it started me reading. The 'young adult' books in those days were pretty much restricted to books in series and, naturally, I read all the Tom Swifts. And I recall the particular pleasure I took in a humor-adventure series by an author named Leo Edwards—the Poppy Ott and Jerry Todd books; nobody talks about them now. When eventually I moved to the adult side of the public library, I ran through the 'Jalna' series, stem to stern, and I read hundreds of books of sea adventure."

Cole graduated from high school in the midst of the economic depression and high unemployment of the 1930s. After studying briefly at a journalism school in Manhattan, he began the difficult task of finding a job. Eventually he moved with his mother to Rye, New York, where he worked first in a deli and then in a bookshop. Cole wrote about this early experience in the book business in *SAAS:* "I loved it; the thrill of those boxes of new books appearing every morning; the excitement of arranging them on the shelves, of ordering new ones from the wholesaler by phone. There I was recommending books to the same ladies I had been slicing liverwurst for the previous week. I was greatly impressed when I met real, live authors, and put together elaborate window displays for local ones. It was a great job for a book-mad boy."

After being promoted to manager of the Rye bookstore in his early twenties, Cole was drafted to serve in World War II. The army opened new doors of opportunity for Cole, as he described in *SAAS:* "I had completed only two weeks of excruciatingly boring 'basic training' when, one morning, I was getting my hair cut. The barber was a particularly friendly Italian-American sergeant, and I told him about working with books and doing some writing in high school. 'Why,' he asked, 'don't you start a regimental newspaper? Good for morale.' He volunteered to ask the colonel about this when he attended to the great man's hair. The colonel agreed, and it changed, if not saved, my life."

Not only did Cole begin a newspaper, *The Old Gray Mare,* for his regiment, he also organized a makeshift library for his fellow recruits. He wrote in *SAAS:* "I'd

So It Goes

In days of yore the dinosaur
Tromped about the forest floor.

He watched the pterodactyl fly
Across the prehistoric sky;

The ichthyosaurus—he was docile—
Is now extinct, or is a fossil.

And in another million years,
Like these, *we'll* be extinct, my dears!

William Cole

Cole often features his own amusing verse in his collections, such as this introduction for *Dinosaurs and Beasts of Yore.* (Illustration by Susanna Natti.)

rounded up some five hundred scruffy books, cadged a large tent, and set up my newspaper office cum library in it. The library didn't have much custom, but it was a good spot to goof-off in and take naps. The books, packed in a large coffinlike box, were supposed to accompany us overseas ... but they disappeared somewhere between Florida and Virginia. To my amazement, the crate surfaced again, mysteriously, on Salisbury Plain. I again set up the library, to the disgust of the eight soldiers who had to carry the box."

Because articles for *The Old Gray Mare* could not be written in the midst of battle, Cole's relatively comfortable position came to an abrupt end once his regiment joined the fighting in Europe. He was assigned the gruesome task of picking up fallen bodies during battles in France and Germany. In *SAAS,* Cole discussed the way in which he adapted his skills to this new situation: "It was snowing and bitter cold, and all extremely basic, sleeping on the ground, eating cold K-rations, washing in water heated in helmets, being scared to death most of the time. My job evolved into being a war correspondent of sorts, interviewing soldiers and sending stories to their hometown papers. I had a knack for this kind of thing, and it 'saved my bacon,' as the saying goes; it kept me from the front lines most of the time."

After the war was over, Cole was chosen by army officials to attend a two-week librarian-training course in Paris. From France he traveled to Ireland and then returned to New York City where his wartime publish-

ing experience helped him secure a position as publicity director at the publishing company Alfred A. Knopf. After eleven years with Knopf he moved to Simon & Schuster as publicity director and editor. Cole launched his career as an anthologist in 1952 by coediting a collection of cartoons from the English humor magazine *Punch.* The book, entitled *The Best Cartoons from Punch: Collected for Americans from England' Famous Humorous Weekly,* is one of several anthologies for adults by Cole, including *The Best Humor from Punch, ... And Be Merry! A Feast of Light Verse and a Soupcon of Prose about the Joy of Eating,* and *New York: A Literary Companion.*

Cole uses many of his own ideas as organizing themes for anthologies and often draws on his own collection of books and clippings for material. He wrote in *SAAS:* "I was born with some of the natural instincts of the pack rat, who, as the dictionary puts it, is 'noted for carrying away small articles which it keeps in its nest.' The articles in my nest are poems, newspaper and magazine stories, files of miscellaneous clippings simply marked 'Interest.' And a couple of files noted as 'Poetry' and 'Light Verse.' It has been my habit, since I was a teenager, to clip and file away anything from a newspaper or magazine that struck my fancy. I had no reason for keeping all this stuff, except I felt that somebody should do it the honor. I now have a large library of books-that-interest-me, mostly poetry, humor, and quotations, and whenever I add a new one to the library, I first read it carefully, pencil in hand, and make light

It's such a shock, I almost screech,
When I find a worm inside my
    peach!
But then, what really makes me
    blue,
Is to find a worm who's bit in two!

WILLIAM COLE

Each of Cole's anthologies for children follows a specific theme—in this case, food. (Illustration by Karen Ann Weinhaus from *Poem Stew,* edited by Cole.)

notations inside the back cover, indicating the page numbers of passages or poems that appeal. So, in a way, my entire library is an anthology."

Much of Cole's work has been as an anthologist of verse for young readers. Refraining from publishing a large general collection of this type of poetry, he has based all of his children's anthologies on specific themes such as animals, nature, magic, and nonsense. One such collection, published in 1967, is *Man's Funniest Friend: The Dog in Stories, Reminiscences, Poems and Cartoons.* This humorous look at canine pets features the verse of writers such as James Thurber, Ogden Nash, and P. G. Wodehouse as well as prose selections, photographs, and cartoons by other contributors. Another animal-oriented poetry anthology is *Dinosaurs and Beasts of Yore,* which a *Horn Book* contributor characterized as full of "good-humored, light-hearted" poems in which "comic speculation ... is expressed at the thought of ancient monsters." Other gatherings of literature for children by

Cole include *Poem Stew* and his 1990 *A Zooful of Animals.*

Cole summed up his profession in *SAAS:* "An anthologist is someone who has a crusading enthusiasm for his subject. He's a practitioner of literary buttonholing, and is continually exclaiming, through the medium of his compilations, 'Hey! Look at *this* one!' An anthology done without enthusiasm is like a TV dinner: frozen, tasteless, and quickly forgotten. In a way, it's a selfish art; the anthologist has the abiding conviction that, if he likes something, other people will. Or *should.* Where research is concerned, he should love his subject so much that he'd be wallowing around in it anyhow, even if he had no anthologistic purpose. His art is infinitely less important than that of the authors he gathers together. Montaigne said, 'I have gathered a posie of other men's flowers, and nothing but the thread that binds them is my own.'"

WORKS CITED:

Cole, William, *Something about the Author Autobiography Series,* Volume 9, Gale, 1990, pp. 89-108.
Review of *Dinosaurs and Beasts of Yore, Horn Book,* August, 1979, p. 431.
Review of *Man's Funniest Friend: The Dog in Stories, Reminiscences, and Cartoons, Horn Book,* April, 1968.

FOR MORE INFORMATION SEE:

PERIODICALS

American Libraries, April, 1976, p. 210.

*   *   *

CONLON-McKENNA, Marita 1956-

PERSONAL: Born November 5, 1956 in Dublin, Ireland; daughter of Patrick J. (a businessman) and Mary (Murphy) Conlon; married James David McKenna (an accountant), August 26, 1977; children: Amanda, Laura, Fiona, James. *Religion:* Roman Catholic.

ADDRESSES: Home—51 Mount Anville Wood, Kilmacud, Dublin 14, Ireland.

CAREER: Writer. Fund raiser for Mount Anville N.S. parents council; affiliated with Kilmacud Children's Summer Project.

AWARDS, HONORS: Reading Association of Ireland Award, International Reading Association award, and Irish Arts Council Bursary award, all 1991.

WRITINGS:

My First Holy Communion, Veritas (Ireland), 1990.
Under the Hawthorn Tree, Holiday House, 1990.
Wildflower Girl, Holiday House, 1992.

WORK IN PROGRESS: Twinkle, Twinkle Little Star, a picture book; text for *The Blue Horse,* completion

MARITA CONLON-McKENNA

expected in 1992; research on "Irish travelers—especially children—how society treats them."

SIDELIGHTS: Marita Conlon-McKenna told *SATA:* "Growing up in Ireland in the 1950s, reading was the key to other places and people—once there was print on paper I would read it. I drove my local librarian crazy constantly looking for books—Heidi on her mountain top with her grandfather, Laura Ingalls Wilder and her family making a life in the American praries, Hans Brinker hoping to win a pair of silver skates. Nothing could make a little girl happier than these marvelous stories. I topped up with Hans Christian Andersen, the brothers Grimm, and the ancient mythology of Greece and Rome. From within Irish stories there were haunting tales like the 'Children of Lir' and the gentle tales of the genius Oscar Wilde. It didn't matter that I lived a quiet life in suburban and safe Dublin—my author friends would send me on magical quests both physical and mental.

"I loved writing almost as much. I enjoyed telling and retelling stories to my young children. Surrounded by them, I began to take an active interest in painting and drawing too. One of my children showed very clear signs of a reading problem early on. Discouraged and fed-up, I was afraid that she was in danger of losing the 'magic of books.' I got a simple sketch pad and a felt-tip pen and drew out a really simple story about a little girl who hates reading and books. She got such pleasure from it that in no time I found myself doing a story about the rest of our family. It seemed incredible to me that 'book writing' for your family could be so easy. *My First Holy Communion* was accepted by the first publisher I sent it to.

"*Under the Hawthorn Tree* came about when I heard of an unmarked children's grave being discovered under a

hawthorn tree beside a country school. I could not shake it from my mind and wondered about these children—would anyone ever remember or think about them again? Then as if possessed I began to write their story—my intention being only that my own children would read and enjoy a story about three Irish children—children they would know and believe walked the roads of Ireland in times gone by. Once again luck crept in and the book got published.

"Everything I write is sparked off by something I hear about. *Wildflower Girl* came about when I read a series of articles about the young Irish girls who left home and friends and family to emigrate to America. I thought about the long hours and hard work, their spirit and energy, their total love of life (for the life of a domestic servant was harsh in the 1850s). There were lots of obstacles to be overcome.

"I began to research the period—few people had bothered to even record their stories. The more I discovered, the more I liked and admired them. And so I was off again with another story to tell.

"My own sister lives in the United States and like so many Irish people I have friends and relations living

Conlon-McKenna's novel *Under the Hawthorn Tree* tells the tale of a young Irish girl who immigrates to the United States to escape famine in her homeland. (Cover illustration by Donald Teskey.)

there. The experience of emigration is still a strong one for us all—even to this day. Saying farewell to a sister or brother stirs up so much feeling. Peggy who was a plucky little girl—*Under the Hawthorn Tree* then demanded the main part—I knew by her she was determined to go to America and so at thirteen years old she sets sail for Boston. She is branded as a 'troublemaker' and has to fight to survive and keep her job in a very new world.

"*Twinkle, Twinkle Little Star* was written about the favorite nursery rhyme—the first my children ever sang, spoke, and wrote. My own little boy was afraid of the dark—after a disastrous visit to a planetarium. I made up the story for him. It is so special for me because he considers it his own. On dark, dark nights we go out and stand in our small garden and look up at that black sky and are no longer afraid."

*   *   *

CREW, Linda 1951-

PERSONAL: Born April 8, 1951, in Corvallis, OR; daughter of Warren (a photographer) and Marolyn (an administrative assistant; maiden name, Schumacher) Welch; married Herb Crew (a farmer), June 22, 1974; children: Miles, William, Mary. *Education:* Attended Lewis and Clark College, 1969-70; University of Oregon, B.A., 1973. *Politics:* Democrat. *Religion:* Presbyterian.

ADDRESSES: Agent—Robin Rue, Anita Diamant Agency, 310 Madison Ave., New York, NY 10017.

LINDA CREW

CAREER: Writer.

MEMBER: Authors Guild, Society of Children's Book Writers, Phi Beta Kappa.

AWARDS, HONORS: Children of the River was chosen as a Golden Kite Honor Book, 1989, a Michigan Library Association Young Adult Honor Book, and an American Library Association Best Book for Young Adults, and received the International Reading Association Children's Book Award in the older readers category.

WRITINGS:

Children of the River, Delacorte, 1989.
Someday I'll Laugh about This, Delacorte, 1990.
Nekomah Creek, illustrated by Charles Robinson, Delacorte, 1991.
Ordinary Miracles (novel for adults), Morrow, 1992.

WORK IN PROGRESS: Research on the history of the Tillamook Burn.

SIDELIGHTS: Linda Crew told *SATA:* "I'm not one of those who can claim a lifelong determination to be a writer. I had plans for several different careers when I was growing up. I wanted to be an artist or maybe a folksinger. Peter, Paul, Mary, and Linda is the sort of thing I had in mind. It only took me two or three years of strumming on the old guitar to figure out that I couldn't sing! Then in high school I was determined to be an actress. This dream dissolved rather abruptly somewhere around my sophomore year at the University of Oregon. The fall play was *A Midsummer Night's Dream,* and the fairies were to be topless. As a potential fairy, this did not appeal to me! Also, as a fourth-generation Oregonian, it had begun to dawn on me that perhaps I would not be happy living in New York City or Los Angeles. I took the bus home and told my parents I thought I should change my major. Unfortunately, I didn't have a clue as to which program I should pursue.

"'Well,' my mother said, 'how about journalism? You've always been a pretty good writer.'

"I'm not here to argue that moms always necessarily know best, but taking her advice (for lack of any better idea) certainly worked out well for me in this case. I loved journalism. Because I'd never taken any similar classes in high school, it was all fresh and new—interviewing, researching, marketing, saying what you have to say without a lot of fuss. But my assignments always ended up full of dialogue, and I had this compelling urge to make each story a little better than the way it really happened. By the time I graduated, I knew fiction was my real love.

"In 1974, I married Herb Crew, and we settled onto a small farm right here in my hometown. It's been a full, busy life with remodeling, working on the farm, raising our three kids. It hasn't always been easy finding time to write, but being a writer has certainly fit into all of this better than being an actress would have!

Working with a family of Cambodian refugees on her family farm provided Crew with the inspiration for *Children of the River*, which details an immigrant girl's struggle to reconcile her new life in the United States with her family's traditions.

"My life on the farm and my family have provided me with much of my material. In 1980, a family of Cambodian refugees came to work for us during harvest. We became friends, and their stories ultimately inspired my first novel, *Children of the River*. My second book, *Someday I'll Laugh about This*, grew around the setting of my grandfather's beach cabin in Yachats, Oregon. I liked the idea of so many family memories, so many little family dramas, being associated with this one place. My third book, *Nekomah Creek*, is a story of happy family chaos. With an eight-year-old, twin toddlers, and a fun-loving dad egging them on right outside my study door, this book seemed, at the time, the only thing I *could* write. I'm confident my husband and children will continue to provide me with more material in the future!"

*   *   *

CROSS, Gillian (Clare) 1945-

PERSONAL: Born December 24, 1945, in London, England; daughter of (James) Eric (a scientist and musician) and Joan (an English teacher; maiden name, Manton) Arnold; married Martin Cross (an examina-

tions director of the Royal Society of Arts), May 10, 1967; children: Jonathan George, Elizabeth Jane, Colman Anthony Richard, Katherine. *Education:* Somerville College, Oxford, B.A. (with first-class honors), 1969, M.A., 1972; University of Sussex, D.Phil., 1974. *Hobbies and other interests:* Playing the piano, orienteering, "which involves running around strange forests, map and compass in hand, looking for control flags."

ADDRESSES: Home—41 Essex Rd., Gravesend, Kent DA11 0SL, England.

CAREER: Author of juvenile and young adult books. Also worked as teacher, assistant to old-style village baker, office clerical assistant, and assistant to Parliament member.

MEMBER: Society of Authors.

AWARDS, HONORS: The Dark behind the Curtain was a Carnegie highly commended book, 1982, and a Guardian Award runnerup, 1983; *On the Edge* was listed among American Library Association's (ALA) best books for young adults, 1984, was a Whitbread Award runnerup, 1984, was listed among ALA's notable books of the year, 1985, and was an Edgar Award runnerup, 1986; *Chartbreaker* was a Carnegie commended book, 1986, and listed among ALA's best books for young adults, 1987; *Roscoe's Leap* was listed among ALA's notable books of the year, 1987.

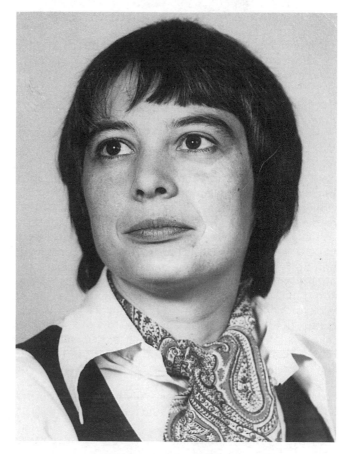

GILLIAN CROSS

WRITINGS:

JUVENILE FICTION

The Runaway, illustrations by Reginald Gray, Methuen, 1979.

The Iron Way, illustrations by Tony Morris, Oxford University Press, 1979.

Revolt at Ratcliffe's Rags, illustrations by T. Morris, Oxford University Press, 1980.

Save Our School, illustrations by Gareth Floyd, Methuen, 1981.

A Whisper of Lace, Oxford University Press, 1981, Merrimack, 1982.

The Dark behind the Curtain, illustrations by David Parkins, Oxford University Press, 1982.

The Demon Headmaster (also see below), illustrations by Gary Rees, Oxford University Press, 1982.

The Mintyglo Kid, illustrations by G. Floyd, Methuen, 1983.

Born of the Sun (Junior Literary Guild selection), illustrations by Mark Edwards, Holiday House, 1984.

On the Edge (Junior Literary Guild selection), Oxford University Press, 1984, Holiday House, 1985.

The Prime Minister's Brain (sequel to *The Demon Headmaster*), Oxford University Press, 1985.

Swimathon!, illustrations by G. Floyd, Methuen, 1986.

Chartbreak, Oxford University Press, 1986, published as *Chartbreaker,* Holiday House, 1987.

Roscoe's Leap (Junior Literary Guild selection), Holiday House, 1987.

A Map of Nowhere, Oxford University Press, 1988, Holiday House, 1989.

Twin and Super-Twin, illustrations by Maureen Bradley, Holiday House, 1990.

Wolf, Holiday House, 1991.

Regular contributor of children's book reviews to *British Book News* and *Times Literary Supplement.*

SIDELIGHTS: English author Gillian Cross combines realism, suspense, history, and entertainment in her juvenile fiction and young adult novels. Popular in England and America since the early 1980s, Cross has gained a reputation for knowing how to capture a reader's interests. One of her secrets is keeping a specific audience in mind when writing. "My imaginary, internalised reader-over-the-shoulder is ... the practical, unliterary one who doesn't usually read, but who might—just might—pick up one of my books," Cross wrote in 1991 in *School Librarian.* "All the time, at the back of my mind, I'm aware of him as I write. I'm almost holding my breath, trying not to write something that would break the spell, that would make him remember that he's reading and put the book down." Judging by the number of her works that remain in print and find their way onto various "best book" lists, many readers apparently have been unable to "break the spell" cast by Cross in her juvenile fiction.

Born in London, England, Cross grew up in postwar Britain in a home filled with stacks of books. Besides being an avid reader, Cross loved to invent stories for

In young adult books such as her award-winning *Chartbreaker,* Cross strives to capture the attention of even the most reluctant readers. (Cover illustration by Mark Salwowski.)

her family and friends. Throughout her school years she created stories and wrote many of them down in a private journal. Her pace slowed down somewhat in college when she studied English literature and began to feel somewhat intimidated by the classics. It was during these university years that Cross found a new audience for her stories when she married and started a family. Upon graduating she resolved to try writing full time: "What really made me into a writer was finishing my doctoral thesis," she once commented in *Contemporary Authors.* "Suddenly, I was no longer a student. For the first time in my life I had lots of free time and no 'official' writing to do. And I was up to my knees in stories. I had two children by then, and I was always making up stories for them and making them small, illustrated books. I'd also helped to start a children's book group in Lewes, the small town where I was living by then. So I decided it was time I had a go at some proper writing. Thanks to my thesis I knew how to handle something long and, very tentatively, I began my first real book. It has never been published (quite rightly!), but by the time I'd finished it I was hooked and I went straight on to the next one. Four years later, when I had five finished books and a whole host of rejection slips, two of my books were accepted simultaneously, by two different publishers."

Cross has since produced more than a dozen books that cover a range of subjects and settings. Though not her personal favorites, her two most popular books have been *The Demon Headmaster* and its sequel, *The Prime Minister's Brain.* The first tells of a group of schoolchildren who attempt to break a spell cast by a diabolical headmaster; the second finds the same headmaster organizing a computer contest for kids—a veiled ruse to bait someone into figuring out the computer codes that access the computer and brain of the Prime Minister. One of Cross's most critically acclaimed works is *On the Edge,* a modern-day story of a London teenage boy kidnapped by terrorists who want to abolish the family unit. Tug, the boy, has part of his memory erased by the kidnappers, who later claim to be his parents. What follows is a psychological thriller with Tug trying desperately to maintain his identity and not succumb to the terrorists' brainwashing. "The loneliness of Tug's struggle and his extraordinary will power make for powerful reading," affirmed Claudia Lepman-Logan in *Horn Book.*

Reviewers have noted that Cross's willingness to deal with the harsh, even malevolent, side of life in her fiction accounts for much of her success. "In all her writing Gillian Cross reveals a certain darkness that is sometimes shown as pure evil and sometimes a symptom of human weakness or need," remarked Sarah Hayes in *Times Literary Supplement.* Hayes continued: "What makes her work increasingly interesting is that the darkness is now so often ambivalent." Writing about the underside of life in a realistic manner reflects Cross's philosophy that elements such as violence belong in children's literature. "I think [violence is] crucial to the nature of children's fiction. Death and danger and injury are hard, definite, dramatic things," Cross observed in *School Librarian.* "Human life is taxing and fulfilling and—absolute. In the last ten years or so, I've begun to see the old dramatic virtues and vices standing out sharply. Love. Hate. The struggle for power. Irrevocable choices. Physical damage. And I've thought, 'So the stories didn't exaggerate after all. It's all there. As absolute, as heroic in its dimensions as anything in Tolkien—or Shakespeare.'"

Cross's decision to feature some of the darker aspects of life in her fiction does not mean that her work is depressing. She believes individuals are capable of confronting difficult problems, making decisions, and living happier, more informed existences as a result. "I like to write for children and young people because then I feel free to write about important things: love, death, moral decisions," Cross once noted in *Contemporary Authors.* "I find a lot of adult fiction is cynical and despairing, concerned with illustrating the powerlessness and unimportance of ordinary people. I believe that ordinary people *are* important and that everyone has the power to influence his own life. I think the young know that too."

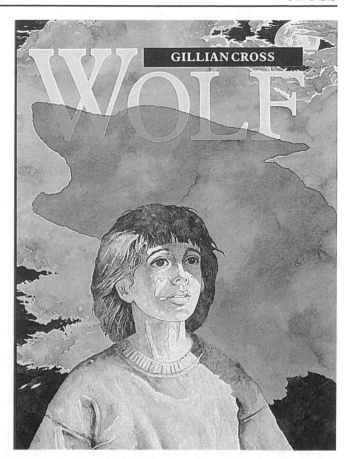

Cross's suspenseful novel, *Wolf,* exemplifies the author's willingness to deal with the malevolent side of life while maintaining a positive outlook. (Cover illustration by Mike Allport.)

WORKS CITED:

Cross, Gillian, "Twenty Things I Don't Believe about Children's Books," *School Librarian,* May, 1991, pp. 44-46.

Hayes, Sarah, review of *Born of the Sun, Times Literary Supplement,* September 30, 1983.

Lepman-Logan, Claudia, "Books in the Classroom: Moral Choices in Literature," *Horn Book,* January-February, 1989, p. 110.

FOR MORE INFORMATION SEE:

BOOKS

Carpenter, Humphrey, and Mari Prichard, *The Oxford Companion to Children's Literature,* Oxford University Press, 1984.

Sixth Book of Junior Authors and Illustrators, edited by Sally Holmes Holtze, H. W. Wilson, 1989, pp. 66-67.

Twentieth-Century Children's Writers, edited by Tracy Chevalier, third edition, St. James, 1989, pp. 247-48.

PERIODICALS

Bulletin of the Center for Children's Books, September, 1983; March, 1985; June, 1985; July-August, 1986; March, 1987; January, 1988.

Junior Literary Guild, October, 1987-March, 1988.

—*Sketch by James F. Kamp*

* * *

CUMMINGS, Pat (Marie) 1950-

PERSONAL: Born November 9, 1950, in Chicago, IL; daughter of Arthur Bernard (a management consultant) and Christine M. (a librarian; maiden name, Taylor) Cummings; married Chuku Lee (a magazine editor, lawyer, and real estate appraiser), 1975. *Education:* Attended Spelman College, 1970-71, and Atlanta School of Art, 1971-72; Pratt Institute, B.F.A., 1974. *Religion:* "Raised Catholic but practice no religion in an organized way now." *Hobbies and other interests:* Travel and foreign languages (especially French and Italian), swimming.

ADDRESSES: Home and office—28 Tiffany Pl., Brooklyn, NY 11231.

CAREER: Free-lance author and illustrator, 1974—. *Exhibitions:* Restoration Corp., Brooklyn, NY, 1974; Black Enterprise Gallery, New York City, 1980; CRT Gallery, Hartford, CT, 1981; Master Eagle Gallery, New York City, 1984, 1985, and 1986; Akbaw Gallery, Mt. Vernon, NY, 1985; Society of Illustrators group show, 1990 and 1991; Museum of Fine Arts, Grand Rapids, MI, 1991; National Museum of Women in the Arts group show, 1992.

MEMBER: Society of Children's Book Writers, Graphic Artists Guild, Children's Book Illustrators Group, Black Art Directors Group of New York.

AWARDS, HONORS: Citation as notable children's trade book in the field of social studies, joint committee of Children's Book Council and National Council on the Social Studies, 1982, for *Just Us Women;* Coretta Scott King Honorable Mention certificate, American Library Association, 1983, for *Just Us Women,* and 1987, for *C.L.O.U.D.S.;* Coretta Scott King Award, 1984, for *My Mama Needs Me;* Black Women in Publishing Illustration Award, 1988; *Boston Globe/Horn Book* Award for nonfiction, 1992, for *Talking with Artists.*

WRITINGS:

SELF-ILLUSTRATED BOOKS FOR JUVENILES

Jimmy Lee Did It, Lothrop, 1985.
C.L.O.U.D.S., Lothrop, 1986.
Clean Your Room, Harvey Moon!, Bradbury, 1991.
Petey Moroni's Camp Runamok Diary, Bradbury, 1992.

ILLUSTRATOR

Eloise Greenfield, *Good News,* Coward, 1977.
Trudie MacDougall, *Beyond Dreamtime: The Life and Lore of the Aboriginal Australian,* Coward, 1978.
Cynthia Jameson, *The Secret of the Royal Mounds,* Coward, 1980.
Jeanette Caines, *Just Us Women,* Harper, 1982.
Mildred Pitts Walter, *My Mama Needs Me* (Reading Rainbow book), Lothrop, 1983.
Cathy Warren, *Fred's First Day,* Lothrop, 1984.
Caines, *Chilly Stomach,* Harper, 1986.
Warren, *Springtime Bears* (also known as *Playing with Mama*), Lothrop, 1986.
Caines, *I Need a Lunch Box,* Harper, 1988.
Mary Stolz, *Storm in the Night,* Harper, 1988.
Barrett, Joyce Durham, *Willie's Not the Hugging Kind,* Harper, 1989.
Walter, *Two and Too Much,* Bradbury, 1990.
Stolz, *Go Fish,* HarperCollins, 1991.

OTHER

(Editor and compiler) *Talking with Artists,* Bradbury, 1991.

SIDELIGHTS: Pat Cummings is a children's author and illustrator whose works feature people of various races taking positive, constructive approaches to everyday problems. Her interest in diversity developed after spending her childhood living in Germany and Japan and such U.S. states as Illinois, New York, Virginia, Kansas, and Massachusetts; her father's career with the U.S. Army involved moving to a new base every two or three years. Being immersed in different cultures as a child sensitized Cummings to the importance of including people of all races in her work as an adult. "I've chosen at times not to illustrate stories that contained what seemed to be negative stereotypes," Cummings affirmed in *Something about the Author Autobiography Series* (*SAAS*). "When the vast majority of books published for children still reflects a primarily white, middle-class reality, I've always felt it was essential to show the spectrum of skin tones that truly make up the planet. I want any child to be able to pick up one of my books and find something of value in it, even if only a laugh. The stories have truly universal themes: a jittery

PAT CUMMINGS

Cummings's self-illustrated *Clean Your Room, Harvey Moon!* is the story of the unusual things a boy keeps in his room.

first day of school, the arrival of a new baby, attacking a messy room."

Born in 1950 in Chicago, Illinois, Cummings was the second of four children. Her brother and sisters were her closest friends while she was growing up, mainly because moving so often made it difficult to develop lasting friendships. She had already moved to Virginia and back to Chicago by the age of five, when she first left American soil to live in Germany. She recalled the impact of living in a foreign country in *SAAS:* "I remember exotic little details from Germany: the strange-smelling gnomelike dolls from the Black Forest, seeing my first gingerbread house one Christmas, and climbing castles that stood along the Rhine River. My mother read fairy tales to us from a book that I believe was called *Tales of the Rhine*.... What I realized later, when I began illustrating children's books, was that the thin line between fantasy and reality began for me when I climbed those castle steps that seemed fashioned right out of the fairy tales my mother had read to us."

One memorable event happened in Germany that proved to have a lasting effect on Cummings's life and career. While out one day with Linda, her older sister, Cummings decided to hop on board a school bus—uninvited—with other girls after Linda had left her alone for a moment. The bus traveled deep into Germany's Black Forest and stopped at a ballet school. Cummings got out with the other girls, pretending to belong, and spent an enchanting afternoon practicing

ballet. When she finally returned home, she discovered that her distraught mother had alerted the German and army police. She was grounded for a long time after that incident. "As it turned out, I found myself with quite a bit of time on my hands to practice drawing," she recollected in *SAAS*. "I was not allowed out alone for thousands of years after that, and stuck in my room, I began drawing ballerinas. They all had pinpoint waists and enormous skirts.... As I perfected my ballerinas, I found that my classmates would pay me for them. I got a nickel for a basic ballerina, a dime for the more elaborate ones. If they had glitter, or were special requests (hearts on Valentine's Day or monsters for Halloween, for example), I might even get some M & Ms or Twinkies as payment. Candy was as good as money in those days. So, at a very early age, I made a connection between artwork being thoroughly enjoyable and good business as well."

Cummings went on creating ballerinas and other works of art throughout her school years. She never spent two years in a row at the same school, except for her junior and senior years of high school. Though many of her school experiences were positive—she used her artistic talents to help out with school projects and meet new friends—one incident at a Virginia elementary school taught her some of the harsh realities of life. "At recess I ran to the playground and hopped on a merry-go-round," she wrote in *SAAS*. "One of the nuns hastily came and led me away from the slides and see-saws, jungle gyms and sandbox I had my sights on next. She took me over to a dirt lot where there was a lone basketball hoop. My sister Linda was there. The nun told me that this was 'my' playground but that seemed ridiculous. There was nothing there. I remember that Linda was crying, having probably just found out the same on our first day. I always expected Linda to explain things, to know everything before I did, but she couldn't tell me what we had done to get kicked out of the 'real' playground. We were black and we couldn't play with the white kids we sat next to in the classroom. That wasn't clear to me then, even looking around at the other black children that had been steered to the dirt lot. It took me several years and more of such encounters to make any connection.... That non-inclusion puzzled me, troubled me, and finally, as I was growing up, led me to an awareness of America's deeply rooted racism." This experience laid the foundation to Cummings's professional goal of creating works that appeal to people of all races.

After graduating from high school in 1968, Cummings decided to attend Pratt Institute in New York City. She majored in fashion because illustration was not offered as a major at that time. Though she dropped out of Pratt, worked for a year, and traveled to Georgia to attend Spelman College and the Atlanta School of Art, Cummings eventually returned to Pratt to earn her degree in fine arts in 1974. During her last year of school she began working as a free-lance commercial artist. She landed her first job after a man in a car saw her hauling her portfolio down the street after school. He informed her that a job awaited her if she would get in the car. "I

Cummings's illustrations of family life in Mildred Pitts Walter's *My Mama Needs Me* reflect her philosophy that children's books should encourage a positive approach to life.

sized up the situation, took a chance and went with him. That was exactly the sort of thing my parents had worried about when I went to New York. But I had developed, I thought, a fairly reliable intuition by that time and it proved to be an excellent move," Cummings related in *SAAS*. The job was drawing posters for the Billie Holiday Theatre for Little Folk, and before long Cummings had clients from other theaters as well.

Cummings's break into book illustration came after some of her artwork was featured in a publication distributed by the Council on Interracial Books for Children. Without any experience with books, Cummings was offered the chance to draw the pictures for Eloise Greenfield's *Good News*. Cummings quickly informed her editor that she knew exactly what to do, but in fact she knew nothing about book illustration. Once the job was hers, Cummings drew upon her network of friends to set up a meeting with illustrator Tom Feelings, who gave her a crash course on everything she was expected to know and do. (To this day

Cummings feels a professional debt to Feelings that she tries to repay by helping other beginning artists.) After her lessons with Feelings, she still had trouble starting. "I stared at the blank paper before me," she remarked in *SAAS*. "I was convinced that this book should rival *Alice in Wonderland* and that the art should make Johnny Carson's staff call to book me. I wanted the cover of *Time* magazine. I was dizzy with panic. I finally took a pad of paper into the bedroom . . . . I drew all afternoon. Not artwork that would bump [*Alice in Wonderland* illustrator John] Tenniel out of place, but drawings that began to give shape to the story at hand . . . . I look at it today and see the hundreds of mistakes I made and remember the agony and the ecstasy it produced. When I saw the book on a shelf in Bloomingdale's it was almost like being on Carson."

Since that first book Cummings has gone on to illustrate more than a dozen works for others, and has written some of her own, including *Jimmy Lee Did It*, *C.L.O.U.D.S.*, and *Clean Your Room, Harvey Moon!* All three have strong ties to Cummings's family. The inspiration for *Jimmy Lee Did It* came from Cummings's brother Artie, who during childhood had his own "Jimmy Lee," an imaginary friend conveniently blamed when trouble occurred. Cummings got the idea for *C.L.O.U.D.S.* after sitting on the porch in Virginia with her mother and applauding a stunning sunset. The story's main character, Chuku—the name of Cummings's husband—is a cloud designer for Creative Lights, Opticals, and Unusual Designs in the Sky who finds himself in trouble after spelling out "Hello Down There" over New York City. A tale of the unusual things a boy keeps in his room, *Clean Your Room, Harvey Moon!* is also based on Artie and was produced while Cummings stayed with her younger sister Barbara in Jamaica.

Whether working on her own books or illustrating for others, Cummings maintains her philosophy that children's books ought to encourage optimistic, constructive approaches to life: "There is a responsibility attached to making books for young readers," she stated in *SAAS*. "A lot of stories focus on the children's emotions and scratching up those feelings is pointless unless there is a positive resolution by the book's end. I feel the best stories allow a child to discover a solution or approach to their own situation. My parent's positive outlook on life gave me and my brother and sisters the tools we needed to construct any future we envisioned. I hope to pass that feeling of capability on through the characters I write about or draw."

WORKS CITED:

Something about the Author Autobiography Series, Volume 13, Gale, 1992, pp. 71-88.

—Sketch by James F. Kamp

D–E

DeCLEMENTS, Barthe 1920-

PERSONAL: Born October 8, 1920, in Seattle, WA; daughter of Ralph Clinton (a salesman) and Doris (a housewife; maiden name, Hutton) DeClements; children: Nicole Greimes Southard, Mari DeClements, Christopher Greimes, Roger DeClements. *Education:* Western Washington College, teaching certificate, 1942; University of Washington, B.A. (English composition), 1944, M.Ed. (educational psychology), 1970. *Politics:* Independent.

ADDRESSES: Agent—William Reiss/John Hawkins Associates, 71 West 23rd St., Suite 1600, New York, NY 10010.

CAREER: Medical-Dental Psychiatric Clinic, Seattle, WA, psychologist, 1946-47; Seattle school district, Seattle, school psychologist, 1950-55; Kirkland/Edmonds school district, Edmonds, WA, teacher, grades 4-8, 1960-67, and 1974-78, high school teacher of English, creative writing, and psychology, 1967-74, guidance counselor, 1977-83.

MEMBER: Authors Guild, Authors League of America, Society of Children's Book Writers, PEN Center USA-West.

AWARDS, HONORS: Children's Choice Book designation, International Reading Association, 1981, for *Nothing's Fair in Fifth Grade,* 1983, for *How Do You Lose Those Ninth Grade Blues?,* 1985, for *Sixth Grade Can Really Kill You,* 1986, for *I Never Asked You to Understand Me,* 1987 (with coauthor Christopher Greimes), for *Double Trouble,* and 1988, for *The Fourth Grade Wizards.*

DeClements has received numerous other awards for her books for children, including the California Young Reader's Medal, Iowa Children's Choice Award, and Ohio Buckeye Award.

BARTHE DeCLEMENTS

WRITINGS:

Nothing's Fair in Fifth Grade, Viking Penguin, 1981.
How Do You Lose Those Ninth Grade Blues?, Viking Penguin, 1983.
Seventeen & In-Between, Viking Penguin, 1984.
Sixth Grade Can Really Kill You, Viking Penguin, 1985.

I Never Asked You to Understand Me, Viking Penguin, 1986.

(With son, Christopher Greimes) *Double Trouble,* Viking Penguin, 1987.

No Place for Me, Viking Penguin, 1987.

The Fourth Grade Wizards, Viking Penguin, 1988.

Five-Finger Discount, Delacorte, 1989.

Monkey See, Monkey Do, Delacorte, 1990.

Breaking Out, Delacorte, 1991.

Wake Me at Midnight, Viking Penguin, 1991.

The Bite of the Gold Bug, Viking Penguin, 1992.

Contributor to periodicals, including *Washington Educational Journal* and *Mount Madison Park Mirror.*

WORK IN PROGRESS: The Pickle Song, a book about a young homeless girl.

SIDELIGHTS: Reading any of the popular books by Barthe DeClements is like overhearing a conversation in any middle-school hallway between classes or eavesdropping on a huddle of girls or boys talking excitedly about the events of their day on the playground during recess. DeClements has been repeatedly praised by reviewers for her realistic, engaging characters and the vivid dialogue that characterizes her writing for young adults. DeClements's novels hold a strong appeal for young readers who can hear the echo of their own concerns amidst the pages.

DeClements grew up in Seattle, Washington, and memories of her own childhood help shape the writing she now does for children. In an interview with *Something about the Author* (*SATA*), Declements reminisced: "I have two brothers. There were no girls in the neighborhood—there were a lot of boys. It was just sort of freaky that way and when I was about twelve a girl moved in and I came running home to my mother to tell her. I was so happy to have somebody to play with besides boys!" She credits the time spent with her two brothers, as well as that spent raising two sons of her own, for her ability to create realistic boy characters and narratives throughout her books. Indeed, one of her most likeable characters is a boy named Jerry Johnson who is introduced to the reader in *Five-Finger Discount* as a fifth-grader trying to deal with the stigma of having a father incarcerated in prison. DeClements's readers follow Jerry as he copes with sixth grade, his parents' divorce, and the painful reality that his father is not going to change his ways in *Monkey See, Monkey Do,* and then on to junior high school in *Breaking Out.* In this, the concluding novel of the trilogy, Jerry gains a new stepfather and learns to emotionally separate himself from his real father and establish a sense of his own individuality and self-esteem through an acting role in a locally produced television commercial. Throughout all three books, the conversations between Jerry Johnson, his neighbor and schoolmate Grace, and the many other characters introduced to the reader ring true through DeClements's critically acclaimed ear for dialogue.

As a young girl, DeClements loved to read, so much so that it sometimes got her into trouble. "I remember that my mother and father would go out to dinner on Tuesdays and Thursdays every week and I was the one who was supposed to get the meals. My mother would tell me just what I was supposed to do—macaroni and cheese; when to put it in the oven and how to make a salad—and I would invariably be reading a book while she was telling this to me, and then I would finish my book and I would try to remember: 'What did she say? What was I supposed to make for dinner?'"

Although it sometimes caused problems, reading remained one of DeClements's favorite pastimes. Some of her favorite books as a girl were those incorporating elements of sadness within their plots: *Lassie Come Home, Black Beauty, Heidi,* and *Pollyanna.* Within the books she has gone on to author, she has tried to incorporate these same elements, believing that children enjoy books that carry them through a broader range of feelings than just "fun and games."

Although an avid reader as far back as she can remember, DeClements never had any childhood aspirations of becoming an author in her own right. Not that she didn't write, of course. "I just always wrote. I remember following my mother around in the house and reading a story to her when I must have been about ten years old and my brother was laughing in the living room because

Fifth-grader Jerry Johnson must deal with the stigma of having a father in prison in DeClements's *Five-Finger Discount*. (Cover illustration by Diana Vayas.)

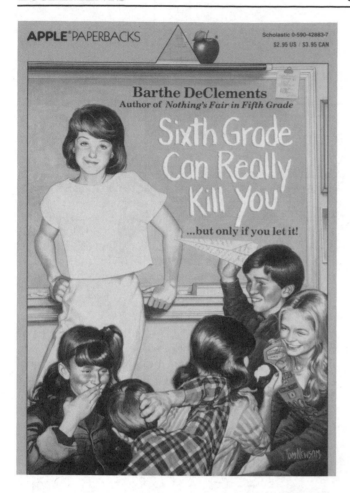

DeClements's experiences as a middle-school teacher and guidance counselor have inspired and informed novels such as *Sixth Grade Can Really Kill You,* which are noted for their realistic characters and accurate dialogue. (Cover illustration by Tom Newsom.)

I had my hero in a terrible wreck one day and had him well the next day.... [Later] when I was in grade school, I wrote plays and the kids put them on and when I went to high school I thought it was just marvelous because I had two study halls and everybody had to be very quiet and so there I was a whole hour with quiet time so I just wrote story after story and of course when the report cards came up that was the end of that. It never occurred to me to show the stories to my English teacher or do anything with them other than write them. I didn't think of myself as a writer. I just wrote stories."

Although DeClements didn't think of herself as a "writer," she was publishing a column in a local newspaper by the time she was sixteen and went on to write for the humor magazine when she became a student at the University of Washington. In college, she decided to train for a career in teaching because it was felt that she didn't have the skills necessary to work in an office. As she once recalled, "[Throughout my school years] on each grade school report card there was an F in spelling.... Because I excelled in other subjects, my parents regarded my failures in spelling ... as idiosyncracies of my personality, to be duly noted but not to be fussed over. At nineteen, after an eleven month marriage to a brutal man, I remember sitting on the floor in my parents' living room while they and my older brother discussed my future. 'She spells poorly and she types poorly. She'll never succeed in an office,' I remember my mother saying. Her opinion was respected on this matter because she had taught business school. It was decided that I should return to college to prepare for a career in teaching. Fortunately for the children and me, I found teaching exhilarating."

"Junior high was a raucous adventure. I liked the students and they liked me, but, as thirteen- and fourteen-year-olds tend to do, they appraised me with clearer eyes than the sixth graders had," DeClements found, recalling for *SATA* her experience with one junior high school class in particular. "When I taught school and wrote on the blackboard I would keep a dictionary on my desk behind me and I would have to turn and refer to it. One time when I was teaching a new boy came into the room and when they were doing a composition he asked me how to spell a word. There was a very bright boy in the class—I mean he was the smartest and his name was Jim Walker—and when the boy asked me how to spell a word one kid piped up, 'Don't ask her, she don't know, ask Jim Walker—he can spell.'"

DeClements views her books as potential lessons for both teachers and parents as well as entertaining reading for children and young adults. Many of the plots for her novels come not only from many years as a teacher, but from her experiences as a school guidance counselor in Edmonds, Washington. "My view is that when kids act badly, they feel bad. In *The Fourth Grade Wizards,* I'm trying to say 'Look, how could this little girl do her work? Her mother died, she's devastated.'" The story's roots lie in an experience DeClements encountered during a testing session at a school for special education when she served as a psychologist. "I came upon this girl and when we were about half way through—by that time I had probably given about one thousand tests and you know pretty well by the time you're half way through what scores they're going to get; whether they would be average, dull average, bright normal, or whatever. I was aware the girl was going to come out average and I thought that this was really strange; but while she was doing the blocks I looked back in her file. She'd done fine in the first couple of grades in school, and then all of a sudden she couldn't function. So when we finished the test I asked her, 'What happened that you started having trouble in school?' She said 'That's the year my mother died,' and I asked 'What's happened this year?' She said, 'My father got married again.' I said, 'What do you call your new step-mother?' She said, 'I call her mom.' I said, 'What does she call you?' She bowed her head and said 'Honey.' So that became the plot of *The Fourth Grade Wizards.*"

DeClements's experiences with the emotional problems that contemporary society imposes upon young people figure strongly in the pages of her books. Consequently her subject matter has sometimes been considered by

The Fourth Grade Wizards **details the attempts of a young girl to succeed in school despite having to cope with the death of her mother.** (Cover illustration by Paul Casale.)

publishers and critics to be too controversial for a young adult audience. One of her greatest disappointments as an author was in the published version of *I Never Asked You to Understand Me*. Recalling her original manuscript, DeClements said: "It was my favorite book. When I wrote it I was counseling in an alternative school and I felt very strongly toward the girls who had suffered from sexual abuse. They are very damaged and they blame it on themselves. They think it was something that they did and they think their family is weird and that it only happens to them. I wrote that book for those girls and unfortunately [publishers] weren't ready for it—it went through eight editors and five years, and by the time the five years were up *Something About Amelia* had been on TV [1984] and the girls didn't need the book as much as they had needed it when I first wrote it. And that's too bad because it never got to them until it was too late."

Also about kids growing up in families with problems is *Nothing's Fair in Fifth Grade*. Her first published book for children and the winner of numerous awards for children's literature, this popular novel introduces readers to the character Elsie Edwards. The "new girl in

school," Elsie doesn't just have to prove herself to a whole new crowd of kids but must also overcome the immediate dislike of her classmates due to the fact that she is very overweight. Constantly threatened with boarding school by a mother who has no patience or understanding and despite a series of mishaps, Elsie learns to control her eating habits and to get along with her schoolmates with the support of some new friends. However, underlying tensions between Elsie and her mother are not resolved, and continue through the book *How Do You Lose Those Ninth Grade Blues?* DeClements commented: "Elsie is paranoid because of the rejection from her mother and it isn't till *Seventeen & In-Between*—six years later—that Elsie and her mother come to any kind of peace between themselves." Through their evolving relationships with other people—Elsie with a boy named Craddoc and Mrs. Edwards with a man named Sam—the difficulties in the mother-daughter relationship come out into the open when Elsie's mother begins to take responsibility for her

Elsie Edwards must deal with the perplexing problems of adolescence while trying to resolve her strained relationship with her mother in *Seventeen and In-Between*. (Cover illustration by Joe DiCesare.)

behavior: "'I know I've made a lot of mistakes with you.... It's funny. We're mother and daughter and I don't even know how to begin this conversation.' 'Maybe because you haven't had much practice talking to me.' 'Elsie, a lot of it is that you remind me of myself. And I guess that I mix us up and treat you the way my mother treated me.' 'I am not you.' 'I know, but. When you're feeling bad... when you're unhappy you don't act very well. Do you understand?' 'Perfectly,' [Elsie] replied icily."

DeClements's own family has been very supportive of her work as a writer. Her daughters have provided their objective opinions on manuscripts as well as a knack for catching the odd mis-spelled word that DeClements admits she will never have. And the book *Seventeen & In-Between* marked the first collaboration between De-Clements and her son, Christopher Greimes. "He wrote the letters that Jack wrote in that book. I thought it would be more realistic to have him write them than for me to write them. It was fun and it worked out." Christopher and his mother went on to collaborate on the book *Double Trouble,* which was organized as a series of letters between Phillip and Faith, twins able to

Double Trouble, the story of psychic twins, was written in letter format, with DeClements and her son Christopher Greimes each writing the part of one twin. (Illustration by Gray.)

communicate with each other through their thoughts when circumstances force them to live apart. DeClements describes the way the book came about to *SATA:* "He took the boy character and I took the girl character and he said, 'I don't want to know what your chapter is or what you're going to write ahead of time, just give me a chapter at a time and I'll respond to it.' So we did it that way." Describing her son as "sort of tomorrow ... or tomorrow" due to the fact that he was constantly busy with other projects—including performing with a band—at the time, she added, "I would have my chapter done and he would be off doing music with the band or something." Even with his busy schedule, Christopher has found the time to edit most of DeClements' books: "He has the ability to close his eyes and visualize the perfect sentence to replace my clumsy one."

For DeClements, being an author is a full-time job—she sits down at the computer and writes for most of each morning, stopping only for a quick breakfast a few hours into her work. "I write only when I do have energy because, [as has been said,] the energy from you goes on to the paper and then goes off to the reader, and if you try to write past that it gets rather bland. And I do not think the reader would really have an experience reading it—I want people to have meaningful experiences when they read my books. When the words stop coming, I'll go into my bedroom and lay on my bed until they come up again. That's been described different ways, like filling up the well or whatever. You wait till words bubble up and then you can go back and write. When they stop I quit writing." She also keeps a paper and pencil ready at her bedside, in case an idea comes to her during the night: "It was Saul Bellow who said, 'You never have to change anything you got up in the middle of the night to write.'"

DeClements has met many young writers in her many years working with school children and has always offered advice and encouragement. "The first thing [kids] need to do is learn to write about what they know about. Sometimes children think they should write about movie-stars or astronauts, and what they need to do is also keep a journal and write about their feelings—not only what happens to them but how they feel about what happens to them—because that's what's going to be precious to them later. I kept a journal when I was seventeen and when I was in my twenties I read it over and I thought, 'Oh, this is so stupid,' and I threw it in the fireplace, and I would have given anything to have that journal when I was writing *Seventeen & In-Between....* But actually, as far as giving advice to writers, I don't think you can stop singers from singing and I don't think you can stop artists from drawing or dancers from dancing. And if they're going to be a writer, they're going to be writing."

WORKS CITED:

DeClements, Barthe, *Seventeen & In-Between,* Viking Penguin, 1984.

DeClements, Barthe, in an interview for *Something about the Author,* June, 1992.

FOR MORE INFORMATION SEE:

PERIODICALS

New York Times Book Review, November 13, 1988, p. 44.
School Library Journal, October, 1986, p. 189; August, 1987, p. 92; April, 1989, p. 101; August, 1991, p. 164.

*   *   *

DESJARLAIS, John 1953-

PERSONAL: Surname is pronounced "dezh-ahr-*lay*"; born March 19, 1953, in Bad Kreuznach, Germany; son of Alfred (a surgical nurse) and Emma (a homemaker; maiden name, Yaczko) Desjarlais; married Virginia Wolff (a homemaker), August 26, 1978; children: Matthew. *Education:* University of Wisconsin—Madison, B.A., 1976; Columbia University, M.A., 1984. Attended Gordon-Conwell Theological Seminary, 1982, and Regent College, Vancouver, British Columbia, 1991.

ADDRESSES: Home—5702 Barton Rd., Madison, WI 53711. *Office*—c/o Intervarsity, 6400 Schroeder Rd., Madison, WI 53711. *Agent*—Donald Brandenburgh, Murrieta, CA.

CAREER: 2100 Productions, Madison, video producer, 1984—; University of Wisconsin—Madison, fiction instructor, 1991—.

MEMBER: American Association of Museums, Association for Educational Communications and Technology.

AWARDS, HONORS: Gold Medal, International Multi-image Festival, 1980, for show *Habakkuk; Christianity Today* Readers Choice Award nomination, 1991, for *The Throne of Tara.*

WRITINGS:

The Throne of Tara (novel), Crossway Books, 1990.

Also author of scripts for documentary films and videos. Creator of "multi-image shows," including *Beyond Human Control,* 1986, and *Habakkuk.*

WORK IN PROGRESS: Relics, a novel of high-medieval France; research on the Crusades and seventeenth-century Jesuit missions in the Great Lakes area.

SIDELIGHTS: John Desjarlais told *SATA:* "In high school I wrote a series of spy novels. None were published but my English teacher encouraged me to enter essay contests and to work for the school newspaper, magazine, and yearbook. I saved the stack of the *Writer* magazines she gave to me, and referred to them when I began my novel. Thanks, Mrs. Masse, wherever you are.

JOHN DESJARLAIS

"For over ten years I have scripted and produced documentary film, video, and multi-image. But writing fiction has been the most difficult, most challenging, and most satisfying work I have done. Fiction writers are professional liars who point to the deeper truths of both the seen and the unseen worlds."

*   *   *

DIAS, Ron 1937-

PERSONAL: Full name, Ronald Lionel Dias; born February 15, 1937, in Honolulu, HI; son of Lionel (an electrician) and Eva (a homemaker) Dias; married Harriet Farrell (divorced); children: Greg, Steve. *Education:* Honolulu Academy of Arts, fine arts and illustration degree, c. 1954; took correspondence course drafted by Famous Artists School, Westport, CT. *Politics:* Democrat. *Religion:* Catholic.

ADDRESSES: Home—Burbank, CA. *Office*—Walt Disney Television Animation, 500 South Buena Vista, Burbank, CA 91521.

CAREER: Illustrator. Walt Disney Productions, worked on animation for film *Sleeping Beauty,* 1956-57; worked in scenic art department for Columbia Pictures, Twentieth Century-Fox, Warner Bros., and Metro-Goldwyn-Mayer Pictures, 1958-1960; Phil Duncan Productions, assistant animator, 1961; Eagle Animation Corp.-Dale Robertson, background artist for film *The Man from Buttonwillow,* 1962-63; Hanna-Barbera Productions, Inc., background artist for film *Hey There, It's Yogi Bear,* 1964, television series *Johnny Quest,* 1965, televi-

RON DIAS

sion special _Alice in Wonderland_ (also known as _What's a Nice Kid Like You Doing in a Place Like This?_), 1966, film _The Man Called Flintstone,_ 1966, television special _Jack and the Beanstalk,_ 1967, television series _The New Adventures of Huckleberry Finn,_ 1968, and television special _A Flintstone Christmas,_ 1977; DePatie-Freleng Enterprises, background artist for theatrical shorts featuring Pink Panther, Daffy Duck, and Speedy Gonzales, 1965, and for film _The Wang Doodle,_ 1978; U.P.A. Pictures, Inc., background artist for television special _Uncle Sam Magoo,_ 1970; Vaccaro Associates Film Educational Films, painter of backgrounds for medical association film _Dizziness—the Inner Ear,_ 1970-73; Paul Carlson Caroons Commercial and Educational Films, character designer and key background artist for films for Moody Institute and General Electric, 1974-75; Sanrio Film Corp. of America, background artist for film _Winds of Change,_ 1975-76; Bakshi Productions, affiliated with film _The Lord of the Rings,_ 1977; Chuck Jones Enterprises, key background artist for television specials _The Pumpkin That Couldn't Smile, Duck Dodgers in the 24 1/2 Century,_ and _Bugs Bunny Busting Out All Over,_ 1978-80; Fantasy Fair, Inc., character and set designer for _The World of Hans Christian Andersen,_ 1978; Ron Campbell, background artist for television special _Treasure Island,_ 1978; Stribling-Ludwig Productions, art director for film _Charlie the Leprechaun,_ 1979; Don Bluth Productions, Inc., background artist for film _The Secret of Nimh,_ 1980-83, and for arcade games _Dragon's Lair_ and _Space Ace,_ 1984; Tom Carter Productions, background artist for film _Hucks Landing,_ 1983; Ruby-Spears Enterprises, Inc., key background artist for television special _Space Ace,_ 1984; Bagdasarian Produc-

tions, key background artist for film _The Chipmunk Adventure,_ 1985-86; Touchstone/Disney Pictures/ Amblin Entertainment, key background artist for Toontown section of _Who Framed Roger Rabbit,_ 1987-88; Warner Bros. and Hyperion Productions, color stylist for background art of film _Rover Dangerfield,_ 1990-91; Disney Television Animation, affiliated with television special _The Little Mermaid,_ 1992, and film _The Little Mermaid._

AWARDS, HONORS: Won national contest for design of U.S. "Children's Friendship" postage stamp, 1956.

ILLUSTRATOR:

WITH BILL LANGLEY

Justine Korman (adapter), _101 Dalmatians Escape from Danger: A Book about Cooperation,_ Western Publishing, 1988.
Teddy Slater (adapter), _Lady and the Tramp through Thick and Thin: A Book about Loyalty,_ Western Publishing, 1988.
Korman, _Sleeping Beauty and the Prince: A Book about Determination,_ Western Publishing, 1988.
Walt Disney's 101 Dalmatians, Western Publishing, 1991.
Slater (adapter), _Walt Disney's Lady and the Tramp,_ Western Publishing, 1991.

WITH WILLY ITO; WRITTEN BY KORMAN

Oliver & Company, Western Publishing, 1988.
(And with Al White Studios) _Oliver & Company: Movie Storybook,_ Western Publishing, 1988.
Oliver & Company: The More the Merrier, Western Publishing, 1988.

OTHER

Slater (editor), _Dumbo,_ Western Publishing, 1988.
Eugene Bradley Coco (adapter), _Walt Disney's Peter Pan,_ Western Publishing, 1989.
Michael Teitelbaum (adapter) _Walt Disney Pictures Presents the Little Mermaid,_ Western Publishing, 1989.
Walt Disney's Mickey's Christmas Carol, Western Publishing, 1990.
A. L. Singer (editor), _Disney's Beauty and the Beast,_ Disney Press, 1991.
Gina Ingoglia, _Pinocchio,_ Western Publishing, 1992.

Also illustrator of books featuring the characters Bambi, Cinderella, Roger Rabbit, and Sleeping Beauty, all for Western Publishing; illustrator of numerous book covers and posters.

WORK IN PROGRESS: Re-creating artwork from Disney classic animated films for a limited art edition.

SIDELIGHTS: Throughout his career as an illustrator, Ron Dias has worked on artwork for various media, including cinema, television, and books. In the late 1980s Dias served as key background artist for _Who Framed Roger Rabbit,_ a film that was praised for its skillful blending of live action and animation. His association with the project was the culmination of

Dias's long association with Walt Disney Productions has led to beautiful pieces such as this poster art for the 1991 film *Beauty and the Beast*.

years as an artist for commercial films. In addition to his work on motion pictures Dias has illustrated numerous books that include characters originally featured in popular Walt Disney films. His illustrations for a print version of Disney's *Beauty and the Beast* were instrumental in helping it to become the first in a long line of books published by Disney Press to achieve best-seller status—a listing in the top ten—in the *New York Times Book Review* and in the picture book category on the *Publishers Weekly* children's book survey.

From as early as the age of six—when he saw the classic Disney film *Snow White and the Seven Dwarfs*—Dias had dreams of becoming an illustrator. He attended the Honolulu Academy of Arts, where he developed his creative skills, and took a correspondence course developed by the Famous Artists School, located in Westport, Connecticut. Dias told *SATA:* "In 1956 an eighteen-year-old kid fresh from Hawaii—and I do mean fresh—came to Hollywood to work for Disney.... Well it was not that easy. Even with all the letters (and they answered every one) I couldn't get in the door. My art schools meant nothing to them. I was working on my third portfolio to submit, *again*—you will never know how close I was to going home to Hawaii—when late one afternoon a knock on the motel door where I had a job (signing people in, to cleaning toilets) was heard. I opened it to flash cameras going off in my face and reporters yelling at me: 'How does it feel winning the contest?,' 'Did you think you had a chance?,' etc I

had just won a national contest for the design of a 'Children's Friendship' U.S. postage stamp."

While in high school, Dias had submitted artwork as part of a governmentally sponsored competition devised to produce a stamp that would encourage harmony among children of all nations. His design, set beneath the words "Friendship—The Key To World Peace," shows a cluster of youngsters from different countries bathed in light issuing from a large golden key. After winning the contest Dias traveled to Washington, D.C., where he met President Dwight D. Eisenhower and First Lady Mamie Eisenhower as part of a dedication ceremony for the stamp. The trip to the nation's capital was not the only benefit that Dias derived from his efforts. He told *SATA* that on the morning after the contest results were printed in newspapers, "I got a call from the Disney studio—not from the art department, or the animation department, but from the publicity department—asking me if I wanted to work for Disney. That's how I started at Disney's. Every paper asked me why I had left paradise. And I told every one I wanted to make my dream come true and work for the Walt Disney Studios."

Dias has been associated with Disney for more than thirty years on an intermittent basis as assistant anima-

Daisy, Huey, Dewey & Louie, Scrooge McDuck, Grandma Duck, and Chip & Dale help the birthday duck celebrate in Dias's original tribute to Donald Duck.

tor for the film *Sleeping Beauty* and for numerous print adaptations of Disney films, such as *Lady and the Tramp, Bambi,* and *Pinocchio.* In addition to working on movies and books associated with the Walt Disney Company, the illustrator has also assisted with projects affiliated with numerous animation studios in southern California. As a testament to the value of Dias's work, four pieces of his artwork—*Pinocchio, Mickey and Minnie Mouse, Donald Duck,* and *Ferdinand the Bull*—were sold at record prices at the world-famous Christie's auction held in New York during the 1980s.

* * *

EDEY, Maitland A(rmstrong) 1910-1992

OBITUARY NOTICE—See index for *SATA* sketch: Born February 13, 1910, in New York, NY; died of a brain hemorrhage, May 9, 1992, in Martha's Vineyard, MA. Editor, conservationist, and writer. Edey was an editor for *Life* magazine from 1941 to 1955. He later moved to Time-Life Books, where he served as a series editor from 1960 to 1966 and editor in chief from 1966 to 1972. Edey was principally known for scientific and environmental writings that were accessible to the nonscientific public. He wrote about natural history, archaeology, and held a particular interest in the evolution of human beings. His 1981 book, *Lucy: The Beginnings of Humankind,* written with Donald C. Johanson, depicted the discovery of a three-million-year-old skeleton of an apelike creature. The winner of a National Book Award, *Lucy* also became the center of heated scientific controversy about evolution. Edey's other books include *American Songbirds, The Cats of Africa, The Northeast Coast, The Missing Link,* and *The Lost World of the Aegean.*

OBITUARIES AND OTHER SOURCES:

BOOKS

Who's Who in America, 46th edition, Marquis, 1990.

PERIODICALS

New York Times, May 13, 1992, p. D24.

F

FREEDMAN, Russell 1929-

PERSONAL: Full name is Russell Bruce Freedman; born October 11, 1929, in San Francisco, CA; son of Louis N. (a publisher's representative) and Irene (an actress; maiden name, Gordon) Freedman. *Education:* Attended San Jose State College (now University), 1947-49; University of California, Berkeley, B.A., 1951. *Hobbies and interests:* Travel, photography, filmmaking.

ADDRESSES: Office—c/o Clarion Books, 215 Park Ave. South, New York, NY 10003.

CAREER: Associated Press, San Francisco, CA, reporter and editor, 1953-56; J. Walter Thompson Co. (advertising agency), New York City, publicity writer for television, 1956-60; Columbia University Press, New York City, associate staff member of *Columbia Encyclopedia,* 1961-63; free-lance writer, particularly for juveniles, 1961—; Crowell-Collier Educational Corp., New York City, editor, 1964-65; New School for Social Research, New York City, writing workshop instructor, 1969-86. *Wartime service:* U.S. Army, Counter Intelligence Corps, 1951-53; served in Korea.

MEMBER: Authors Guild, PEN, Society of Children's Book Writers.

AWARDS, HONORS: Western Heritage Award, National Cowboy Hall of Fame, 1984, for *Children of the Wild West;* Spur Award Honor Book, Western Writers of America, 1985, and Jefferson Cup Award Honor Book, 1986, both for *Cowboys of the Wild West;* Jefferson Cup Award Honor Book, 1988, for *Indian Chiefs;* Golden Kite Award Honor Book, Society of Children's Book Writers, 1987, Newbery Medal, American Library Association, and Jefferson Cup Award, both 1988, all for *Lincoln: A Photobiography;* Golden Kite Award Honor Book, 1988, for *Buffalo Hunt;* Golden Kite Award Honor Book, 1990, Orbis Pictus Award, National Council of Teachers of English, and Jefferson Cup Award, both 1991, all for *Franklin Delano Roosevelt;* Golden Kite Award, 1991, Jefferson Cup Award, and Newbery Honor Book, both 1992, all for *The Wright*

Brothers: How They Invented the Airplane; Washington Post/Children's Book Guild Nonfiction Award for distinguished work in the field of nonfiction for children, 1992.

Freedman's books have appeared on various "best" or "outstanding" book lists, including lists compiled by such organizations as the American Library Association, the Junior Literary Guild, the Child Study Association

RUSSELL FREEDMAN

of America, and the Children's Book Council, and such periodicals as *School Library Journal, Horn Book,* and *Booklist.*

WRITINGS:

NONFICTION BOOKS FOR JUVENILES, EXCEPT WHERE INDICATED

Teenagers Who Made History, portraits by Arthur Shilstone, Holiday House, 1961.
Two Thousand Years of Space Travel, Holiday House, 1963.
Jules Verne: Portrait of a Prophet, Holiday House, 1965.
Thomas Alva Edison, Study-Master, 1966.
Scouting with Baden-Powell, Holiday House, 1967.
(With James E. Morriss) *How Animals Learn,* Holiday House, 1969.
(With Morriss) *Animal Instincts,* illustrated by John Morris, Holiday House, 1970.
Animal Architects, Holiday House, 1971.
(With Morriss) *The Brains of Animals and Man,* Holiday House, 1972.
The First Days of Life, illustrated by Joseph Cellini, Holiday House, 1974.
Growing Up Wild: How Young Animals Survive, illustrated by Leslie Morrill, Holiday House, 1975.
Animal Fathers, illustrated by Cellini, Holiday House, 1976.
Animal Games, illustrated by St. Tamara, Holiday House, 1976.
Hanging On: How Animals Carry Their Young, Holiday House, 1977.
How Birds Fly, illustrated by Lorence F. Bjorklund, Holiday House, 1977.

Freedman's works include more than twenty books on animal behavior, a subject that has fascinated him since childhood. (Illustration by Leslie Morrill from *Dinosaurs and Their Young.*)

Getting Born, illustrated with photographs and with drawings by Corbett Jones, Holiday House, 1978.
How Animals Defend Their Young, Dutton, 1978.
Immigrant Kids, Dutton, 1980.
Tooth and Claw: A Look at Animal Weapons, Holiday House, 1980.
They Lived with the Dinosaurs, Holiday House, 1980.
Animal Superstars: Biggest, Strongest, Fastest, Smartest, Prentice-Hall, 1981.
Farm Babies, Holiday House, 1981.
When Winter Comes, illustrated by Pamela Johnson, Dutton, 1981.
Can Bears Predict Earthquakes? Unsolved Mysteries of Animal Behavior, Prentice-Hall, 1982.
Killer Fish, Holiday House, 1982.
Killer Snakes, Holiday House, 1982.
Children of the Wild West, Clarion Books, 1983.
Dinosaurs and Their Young, illustrated by Morrill, Holiday House, 1983.
Rattlesnakes, Holiday House, 1984.
Cowboys of the Wild West, Clarion Books, 1985.
Holiday House: The First Fifty Years (adult), Holiday House, 1985.
Sharks, Holiday House, 1985.
Indian Chiefs, Holiday House, 1987.
Lincoln: A Photobiography, Clarion Books, 1987.
Buffalo Hunt, Holiday House, 1988.
Franklin Delano Roosevelt, Clarion, 1990.
The Wright Brothers: How They Invented the Airplane, photographs by Orville and Wilbur Wright, Holiday House, 1991.
An Indian Winter, paintings and drawings by Karl Bodmer, Holiday House, 1992.
Eleanor Roosevelt: A Life of Discovery, Clarion, in press.

Contributor to *Columbia Encyclopedia,* third edition, and to the *New Book of Knowledge Annual,* 1981-89. Also contributor to periodicals, including *Cricket, Ranger Rick, Horn Book,* and *School Library Journal.*

ADAPTATIONS: Lincoln: A Photobiography (filmstrip and video), McGraw-Hill Media, 1989.

SIDELIGHTS: Russell Freedman is the respected author of more than thirty-five nonfiction books written for children and young adults. With subjects such as famous teenagers, animal behavior, and American presidents, his books are noted for their understandable and entertaining presentation of often complex information. Freedman has been recognized as one of the more prolific and talented writers in his field. In 1988 he was awarded the prestigious Newbery Medal for his book *Lincoln: A Photobiography,* a factual history of the sixteenth president of the United States, Abraham Lincoln. Freedman was the first nonfiction author in thirty-two years to win the Newbery and one of only a handful of nonfiction authors to be honored with the medal since it was first presented in 1922.

Born in San Francisco, California, Freedman was exposed to literature at an early age. His father, whom Freedman has described as a "great storyteller," was a publishing representative for Macmillan and filled the

Freedman's "photobiographies" are noted for their use of unique, illuminating pictures, such as this rare photograph of President Franklin D. Roosevelt in a wheelchair. (Photograph by Margaret Suckley from *Franklin Delano Roosevelt.*)

Freedman home with books. Because of his father's occupation, Freedman had the rare experience of personally meeting some of the twentieth century's greatest authors—right in his own home. Authors such as John Steinbeck, William Saroyan, and John Masefield were frequent dinner guests of the Freedman family.

Freedman's early association with books went beyond dining with literary greats, for he was also an avid reader. As a youth two of his favorite books were Robert Louis Stevenson's novel *Treasure Island* and Ernest Thompson Seton's natural history book *Wild Animals I Have Known.* Freedman related his boyhood perception of those books in *Horn Book:* "In those innocent days I didn't worry about distinctions like fiction and nonfiction . . . . I did know that I was thrilled by both of those

books." However, what became significant to Freedman as he matured was that a nonfiction book like Seton's could entertain him as thoroughly as a fictional tale such as *Treasure Island.* "What is important is that I read *Wild Animals I Have Known* with as much pleasure and satisfaction as I have any novel or story," Freedman recalled in *Horn Book.* He remembers Seton's book as a starting point in his interest for nonfiction reading—an interest that contributed to his decision to become a professional writer.

Freedman held several writing positions, including jobs with the Associated Press and Columbia University Press. Although he acknowledges that those jobs were where he "really learned to write," he related in *Sixth Book of Junior Authors and Illustrators* that he "wanted to write about people and things that I cared about." One day Freedman came across a *New York Times* article about a blind sixteen year old who had invented a Braille typewriter. Reading further, he learned that Louis Braille had also been sixteen when he had invented the Braille alphabet, a system that allows blind people to read with their hands. This information led Freedman to wonder what other significant achievements had been made by young people. His curiosity eventually led to the writing of his first book, *Teenagers Who Made History,* a collection of biographies of such influential young people as classical music conductor Arturo Toscanini and professional golfer and athlete Babe Didrikson Zaharias. Freedman followed *Teenagers* with several other books, including *Two Thousand Years of Space Travel* and *Jules Verne: Portrait of a Prophet,* before he began writing the books that comprise the bulk of his career: animal books.

Since the late sixties Freedman has written more than twenty books on animal behavior, a subject that has interested him since his youth. He collaborated with James E. Morriss on a series of books that seeks to explain, in simple language, some of the scientific concepts of the animal kingdom. As the titles indicate, the books cover subjects such as *How Animals Learn, Animal Instincts,* and *The Brains of Animals and Man.* The books were well received by the educational community, as reflected in the books' appraisal in *Science Books: A Quarterly Review,* which stated that Freedman and Morriss's "*How Animals Learn* and *Animal Instincts,* are among the best for beginning naturalists." Freedman followed these books with further explorations of the animal kingdom, including such titles as *The First Days of Life, Animal Fathers,* and *How Birds Fly.* Some of these books feature detailed drawings that illustrate Freedman's words. However, near the end of the seventies Freedman made a significant switch to photographs. Freedman explained in *Horn Book* that he views the photos as an enhancement to his text: "They're an essential part of the story I want to tell, the information I want to convey. Ideally, the photographs should reveal something that words alone can't express." *Hanging On: How Animals Carry Their Young* was one of his initial books to utilize photography. Readers reacted favorably to the book, citing its unusual subject matter as a point of interest. Paul R. Boehlke, writing in *Science Books and Films,* commented that "*Hanging On* is unique and very well done."

In 1980 Freedman took a break from chronicling wildlife to write a book on a different kind of animal— the human. While attending a photographic exhibit at the New York Historical Society, Freedman was struck by the photographs of children in nineteenth- and early twentieth-century America. "What impressed me most of all was the way that those old photographs seemed to defy the passage of time," he wrote in *Horn Book.* Freedman decided to tell the story behind the photographs, attempting to convey through his words—and some of those very same pictures—a sense of what life was like in those suspended moments of history. The resulting book was titled *Immigrant Kids.* The book

proved to be a turning point; Freedman continued to produce books on animals, but he was increasingly turning his writing attention to people. The books *Children of the Wild West* and *Cowboys of the Wild West* followed, earning praise for their accurate portrayal of life in the old West. Richard Snow, for example, wrote in the *New York Times Book Review* that *Children of the Wild West* is "a good introduction for young readers to the patterns of life in a Wild West that had nothing at all to do with gambling halls and shootouts."

After discovering the truth behind the myths associated with life in the old West, Freedman decided to separate fact from fiction with respect to one of American history's most intriguing characters, Abraham Lincoln. In his quest to accurately research the book that would become *Lincoln: A Photobiography,* Freedman travelled to Lincoln's birthplace in Kentucky, then to the numerous Lincoln historical sites in Springfield, Illinois, and finally to the fated Ford's Theatre in Washington, DC, where Lincoln was assassinated. Freedman was also allowed to examine some of the former president's original handwritten documents, including a letter to Lincoln's wife, Mary, and first draft notes on his famed Emancipation Proclamation. Freedman's commitment to presenting the facts paid off; critical and popular response toward the book was very favorable. Elaine Fort Weischedel proclaimed in *School Library Journal:* "Few, if any, of the many books written for children about Lincoln can compare with Freedman's contribution." Freedman summarized his view of *Lincoln* in his

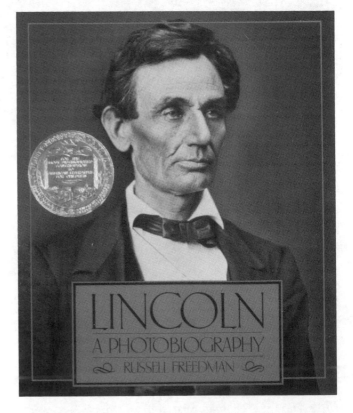

Freedman's balanced biography of America's sixteenth president was the first nonfiction book in over thirty years to be awarded the prestigious Newbery Medal.

Newbery Medal acceptance speech, quoted in *Authors and Artists for Young Adults:* "I was never tempted to write an idealized, hero-worshiping account. A knowledge of Lincoln's weaknesses throws his strengths, and his greatness, into sharper relief."

Following the success of *Lincoln,* Freedman continued to write on historical figures in "photobiographies," including *Franklin Delano Roosevelt* and *The Wright Brothers: How They Invented the Airplane.* Freedman's talent for creating entertaining and informative books has earned him several awards and made him one of the most respected authors for juvenile readers. He enjoys being in a position where he can inform curious young minds. As Freedman explained in his Newbery acceptance speech: "One of the great joys of writing nonfiction for youngsters is the opportunity to explore almost any subject that excites your interest."

WORKS CITED:

Review of *Animal Instincts, Science Books: A Quarterly Review,* May, 1970, pp. 2-3.
Authors and Artists for Young Adults, Volume 4, Gale, 1990, pp. 95-105.
Boehlke, Paul R., review of *Hanging On, Science Books and Films,* December, 1977, p. 166.
Freedman, Russell, "Newbery Medal Acceptance," *Horn Book,* July/August, 1988.
Freedman, Russell, "Perusing the Pleasure Principle," *Horn Book,* January/February, 1986, pp. 444-51.
Sixth Book of Junior Authors and Illustrators, H. W. Wilson, 1989, pp. 89-91.
Snow, Richard, "Prairie Smarts," *New York Times Book Review,* November 13, 1983, p. 52.
Weischedel, Elaine Fort, review of *Lincoln: A Photobiography, School Library Journal,* December, 1987, pp. 93-94.

FOR MORE INFORMATION SEE:

BOOKS

Children's Literature Review, Volume 20, Gale, 1990, pp. 71-89.

PERIODICALS

Bulletin of the Center for Children's Books, May, 1987; January, 1988.
Horn Book, July/August, 1988, pp. 452-56.
Junior Literary Guild, October, 1987-March, 1988.
New York Times Book Review, January 24, 1988.*

—*Sketch by David Galens*

*   *   *

FRIESNER, Esther M. 1951-

PERSONAL: Born July 16, 1951, in New York, NY; daughter of David R. (a teacher) and Beatrice (a teacher; maiden name, Richter) Friesner; married Walter Stutzman (a software specialist), December 22, 1974; children: Michael Jacob, Anne Elizabeth. *Education:* Vassar College, B.A. in Spanish and Drama (cum laude), 1972; Yale University, M.A. in Spanish, 1975, Ph.D. in Spanish, 1977.

ADDRESSES: Home—53 Mendingwall Circle, Madison, CT 06443. *Agent*—Richard Curtis Literary Agency, 171 East 74th Street, New York, New York 10021.

CAREER: Writer. Yale University, New Haven, CT, instructor in Spanish, 1977-79, and 1983.

MEMBER: Science Fiction Writers of America.

AWARDS, HONORS: Named Outstanding New Fantasy Writer by *Romantic Times,* 1986; Best Science Fiction/Fantasy Titles citation, *Voice of Youth Advocates,* 1988, for *New York by Knight.*

WRITINGS:

FANTASY NOVELS

Harlot's Ruse, Popular Library, 1986.
New York by Knight, New American Library, 1986.
The Silver Mountain, Popular Library, 1986.
Elf Defense, New American Library, 1988.
Druid's Blood, New American Library, 1988.
Sphynxes Wild, New American Library, 1989.
Gnome Man's Land (first volume in trilogy), Ace, 1991.
Harpy High (second volume in trilogy), Ace, 1991.
Unicorn U (third volume in trilogy), Ace, 1992.

ESTHER M. FRIESNER

Yesterday We Saw Mermaids, Tor Books, 1992.
Wishing Season (young adult), Atheneum, 1993.
Majik by Accident, Ace, 1993.
(With Laurence Watt-Evans) *Split Heirs,* Tor Books, 1993.

"CHRONICLES OF THE TWELVE KINGDOMS"; FANTASY NOVELS

Mustapha and His Wise Dog, Avon, 1985.
Spells of Mortal Weaving, Avon, 1986.
The Witchwood Cradle, Avon, 1987.
The Water Kings' Laughter, Avon, 1989.

"DEMONS" SERIES; FANTASY NOVELS

Here Be Demons, Ace, 1988.
Demon Blues, Ace, 1989.
Hooray for Hellywood, Ace, 1990.

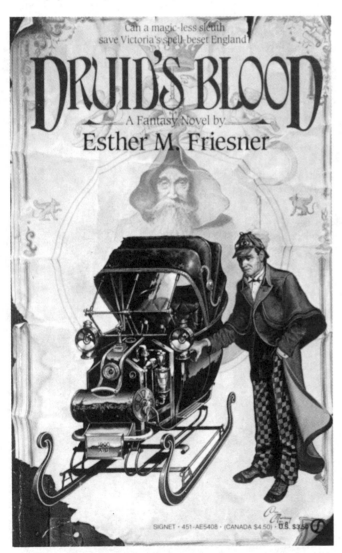

Friesner combines mystery, fantasy, and an alternate nineteenth-century England in which magic works in *Druid's Blood,* the tale of how the counterparts to Sherlock Holmes and Dr. Watson attempt to retrieve Queen Victoria's stolen book of magic. (Cover illustration by Morrissey.)

SIDELIGHTS: "Esther M. Friesner," writes Fred Lerner in *Voice of Youth Advocates,* "has established herself as one of the most prolific writers of fantasy fiction, and one of the funniest." She overturns many of the conventions of modern and traditional fantasy in books ranging from *New York by Knight,* in which a dragon and his armored pursuer bring their ages-old battle to the streets of modern-day New York, and *Elf Defense,* in which a mortal woman seeks to escape her marriage to the king of Elfhame by hiring a divorce lawyer, to the "Gnome Man's Land" trilogy—where a high-school student from a single-parent home must cope not only with adolescence but with successive invasions of "little people" from folklore, exotic monsters, and gods. Friesner's works, Lerner continues, "open new territory. She has made a specialty of ferreting out obscure creatures from the mythologies and demonologies of the world and turning them loose on unsuspecting places like Brooklyn, New Haven, and Hollywood."

"I was born in New York (Brooklyn, to be specific)," Esther Friesner states in an interview for *Something about the Author.* "My mother was an English teacher in the Brooklyn public junior high schools. She later became a reading specialist. My father also started out teaching in the Brooklyn junior high schools, then went on to teach in the high schools. His main speciality was Spanish, but he also taught Latin, Italian, algebra, and he coached soccer in the Brooklyn high schools.

"My mother told me stories when we were going on long car trips—stories from the works of Washington Irving, for instance. She'd tell me 'The Legend of Sleepy Hollow,' and I kept saying, 'I want another story, I want another story.' Finally she said, 'Look, learn to read and you can have all the stories you want.' So I thought 'That sounds like a good idea,' and I learned to read. Instead of bedtime stories, my father would sit down and read me collections of the *Pogo* comic strip by Walt Kelly. That was wonderful. It totally warped my sense of humor in just the right way. I didn't understand a lot but I certainly knew that what Kelly was doing with the language was wonderful.

"I liked to write at an early age. In fact, I started making stories when I was three years old. I couldn't write them down, but I cornered my mother and said, 'Would you please write this down for me?' I'd tell myself a story while drawing a picture, and that would help me know what to put into the picture next. I'd take a pack of index cards and create a series of cartoons that would tell a story about the characters. The main character started out on the first card and then I went through the character's routines, waking up in the morning, getting ready for school. The character in question was a little stick figure bird for some reason (probably because if I drew wings I didn't have to worry about drawing fingers, which I could not draw; and a bird's legs are stiff so you don't have to worry where the knees go) wearing shorts and a little baseball cap. Of course the mother looked like Mary Tyler Moore on *The Dick Van Dyke Show* drawn as a bird.

"We had books all over the place. My mother said to me, 'Oh, you *have* to read [Frances Hodgson Burnett's] *The Secret Garden*.' When a parent says 'Oh, you have to read something,' immediately the child thinks 'Oh yeah?!' But I tried it and it was wonderful. I got to love Kipling. Then as I got a little older my father said 'I adore Jack London,' so I tried some Jack London and wound up reading everything he ever wrote. Another favorite author was E. Nesbit, who did *Magic by the Lake,* and *The Time Garden.* It was one of the few times that I read something and actually wished it would happen to me.

"Because the bookshelf had my parents' books on it as well, if I got bored I could look at the selection and think, 'Well, this looks kind of interesting; maybe I'll like it, maybe I won't.' One time I wound up reading *Emily Post's Etiquette.* I was fascinated. One of the rules stated that 'young ladies may not accept gifts from a gentleman,' and I thought, 'Why not?' I didn't understand half of what was going on and I never even thought to ask questions about it. I just thought, 'My goodness, things get complicated when you get older.'

"In school I mostly concentrated on reading. I did not like sports. I was nearsighted (I wore glasses from age six) but I liked to dance. In the first grade we had a talent show and I actually got up in front of everybody and improvised a dance. The teacher was shocked because I was very quiet and she did not think I would have the nerve to get up in front of everybody as if there was no such thing as stage fright.

"Because I was an only child, I didn't have anyone to tell stories to. Once, however, my parents took me visiting, and the people we were visiting had a girl a little younger than I was. I started to amuse her by telling her stories about the different objects in her room. For instance, she had a very nice statue of a Siamese cat with one eye as a jewel and the other eye as plain white ceramic, so I told her the story of the statue's magical eye: how it would protect people or how the evil people who tried to steal it got fricasseed (the evil people always had to get fricasseed).

"I got a very strange sense of power knowing I could scare somebody else. Of course this came back to haunt me when I was in high school. I once read a story called 'The Screaming Skull' that terrified me so badly that it haunted me. I couldn't get rid of that story until I took a friend aside and said 'I read the worst story, you've got to hear this story,' and told it to her with as much of the horror as I could. That night I slept peacefully for the first time in weeks. The next day she came into school and said, 'Thanks a *lot*.' She hadn't slept.

"I attended Hunter College High School from seventh grade on. It was a combined junior high and high school. At the time, Hunter College High School was an all girls school, the equivalent and sister school of places like Stuyvesant and Brooklyn Tech for boys. Entrance was by examination, and the school drew girls from all over the five boroughs."

A college freshman's discovery that he has a gift for sorcery leads to amusing complications in *Demon Blues,* one of Friesner's "Demons" series. (Cover illustration by Walter Velez.)

After graduating from high school, Friesner went on to Vassar College where she studied Spanish and Drama. She chose Spanish, she told *SATA,* "because I thought that no matter *what* I wanted to be, I ought to have something practical that I could fall back on. I wanted to have a skill that would be useful, and I knew I could teach Spanish or use it in business. But I enjoy Spanish, both the culture and the literature. It's a wonderfully rich body of literature that a lot of people unfortunately aren't familiar with. I concentrated on Castilian (I wasn't a Latin American Spanish major), and specialized in the Golden Age of the late 16th and early 17th centuries, especially on the playwright Lope De Vega.

"It was a fascinating time—the romantic movement in Spain was marvelous too—but most people in the United States aren't familiar with it. The ballad of El Cid is a magnificent epic, but the only thing most people will know about the story is if they saw the Charlton Heston-Sophia Loren movie. On the other hand, they do know King Arthur, which is why fantasy books based on the King Arthur cycle are more accessible. Yet there is a whole body of literature that people do not know about because they haven't been introduced to it.

"Drama, on the other hand, was the result of a strange occurrence. When I started out at Vassar I had taken advanced placement examinations in both Spanish and English. Later I found out that if I had taken a third AP exam I could have skipped a whole year of college. I thought that would have been a wonderful saving of money for my parents. So I asked my guidance counselor, 'How can I accelerate?' and we worked out a program.

"I crammed so many credits into my second year it was appalling. Later, when I told my parents I was accelerating my coursework to save them money, they said 'Dear, college can be some of the best years of your life. We're in no hurry; we've saved our money, we can afford this. *De*celerate! You're putting yourself under too much pressure.'

"So there I was with a nearly empty program. I found I could do anything I wanted with the next two years of education. I thought, 'Well, I'm enjoying the drama course I'm taking. Maybe I could turn all these empty slots into a second major.' I love drama, and I enjoyed acting, but I was certainly not good enough to make a living at it. Still, I could take the major and enjoy drama just for its own sake instead of looking at it as a possible career.

"And, heaven knows, at the time I was at Vassar there was a shining light of pure talent: Meryl Streep. When you are a drama major you have got to participate in every official drama department production. If you audition and get a part in the particular production, that's your participation; otherwise you have to be on one of the crews: the prop crew, the tech crew, the lighting crew, the publicity crew.... Well, the rule also was that you had to serve at least once on a crew. I got a part in a departmental production (Rosita, the aging street walker, in Tennessee William's *Camino Real*) once when Meryl Streep had to do her compulsory crew. She was on makeup crew. So there I sat in a crummy aqua satin dress with my hair all bedraggled, while Meryl Streep said things like, 'Now let me put on some black tooth wax so that you'll have a blotted out tooth.' Meanwhile, I'm sweating bullets because my parents are in the audience. I tried to explain, 'Mom, Dad, just because I'm playing a hooker doesn't mean anything.' They said, 'We know, dear. Just do the best you can.'

"Meryl is a very lovely person, absolutely wonderful. She wound up going to the Yale Drama School at the same time I was in the Yale Grad School. I was always in awe of her, but really she was just another human being. She would have been very friendly, but I was so awestricken and full of admiration and a degree of hero worship that I never even thought to approach her as a potential friend."

In Friesner's "Gnome Man's Land" trilogy, the typical problems of an adolescent are compounded ...

Yale also introduced Friesner to her future husband, Walter Stutzman. "When I first came to Yale," she explains, "I couldn't get into student housing. Midway through my first year a woman got married and I got into her room. But I was in a dormitory, I didn't know anybody in the cafeteria and it was very lonely eating by myself. Finally a girl from Vassar who knew me, recognized me and said, 'Come on over to our table' and there was Walter, one of the gang at the table. We became friends, we ate together, went to the movies together and hung out together, and by the second year we weren't just friends anymore.

"It was sort of a cross between *When Harry Met Sally* and *The Big Chill,* although I also never found Walter to be initially obnoxious the way Sally felt about Harry. I thought he was a very charming person. One of the advantages in being nearsighted is that you can really say that looks aren't everything. Walter happens to be incredibly handsome but I had no idea that was so until somebody said 'Oh boy,' and I looked very closely and said, 'Oh my goodness, you're *right!*' I actually liked him for his personality because I couldn't see anything else.

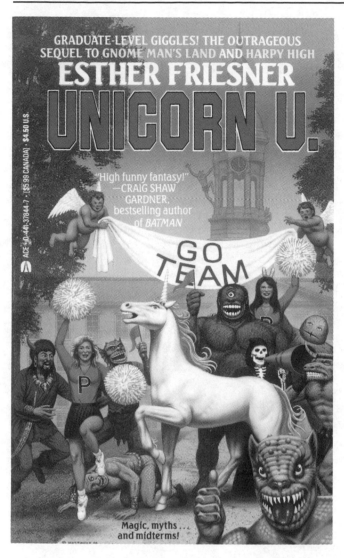

... by the appearances of exotic mythological creatures. (Cover illustrations by David Mattingly.)

"I love reading Dr. Samuel Johnson's quotation about *no man but a blockhead ever wrote, except for money.* I always knew that I wanted to write, but I did want to write for money. I was trying to get published while I was in college, but it wasn't until I was in grad school that I got very serious about it. The first item I ever sold was a nonfiction article with the photos—I sold the photos, too—to *Cats Magazine.* I also sold an article to *Brides Magazine* about how to get through the first year of your marriage without shooting anybody. (It was hard to survive all the advice). The editors of the magazine said 'Put in lots of examples,' so I did, and various people came around and said 'I *know* you meant me.' I'm not up on a murder rap so I think it worked out pretty well.

"But fiction was my main love. I wanted to write fiction and I tried and tried and tried.... I'd written two novels that didn't sell; one was a murder mystery which came close but didn't make it, and the other one was an historical that I really didn't send out much. The first time I got an encouraging rejection slip (saying 'We are not buying this, but this is why,') was from George

Scithers of *Isaac Asimov's Science Fiction Magazine.* I continued to send to him and he continued to send me back rejection slips, but always telling me what was wrong. Finally I made my first sale to *IASFM* as a result of his encouragement. I appreciated it and I won't forget it. He was very, very good. His criticism was excellent, never the *because I said so* type of criticism.

"That was a short story, but I got into writing full-length fantasy thanks to a group at Yale. In the grad school there was a woman who is now also a published science fiction and fantasy author. She is now famous for the hard science fiction she writes, but she started out writing a fantasy. Her name is Shariann Lewitt, but she publishes under the name S. N. Lewitt because unfortunately at the time there was a lot of prejudice against women writing hard SF. There was a real fear that people would say 'What can a woman know about this? I won't buy the book.' So Shariann was working on her first fantasy novel, and we saw her building a whole world, working out all the details on a big legal pad she had. This was quite different from writing a short story. I thought, 'Oh, building a world. I get to be God! How nice. I'm going to try that.' And that was how I got started on fantasy novels.

"The novel I wrote from my first world-building was actually the second book I sold. It was *Spells of Mortal Weaving,* in the 'Chronicles of the Twelve Kingdoms' series. In its original version, however, it was a little too off-the-wall (at least, that was the response I got on it), so I did a rewrite, calming it down a bit, and it came out much better. It did sell eventually, but it was not the first one that sold." Friesner's first published book was *Mustapha and His Wise Dog,* an Arabian Nights-style adventure "enlivened by an exotic and evocative fantasy setting, and a pair of captivating characters," declares Don D'Ammassa in *Twentieth-Century Science-Fiction Writers.* The series, continued in *The Witchwood Cradle* and *The Water King's Laughter,* follows the struggles of various mortals to overthrow Morgeld, an evil demigod. "Although Friesner followed traditional forms for the most part in this series," D'Ammassa concludes, "her wry humor and gift for characterization marked her early as someone to watch."

"When I write," Friesner tells *SATA,* "I try to make the story so interesting that I wouldn't mind rereading it myself. This is actually a very good thing. It's important to interest your readers because if you don't you won't have readers anymore. But if you don't interest yourself in what you're writing.... Well, the process of going from the first draft to the published book takes an awfully long time. You will have to look at that story and those characters a lot—you'll have to do another draft, perhaps even a third, then the editor will go over it, then the copy editor. Every time you're going to be reading the same words. If they aren't good words, you're going to get the feeling of being trapped at a party with people you don't like.

"Now Walter is a published writer too. He is the person who pushed me to go from the typewriter to the

Spells of Mortal Weaving, her second novel to be sold, was the result of Friesner's first attempt at "world-building."

computer for writing. Now whenever I have a problem with the computer I don't reach for the manual; I just say, 'Oh *hon*ey!' And a few years back, while we were sitting around just joking about these ads on TV—the ones for Ronco or Ginsu blades that will cut through anything, or for Elvis Presley's Greatest Hits—we started to write a fantasy parody titled 'But Wait, There's More,' which was later published. He contributed as much as I did. Again, recently I was asked to participate in an anthology called *Whatdunnit: Science Fiction Mysteries.* The editor gave me my choice of scenarios but I said, 'Could I please have Walter help me on this, because he's a mystery fan?' (I'm the one who looks at the last page to find out who done it and then decides if I'm going to read the book or not). I did the actual writing but Walter was the plotter. Now I'm trying to drag him into writing a full length science mystery with me. I'm also going to try and drag our poor innocent thirteen-year-old son in. He's becoming a young computer expert and he likes to do computer gaming and I'd like to make the project a family thing. I may drag my daughter in at some point, too. The cat is still safe."

WORKS CITED:

D'Ammassa, Don, "Esther M. Friesner," *Twentieth-Century Science-Fiction Writers,* 3rd edition, St. James, 1991.

Friesner, Esther, interview with Kenneth R. Shepherd for *Something about the Author,* May 11, 1992.

Lerner, Fred, "The Newcomer," *Voice of Youth Advocates,* December, 1991, p. 294.

FOR MORE INFORMATION SEE:

PERIODICALS

Analog, December, 1989, pp. 184-85; September, 1991, pp. 166-67.

Locus, April, 1989, pp. 25-27; January, 1990, p. 25.

Science Fiction Chronicles, June, 1990, p. 37; October, 1991, p. 41.

Voice of Youth Advocates, April, 1991, p. 42.

G

GEAR, Kathleen O'Neal 1954-
(Kathleen M. O'Neal)

PERSONAL: Born October 29, 1954, in Tulare, CA; daughter of Harold A. (a farmer and writer) and Wanda Lillie (a journalist; maiden name, Buckner); married W. Michael Gear (an anthropologist, archaeologist, and writer), October 1, 1982. *Education:* Attended Hebrew University of Jerusalem, 1976-77; California State University, Bakersfield, B.A., 1977; California State University, Chico, M.A., 1979; doctoral coursework at University of California, Los Angeles, 1979-80. *Politics:* Libertarian. *Religion:* "Native American."

CAREER: Archaeologist for excavations conducted at Sea of Galilee, Israel, 1976; Museum of Cultural History, Los Angeles, CA, senior museum preparator, 1980; City of Cheyenne, Cheyenne, WY, historian, 1980-81; U.S. Department of the Interior, Bureau of Land Management, Washington, DC, state historian in Cheyenne, 1981-82, archaeologist in Casper, WY, 1982-86; Wind River Archaeological Consultants, Dubois, WY, principal investigator, 1987—; writer.

MEMBER: Society for Historical Archaeology, Western Writers of America, Science Fiction Writers of America, Wyoming Writers.

AWARDS, HONORS: Special Achievement awards, U.S. Department of the Interior, 1984 and 1985, for "outstanding management" of America's cultural resources.

WRITINGS:

WITH HUSBAND, W. MICHAEL GEAR

People of the Wolf, Tor Books, 1990.
People of the Fire, Tor Books, 1991.
People of the Earth, Tor Books, 1992.
People of the River, Tor Books, 1992.
People of the Lakes, Tor Books, in press.
People of the Sea, Tor Books, in press.

The authors' works have been translated into Dutch, German, Polish, and Spanish.

"POWERS OF LIGHT" SERIES; WRITTEN UNDER THE NAME KATHLEEN M. O'NEAL

An Abyss of Light, Daw Books, 1990.
Treasure of Light, Daw Books, 1990.
Redemption of Light, Daw Books, 1991.

OTHER

Sand in the Wind, Tor Books, 1990.
This Widowed Land, Tor Books, in press.

Contributor of over forty articles on historical, archaeological, and biological subjects to journals and periodicals.

ADAPTATIONS:

People of the Wolf was adapted for audiocassette by Audio Renaissance, 1990; *People of the Fire* was adapted for audiocassette, 1991; *People of the Earth* and *People of the River* were adapted for audiocassette, 1992.

WORK IN PROGRESS: Research on Anasazi archaeoastronomy.

SIDELIGHTS: Kathleen O'Neal Gear and her husband, W. Michael Gear, have collaborated on several novels for young adults. Please refer to W. Michael Gear's sketch in this volume for Sidelights.

*   *   *

GEAR, Kathleen M. O'Neal
See GEAR, Kathleen O'Neal

*   *   *

GEAR, W. Michael 1955-

PERSONAL: Born May 20, 1955, in Colorado Springs, CO; son of George William Gear (a news anchor) and Katherine Mable Cook (an artist; maiden name, Perry);

The anthropologist/archaeologist husband-and-wife team of W. Michael Gear and Kathleen O'Neal Gear begin their Ice Age saga with the story of twin brothers whose lives take very different paths. (Cover illustration by Royo.)

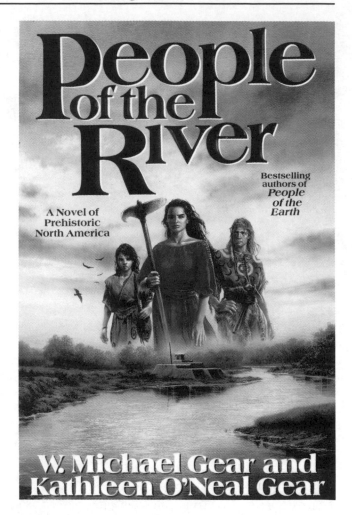

The Gears continue their portrayal of early Native Americans in *People of the River.* (Cover illustration by Royo.)

married Kathleen O'Neal (an archaeologist and writer), October 1, 1982. *Education:* Colorado State University, B.A., 1976, M.A., 1979. *Politics:* Libertarian. *Religion:* "Native American."

CAREER: Physical anthropologist, paleopathologist, archaeologist, and cultural resource management specialist; writer.

WRITINGS:

WITH WIFE, KATHLEEN O'NEAL GEAR

People of the Wolf, Tor Books, 1990.
People of the Fire, Tor Books, 1991.
People of the Earth, Tor Books, 1992.
People of the River, Tor Books, 1992.
People of the Lakes, Tor Books, in press.
People of the Sea, Tor Books, in press.

The authors' works have been translated into Dutch, German, Polish, and Spanish.

"SPIDER" TRILOGY; SCIENCE-FICTION NOVELS

Warriors of Spider, Daw Books, 1988.
Way of Spider, Daw Books, 1989.
Web of Spider, Daw Books, 1989.

OTHER

Big Horn Legacy, Pinnacle Books, 1988.
Long Ride Home, Tor Books, 1988.
The Artifact, Daw Books, 1990.
Starstrike, Daw Books, 1990.
Requiem for the Conqueror, Daw Books, 1991.
Relic of Empire, Daw Books, 1992.
Countermeasures, Daw Books, in press.

ADAPTATIONS:

People of the Wolf was adapted for audiocassette by Audio Renaissance, 1990; *People of the Fire* was adapted for audiocassette, 1991; *People of the Earth* and *People of the River* were adapted for audiocassette, 1992.

WORK IN PROGRESS: Five more North American prehistory novels, for Tor Books; book three in the "Forbidden Borders" trilogy, for Daw Books; a science-fiction novel; research on North American prehistory, western American history, and astrophysics.

SIDELIGHTS: Anthropologist W. Michael Gear and his wife, Kathleen O'Neal Gear, have collaborated on several books, including *People of the Wolf* and *People of the Fire,* that begin when explorers discover artifacts of ancient people who once occupied the land. *People of the Wolf* focuses on native Americans living in Canada at the end of the Ice Age. The two main characters, twin brothers Raven Hunter and Runs-in-Light, are the offspring of a random encounter between a female member of the "People," the tribe in which they are raised, and a male warrior of the "Other," a rival clan. Raven Hunter becomes a leader among the People, and his pride causes him to mount attacks against the Other during which several members of the victim tribe are killed. Eventually, Raven Hunter becomes an enemy to members of his own group.

Runs-in-Light, on the other hand, becomes a visionary who dreams that a wolf—a revered animal among the People—leads him away from barren hunting grounds to fertile land. Renamed Wolf Dreamer, the young man comes to know of the significance of dreams from a female sage of the clan. Inspired by her wisdom, Runs-in-Light walks through a hole in an ice formation and discovers a rich land which he believes would make an ideal new home for his tribe. In reviewing *People of the Wolf,* Carolyn Cushman of *Locus* declared that the book "should prove rewarding reading to anyone interested in exploring the lives of the earliest inhabitants of North America."

The Gears' second book, *People of the Fire,* focuses on Little Dancer, another dreamer among a race of ancient people. The young man is sheltered and befriended by Two Smokes, an outcast member of the tribe, and trained as a visionary by a medicine woman named White Calf. He becomes a husband and father but must abandon his family out of a sense of responsibility to follow the messages of his dreams and lead his tribe. Little Dancer must also face Heavy Beaver, a power-hungry visionary who tries to mislead the tribe with false dreams. Sister Mary Veronica of *Voice of Youth Advocates* enjoyed *People of the Fire,* stating that "the action is intense and satisfying and the characters are vividly portrayed."

WORKS CITED:

Locus, July, 1990, p. 23.
Voice of Youth Advocates, June, 1991, pp. 95-96.

* * *

GOLDBERG, Susan 1948-

PERSONAL: Born January 1, 1948, in Brooklyn, NY; daughter of Sidney (a furrier) and Pearl (a bookkeeper;

maiden name, Weiss) Lehman; married Jacob J. Goldberg, July 25, 1968 (divorced, June 21, 1989); children: Jennifer Ellen, Jonathan Michael. *Education:* Queens College, B.A., 1968. *Politics:* Independent. *Religion:* Jewish.

ADDRESSES: Home—29 Great Hills Rd., Short Hills, NJ 07078.

CAREER: Kindergarten teacher at public schools in Marblehead, MA; teacher of computer science at Millburn Public Schools. Temple B'nai Jeshurun, youth adviser, 1985-87; Bronx Zoo, docent, weekend chair, 1978, day captain, 1981-83, materials chair, 1992—.

WRITINGS:

(With Joyce Altman) *Dear Bronx Zoo,* Macmillan, 1991.

WORK IN PROGRESS: Research on baseball parks and zoos across the country.

SIDELIGHTS: Susan Goldberg told *SATA:* "When I was an elementary student, I'm afraid I wasn't a choosy reader. Oh, I bought every copy of the Bobbsey twins and Nancy Drew and read them all. But the wonderful classic books for children I didn't discover until I was studying the teaching of reading, in college. Then I began to share these books, like *The Borrowers* and *Wind in the Willows,* with my mother, who hadn't been exposed to any of these books either. By the time I had

Susan Goldberg and children.

my own children, reading aloud, especially at bedtime, became an important part of every day. We read all kinds of books, including long ones like *The Hobbit* and *Mary Poppins*. Eventually, everyone was able to take turns reading out loud. This sharing continued, as my daughter brought me all the authors she enjoyed, so I could 'discover' Ursula LeGuin, Bette Greene, Madeline L'Engle, and others. My children are now in college, and my son recently brought home yet another book for Mom to read!

"My interest in animals, though, did begin at an early age. There were always books about them, and toy dogs and cats to play with. We visited the zoo in Brooklyn a lot, but my mother never let me bring home the sheep! Summertimes, when we visited the country, there were frogs and turtles that we'd catch and watch for the day before we let them go. And one of my grandfathers had an egg farm. The chicks and puppies and cats provided moments of real delight that were hard to duplicate with toys. In fourth grade, one of the girls brought her guinea pig to school, and I remember vividly that the teacher, who otherwise did not impress me, kissed the rodent. A picture in my mind remains to this day, and my fourth grade teacher became suddenly someone to admire. Eventually, in spite of my mother's fears, our family shared the house with dogs, who surely provided more enjoyment for me than the untouchable tropical fish and the fragile birds.

"In between early childhood and motherhood also came a love for baseball and a strong interest in writing about it. I may have played with stuffed animals, and wished for pets, but I dreamed of being a sports writer. I read everything written about the Yankees, clipped all the articles, and then wrote my own articles and commentaries. I started writing short stories about baseball that I thought school kids would like. But I never did anything with these writings, except to share them with my brother or a friend, and to store them away in a box. In college I took a course in broadcasting and extended my dream to the sportscast booth. Women were just about to break into the business, but I didn't know it, and I wasn't daring enough to try to live my dream. (I wasn't even daring enough to take biology classes to foster my interest in animals or working with them.) Taking risks just wasn't something I was ready to do.

"I became a teacher, something I'd intended to do since I was six years old, and brought my interests along with me into the classroom. In fact, now animals and sports find many ways to creep, to crawl, and steal into my computer curriculum. When I ventured out of the classroom, it was to the Bronx Zoo, where I could learn about animals, occasionally work with them, and teach too. The zoo provided a living classroom. It was only natural that my friend Joyce and I would think of writing down some of the things we had been teaching people for many years. And it was fun doing the research about our favorite animals and sharing our new knowledge.

"Spending the last fifteen years working at the zoo, I discovered that it was easy to wander 'down the road' to watch the Yankees. My son and I have done a lot of that! (For my daughter I compromise, and visit the Mets.)

"Someday soon, I think it would be great to pursue my dream again. Maybe you'll find me visiting baseball parks at night, and zoos during the day. I don't think there's anyone doing 'field' research that covers all those bases!"

* * *

GRAMBLING, Lois G. 1927-

PERSONAL: Born August 20, 1927, in Elizabeth, NJ; daughter of Arthur and Ethel Goodwin; married F. Arthur Grambling, January 21, 1949; children: Jeffrey, Mark. *Education:* Drew University, B.A., 1949; Central State College, M.A., 1966.

ADDRESSES: Home—48 Blackstone Ave., Binghamton, NY 13903.

CAREER: Elementary teacher in Denver, CO, 1950-52, Milwaukee, WI, 1953-56, and Oklahoma City, OK, 1963-65; school social worker in Oklahoma City, 1965-67, and Binghamton, NY, 1967-89; writer. Leader of workshops for professional education groups and at

LOIS G. GRAMBLING

So the two friends sat together in their favorite chair and read *The Night Before Christmas*.

Grambling uses holiday preparations to develop the special relationship between an elephant and a mouse in *Elephant and Mouse Get Ready for Christmas*. (Illustration by Deborah Maze.)

schools and libraries in New York, Pennsylvania, and New Jersey.

WRITINGS:

A Hundred Million Reasons for Owning an Elephant, illustrated by Vickie M. Learner, Barron's, 1990.
Elephant and Mouse Get Ready for Christmas, illustrated by Deborah Maze, Barron's, 1990.
Elephant and Mouse Get Ready for Easter, illustrated by Maze, Barron's, 1991.
Elephant and Mouse Celebrate Halloween, illustrated by Maze, Barron's, 1991.
An Alligator Named ... Alligator, illustrated by Doug Cushman, Barron's, 1991.

Also contributor of stories to *Cricket, Hopscotch,* and *Jack and Jill.*

SIDELIGHTS: Lois G. Grambling told *SATA:* "My first really vivid childhood memory is that of getting my very own library card—no easy feat for a not quite five-year-old who was definitely not into printing or writing or spelling, yet. With card in hand my enthusiasm was boundless. Suddenly all those books on the library shelves were *mine,* too! I could take them home and read them. And I did—by the dozens. I've been taking them home and reading them by the dozens ever since.

"As a writer, I was a late bloomer. I never gave much thought to putting pen to paper to express my feelings or

to share my experiences until our first grandchild, Lara, was born in 1984. Then I had someone very important to write to and for. In 1987 Lara's brother Tyler was born. Then I had another very important someone to write to and for. Now that I have started writing I find that I can't stop! Writing has become an integral part of my life. I love it. I look forward to it. And if a day goes by when I haven't been able to do some writing, I miss it. Yes, I really do put pen to paper. I don't use a computer.

"In 1990 my first book, *A Hundred Million Reasons for Owning an Elephant,* was published. (And believe me, there is nothing more exciting than holding your very first book in your hands!) *A Hundred Million Reasons ...* is great fun for reading aloud to groups of kids. It seems to get their imaginative juices flowing. And their reasons for owning an elephant are absolutely marvelous. Much better than mine. Maybe I should rewrite the book?

"That same year, 1990, *Elephant and Mouse Get Ready for Christmas* was published. I fell in love with Elephant and Mouse and their special relationship. So I wrote *Elephant and Mouse Get Ready for Easter* and then *Elephant and Mouse Celebrate Halloween,* both in 1991. Holidays tend to bring out the best in all of us and Elephant and Mouse in this series, I hope, prove it.

"After completing the Elephant and Mouse series, I felt I wanted to write something absolutely wacky. So I did. And that's when *An Alligator Named ... Alligator* was born. Published in 1991, it is an easy reader. I had such fun writing about Alligator that I missed him terribly when the book was completed. So I went out and got myself two alligator eggs. I don't miss Alligator so much now."

*   *   *

GUIBERSON, Brenda Z. 1946-

PERSONAL: Surname is pronounced "*guy*-berson"; born December 10, 1946, in Denver, CO; daughter of Carl Nicholas (a civil engineer) and Ruth Ellen (a homemaker; maiden name, Schenker) Zangar; married William R. Guiberson (a business agent), August, 1973; children: Jason Carl. *Education:* Received B.A.'s in art and English from University of Washington.

ADDRESSES: Home—20130 Eighth Ave. N.W., Seattle, WA 98177.

CAREER: Writer. Worked as a copywriter, letter carrier, stained glass worker and woodworker, manager, and counselor.

AWARDS, HONORS: Turtle People was named a Junior Literary Guild selection.

WRITINGS:

Turtle People, Atheneum, 1990.
Cactus Hotel, illustrated by Megan Lloyd, Holt, 1991.

BRENDA Z. GUIBERSON

Instant Soup, Atheneum, 1991.

WORK IN PROGRESS: Master Detective, a novel; *Spoonbill Swamp*, a nonfiction picture book, completion expected in 1992; *Winter Wheat* and *Lobster Boat*, nonfiction picture books, completion of both expected in 1993. Research on rain forests and floods.

SIDELIGHTS: Brenda Z. Guiberson told *SATA:* "Becoming a writer was not on my mind as a child. I had five sisters and two brothers and, for a while, three foster children in the family. We never sat around much and were usually out along the Columbia River, which ran past our backyard in Richland, Washington.

"In high school and college I took many science classes and was a little surprised to finally end up with degrees in fine art and English. Along the way, I tried out several

things: copywriter, letter carrier, stained glass and woodworker, manager, and counselor.

"The idea of creating children's books started with my son, Jason. He used to bring home dozens of books from the library and ask to hear them over and over again. We were having a good time and it sank in. After years in this training ground, I finally got up the courage to write. Now I don't want to stop.

"I like to write both fiction and nonfiction. I like to write about subjects that are interesting and exciting to me. Writers can make anything happen and write about places that they would like to go.

"Experiences of my childhood came up in the novel *Turtle People*. I spent many hours swimming in the Columbia River. Occasionally, we found Indian artifacts. I only found chips and arrowheads, but my sister Cathy found the real turtle bowl, on an island in the Snake River. I was the one who took it around to museums and collectors for information.

"*Cactus Hotel* was written after a trip to the Sonoran Desert in Arizona. *Spoonbill Swamp* began after trips out into the waterways of Louisiana and Florida. I thought about these places quite a bit and wanted to know about the action and drama that went on in all those moments that I could not be there. I wanted to know why cacti have holes and what happens when all the sleeping creatures wake up hungry.

"It takes a lot of research to write about what might happen at some random moment in time. A writer can't say that a kangaroo rat stops for a drink of water when research reveals that this creature never drinks. And if an alligator is cold-blooded, then how does it behave? It takes a lot of digging into other books to find out. This is something I like to do. In writing *Turtle People*, I ended up reading the entire journals of Lewis and Clark, plus additional books on Sacajawea [their native American guide during part of their expedition] and others.

"For someone who has always been interested in science and the visual arts, the process of writing a book combines many things that I like to do. It's hard work but fun and surprises pop up all along the way."

H

HARRIS, Alan 1944-

PERSONAL: Born August 3, 1944, in Portland, OR; son of (James) Stewart (a dry cleaner) and Jane Ann Gordon (a dry cleaner) Harris; married Rose Marie (a classroom aide; maiden name, Spitt), August 22, 1970; children: (William) Donald, David S., Catherine R. *Education:* California Institute of Technology, B.S., 1966; University of California, Los Angeles, M.S., 1967, Ph.D., 1975. *Politics:* Democrat. *Religion:* None.

ADDRESSES: Home—4603 Orange Knoll, La Canada, CA 91011. *Office*—Jet Propulsion Lab, MS 183-501, Pasadena, CA 91109. *Agent*—RGA Publishing Group, 1875 Century Park E., Suite 220, Los Angeles, CA 90067.

CAREER: Jet Propulsion Lab, Pasadena, CA, member of technical staff, 1975-91, senior member of technical staff, 1991—. Assistant scoutmaster with Boy Scouts of America.

MEMBER: American Astronomical Society (member of dynamical astronomy division executive committee, 1978-80, divisional vice-chairman, 1990-91, divisional chairman, 1991-92), International Astronomical Union, Commission 15 (organizing commissioner, 1985-88; vice president, 1988-91; president, 1991—).

AWARDS, HONORS: Alan Harris's last name was given to "Asteroid (2929)" by the International Astronomical Union.

WRITINGS:

(With Paul Weissman) *The Great Voyager Adventure,* Silver Burdett, 1990.

Also author of about one hundred technical papers and book chapters on astronomical subjects.

WORK IN PROGRESS: Proceedings of an international conference, "Asteroids, Comets, Meteors, 1991," a technical work for scientists; research for a children's book on the history of space exploration.

ALAN HARRIS

SIDELIGHTS: Alan Harris told *SATA:* "I have been interested in astronomy since I was a small child, especially in the planets and spaceflight. In the time before Sputnik [satellites launched by the Soviet space program], there were few books about space that were informative and factually accurate for young readers. The authors of the few books I could find were among my childhood heroes.

"After completing my university and graduate training, I began my research career at the Jet Propulsion Laboratory, where most planetary spacecraft have been built—including the Ranger and Surveyor probes to the moon; the Mariners to Mercury, Venus, and Mars; Viking to Mars; and, of course, the Voyagers that went to Jupiter, Saturn, Uranus, and Neptune and are now exploring the far reaches beyond the known planets. One of the most rewarding experiences I have had in my career has been to meet and get to know some of those early childhood heroes who wrote the books that launched me on my path of research.

"I remember one such incident clearly. I was about thirteen years old and had gone to Portland (about twenty-five miles from my home in Oregon) on the bus to an appointment at the orthodontist. After my dentist appointment, I took advantage of the visit to the 'big city' to browse a technical bookstore for any new interesting material. I found a book, *The Moon and the Planets,* and bought it. Then I went to the nearby Woolworth's lunch counter to get something to eat before catching the bus home. It was only after eating half my lunch that I remembered with horror that I had spent my lunch money on that book! Fortunately, a kindly lady saved me further embarrassment and paid for my lunch. I still have the book. A few months ago, I was honored to have in attendance at a meeting I had organized, the author of that book, Fred Whipple, now professor emeritus at Harvard/Smithsonian Observatory. More than thirty years after buying the book, I now have it autographed! These people are still my heroes.

"As a part of my profession, I write research papers for technical journals and books. But those papers, longer and more complicated to write, reach few readers—maybe less than one hundred researchers interested in a specialized topic. By comparison, a book for general readers will be read by thousands of people, even hundreds of thousands. So in that sense, more communication occurs from one small book for children than all the papers I will ever write for my scientific colleagues. It was this realization, plus my childhood admiration for the authors who inspired my career, that encouraged me to write a book."

*　　*　　*

HARRIS, Robin
See SHINE, Deborah

*　　*　　*

HARSHMAN, Marc 1950-

PERSONAL: Born October 1, 1950, in Randolph County, IN; son of William L. Harshman and Janice Maloon Wells; married Cheryl Ryan (a librarian and writer), August 25, 1976; children: Sarah Jayne. *Education:* Bethany College, B.A., 1973; Yale University Divinity School, M.A.R., 1975; University of Pittsburgh, M.A., 1978. *Religion:* Protestant.

ADDRESSES: Home—Moundsville, WV. *Office*—c/o Rosanne Lauer, Cobblehill Books, 375 Hudson St., New York, NY 10014.

CAREER: Writer. Professional storyteller, 1978—; elementary teacher in West Virginia, 1985—.

WRITINGS:

FOR CHILDREN

A Little Excitement, illustrated by Ted Rand, Cobblehill Books/Dutton, 1989.
Snow Company, illustrated by Leslie W. Bowman, Cobblehill Books/Dutton, 1990.
(With Bonnie Collins) *Rocks in My Pockets,* Cobblehill Books/Dutton, 1991.
Only One, Cobblehill Books/Dutton, in press.
Uncle James, Cobblehill Books/Dutton, in press.

A Little Excitement has been translated into Swedish and Danish.

POEMS

Turning out the Stones, State Street Press, 1983.

Also contributor of poems to periodicals.

WORK IN PROGRESS: Moving Days, a picture book about a family leaving their home, for Cobblehill Books/Dutton, 1994; *The Luck of the Squirrels,* a full-length collection of poems for adults.

SIDELIGHTS: Marc Harshman told *SATA:* "I believe our language holds the power to challenge and persuade, comfort, inform, and ultimately to reveal truths about who we are. Through our language the best of who we are is preserved. An artist's manipulation of words through rhythms, images, and countless other figures is a high calling. It is my duty to remind others that the language is their language, a living thing renewed by what they—its speakers and writers—bring to it. As a

MARC HARSHMAN

children's writer, I also see an opportunity to promote a vision of writing and storytelling that is natural to everyday living, giving children a means of responding to the world.

"It always brings me great pleasure to visit with children. I love being able to tell them stories and to talk with them about writing and books. I enjoy seeing them discover that writers are real people who use the same language that they do. I want them to see that they have at their fingertips possibilities for creating new visions of themselves and their world, visions that will not only help them be better writers, but be better people as well.

"My poems are frequently narrations springing from specific and local geographies, be they the rural Indiana where I was raised, the West Virginia where I have lived my adult life, or the towns and farms of Canada and England where I have traveled. I believe the poems reveal perceptions of value gleaned from the bleaker aspects of lives lived either alone or in communal isolation from the mainstream. The free verse in which I compose is intended to be voiced, to be heard, and is informed by the harmonies and rhythms of traditional verse and pushed toward new hearing by the emotional pressures of the breath itself."

*   *   *

HARVEY, Roland 1945-

PERSONAL: Born December 11, 1945, in Melbourne, Victoria, Australia; son of Herbert Bruce (a graphic artist) and Eveline Anne (a graphic artist) Harvey; married Rona Judith Sharpe (a teacher and astrologer), 1977; children: Sally Christina, Timothy Piers, Roland James, Sara Jane. *Education:* Royal Melbourne Institute of Technology, B. Environmental Science, 1974, student of architecture, 1973-77. *Politics:* Green. *Religion:* None.

ADDRESSES: Home—11 Selbourne Rd., Kew, Victoria 3101, Australia. *Office*—125 Auburn Rd., Hawthorn, Victoria 3122, Australia.

CAREER: Worked as a cadet executive for a corporation in Victoria, Australia, 1964-68; affiliated with Colonial Sugar Refining Co., Victoria, 1968-72; Roland Harvey Studios/The Five Mile Press, Collingwood, Victoria, managing director, 1977-90; Roland Harvey Studios/The Periscope Press, Hawthorn, Victoria, managing director, 1991—; writer and illustrator.

MEMBER: Black and White Illustrators Club, Icicles Ski Club, Gippsland Lakes Yacht Club.

AWARDS, HONORS: Commendation, Children's Book Council of Australia (CBC), 1984, and shortlisted for best picture story book, Young Australians Best Book Award Council, 1986, both for *The Friends of Emily Culpepper;* Clifton Pugh Award, CBC, and shortlisted for the Junior Book of the Year Award, CBC, both 1986, for *Burke and Wills;* children's picture book of the year

ROLAND HARVEY

finalist, CBC, 1989, for *My Place in Space,* which also was named a CBC honor book.

WRITINGS:

SELF-ILLUSTRATED

Roland Harvey's Book of Christmas, Five Mile Press, 1982.
Roland Harvey's First Ever Book of Things to Make and Do, Roland Harvey Studios, 1982.
Roland Harvey's Second Ever Book of Things to Make and Do, Roland Harvey Studios, 1983.
Roland Harvey's Incredible Book of Almost Everything, Five Mile Press, 1985.
Burke and Wills, Five Mile Press, 1985.
Roland Harvey's New Book of Christmas, Five Mile Press, 1986.
Roland Harvey's Only Joking Take-Away Fun Book!, Ashton Scholastic, 1987.
The Real Me Book, Five Mile Press, 1989.
(Author with Scott Riddle) *Crisis on Christmas Eve,* Periscope Press, 1991.

ILLUSTRATOR

Lorraine Milne, *The Fix-It Man: Songs for Schools,* Macmillan, 1979.
Michael Dugan, compiler, *More Stuff and Nonsense,* Collins, 1980.
Alan Boardman, *Eureka Stockade,* Five Mile Press, 1981.

Harvey often fills his pictures with numerous details that tell unique stories of their own, as in this illustration from Robin and Sally Hirst's *My Place in Space.* (Illustration by Harvey and Joe Levine.)

Boardman, *The First Fleet,* Five Mile Press, 1982.

Jean Chapman, *The Great Candle Scandal,* Hodder and Stoughton, 1982.

Ann Coleridge, *The Friends of Emily Culpepper,* Five Mile Press, 1983.

Boardman, *The Crossing of the Blue Mountains,* Five Mile Press, 1985.

Boardman, *Great Events in Australia's History,* Five Mile Press, 1985.

Jim Converse, *The Book of Australian Trivia,* Five Mile Press, 1985.

Nette Hilton, *Dirty Dave the Bushranger,* Five Mile Press, 1987.

(With Joe Levine) Robin Hirst and Sally Hirst, *My Place in Space,* Five Mile Press, 1988.

Marcia Vaughan, *Milly Fitzwilly's Mousecatcher,* Periscope Press, 1991.

OTHER

My Place in Time, Periscope Press, in press.

WORK IN PROGRESS: A book on philosophy for children, for Periscope Press.

SIDELIGHTS: Roland Harvey told *SATA:* "Some of my earliest memories are of our holiday house in the mountains. We were fifty meters from the edge of the forest, and the name of our house, 'Joalah' meant 'home of the lyrebird.' We spent most of our time there listening to and feeding those beautiful birds, climbing waterfalls, and generally getting very dirty. I wrote my

first books here: exercise books with bits of leaf, fern, feathers, and sometimes whole logs stuck in them.

"My parents were both graphic artists, which gave me a lot of confidence in my drawing. It also stalled my entry into the real world of illustrating: my mum and dad had suffered in the Great Depression. So I tried a number of other careers and finally architecture, which I loved. Ironically, another depression in the building trade pushed me from architecture into illustrating, then writing and illustrating, and then publishing, writing, and illustrating. I love that even more.

"My first real success came with an attempt to present history in an interesting way. It was on that project that I discovered I work best in a team. *Eureka Stockade,* the true story of the Gold Rush in Australia and the miner's struggle against repression, was developed with Alan Boardman and was really the birth of my 'style.' In the illustrations of that book, little challenges and questions lurk in every corner, tiny tragedies and comedies are enacted off center stage. I later worked on other history books as well as *My Place in Space,* an interesting collaboration between two astronomers (Robin and Sally Hirst), an airbrush wizard (Joe Levine) and me. I hope to extend the concept in order to tackle even more difficult subjects like 'time,' all the while trying to make such difficult subjects accessible and fun.

"I don't feel bound to book illustrating; a lot of my time goes toward developing my very Australian cards, kid's calendars, posters and 'other things.'

"I listen a lot to what my kids say about my books, such as 'Dad—you can't say that!' or 'The reindeer wouldn't be rude to Santa!' I also notice kids laugh at anything to do with toilets."

* * *

HISER, Constance 1950-

PERSONAL: Born November 14, 1950, in Joplin, MO; daughter of Herman A. (a civil engineer) and Joyce M. (a homemaker; maiden name, Wommack) Harrington; married Ronald G. Hiser (a freelance writer), December 23, 1972; children: Jeannie, James. *Education:* Missouri Southern State College, B.A., 1973. *Politics:* Republican. *Religion:* Southern Baptist. *Hobbies and other interests:* Reading, classical music (singing and piano), exercise sports (aerobics and freeweights).

ADDRESSES: Home and office—P.O. Box 289, Webb City, MO 64870.

CAREER: Freelance writer of greeting cards, 1978-86; American Greetings, Cleveland, OH, contract writer, 1986-87; Gibson Greetings, Cincinnati, OH, contract writer, 1987—. Speaker at schools, churches, and clubs; active in church.

MEMBER: Society of Children's Book Writers.

WRITINGS:

"JAMES AND GANG" SERIES

No Bean Sprouts, Please!, Holiday House, 1989.
Ghosts in Fourth Grade, Holiday House, 1991.
Dog on Third Base, Holiday House, 1991.
Critter Sitters, Holiday House, 1992.

OTHER BOOKS FOR CHILDREN

Sixth-Grade Star, Holiday House, 1992.
Scoop Snoops, Holiday House, in press.

WORK IN PROGRESS: Work on several short chapter books; a novel under revision.

SIDELIGHTS: Constance Hiser told *SATA:* "All through elementary school I was the 'Invisible Girl'— the one who couldn't jump rope or hit a ball. To make matters worse, I was also the class bookworm, having been taught to read at the age of three by my grandmother, who was a first grade teacher. Talk about misfits! This unhappy state of affairs lasted until the fifth grade, when, for an English assignment, I wrote my first story. After I read my story out loud the class actually clapped their hands! I was hooked. I spent much of my time writing stories—in the margins of spelling tests and the backs of history papers. That year I also completed my first 'book'—a novel based on Oliver Cromwell and the English Revolution. I knew nothing about the subject, but I didn't let that stop *me.*

"From that starting point, my 'career' took its first big leap when I met my husband, Ron, then a writer for Hallmark greeting cards. With his help and encouragement, I began selling card verses to most of the major greeting card companies. I eventually wound up in a cozy niche with Gibson Greetings. It's especially nice to be able to work at home, with only an occasional trip to Cincinnati to touch bases."

While Hiser had job security with her greeting card work, she continued to write fiction, hoping to get her work published. She recalled the process of writing and selling *No Bean Sprouts, Please!:* "I lucked into my first book sale. I got the idea for the book from the realization that my son would *never* like anything I fixed for his lunch box. This was the germ for *No Bean Sprouts, Please!,* the first of my 'James and Gang' series for Holiday House. I would like to stress to kids that this book was my *thirteenth* attempt to publish a children's book. Sometimes I still shudder when I imagine what would have happened if I'd given up after the twelfth flop!

"In fact, if there's any idea I'd like to get across to the kids I meet, it's this: It takes more than dreaming to make dreams come true. I think I work *harder* at writing than I'd work at any 'real job'—but the satisfaction I receive each time I hold a new copy of one of my books makes it all worthwhile. There is *nothing* a kid can't accomplish—I feel I'm proof of that!"

CONSTANCE HISER

HOWE, James 1946-

PERSONAL: Born August 2, 1946, in Oneida, NY; son of Lee Arthur (a clergyman) and Lonnelle (a teacher; maiden name, Crossley) Howe; married Deborah Smith (a writer and actress), September 28, 1969 (died, June 3, 1978); married Betsy Imershein (a photographer), April 5, 1981; children: (second marriage) Zoe. *Education:* Boston University, B.F.A., 1968; Hunter College of the City University of New York, M.A., 1977. *Hobbies and other interests:* Bicycling, hiking, skiing, movies, theater, traveling, reading.

ADDRESSES: Agent—Amy Berkower, Writers House Inc., 21 West 26th St., New York, NY 10010.

CAREER: Free-lance actor and director, 1971-75; Lucy Kroll Agency, New York City, literary agent, 1976-81; children's writer, 1981—. Member of advisory board, Hospice of St. Vincent's Hospital, 1979-81, and Ethnic Heritage Program, Henry Street Settlement, 1980-83; member of board of trustees, Village Temple, 1980-85; member of board of directors, Hastings Creative Arts Council, 1991—. *Wartime service:* Civilian public service, 1968-70.

MEMBER: Authors Guild, PEN American Center, Mystery Writers of America, Society of Children's Book Writers, Writers Guild of America, East.

AWARDS, HONORS: Notable book citation, American Library Association (ALA), 1979, and Pacific Northwest Young Readers' Choice Award, 1982, both for *Bunnicula: A Rabbit-Tale of Mystery; Bunnicula* has also received twelve other Children's Choice awards from various states, including Florida, Hawaii, Illinois, and Vermont, and a listing among *Booklist*'s "Fifty All-Time Favorite Children's Books"; Honor Book in Nonfiction, *Boston Globe-Horn Book,* notable book citation, ALA,

JAMES HOWE

and Children's Book of the Year citation, Library of Congress, all 1981, and nonfiction nominee, American Book Award in Children's Books (now National Book Award), 1982, all for *The Hospital Book;* CRABbery honor book, 1984, for *The Celery Stalks at Midnight.*

Howe's works have been cited by such periodicals as *School Library Journal* and *Booklist,* and by such organizations as the Junior Literary Guild, the American Booksellers Association, the Child Study Children's Book Committee, the Children's Book Council, the National Science Teachers Association, and the International Reading Association; they have also received numerous other children's choice awards.

WRITINGS:

FOR CHILDREN

(With Deborah Howe) *Teddy Bear's Scrapbook,* illustrated by David S. Rose, Atheneum, 1980.
The Hospital Book (nonfiction), photographs by Mal Warshaw, Crown, 1981.
Annie Joins the Circus (spin-off from movie *Annie*), illustrated by Leonard Shortall, Random House, 1982.
The Case of the Missing Mother, illustrated by William Cleaver, Random House, 1983.
A Night without Stars, Atheneum, 1983.
The Muppet Guide to Magnificent Manners; Featuring Jim Henson's Muppets, illustrated by Peter Elwell, Random House, 1984.
How the Ewoks Saved the Trees: An Old Ewok Legend (spin-off from movie *Return of the Jedi*), illustrated by Walter Velez, Random House, 1984.
Morgan's Zoo, illustrated by Leslie Morrill, Atheneum, 1984.
The Day the Teacher Went Bananas (picture book), illustrated by Lillian Hoban, Dutton, 1984.
Mister Tinker in Oz ("Brand-New Oz" adventure series), illustrated by D. Rose, Random House, 1985.
When You Go to Kindergarten, photographs by wife Betsy Imershein, Knopf, 1986.
There's a Monster under My Bed (picture book), illustrated by D. Rose, Atheneum, 1986.
A Love Note for Baby Piggy, Marvel, 1986.
(Reteller) *Babes in Toyland* (adaptation of 1903 operetta by Victor Herbert and Glen MacDonough), illustrated by Allen Atkinson, Gulliver Books, 1986.
(Reteller) *The Secret Garden* (adaptation of the classic by Frances Hodgson Burnett), illustrated by Thomas B. Allen, Random House, 1987.
I Wish I Were a Butterfly (picture book), illustrated by Ed Young, Gulliver Books, 1987.
Carol Burnett: The Sound of Laughter ("Women of Our Time" series), illustrated by Robert Masheris, Viking, 1987.
(Adaptor) *Dances with Wolves: A Story for Children* (adapted from the screenplay by Michael Blake), Newmarket Press, 1991.

"BUNNICULA" SERIES

(With D. Howe) *Bunnicula: A Rabbit-Tale of Mystery,* illustrated by Alan Daniel, Atheneum, 1979.

Howliday Inn, illustrated by Lynn Munsinger, Atheneum, 1982.

The Celery Stalks at Midnight, illustrated by Leslie Morrill, Atheneum, 1983.

Nighty-Nightmare, illustrated by L. Morrill, Atheneum, 1987.

Harold and Chester in The Fright before Christmas, illustrated by L. Morrill, Morrow, 1988.

Harold and Chester in Scared Silly: A Halloween Treat, illustrated by L. Morrill, Morrow, 1989.

Harold and Chester in Hot Fudge, illustrated by L. Morrill, Morrow, 1990.

Harold and Chester in Creepy-Crawly Birthday, illustrated by L. Morrill, Morrow, 1991.

Return to Howliday Inn, illustrated by A. Daniel, Atheneum, 1992.

"SEBASTIAN BARTH" MYSTERY SERIES

What Eric Knew, Atheneum, 1985.

Stage Fright, Atheneum, 1986.

Eat Your Poison, Dear, Atheneum, 1986.

Dew Drop Dead, Atheneum, 1990.

"PINKY AND REX" SERIES

Pinky and Rex, illustrated by Melissa Sweet, Atheneum, 1990.

Pinky and Rex Get Married, illustrated by M. Sweet, Atheneum, 1990.

Pinky and Rex and the Spelling Bee, illustrated by M. Sweet, Atheneum, 1991.

Pinky and Rex and the Mean Old Witch, illustrated by M. Sweet, Atheneum, 1991.

Pinky and Rex Go to Camp, illustrated by M. Sweet, Atheneum, 1992.

OTHER

My Life as a Babysitter (television play), The Disney Channel, 1990.

Also compiler of *365 New Words-a-Year Shoelace Calendar for Kids,* Workman Publishing, 1983-85. Contributor to *Horn Book* and *School Library Journal.*

Some of Howe's works have been translated into French, German, Swedish, Danish, Italian, Japanese, Spanish, and Dutch.

ADAPTATIONS: Bunnicula has been adapted into an animated television movie, produced by Ruby-Spears Productions, ABC, 1982, a sound recording, narrated by Lou Jacobi, Caedmon Records, 1982, and a videocassette, World Vision Home Video; *Howliday Inn* has been adapted into a sound recording, narrated by Jacobi, Caedmon Records, 1984; *The Celery Stalks at Midnight* has been adapted into a sound recording, 1987; *Nighty-Nightmare* has been adapted into a sound recording, narrated by George S. Irving, Caedmon, 1988.

WORK IN PROGRESS: Rabbit-Cadabra! (part of the "Bunnicula" series), illustrated by A. Daniel, publication by Morrow expected in 1993; *Pinky and Rex and*

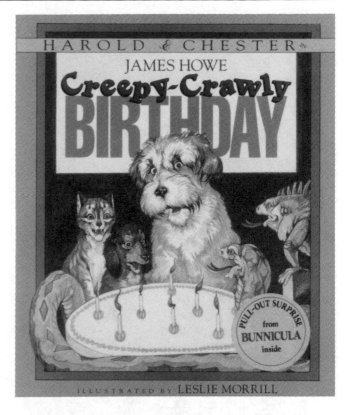

Harold, a shaggy dog with a literary bent, and Chester, a conceited cat with an overdeveloped imagination, team up to solve mysteries in Howe's "Bunnicula" series. (Cover illustration by Leslie Morrill).

the New Baby, illustrated by M. Sweet, publication by Atheneum expected in 1993.

SIDELIGHTS: James Howe is a versatile children's author who likes to challenge and entertain his young readers through word play, suspense, and humor. Best known for his comical "Bunnicula" series—about a pet rabbit suspected of possessing vampire tendencies—Howe combines witty and engaging dialogue with fast-paced and often absurd story lines. He traces his creative impulses back to his youth, when he concocted tales with his friends, and credits his family with inspiring in him an early love of language. "Words played an important part in my growing up," he revealed in *Sixth Book of Junior Authors and Illustrators.* "Not only the written word . . . but words that flew through the air—jokes, riddles, puns. My family was always playing with words. It is little wonder that even after I got serious about writing, I've had a hard time getting serious about words."

"I don't believe I was born to write," Howe once admitted. "But the creative itch *has* been with me for as long as I can remember. And it has always been strong enough that it demanded to be scratched." He was born in Oneida, New York, in 1946, and from the first he considered writing simply entertainment—not a serious endeavor. He wrote and performed in his first play at the young age of seven. Short stories, a self-published newspaper (called *The Gory Gazette*), and humor col-

who relishes horror stories, and Harold, a lumbering, shaggy dog who narrates the tale under the pseudonym Harold X. (to protect the innocent). The sleuths team up when their owners, the Monroes, innocently adopt a bunny abandoned at a movie theater and name it Bunnicula, after the chilling film *Dracula* that had been playing there. Convinced that Bunnicula is really a vampire rabbit—it does have oddly-shaped teeth resembling fangs *and* the vegetables in the house have been mysteriously drained of their color soon after Bunnicula's arrival—the cat-and-dog twosome attempt to warn the unsuspecting Monroes. *Bunnicula*'s "stylish, exuberant make-believe," observed a reviewer in *Publishers Weekly,* arises from the Howes' "unreined imagination and ... glinting sense of humor."

"Bunnicula" soon evolved into a series, with the completion of such light-hearted and comic tales as *Howliday Inn, The Celery Stalks at Midnight, Nighty-Nightmare, Harold and Chester in Creepy-Crawly Birthday,* and *Return to Howliday Inn.* Chateau Bow-Wow provides the locale for *Howliday Inn* (so named because Chester is convinced it shelters werewolves). In the story Chester and Harold are lodged at a boarding house,

Chester's suspicions of werewolves and the mysterious disappearances of pets transform the "Chateau Bow-Wow" into the "Howliday Inn" in this second tale of the "Bunnicula" series. (Illustration by Lynn Munsinger.)

umns for his high school paper followed. He entered college, though, intent on becoming an actor, not a writer. "You see," he explained in *Sixth Book of Junior Authors and Illustrators,* "as much as I loved writing plays, I loved performing in them even more." At Boston University he earned a degree in fine arts in 1968, then promptly became a social worker—in lieu of combat duty during the Vietnam War. He worked variously as a free-lance actor and director a few years later and also returned to graduate school, where a playwriting seminar revived his childhood love of writing. "It was during this time in my life," Howe recalled, "that ... my late wife, Deborah, suggested that we collaborate on a children's book based on a character I had created several years earlier in an uncontrolled fit of whimsy, Count Bunnicula. And so we did."

Published in 1979, *Bunnicula: A Rabbit-Tale of Mystery* quickly became a favorite among children, winning more than ten children's choice awards, including the Dorothy Canfield Fisher Award and the Nene Award. The story revolves around Chester, an arrogant, lofty cat

The author's passion for puns and word play demonstrates itself throughout his books, especially in this "Bunnicula" mystery about vampire vegetables. (Cover illustration by Morrill.)

from which cats and dogs strangely disappear almost daily. Frantic when even Louise, the French poodle, vanishes, the distressed pair fears the work of a villainous murderer. "Wonderfully witty dialogue and irresistible characters" fill the story, decided a *Publishers Weekly* reviewer. *The Celery Stalks at Midnight* follows the duo's efforts to track Bunnicula, who has disappeared from his cage in the Monroe house. Along with Howie, a tiny pup who insists Chester is his "pop," the three also join forces to destroy (puncture with toothpicks) the vegetables Chester is sure have been transformed into killer zombies by the vampire rabbit.

Most reviewers especially praised the slapstick humor and abundant puns that fill *Celery:* "Hare today, gone tomorrow," quips young Howie to his reluctant feline father. Or "A vampire," explains Harold to the naive puppy, "is the person who calls the rules during a baseball game." And "I just had a thought," says the agitated Chester to Harold. "What if Bunnicula's met up with one of his own kind? You know how they multiply ... " "Well, I don't really," the bumbling dog earnestly replies, "but if they're like everybody else these days, they probably use those little pocket calculators."

In addition to the "Bunnicula" series, Howe has created two other series, "Pinky and Rex," about two young best friends, and "Sebastian Barth," about a junior high school sleuth whose appetite for mystery leads to dangerous, and sometimes comical, situations. In *Eat Your Poison, Dear,* for example, Sebastian discovers that the flu epidemic suffered by his eighth-grade classmates is actually a case of premeditated food poisoning. Among his suspects? Miss Swille, the seasoned cafeteria manager. However in *Dew Drop Dead,* the author reveals his versatility by interweaving a serious theme—homelessness—into the tale. Sebastian and his friends uncover a dead body, possibly a murder victim, concealed in an abandoned inn, and as the narrative unfolds, a homeless man from a neighboring shelter becomes the chief suspect. Many reviewers commended Howe for portraying the homeless as individuals: from Marcus, a silent and moody teenager, to Abraham, a mentally ill man who experiences visions. "In spite of the overall light tone of the novel," observed Frances Bradburn in *Wilson Library Bulletin,* "[Howe] forces [his] readers to at least become aware of one of our great national tragedies."

Depicting serious themes such as homelessness seems to confirm a commitment Howe feels toward his young readers: to be open and honest with them. "It is the writer's privilege and responsibility," he stated in a 1985 *Horn Book* article, "to give children a world they can enter, recognize, at times be frightened of, but which ultimately, they can master and control.... We must not leave them feeling stranded in an unfamiliar world where the questions, let alone the answers, are beyond their grasp." Howe's philosophy is reflected in *The Hospital Book,* which was nominated for the 1982 National Book Award in nonfiction. The work details hospital procedures from a child's point of view, and

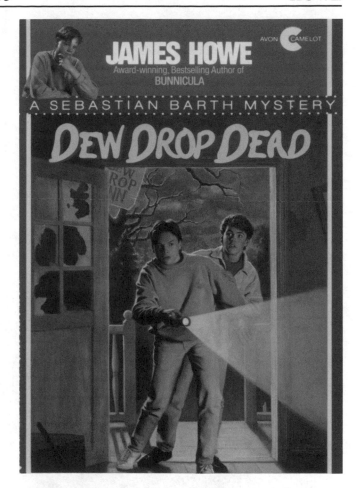

While Howe's works are noted for their humor and suspense, novels such as *Dew Drop Dead* also demonstrate his ability to treat serious themes such as homelessness.

most critics agree that it provides one of the best sources of comprehensive and candid information on its subject. "This is the finest book of its kind available," stated Karen Harris in *School Library Journal.* Howe has also written *A Night without Stars,* a fictionalized account of a young patient's fear of open-heart surgery.

Prevalent throughout most of Howe's books, though, are the laughs. *The Day the Teacher Went Bananas,* for instance, features an unusual elementary schoolteacher—a gorilla—who teaches his eager kindergartners to dangle from tree branches, count with their toes, and romp in the mud. "Humor is the most precious gift I can give to my reader," the author stressed in his 1985 *Horn Book* article, "a reminder that the world is not such a terribly serious place. There is more than video games and drugs and nuclear threats; there is laughter—and there is hope."

Howe noted: "I'm one of the fortunate ones. My personal and work lives are totally entwined. I get up in the morning, have breakfast with my family, walk to the other end of the house, and sit down at my desk. Later, I'll take breaks to read a book to my daughter or a chapter of a book to myself, have lunch, go for a walk, or play with the cat. All the while my writer's mind is

Pinky and Rex are best friends, and they want their friendship to be forever

Pinky and Rex Get Married

JAMES HOWE
Author of **Bunnicula**

AVON
C
CAMELOT
0-380-71191-5
$3.50 U.S.
$4.25 CAN

Illustrated by Melissa Sweet

The author's works also include the lighthearted "Pinky and Rex" series, about two young friends; Howe says it's a "challenge" to keep his series fresh and interesting. (Cover illustration by Melissa Sweet.)

ticking away, thinking about the book I'm working on or ideas for new stories.

"Most of my stories are humorous, but they almost always have something serious going on in them as well. That's because I can no more separate my serious concerns about the world from my cockeyed way of seeing it than I can keep apart my personal and professional selves.

"Since my work is a part of everything I am, it is important that I allow it to grow and change. One of the difficult things about doing sequels and series—and it's a juggling act, in a way—is keeping alive the elements that made the first book funny and popular while writing as the person I am now. That's been one of the greatest challenges of my work.

"But challenge is much of what work is about—at least it is if one's work is going to be rich and satisfying. I look forward to the challenges ahead, the changes and the unknowns. Readers expect to be surprised by writers. What's fun—and crucial—for writers is that we surprise ourselves."

WORKS CITED:

Bradburn, Frances, "Middle Books," *Wilson Library Bulletin,* June, 1990, pp. 116-17.
Review of *Bunnicula: A Rabbit-Tale of Mystery, Publishers Weekly,* March 19, 1979, p. 94.
Harris, Karen, review of *The Hospital Book, School Library Journal,* May, 1981, p. 56.
Howe, James, *The Celery Stalks at Midnight,* illustrated by Leslie Morrill, Atheneum, 1983, pp. 7, 20, 48.
Howe, James, "James Howe," *Sixth Book of Junior Authors and Illustrators,* edited by Sally Holmes Holtze, H. W. Wilson, 1989, pp. 135-37.
Howe, James, "Writing for the Hidden Child," *Horn Book,* March/April, 1985, pp. 156-61.
Review of *Howliday Inn, Publishers Weekly,* March 19, 1982, p. 71.

FOR MORE INFORMATION SEE:

BOOKS

Children's Literature Review, Volume 9, Gale, 1985, pp. 54-60.

PERIODICALS

Booklist, April 15, 1990, p. 1631.
Bulletin of the Center for Children's Books, June, 1983; October, 1983; January, 1985, pp. 87-88; September, 1986, p. 10; October, 1986, p. 28; November, 1986, p. 51.
Horn Book, July/August, 1986; July/August, 1987, p. 462; March/April, 1988, p. 193; March/April, 1990, pp. 178-83.
New York Times Book Review, May 17, 1992.
Publishers Weekly, April 13, 1992.
School Library Journal, March, 1985, pp. 167-68; May, 1986, pp. 76-77; December, 1986, pp. 103-04; April, 1987, p. 96; July/August, 1987, p. 26; October, 1987, p. 133; November, 1987, p. 91; April, 1990, p. 120.
Wilson Library Bulletin, September, 1987, pp. 68-69.

—*Sketch by Denise E. Kasinec*

* * *

HUGHES, Libby

PERSONAL: Born in Pittsburgh, PA; daughter of Lloyd A. (in business and engineering) and Vera (Walker) Pockman; married R. John Hughes (in the newspaper business), August 20, 1955 (divorced, 1987); children: Wendy E., Mark E. *Education:* University of Alabama, B.A., 1954; Boston University, M.F.A., 1955. *Politics:* Independent. *Religion:* Christian Science. *Hobbies and other interests:* "I am a twenty-four hour news junkie. I also enjoy reading biographies and suspense thrillers. Work is my life, except for children and animals."

ADDRESSES: Home—2523 Mountain Brook Circle, Birmingham, AL 35223.

CAREER: Actress in Kenya, East Africa, and South Africa, 1955-58; freelance writer in Asia, 1964-70; assistant publisher, publisher, writer, and drama critic,

1977-85, for New England newspapers; playwright, 1977—. Affiliated with board of National Society of Arts and Letters, 1982-84; affiliated with Alabama Wildlife Rescue Service and Bookmarkers Literary Club.

MEMBER: Dramatists Guild, Authors Guild.

AWARDS, HONORS: Winner, Maxwell Anderson Playwrights Series competition, 1984, for *Cabbie.*

WRITINGS:

BOOKS

Bali, Paul Hamlyn, 1969.
Madame Prime Minister, Dillon, 1989.
Benazir Bhutto: From Prison to Prime Minister, Dillon, 1990.
(Editor), *Ginger* (Ginger Rogers's autobiography), HarperCollins, 1991.
Nelson Mandela, Dillon, 1992.
General H. Norman Schwarzkopf, Dillon, 1992.
West Point, Dillon, 1992.
(And illustrator) *Good Manners for Children* (coloring book), Fruition Press, 1992.

PLAYS

Cabbie, Maxwell Anderson Playwrights Series, 1984.
The Tortured Triangle, produced in New York City, 1984.
The Opening, produced in New York City, 1985.
White House Secrets, produced in Palm Desert, CA, 1987.

LIBBY HUGHES

Author of other plays, some of which have been produced off-off-broadway.

WORK IN PROGRESS: Bookscript for a musical.

SIDELIGHTS: Libby Hughes told *SATA:* "I was born in Pittsburgh, Pennsylvania, but because my parents were constantly on the move, I grew up in a variety of places. We lived in Glen Ridge and Montclair, New Jersey, Swarthmore, Pennsylvania, and Elmira, New York. When I was fifteen my parents shipped me off to the Emma Willard boarding school in Troy, New York. I attended the school for three years. It was at Emma Willard that I first became interested in writing. However, I transferred my literary desires to the world of theater and acting. Meanwhile, my parents had moved to Alabama, and upon graduation from high school I entered the University of Alabama as an acting major. From the University of Alabama, I headed to New York City in an attempt to make it on Broadway. While at a Carnegie Hall audition, I won a full scholarship to Boston University, where I later received an M.F.A. in acting and directing. While I was in Boston, Elliot Norton—a famous drama critic—told me I should be a writer, but at that time I was far too involved with theater to make a change.

"After acting professionally in summer theater, I married a newspaperman and headed first to Africa and then to Asia. During that time I acted and did freelance writing for American newspapers. Upon returning to the United States, I became part owner of some newspapers on Cape Cod. I wrote theater reviews and interviewed celebrities for the papers. From there I began writing plays, more than twenty in all, some of which would be produced off-off-Broadway. In 1986, I moved back to Alabama and began writing biographies of international heroes and heroines for Dillon Press.

"In 1989 I was asked by Dillon Press to write a biography on Margaret Thatcher, the former prime minister of Great Britain. I flew to England and visited her hometown of Grantham and the schools she attended. I also visited her constituencies and the House of Commons. Also in 1989, actress, singer, and dancer Ginger Rogers, a close personal friend of mine, asked me to come to her home in California to help her edit her autobiography, which was published by HarperCollins in 1991.

"In 1990 Dillon Press invited me to write another biography, this time on the prime minister of Pakistan, Benazir Bhutto. I travelled to Pakistan to visit the schools she attended and the various prisons where she had been held over a ten-year period. I interviewed many of Bhutto's friends and teachers and was fortunate enough to have a forty-minute interview with the prime minister herself.

"In 1990 I travelled to South Africa to research a book on Nelson Mandela. I spent an evening in the Mandela home, in the township of Soweto, with Mr. Mandela and his wife Winnie, their daughters, and their grandchildren. We drove to Mr. Mandela's villages in the Transkei and visited his schools. I also talked to his friends, his colleagues, and government officials in Pretoria, Cape Town, and Johannesburg.

"Following my work on the Mandela book, my publishers asked me to write two more books for them in 1992: A book on the military academy West Point and a book on the commander of the U.S. troops during Operation Desert Storm, General H. Norman Schwarzkopf. For the first book, I spent time at West Point during Plebe Day, when the new students first arrive, and on alumni weekend. In researching General Schwarzkopf, I spent a day in the Pentagon and visited the War College at Carlisle, Pennsylvania. I also went to Schwarzkopf's hometown of Lawrenceville, New Jersey, visited the Valley Forge Military Academy, and travelled to seven of his posts, including Fort Richardson in Alaska. I also interviewed many of Schwarzkopf's friends and colleagues.

"Although I had not written for twelve- to eighteen-year olds prior to these books, I found it challenging to gather files and files of research and condense it to its simplest terms. Each person that I have written about is fascinating. Each inspires young people to overcome hardships and obstacles to achieve success. I feel compelled to travel to the places where my subjects grew up—in order to give my readers authentic depictions. My background in journalism was a tremendous help in writing these biographies. For me, the best part of these projects has been the research. Going to different countries and meeting such interesting people makes for an exciting adventure."

*   *   *

HUMPHREYS, Martha 1943-

PERSONAL: Full name, Martha Mason Humphreys; born September 24, 1943, in Washington, DC; daughter of John Nedwell (an attorney) and Ethel (a bookkeeper; maiden name, Nock) Mason; married John T. Humphreys (in management), June 18, 1971. *Education:* Hiram College, B.A., 1965; University of Indiana, M.A., 1967. *Hobbies and other interests:* "Theatre activities, reading, movies, and some television. I'm addicted to *All My Children*."

ADDRESSES: Home and office—3503 Lakin Circle, SE Huntsville, AL 35801. *Agent*—Kay Kidde, Kidde, Hoyt & Picard, 335 East Fifty-first St., New York, NY 10022.

CAREER: Office worker, typist, and waitress during 1960s; Ideal Publishing, New York, assistant editor of *Movie Life Magazine,* 1967-68; Department of Social Services, Brooklyn, NY, caseworker, 1968-69; *London Daily Express,* New York offices, researcher and writer, 1969; Alabama Agricultural and Mechanical University, Huntsville, assistant professor of speech, 1969-81; freelance writer, 1977—; University of Alabama in Huntsville, part-time instructor, 1981—. Variously served as president, secretary, treasurer, director, actor, and house manager of Huntsville Little Theatre, 1970—.

MARTHA HUMPHREYS

WRITINGS:

NOVELS FOR JUVENILES

Side by Side (romance), Silhouette, 1984.
A Broken Bow (romance), Silhouette, 1986.
Until Whatever, Clarion, 1991.

PLAYS

Offstage, published by Contemporary Drama Services, 1978.
Sweet Thing, staged reading by Reckless Dialogue and The University of the Streets, New York, 1986, produced by Gettysburg College, Gettysburg, PA, 1988.
The Family Way, produced by Twickingham Repertory Company, Huntsville, AL, 1987.
Loco, but Not Too Motive, produced by The Actors' Company, Los Angeles, CA, 1989.
Sunday Tea, produced by Heights Showcase, New York City, 1990.
Margaret Tillinghouse Died Next Week, produced by Huntsville Little Theatre, Huntsville, 1991.

Also author of *The Saga of Princess Ugly,* 1981.

OTHER

Contributor of numerous short stories and nonfiction articles to periodicals, including *True Romance, Real*

Confessions, True Love, Odyssey, Travel Smart, and *True Experience.*

WORK IN PROGRESS: Two teenage novels, *Geek Adventure* and *Just Like Romeo and Juliet;* two farces, *Just Vamp It!* and *Cruisin'.*

SIDELIGHTS: Martha Humphreys told *SATA:* "As a child I read voraciously and eventually started to write. My first project was to improve on Nancy Drew. She always got into trouble at the end of chapter twenty-four in all of her books—that wasn't enough for me. My mystery heroine was seriously threatened at the end of every chapter I wrote.

"I didn't write in high school. There wasn't time. I was too busy trying to fit in with the cool crowd. I did, however, still read. In college I took an occasional writing course, but I wasn't—or my stories weren't—deep, intellectual, or exquisitely symbolic. Consequently I never received the feedback or encouragement that was reaped by those who were deep, intellectual, or exquisitely symbolic.

"After graduate school I lived in New York, where I had two jobs that involved nonfiction writing. I occasionally toyed with fiction, but I lacked the motivation or discipline to stick with it. Years later, in Huntsville, Alabama, my job became horrible and provided me with the motivation and discipline I needed. I wrote every day; I still write every day. Besides providing a diversion from my job, the writing became a godsend in another way. At the time I quit the horrible job, I was diagnosed with multiple sclerosis. Now, ten years later, despite several chemotherapies, countless rounds of steroids, and a persistence that has surprised even me, the disease—no longer multiple sclerosis but an undiagnosable neurological disorder—forces me to live in a wheelchair. But during those ten years my writing kept me sane, as it does even now, providing both a sanctuary when reality is unpleasant and a goal to be reached."

*   *   *

HURWITZ, Johanna 1937-

PERSONAL: Born October 9, 1937, in New York, NY; daughter of Nelson (a journalist and bookseller) and Tillie (a library assistant; maiden name, Miller) Frank; married Uri Levi Hurwitz (a writer and college teacher), February 19, 1962; children: Nomi, Benjamin. *Education:* Queens College (now Queens College of the City University of New York), B.A., 1958; Columbia University, M.L.S., 1959. *Politics:* Liberal. *Religion:* Jewish.

ADDRESSES: Home—10 Spruce Pl., Great Neck, NY 11021.

CAREER: New York Public Library, New York City, children's librarian, 1959-63; Queen's College of the City University of New York, Flushing, NY, lecturer on children's literature, 1965-68; Calhoun School, New York City, children's librarian, 1968-75; Manor Oaks

School, New Hyde Park, NY, children's librarian, 1975-77; Great Neck Library, Great Neck, NY, children's librarian, 1978—; writer. New York Public Library, visiting storyteller, 1964-67.

MEMBER: PEN, Authors Guild, Society of Children's Book Writers, American Library Association, Amnesty International, Beta Phi Mu.

AWARDS, HONORS: Parents' Choice Award, Parents' Choice Foundation, 1982, for *The Rabbi's Girls,* and 1984, for *The Hot and Cold Summer;* Texas Bluebonnet Award and Wyoming Indian Paintbrush Award, both 1987, both for *The Hot and Cold Summer;* Kentucky Bluegrass Award, West Virginia Children's Book Award, and Mississippi Children's Book Award, all 1989, all for *Class Clown;* Florida Sunshine State Award, 1990, and New Jersey Garden State Award, 1991, both for *Teacher's Pet.*

WRITINGS:

FICTION FOR CHILDREN AND YOUNG ADULTS; ALL PUBLISHED BY MORROW, EXCEPT AS INDICATED

Busybody Nora, illustrated by Susan Jeschke, 1976, new edition illustrated by Lillian Hoban, 1990.

Nora and Mrs. Mind-Your-Own-Business, illustrated by Jeschke, 1977, new edition illustrated by Hoban, 1991.

The Law of Gravity, illustrated by Ingrid Fetz, 1978, published as *What Goes up Must Come Down,* Scholastic/Apple, 1983.

Much Ado about Aldo, illustrated by John Wallner, 1978.

JOHANNA HURWITZ

Johanna Hurwitz
"E" IS FOR ELISA
Illustrated by Lillian Hoban

Hurwitz's optimistic stories portray children in everyday situations; in *"E" Is for Elisa* the title character tries to keep up with an older brother despite his constant teasing. (Cover illustration by Lillian Hoban.)

Aldo Applesauce, illustrated by Wallner, 1979.
New Neighbors for Nora, illustrated by Jeschke, 1979, new edition illustrated by Hoban, 1991.
Once I Was a Plum Tree, illustrated by Fetz, 1980.
Superduper Teddy, illustrated by Jeschke, 1980, new edition illustrated by Hoban, 1990.
Aldo Ice Cream, illustrated by Wallner, 1981.
Baseball Fever, illustrated by Ray Cruz, 1981.
The Rabbi's Girls, illustrated by Pamela Johnson, 1982.
Tough-luck Karen, illustrated by Diane de Groat, 1982.
Rip-roaring Russell, illustrated by Hoban, 1983.
DeDe Takes Charge!, illustrated by de Groat, 1984.
The Hot and Cold Summer, illustrated by Gail Owens, 1985.
The Adventures of Ali Baba Bernstein, illustrated by Owens, 1985.
Russell Rides Again, illustrated by Hoban, 1985.
Hurricane Elaine, illustrated by de Groat, 1986.
Yellow Blue Jay, illustrated by Donald Carrick, 1986, published as *Bunk Mates,* Scholastic, 1988.
Class Clown, illustrated by Sheila Hamanaka, 1987.
Russell Sprouts, illustrated by Hoban, 1987.
The Cold and Hot Winter, illustrated by Carolyn Ewing, 1988.
Teacher's Pet, illustrated by Hamanaka, 1988.

Hurray for Ali Baba Bernstein, illustrated by Owens, 1989.
Russell and Elisa, illustrated by Hoban, 1989.
Class President, illustrated by Hamanaka, 1990.
Aldo Peanut Butter, illustrated by de Groat, 1990.
"E" Is for Elisa, illustrated by Hoban, 1991.
School's Out, illustrated by Hamanaka, 1991.
Roz and Ozzie, illustrated by McKeating, 1992.
Ali Baba Bernstein: Lost and Found, illustrated by Karen Milone, 1992.

NONFICTION FOR CHILDREN AND YOUNG ADULTS

Anne Frank: Life in Hiding, illustrated by Vera Rosenberry, Jewish Publication Society, 1988.
Astrid Lindgren: Storyteller to the World, illustrated by Michael Dooling, Viking, 1989.

OTHER

Contributor to periodicals, including *Horn Book.*

WORK IN PROGRESS: A biography of composer and conductor Leonard Bernstein; two picture books.

SIDELIGHTS: Johanna Hurwitz is author of more than thirty books for young people. Among her most popular works are lighthearted novels for elementary and junior high school readers that are characterized by endearing and eccentric protagonists who face the universal difficulties of childhood. Hurwitz's books are loosely connected, as a minor character in one novel will often become the central figure of another. *Aldo Applesauce,* for instance, is about a fourth-grader, while *Tough-luck Karen* and *Hurricane Elaine* feature his older sisters. Though Hurwitz tackles some serious issues, such as divorce in *DeDe Takes Charge!* and prejudice in *The Rabbi's Girls,* her fiction is laced with trademark humor and irony, and her protagonist's main problems are often resolved by book's end. Hurwitz's optimistic approach, fast-paced narratives, and frequent depictions of strong family relationships have made her books appealing to readers and reviewers alike.

Hurwitz grew up in a New York City apartment where the walls were lined with books. Her parents (who met in a bookstore) passed their love of reading on to their daughter; Hurwitz remembers being interested in books from an early age. She secured a library card as soon as she was able to and by age ten decided that she would someday become a librarian and a writer. Hurwitz once recalled: "When I was five years old, an accident resulted in a head injury and a lot of blood. My mother telephoned for an ambulance. When the medical attendants arrived at our apartment, they gaped in amazement at our books. 'Hurry, hurry!' my mother shouted. She was afraid I would die. But they just stared speechless at the number of books. 'Gee lady, you must like to read,' said one of the men without moving. And it was true, we all did."

Hurwitz began working at the New York Public Library while still in high school and, after attending Queens College and Columbia University, she became a full-time children's librarian in 1959. Though she began writing poems and stories at an early age, it was not until 1976 that she published her first book, *Busybody Nora,* which was derived from her experiences raising a family in a New York City apartment. "It seems as if all my fiction has grown out of real experiences," Hurwitz revealed in the *Sixth Book of Junior Authors.* "Whether it is my children's passion for baseball (*Baseball Fever*), my own childhood at the end of World War II (*Once I Was a Plum Tree*), my mother's childhood (*The Rabbi's Girls*) or a summer vacation in Vermont (*Yellow Blue Jay*), I have found ample material close at hand. Even my cats and their fleas have made it into a book (*Hurricane Elaine*). It took me many years to realize that my everyday life contained the substance for the books I fantasized I would write."

A book for early elementary school readers, *Busybody Nora* focuses on the everyday adventures of the inquisitive seven-year-old title character who lives in a large New York City apartment building with her parents and younger brother, Teddy. The heroine's further escapades are chronicled in *Nora and Mrs. Mind-Your-Own-Business* and *New Neighbors for Nora.* Five-year-old Teddy is also featured in later works, including *Superduper Teddy,* where, bolstered by his superhero cape and outgoing sister, he learns to overcome his shyness.

Several of Hurwitz's books revolve around the life of fourth-grader Aldo Sossi, including this work about Aldo's attempts to sample every flavor of ice cream during his summer vacation. (Cover illustration by John Wallner.)

The author's books are often connected, with minor characters from one story being featured in others; in *Tough-Luck Karen,* for instance, Aldo's thirteen-year-old sister must learn to accept responsibility for her actions. (Cover illustration by Diane de Groat.)

Hurwitz develops similar themes in her books about Russell and his younger sister, Elisa, who live in the same apartment building as their friends Nora and Teddy. In *Rip-roaring Russell,* the title character begins nursery school, which is at first a source of anxiety and temper tantrums. His sixth birthday party is the main event of *Russell Rides Again,* and *Russell Sprouts* revolves around his adventures in first grade. In *Russell and Elisa* Russell deems his sister a cause of embarrassment, especially when she tags along to his baseball game with her doll, Airmail. The young heroine wants to do everything her older brother can in *"E" Is for Elisa,* such as go on cookouts with the Cub Scouts. In the course of the book, Elisa breaks her arm, wears her bathing suit in the winter, and endures Russell's teasing.

Hurwitz's works involving Nora, Teddy, Russell, and Elisa have been praised for their light, humorous glimpses into the world of children, replete with minor disasters and triumphant successes. The books are considered especially suitable for reading aloud, as their chapters are short and self-contained while relating to a more general plot. In a *Bulletin of the Center for Children's Books* review of *Russell and Elisa,* Ruth Ann

JOHANNA HURWITZ
SCHOOL'S OUT

ILLUSTRATED BY
SHEILA HAMANAKA

While Hurwitz's works in general are popular with readers and critics for their humor, strong characterizations, and positive portrayals of family life, reviewers reserve special praise for books such as *School's Out,* in which the protagonists grow and learn. (Cover illustration by Sheila Hamanaka.)

Staitl commented: "Hurwitz excels in conveying the young child's point of view without any condescension. The moments of laughter in this family story ring true."

A number of Hurwitz's books for upper elementary and junior high school readers concern another family, the Sossis. Aldo, a fourth-grader, is featured in several books, such as *Aldo Ice Cream,* where his summer activities include sampling every flavor at the local ice cream parlor, and *Aldo Peanut Butter,* in which he experiences the joys and frustrations of raising puppies (named Peanut and Butter). Aldo's thirteen-year-old sister is the focus of *Tough-luck Karen,* in which she encounters some "bad luck" after neglecting her homework in favor of cooking, writing to pen pals, and babysitting. Eventually however, Karen recognizes her carelessness and begins to take responsibility for her actions. Another sister is the main character of *Hurricane Elaine,* where the fifteen-year-old begins dating, looks forward to high school, and learns to curb the impulsive behavior that gets her into trouble at school and at home.

Critics have praised Hurwitz's works where, as in *Tough-luck Karen* and *Hurricane Elaine,* the protagonist achieves noticable personal growth. Another example is *School's Out,* in which class clown Lucas Cott delights in getting the best of his new French babysitter, Genevieve, during summer vacation. As the weeks go by, however, Lucas comes to like Genevieve and decides that he must become a better influence on his younger twin brothers.

In addition to fiction, Hurwitz has published two nonfiction works. *Anne Frank: Life in Hiding* introduces Anne and the Frank family to elementary school readers, gives an explanation of the political and economic background of the Holocaust of World War II, and describes the significance of the diary that was published after Anne's death. And in *Astrid Lindgren: Storyteller to the World* Hurwitz recounts the life and career of the creator of the beloved character Pippi Longstocking.

Though she has penned a variety of works for young readers, Hurwitz does not expect to write for adults someday. "I get angry when people ask me when am I going to write a book for adults," the author once commented. "I do not feel that my writing for children

A young boy's overactive imagination leads him into embarrassing situations in Hurwitz's *The Adventures of Ali Baba Bernstein.* (Illustration by Gail Owens.)

is practice for that. I write for children because I am especially interested in that period of life. There is an intensity and seriousness about childhood which fascinates me."

WORKS CITED:

Sixth Book of Junior Authors, H. W. Wilson, 1989, pp. 144-146.
Staitl, Ruth Ann, review of *Russell and Elisa, Bulletin of the Center for Children's Books,* January, 1990, p. 111.

FOR MORE INFORMATION SEE:

PERIODICALS

Booklist, October 15, 1988, p. 409.
Bulletin of the Center for Children's Books, January, 1980; June, 1980; November, 1984; June, 1985; October, 1985; December, 1986; April, 1987; April, 1991, p. 197.
Horn Book, December, 1976, p. 663; December, 1981, p. 664; June, 1982, p. 288; October, 1982, p. 517; December, 1983, p. 710; September/October, 1987, p. 605.
Publishers Weekly, January 30, 1981; June 29, 1984, p. 104; July 8, 1988, p. 56; March, 30, 1990, p. 62; August 10, 1990, p. 444.
School Library Journal, October, 1978, p. 129, 134; September, 1979, p. 113; February, 1980, p. 57; December, 1980, p. 53; January, 1983, p. 76; May, 1984, p. 81; November, 1984, p. 126; September, 1988, p. 183; March, 1989, p. 163; August, 1989, p. 146; February, 1990, p. 103; May, 1990, p. 106; May, 1991, p. 93.

J

JACKSON, Guida M. 1930-

PERSONAL: Given name is pronounced "*guy*-da"; born August 29, 1930, in Clarendon, TX; daughter of James Hurley (a merchant) and Ina (a homemaker; maiden name, Benson) Miller; married Prentice Lamar Jackson (an anesthesiologist), June 15, 1951 (divorced, January, 1986); married William Hervey Laufer (an artist), February 14, 1986; children: (first marriage) Jeffrey Allen, William Andrew, James Tucker, Annabeth Jackson Ramos. *Education:* Attended Musical Arts Conservatory, Amarillo, TX, 1945-47; Texas Technological College (now Texas Tech University), B.A., 1951, graduate study, 1952; graduate study at University of Houston, 1953; California State University, M.A., 1984; graduate study at Union Graduate School, 1986-87; Greenwich University Institute of Advanced Studies, Ph.D., 1989.

ADDRESSES: Home—The Woodlands, Texas. *Office*—*Touchstone,* P.O. Box 8308, Spring, TX 77387.

CAREER: Houston secondary schools, Houston, TX, English teacher, 1951-53; Fort Worth secondary schools, Fort Worth, TX, English teacher, 1953-56; music teacher and freelance writer, Houston, 1956-71; Monday Shop (antiques store), Houston, owner, 1971-75; *Houston Town and Country* (magazine), Houston, contributing editor, 1975; *Texas Country* (magazine), Houston, editor in chief, 1976-78; *Touchstone,* Houston, managing editor, 1978—; freelance writer, 1978—. University of Houston, Houston, English lecturer, 1986-89; guest lecturer at University of St. Thomas and Rice University; creative writing instructor at St. John's School, University of Houston at Clear Lake, Alvin Community College, and Southwest Texas Junior College.

MEMBER: International Women's Writing Guild, Dramatists Guild, Women in Communications, Eudora Welty Society, Authors UNLTD of Houston, Houston Writers Guild, Houston Novel Writers, Woodlands Writers Guild.

GUIDA JACKSON

AWARDS, HONORS: First place, Faulkner short fiction competition; first place, Allen Tate poetry competition; first place, Percy nonfiction competition; first place, Berthold nonfiction competition; first place, Porter short story competition.

WRITINGS:

Passing Through (novel), Simon & Schuster, 1979.
A Common Valor, Simon & Schuster, 1980.
Voices of Women, Touchstone Books, 1985.
The Lamentable Affair of the Vicar's Wife (play), I. E. Clark, 1988.
An Evening with Eve, I. E. Clark, 1989.
Heart to Hearth, Prism, 1989.
Women Who Ruled, ABC-CLIO, 1990.
(Compiler and editor) *African Women Write,* Touchstone Press, 1991.
Hardships of War, Heritage, 1992.

Favorite Fables from around the World, Prism, 1992.

Editor for *Texas Anesthesiologists Quarterly,* 1972-80, *TSA Newsletter,* 1974-82, *Touchstone Literary Quarterly,* and Mexican American Studies department, University of Houston. Contributor to *The Three Ingredient Cookbook,* compiled by Phyllis Stillwell Prokop, Broadman, 1981. Contributor to periodicals.

WORK IN PROGRESS: "How land (i.e., the plains or islands) shapes the literature of the people living there."

SIDELIGHTS: Guida M. Jackson told *SATA:* "I have taken to heart what Carlos Fuentes has been saying for years: We in this country are not immersed in our history. I feel an obligation to be a connector between the past and the present—maybe even the future, if I do my job well enough. Like all writers, I developed an early passion for reading. More recently, I've come to appreciate the rich oral traditions of tribal peoples, and I applaud the emerging vocation of 'storytelling' in this country. Stories tell us who we are and who other people are. Stories are the ultimate connectors."

*   *   *

JACOBS, Leland Blair 1907-1992

OBITUARY NOTICE—See index for *SATA* sketch: Born February 12, 1907, in Tawas City, MI; died of congestive heart failure, April 4, 1992, in Leonia, NJ. Educator, school administrator, and writer. Jacobs, a professor of education at Columbia University, was known for his work in developing methods for teaching literature to very young children. Jacobs began teaching in a one room schoolhouse in Michigan. After teaching at all levels of elementary, junior high, and high school and serving as an elementary school principal, Jacobs went on to teach education at the undergraduate and graduate level. Besides his textbooks and numerous articles and books on educational methods, Jacobs wrote stories and poetry for children, always working toward his goal of making reading appealing to young readers. His writings include *Using Literature with Young Children, Poems for Young Scientists, Poetry for Chuckles and Grins,* and *Holiday Happenings in Limerick Land.*

OBITUARIES AND OTHER SOURCES:

BOOKS

Authors of Books for Young People, 3rd edition, Scarecrow, 1990.

PERIODICALS

Chicago Tribune, April 9, 1992, section 3, p. 11.
New York Times, April 7, 1992, p. B7.

*   *   *

JERAM, Anita 1965-

PERSONAL: Born July 13, 1965, in Portsmouth, England; daughter of Dennis Arthur and Eileen Ann (a shop assistant; maiden name, Roberts) Rogers; married

Andrew Jeram (a paleontologist), March 22, 1986; children: Joe. *Education:* Manchester Polytechnic, B.A., 1990. *Hobbies and other interests:* Keeping pets, photography, collecting junk off of the beach.

ADDRESSES: Home—Bangor, County Down, Northern Ireland. *Agent*—c/o Walker Books Ltd., 87 Vauxhall Walk, London SE11 5HJ, England.

CAREER: Factory worker, Portsmouth, England, 1983-84; kennel assistant, Alton, Hampshire, England, 1984-85; shop assistant, Portsmouth, 1985-86; freelance author and illustrator, Bangor, County Down, Northern Ireland, 1990—.

MEMBER: Elefriends.

AWARDS, HONORS: Highly commended in the Benson and Hedges Illustration Awards, 1989.

WRITINGS:

SELF-ILLUSTRATED BOOKS FOR JUVENILES

Bill's Belly Button, Walker Books, 1991.
It Was Jake, Walker Books, 1991.
The Most Obedient Dog in the World, Walker Books, in press.

OTHER BOOKS FOR JUVENILES; ILLUSTRATOR

Dick King-Smith, *All Pigs Are Beautiful,* Walker Books, in press.

WORK IN PROGRESS: Researching mice and frogs.

SIDELIGHTS: Anita Jeram told *SATA:* "I grew up by the sea in Portsmouth, England. At school I was a bit of a disaster and didn't do very well in exams. However, I did like art and English, and my teachers in these subjects encouraged me enough that I felt I could be

ANITA JERAM

good at something. From school I went on to art college. Although I enjoyed the year I spent there, it didn't seem very different from being at school, and by the end of the year I still didn't have the qualifications I needed to apply for a degree course. When I left art college I had no idea what I was going to do next. I can't really remember having had any ambitions when I was young, except that I always loved animals and wanted to be a vet or a zookeeper when I grew up.

"My first employment was at a potato chip factory, where I was supposed to pick out the defective chips as they passed by me on a conveyor belt. I didn't last very long at that job and went on to work in other factories. I did spend one year working at a quarantine kennel and cattery in the country, and that really did cure me from wanting to work in a zoo.

"In 1986 I got married and moved to Manchester, where my husband Andy was researching fossilized scorpions at the university. For a while I worked as a shop assistant but soon decided to return to art college as a mature student. This time around I made the most of the opportunity and did a degree course in illustration, which allowed me to indulge in my favorite pastime—drawing animals.

"My first book, *Bill's Belly Button,* was completed in 1989, my second year at art college. The idea for this story came from when I was very young—at the unanswerable-question-asking age. I recall asking if elephants had belly buttons. As a surprise my older sister wrote to a local zoo to find out the answer for me. The zoo replied that elephants did have belly buttons. I wasn't entirely convinced at the time, and years later I wrote to as many zoos as I could, asking the same question. All the replies were different and amusing, and an idea for a book grew out of those replies.

"1990 was a very busy year. I completed my next book, *It Was Jake,* finished my degree, moved to Northern Ireland where Andy started a new job as a museum curator, and then had a baby boy, Joe—all in the space of three months. Since then I have been working as a freelance illustrator and, when our young son lets me, working on my latest picture books.

"I didn't deliberately set out to write and illustrate children's books, but by my second year in college it became clear that this was something I really enjoyed doing. It's much more fun than working in a potato chip factory. I hope that children have fun reading the finished books."

*   *   *

JOHNSON, Pamela 1949-

PERSONAL: Born November 5, 1949, in Philadelphia, PA. *Education:* Wheaton College, B.A., 1970; attended Dartmouth College, 1970-71.

ADDRESSES: Home and office—Sedgwick, ME 04676.

CAREER: Author and illustrator of books for juveniles.

WRITINGS:

BOOKS FOR JUVENILES; SELF-ILLUSTRATED

How to Draw the Circus, Troll, 1987.
Let's Celebrate St. Patrick's Day: A Book of Drawing Fun, Troll, 1987.
A Mouse's Tale, Harcourt, 1991.

ILLUSTRATOR

Caras, Roger, *A Zoo in Your Room,* Harcourt, 1975.
Hurwitz, Johanna, *The Rabbi's Girls,* Morrow, 1982.

Also illustrated *And Then There Was One,* published by Little, Brown.

*   *   *

JOHNSTON, Janet 1944-

PERSONAL: Born March 16, 1944, in Pittsburgh, PA; daughter of Richard (affiliated with the U.S. Air Force) and Muriel (an elementary school and college teacher; maiden name, Thompson) Johnston; married H. Wallace Teal (a fire chief), June 17, 1944; children: Dawn, Kevin, Beverly, Andrea. *Education:* Southwest Texas State, B.S., 1984. *Politics:* Liberal. *Religion:* "Claim none, respect all." *Hobbies and other interests:* "I like to do things with my friends such as going out to dinner or seeing movies."

JANET JOHNSTON

ADDRESSES: Home—PSC 05, Box 121, APO AA 34005.

CAREER: U.S. Department of Defense, Panama, first grade and kindergarten teacher at Fort Davis Elementary, 1985-88, and English teacher at Cristobal Junior and Senior High School, 1988-92; author of books for juveniles, 1990—.

MEMBER: Society of Children's Book Writers, National Council of Teachers of English.

WRITINGS:

Ellie Brader Hates Mr. G., Clarion, 1991.

WORK IN PROGRESS: A fiction book for sixth- through eighth-graders, titled *Michelle Can Tell Your Future;* legal research for a screenplay about a court case.

SIDELIGHTS: Janet Johnston told *SATA:* "My husband and I have lived in Panama, Central America, for about twenty years. He's a fire chief and I teach school to military and Panama Canal Commission dependents, as well as tuition students. The three main things that I am constantly balancing are teaching full-time (two eighth-grade classes, two senior classes, and one tenth-grade class), teaching part-time at Panama Canal Junior College (I teach at a military post where soldiers attend school at night), and my own writing. Writing has always been private to me—only my family reads my work before I send it in. Though I'm not shy, in most ways I am very private about my work. However, I don't mind sending work to editors because I don't know them."

Due to her busy work schedule, Johnston has to fit her writing time in between her other tasks. As she related: "My daily life would be very happy except that I have too much to do. I get up to write at four-thirty in the morning because I'm too tired to do it after teaching. My idea of heaven would be writing during the day and sometimes teaching a college class. As it is, I cram writing into the time when I'd rather sleep or else write on weekends, when I'd rather have fun. However, if I don't write at those times, it won't get done, and nothing is more disconcerting than that."

Johnston developed a discipline for writing at an early age. Her father, a career officer in the U.S. Air Force, often had to move his family to bases around the world. To help herself adjust to the numerous relocations, Johnston took comfort in her family and in reading and writing. As she explained: "My writing career was shaped by my experiences as a child. I was a military kid. My three brothers and I moved frequently, and perhaps because of this we were, and are, quite close. Reading was very important to me. My favorite words to read were 'Base Library' on the building I always found right away, no matter where we were stationed. I think being the new kid all the time gave me an outsider attitude that led to writing. Once when I was visiting my family in the United States, my sister-in-law, who is an elementary school teacher, gave me tapes made by authors of children's books. I was very excited because I love hearing writers talk about why and how they write. I listened to about twenty tapes in a row, and a *huge* percent of these authors had been military kids like myself. Some had moved for whatever reason, or had perhaps belonged to a religion that was outside the norm, or even had been quite ill, and thus they felt apart from others as children. I think that kind of separation lends itself to a writing bent."

Johnston believes that acting on her "writing bent" helped her through some difficult times in her youth. She maintains that all negatives can be made positive with the correct outlook and initiative. She offers this advice to young people: "I want to say one thing that students should know. When I was in the eighth grade we were stationed in Montana, coming from Germany. I went through a sad time and ended up failing the whole year. So during both years of eighth grade, and about half of ninth grade, I was unhappy (except at home). But at whatever stage you find yourself, if it is painful, it can be altered. Nothing is forever. You can change things."

* * *

JORDAN, Sherryl 1949-

PERSONAL: Born June 8, 1949, in Hawera, New Zealand; daughter of Alan Vivian and Patricia (Eta) Brogden; married Lee Jordan, 1970; children: Kym. *Education:* Attended Tauranga Girls' College, 1962-64; two years of nursing training, 1967-68. *Religion:* Chris-

SHERRYL JORDAN

tian. *Hobbies and other interests:* "Music, friends, conversation, and solitude to write."

ADDRESSES: Home—165 Kings Ave., Matua, Tauranga, New Zealand. *Agent*—Ray Richards, P.O. Box 31-240, Milford, Auckland 9, New Zealand.

CAREER: Illustrator, 1980-85; full-time writer, 1988—. Part-time work as a teacher's aide in primary schools, working with profoundly deaf children, 1979-87.

MEMBER: Children's Literature Association (committee member), Bay of Plenty branch.

AWARDS, HONORS: Winner of national illustrating competition, Whitcoulls, 1980, for *The Silent One;* Choysa bursary, 1988, and AIM Story Book of the Year, 1991, both for *Rocco.*

WRITINGS:

(Self-illustrated) *The Firewind and the Song,* Kagyusha Publishers (Japan), 1984.
Matthew's Monsters, illustrated by Dierdre Gardiner, Ashton Scholastic (New Zealand), 1986.
No Problem Pomperoy, illustrated by Jan van der Voo, Century Hutchinson, 1988.
Kittens (school reader), Shortlands, 1989.
The Wobbly Tooth, Shortlands, 1989.
Babysitter Bear, illustrated by Trevor Pye, Century Hutchinson, 1990.
A Time of Darkness (novel for young adults), Scholastic Inc., 1990, published in New Zealand as *Rocco,* Ashton Scholastic, 1990.
The Juniper Game (novel for young adults), Scholastic Inc., 1991.
The Wednesday Wizard (novel for ten- to twelve-year-olds), Ashton Scholastic, 1991.
Winter of Fire (novel for young adults), Ashton Scholastic, 1992.
Denzil's Dilemma (sequel to *The Wednesday Wizard*), Ashton Scholastic, 1992.
Other Side of Midnight, Ashton Scholastic, in press.

Also author of poem "Plea," published in an anthology featuring New Zealand writings for children entitled *The Magpies Said,* edited by Dorothy Butler.

ILLUSTRATOR FOR JOY COWLEY

The Silent One, Whitcouls, 1981.
Tell-tale, Shortland Publications, 1982.
Mouse, Shortland Publications, 1983.
Mouse Monster, Shortland Publications, 1985.

SIDELIGHTS: Sherryl Jordan told *SATA:* "I am a full-time writer of novels for young adults. I have in the past written picture books for younger children, but because my writing hours are now limited, I write only novels, which gives me greater joy. I visit schools regularly, both primary and collegiate, and discuss books and writing. I have held several workshops on creative writing for adults and children. I have also spoken at seminars on my life and work as a writer.

"In my writing I am drawn to science fiction because I can stretch my imagination to the limits—and then further. I give my characters power, but the power is always possible in reality and available to us all. I hope my books give young people something that is uplifting, encouraging and inspiring.

"I was born in Hawera, New Zealand, in 1949 and have been writing books since I was ten years old. From my earliest days I was also good at art. I began to seriously work on children's books in 1980, when I won a national competition for illustrations for my work on Joy Cowley's book *The Silent One.* I continued to illustrate books until 1985, when I finally admitted to myself that I was miserable working on other people's books and that I had always intended to write and illustrate my own books. I gave up illustrating and began writing, but the path was long and arduous.

"I learned my writing craft through a combination of listening to other writers, attending seminars, criticism and rewriting, and determination and perseverance. During the five years I worked as a serious writer, I

Jordan explores ideas of memory, time travel, and telepathy in her young adult novel *The Juniper Game,* in which two teenagers experience mental contact with a woman of medieval times. (Cover illustration by Joe DiCesare.)

wrote twenty-seven picture books for children and four novels. Of the picture books, three were published. Not one of the novels was published. In 1988 I began work on my fifth novel, deciding that this was going to be the making or breaking of my literary career—if this book was rejected, I would give up writing. The book I wrote is a fantasy for young adults and is titled *Rocco*. I entered *Rocco* in the 1988 Choysa bursary for children's writers—and won.

"All my novels, though called fantasy books, are based on truths that life has taught me. I have always had memory-like impressions of ancient times and places, and these images and visions are the inspiration for many of my books. The Valley of Anshur in *Rocco* was inspired by a dream of a stone age past, and the valley in the book is exactly as I saw it.

"These ancient 'memories' once disturbed me deeply. I do not believe in reincarnation, and for many years I attempted to deny the power and reality of the places I had in my mind. Then one day I read a book about time and how it may not be the way we measure it—how there may be no time at all, but only an eternal 'Now' through which we can travel forwards or backwards. The idea bemused me, fascinated me, and inspired me. Exploring the idea, and all the possibilities that came with it, I wrote a book called *The Juniper Game*.

"*The Juniper Game* is about two teenagers who have a telepathic connection with a woman in medieval times. It is about ancient memory-like experiences and explores an alternative to the idea of reincarnation. Several months after completing *The Juniper Game* I read an article about a British scientist and philosopher, Rupert Sheldrake, who had a new theory about memory and time. Sheldrake's ideas suddenly made everything clear, explained a thousand mysteries in my life, and tore down walls in my mind. I realized that I had *almost*

hit upon his theory in *The Juniper Game*. In one conversation in the book, I mentioned that maybe my characters touched the memories of the medieval woman—in that conversation lay the seed of what I would learn from Rupert Sheldrake.

"In the two years following *The Juniper Game*, I wrote a novel for younger children called *The Wednesday Wizard* and another novel for young adults called *Winter of Fire*. In many ways *Winter of Fire* is the most special of all my books, because it was written when I had RSI (Repetition Strain Injury—or Occupational Overuse Syndrome) and had been told by a specialist that I would never write or type again. It was while I faced that affliction, and fought the greatest battle of my life, that I wrote *Winter of Fire,* a novel about a young slave woman called Elsha.

"I had conceived the story for *Winter of Fire* more than a year before, and Elsha herself had lived in my life as a character for all that time. She was unstoppable, charismatic, and a warrior at soul. It was only because of her that I refused to accept that my writing days were over—only because of her that I picked myself up out of despair and wrote another book. We were warriors together in our battles against the impossible. The story is hers as much as it is mine, and without her strength it would never have been written at all.

"So in all my books there is that lesson that life itself has taught me: whether, as in *Rocco,* it is that the smallest and most insignificant acts can have the greatest consequences, or, as in *The Juniper Game,* that new ideas about supernatural experiences can be explored. I hope all my books will inspire my readers to explore these astounding fields for themselves—to realize that all is not what it seems and that there are no boundaries between fact and fiction, the tangible and the mystical, the real and the truth we imagine."

K

KAYE, Judy
  See BAER, Judy

*   *   *

KELLY, Kathleen M. 1964-

PERSONAL: Born December 8, 1964, in Waterbury, CT; daughter of Thomas J. (a consulting engineer) and Elsa (a nurse; maiden name, Mrazik) Kelly. *Education:* Paier College of Art, B.F.A., 1986. *Religion:* Catholic.

ADDRESSES: Home and office—158 Forest St. #708, Manchester, CT 06040.

CAREER: Kelly Art Studios, Manchester, CT, owner and operator, 1987—. Has also worked in design for The Mind's Eye, Stamford, CT, 1988—, Davidoff White Good, Inc., Westport, CT, 1989-90, Young Associates, Westport, CT, 1990-91, Promotional Innovations, Stamford, CT, 1990-91, and Everett Studios, White Plains, NY, 1991—. Speaker at schools.

MEMBER: Society of Children's Book Writers and Illustrators.

AWARDS, HONORS: First Place Fine Art Award, Paier College, 1986.

WRITINGS:

(Self-illustrated) *River Friends* (picture book), Atheneum, 1988.

ILLUSTRATOR

Harold Bloom, editor, *Modern Critical Views of Thomas Hardy,* Chelsea House, 1986.
Bloom, editor, *Modern Critical Views of Henry David Thoreau,* Chelsea House, 1987.
C. B. Christiansen, *A Small Pleasure,* Atheneum, 1988.
Peg Kehret, *Sisters, Long Ago,* Dutton/Cobblehill, 1990.
Drew Stevenson, *One Ghost Too Many,* Penguin, 1991.

Also contributor of illustrations to *Teaching K-8* magazine.

WORK IN PROGRESS: High in the Sky, in which a young boy sees his world from a new perspective, in preparation; research on winter fun and adventure parks.

SIDELIGHTS: Kathleen M. Kelly writes: "As a child I drew pictures for my Dad. He would stop and really look at them and give me a hug. Later he brought me to painting classes. In high school I attended the Center for Creative Youth at Wesleyan College, where I was inspired by kids my age who loved to dance, sing, act,

KATHLEEN M. KELLY

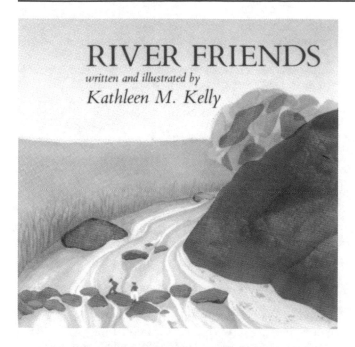

Kelly's first picture book, *River Friends,* demonstrates her positive outlook on life and her desire to share her love of nature with her readers. (Cover illustration by the author.)

draw, play instruments, and photograph. I followed my dream to college, where I worked a full-time job. I wasn't the best in the class, but I think I tried the hardest.

"It wasn't until after I graduated and was on my own that I really started to feel who I am in terms of my art. I trust my art—what it's done for me, the people it has brought me in touch with, how it has helped me to send a child into a world of friendship and nature, mystery and suspense—and most of all, how it has found its way into every cell of my being. I try to look on the positive side of life, keep an 'up' mood, and help others to stay excited about who they are and what lies ahead for them."

FOR MORE INFORMATION SEE:

PERIODICALS

Society of Children's Book Writers, September/October, 1988.

*   *   *

KENDA, Margaret 1942-

PERSONAL: Born November 1, 1942, in Indianapolis, IN; daughter of John I. (a business manager) and Margaret (a teacher; maiden name, Grable) Mason; married William Kenda (a business manager), September 8, 1962; children: John, Ann, Mary. *Education:* Northwestern University, B.S.Ed., 1964; University of Iowa, M.A., 1965, Ph.D., 1971. *Politics:* Democrat. *Religion:* Unitarian.

ADDRESSES: Home—68 Forest St., Sudbury, MA 01776. *Office*—Barron's, 250 Wireless Blvd., Hauppauge, NY 11788.

CAREER: Freelance writer, Sudbury, MA, 1971—. Professor of English, University of Maine, 1967-77.

MEMBER: Authors Guild.

WRITINGS:

(With Phyllis S. Williams) *The Natural Baby Food Cookbook,* Avon, 1972, revised edition, 1981.
(With Williams) *Cooking Wizardry for Kids,* Barron's, 1990.
(With Williams) *Science Wizardry for Kids,* Barron's, 1992.

*   *   *

KINSEY-WARNOCK, Natalie 1956-

PERSONAL: Born November 2, 1956, in Newport, VT; daughter of Frederick (a farmer) and Louise (a day-care provider; maiden name, Rowell) Kinsey; married Tom Warnock (a teacher), May 8, 1976. *Education:* Johnson State College, B.A. in Art/Athletic Training, 1978. *Religion:* Presbyterian.

ADDRESSES: Home—RD 3, Box 36A, Barton, VT 05822. *Agent*—Gina Maccoby, 1123 Broadway #1010, New York, NY 10010.

CAREER: Writer. University of Vermont Extension Service, Newport, VT, energy auditor, 1980-85; Craftsbury Sports Center, Craftsbury, VT, elderhostel director and cross-country ski instructor, 1987-91. Albany Library trustee, 1988-90; leader of East Craftsbury Recreation Program, 1983-89; elder of East Craftsbury Presbyterian Church, 1989—.

AWARDS, HONORS: ALA Notable Book citation, 1989, New York Library's 100 Best Books citation, 1989, and Joan Fassler Memorial Book Award, Association for Children's Health, 1991, all for *The Canada Geese Quilt;* American Booksellers Pick of the List citation, 1991, for *The Night the Bells Rang; The Wild Horses of Sweetbriar* and *The Night the Bells Rang* were both chosen as "Children's Books of the Year" by Bank Street College.

WRITINGS:

The Canada Geese Quilt, Cobblehill Books, 1989.
The Wild Horses of Sweetbriar, Cobblehill Books, 1990.
The Night the Bells Rang, Cobblehill Books, 1991.
Wilderness Cat, Cobblehill Books, 1992.
When Spring Comes, Dutton, 1993.
The Bear That Heard Crying, Cobblehill Books, 1993.
The Fiddler of the Northern Lights, Cobblehill Books, in press.
On a Starry Night, Joy Street Books, in press.

WORK IN PROGRESS: "A book of my grandmother's quilts; *Home before Morning,* a book about a girl and

NATALIE KINSEY-WARNOCK

her family in Barre in the 1920s (her father is a stonecutter); a sequel to *The Canada Geese Quilt* called *Where the Wild Ginger Grows;* a young adult novel set in turn-of-the-century Vermont entitled *Cold Hollow;* 3 other young adult novels; and a picture book entitled *If I Ever See Scotland Again,* based on my ancestors."

SIDELIGHTS: "My Scottish ancestors settled here in the Northeast Kingdom of Vermont almost 200 years ago," writes Natalie Kinsey-Warnock. "It is this land that they settled—where I grew up and still live—that means so much to me and provides the setting for almost all of my stories. I feel a part of this hill country and I'm grateful to the legacy these ancestors passed down.

"I grew up on a dairy farm in the Northeast Kingdom along with a sister and three brothers. This fostered a strong connection to the land, a sense of nurturing and caring for the earth. My father was a baseball and track star before he became a farmer and passed on both his love of sports and of history to us, while my mother, a former teacher, instilled in us her insatiable appetite for books and words. It is because of her that my brother Leland and I are writers.

"My interests are varied—athletics, nature, art and writing—but all of them are rooted to this area where I live. Sports are an integral part of my life: I run 5-10 miles each morning, cross-country ski, mountain bike, swim, play tennis, and I played field hockey all across the country for thirteen years. I love the outdoors, and study and sketch birds and wildflowers which are most often the subjects of my watercolor paintings. The past five years, my husband Tom and I have been building a timber-frame house on this land; both of us enjoy working with wood. Tom shares my love of the land, sports and animals; we have a Morgan horse, 3 dogs and 6 cats (I always wished I could open a shelter for animals). We love gardening and have planted an orchard of old varieties of apples.

"I guess anything to do with history appeals to me. History teaches us who we are, and in all my talks with school groups I encourage every person to record their family histories and stories before they are lost forever. Many of my books come from family stories. My sister Helen is the family genealogist and I have often joined her in reading town histories and walking old cemeteries. Most of my stories take place before I was born; I enjoy putting my characters into time periods I'm interested in. I guess I feel that in some small way I get to live in that time period, at least while I'm writing the story.

"I've had such strong role models in my life—especially strong, enduring women have influenced me: women like my grandmother, Helen Urie Rowell, my great-aunt Ada Urie (who was featured in a book titled *Enduring Women* by Diane Koos Gentry), and down to my mother. I want my books to portray strong female characters, and I hope they honor these women.

"My first children's book, *The Canada Geese Quilt,* grew out of my love and admiration for my grandmother and a special quilt we made together. My grandmother began quilting when she was in her 60s, and over the next fifteen years she made over 230 quilts. I designed about twenty of the quilts, most of them of birds, wildflowers, and starry skies—including one of Canada geese which inspired the book. My grandmother died in February, 1991, at age 89.

"Another book, *The Bear That Heard Crying,* is a collaboration between my sister and me and is the true story of our great-great-great-great-aunt Sarah Whitcher. In 1783, when she was three years old, she was lost in the woods for four days and was found and protected by a bear. *As Long as There Are Mountains* is my longest and most autobiographical book. It centers on twelve-year-old-Iris Simpson and her family on their northern Vermont farm in 1956. Her father wants to pass on the farm to Iris's brother, who wants to be a writer instead. Then her father loses his leg, and the farm must be sold unless her brother can be persuaded to give up his dream and come home."

*   *   *

KORALEK, Jenny 1934-

PERSONAL: Born November 5, 1934, in South Africa; married Paul Koralek (an architect); children: three.

Education: Attended several United Kingdom schools and Sorbonne, University of Paris, France.

ADDRESSES: Agent—Murray Pollinger, 222 Old Brompton Rd., London SW5 0BZ, England.

CAREER: Writer, 1978—. Held "several jobs—secretarial or P.A.—in UK, Switzerland, Canada, and at UNESCO, Paris until motherhood (the primary career for me), then worked—on and off—in play schools and as a freelance translator."

MEMBER: Authors Society.

AWARDS, HONORS: Children's Books of the Year, 1987, for *The Knights of Hawthorn Crescent,* and 1988, for *Message in a Bottle.*

WRITINGS:

John Logan's Rooster, Hamish Hamilton, 1980.
The Song of Roland Smith, Patrick Hardy Books, 1983.
Mabel's Story, Patrick Hardy Books, 1984.
The Knights of Hawthorn Crescent, Methuen, 1986.
Message in a Bottle, Lutterworth Press, 1987.
Going Out with Hatty, Methuen, 1988.
The Friendly Fox, Little, Brown, 1988.
Hanukkah, Walker, 1989.
Stories for the Very Young: The Cletterkin (anthology), Kingfisher, 1989.
The Cobweb Curtain, Holt, 1989.
A Moon, a Star, a Story: Marika's Favourite Story (short stories), Blackie, 1990.
Heartache: Sea Changes, Methuen, 1991.
The Cloth of Dreams: A Fairy Story, Little, Brown, 1992.
Daniel and the Cloth of Dreams (picture book), Walker, 1992.

WORK IN PROGRESS: The What-If Girl.

JENNY KORALEK

SIDELIGHTS: Jenny Koralek writes, "I came to writing in my middle years when my three children were almost grown up and after a very interesting, rich and varied experience of life in various European countries, as well as Canada and the USA. I have always enjoyed children and young people and feel immensely sympathetic to them. I am not a crusader in my writing. I just hope to write stories which are true to the experiences they describe, hoping that children may identify with them or yearn for adventures and experiences of the imagination. I am deeply interested in mythology and traditional tales and hope something of their underlying truths and archetypeness, so to speak, is somewhere in what I write.

"I read all the time in a very eclectic fashion, everything from everywhere (well, almost!): adult classics, modern classics and of course children's books. I can't imagine how one can write if one doesn't also read! I think the Anglo Saxon world has produced children's writers second to none and long may it continue to do so.

"I love my European continent and hope now that more and more stories will come out of the broken walls so that children across the world can share things and learn about each other. But I do believe children's books should primarily present a good story for its own sake.

"I eavesdrop everywhere and talk to children wherever and whenever I can. Two live over my garden wall, and they tell me things that often find their way into my stories. I listen for new slang, new interests (or rather new forms of perennial interests).

"I thoroughly enjoyed being a mother and having a house which was always full of children between the ages of 0 and 20 (and up, because of course some grown ups are not altogether grown up—the ones who have not forgotten what it was like to be a child). I also believe it is very important and enjoyable to mix up generations in life and in stories.

"And now I have a little grandchild and I watch her discovering this world and her developing skills, her fears, her joys, her interests ... and I put them all into my dreams and plans for my books, imagining I am talking to her and all her little friends."

*   *   *

KREMENTZ, Jill 1940-

PERSONAL: Born February 19, 1940, in New York, NY; daughter of Walter and Virginia (Hyde) Krementz; married Kurt Vonnegut, Jr. (a writer), November, 1979; children: Lily. *Education:* Attended Drew University, 1958-59, Columbia University, and Art Students League.

ADDRESSES: Home—228 East 48th St., New York, NY 10017.

CAREER: Free-lance photographer and writer. *Harper's Bazaar,* New York City, secretary, 1959-60; *Glamour,*

Jill Krementz and daughter Lily Vonnegut.

New York City, assistant to features editor, 1960-61; Indian Industries Fair, New Delhi, India, public relations representative, 1961; *Show,* New York City, reporter and columnist, 1962-64; *New York Herald Tribune,* New York City, staff photographer, 1964-65; free-lance photographer in Vietnam, 1965-66; *Status and Diplomat,* New York City, associate editor with status of staff photographer, 1966-67; *New York* (magazine), New York City, contributing editor, 1967-68; Time-Life, Inc., New York City, correspondent, 1969-70; *People* (magazine), Chicago, IL, contributing photographer, 1975—. Work has been exhibited at Madison Art Center (Wisconsin), Morris Museum, University of Massachusetts, Delaware Arts Museum, Newark Museum, Central Falls Gallery in New York, and in permanent collections at Museum of Modern Art and Library of Congress. Chosen to take the official photographs of four members of U.S. Cabinet, 1978.

MEMBER: American Society of Magazine Photographers, PEN, Women's Forum.

AWARDS, HONORS: A Very Young Dancer was named to American Institute of Graphic Artists Fifty Books of the Year List, *School Library Journal* Best Books of the Year List, and the *New York Times* Best Seller List of Children's Books, all 1976; *A Very Young Rider* and *A Very Young Gymnast* were named to the *School Library Journal* Best Books of the Year List, 1978; Garden State Children's Book Award, 1980; *Washington Post*/Children's Book Guild Nonfiction Award, 1984.

WRITINGS:

ALL WITH PHOTOGRAPHS BY KREMENTZ

The Face of South Vietnam (a book of photographs, with text by Dean Brelis), Houghton, 1968.
Sweet Pea: A Black Girl Growing Up in the Rural South, foreword by Margaret Mead, Harcourt, 1969.
Words and Their Masters (a book of photographs, with text by Israel Shenker), Doubleday, 1973.
The Writer's Image: Literary Portraits, preface by husband, Kurt Vonnegut, Jr., David Godine, 1980.
The Fun of Cooking, Knopf, 1985.
Benjy Goes to a Restaurant (juvenile), Crown, 1986.
Taryn Goes to the Dentist (juvenile), Crown, 1986.
A Visit to Washington, D.C., Scholastic Inc., 1987.

"A VERY YOUNG" SERIES

A Very Young Dancer, Knopf, 1976.
A Very Young Rider, Knopf, 1977.
A Very Young Gymnast, Knopf, 1978.
A Very Young Circus Flyer, Knopf, 1979.
A Very Young Skater, Knopf, 1979.
A Very Young Skier, Knopf, 1990.
A Very Young Actress, Knopf, 1991.
A Very Young Gardener, Knopf, 1991.
A Very Young Musician, Knopf, 1991.

"HOW IT FEELS" SERIES

How It Feels When a Parent Dies, Knopf, 1981.
How It Feels to Be Adopted, Knopf, 1982.
How It Feels When Parents Divorce, Knopf, 1984.
How It Feels to Fight for Your Life, Knopf, 1989.
How It Feels to Live with a Physical Disability, Simon & Schuster, 1992.

"GREAT BIG BOARD BOOKS" SERIES

Jack Goes to the Beach, Random House, 1986.
Jamie Goes on an Airplane, Random House, 1986.
Katherine Goes to Nursery School, Random House, 1986.
Lily Goes to the Playground, Random House, 1986.

"TOUGH ENOUGH BOOKS" SERIES

Holly's Farm Animals, Random House, 1986.
Zachary Goes to the Zoo, Random House, 1986.

OTHER

(Editor and compiler) *Happy Birthday, Kurt Vonnegut,* Delacorte, 1982.

Photographs represented in numerous additional works, including *A Poetic Equation: Conversations between Nikki Giovanni and Margaret Walker,* Howard University Press, 1974, and Herman Wouk's *This Is My God: The Jewish Way of Life,* Little, Brown, 1988. Contributor to national and international magazines and newspapers, including *Vogue, Newsweek, Esquire, Holiday, Time, Life,* and *New York Times Book Review.*

SIDELIGHTS: "Whatever I do, I do 100%," said Jill Krementz in *Writer's Digest.* Krementz is one of America's best-known photojournalists and was a pioneer in opening the profession to women. Her photo books have

Ballet master George Balanchine helps two of his junior dancers prepare for a performance of *The Nutcracker*. (Photograph by Krementz from *A Very Young Dancer*.)

ranged from *The Face of South Vietnam,* which conveyed the human tragedy of the Vietnam War, to *A Very Young Dancer,* which showed the efforts of a ten-year-old girl to master the art of ballet. "I've always been curious as to what goes on in other kinds of lives than my own," she said in an interview with *Contemporary Authors.* "Being a journalist is, in a way, a license to go backstage to see how things work."

Throughout her career Krementz has been richly rewarded because she showed determination and a willingness to take risks. While still in her teens she left college and ventured to New York City, ready to fulfill her childhood dream of being a self-supporting career woman—a heady goal for the late 1950s, when most girls were trained to limit their ambitions to marriage and motherhood. Her first office job paid so little that she had to buttress her income by selling robes in a department store, but by age twenty she was reviewing and editing manuscripts for the features editor at *Glamour* magazine. Then an acquaintance came through the office, looking for someone to accompany her on a trip around the world by steamship. Krementz jumped at the chance and invested the money she had saved in New York in order to finance her voyage. During the trip she stopped over in India and worked for several months as a publicist before returning to the United States.

Then Krementz began to move up in the world of journalism. She got an entry-level job at *Show* magazine and, in part because she didn't like working the telephone switchboard, found herself promoted to film and theater reporter. The art director of the magazine encouraged her to take photographs. On November 22, 1963—the day U.S. president John F. Kennedy was assassinated—Krementz discovered her life's work. When news of the assassination reached New York, she was inspired to go out and record the somber reactions of New Yorkers. She photographed people in Bloomingdale's department store as they watched reports over the television sets; she phoned the *New York Times* and got permission to take pictures as headlines describing the assassination rolled off the presses. "I could sense that many of my colleagues felt I was being callous but, even though I was as devastated as everyone else, I still felt a great need to record an event I knew was already becoming history," she told the *Miami Herald.* "I guess that's when I first realized that more than anything else I wanted to be a journalistic photographer."

When *Show* folded in 1964, Krementz quickly joined the *New York Herald Tribune,* becoming the staff's first woman photographer and, at age twenty-four, its youngest as well. Her mentor there was veteran photographer Ira Rosenberg. "[He] taught me everything—the meaning of craftsmanship, how to think on my feet and how to go the extra mile for a good picture," she told the *Miami Herald.* "More than anything else, he taught me that even if I got a page one picture, that today's paper was already yesterday's and I better concentrate on the next assignment. In short: Be a pro." In a year and a half at the *Herald Tribune* Krementz covered everything from riots in Harlem to high fashion and football games and worked with such up-and-coming writers as Jimmy Breslin, Gail Sheehy, and Tom Wolfe.

But she was on her own again by 1965, eager to do freelance work. "Most job challenges can be conquered in about a year, then it's time to find new windmills to knock over," Rosenberg later quoted her in the *Detroit Free Press.* At a dinner party she met one of her favorite photographers, the acclaimed Henri Cartier-Bresson, who suggested to her that the ongoing war in Vietnam was perhaps the most compelling photo story of the time. Krementz went to the troubled country and brought to her coverage of the war her own distinctive style—what she has sometimes called "peripheral" photography. While most photographers concentrated on dramatic combat pictures, Krementz traveled behind the lines, visiting hospitals and orphanages, viewing the everyday lives of both soldiers and civilians. Her resulting photo album, *The Face of South Vietnam,* became a classic, and Krementz found herself endorsed by such renowned members of her profession as Edward Steichen. "She's a pretty damn good photographer," said Steichen in the *Miami Herald.* "Good sharp penetration . . . . When she presses the button, it's happening."

Back in the United States by 1966, Krementz was drawn to the drama of the civil rights movement. While profiling a federal job-training program, she met a young black woman named Emma who had come from the rural South, where black people were struggling to overcome a particularly strong legacy of discrimination and poverty. Krementz wished to take pictures of conditions where Emma lived, and Emma invited the photographer to stay with her family. There Krementz met Sweet Pea, Emma's nine-year-old sister, and decided to create a photo book about her. *Sweet Pea* follows its young title character at school, at church, and at play, making clear that her spirit is unbroken despite the many obstacles that racism has placed in her path. To accompany the photographs Krementz wrote a first-person narration that would give readers the feeling they were hearing from Sweet Pea herself. Observers found Krementz's book eloquent and inspiring. "All of us, wherever we live, have the task of bringing our children closer to people in other towns and states and nations, on the six continents and the islands of the seas," wrote renowned anthropologist Margaret Mead in an introduction to the collection. "This book," she declared, "will help." Krementz and Sweet Pea remained good friends for years thereafter, as Sweet Pea grew up and had a child of her own.

Determined to remain a free-lance photographer as she entered the 1970s, Krementz decided to settle on a specialty: authors. It was another pioneering effort. Traditionally, she explained in *Writer's Digest,* "the publishers would tell the writers to send in a bio form and a couple of snapshots. The authors would rummage through wallets or have neighbors take pictures. I thought they deserved a little better." Krementz, who read up on authors before she went to photograph them, became known for pictures that expressed each subject's personality and interests. She photographed more than a thousand writers, including journalist and children's author E. B. White, commentator William F. Buckley, and Southern novelist and short story writer Eudora Welty. One of her subjects—best-selling novelist Kurt Vonnegut, Jr.—became her husband in 1979. Vonnegut wrote the preface to *The Writer's Image* (1980), a collection of Krementz's photos.

Meanwhile Krementz, who was always interested in new challenges, began a new phase of her career in the mid-1970s by becoming the photographer and author of further books about children. "I've always loved children," she told *Contemporary Authors* in 1987, "and I think I realize now ... that probably it satisfied me on several levels. On one, I enjoyed the work in itself. But I think that on another level it gave me a chance to almost have children of my own, to be involved with them on a very intimate level with enduring relationships. And it was probably the only way I could combine having children in my life and continuing to work professionally and be as involved in my career as I was.... For women who really want to work and who are ambitious, I think it's hard to have children in your early thirties when you're scrambling just to get someplace."

As with *Sweet Pea,* Krementz's new books about children began by chance when she began taking pictures of

a friend's young daughter, simply because the child was photogenic. Krementz then decided to photograph the girl as she practiced and performed at the School of American Ballet. The resulting book—*A Very Young Dancer*—became a tribute to the girl's determination and skill. Clive Barnes, renowned dance critic for the *New York Times,* hailed the work in the *New York Times Book Review* as "quite the best ballet book ever written for children." Krementz, he continued, "has a documentary eye. She catches the atmosphere of classrooms and locker rooms, of rehearsals and ... performances." As in *Sweet Pea* and her subsequent books for children, Krementz accompanied her photos with a first-person narrative designed to portray the feelings of the young subject. "Miss Krementz," Barnes declared, "has caught the very tone and manner of a 10-year-old girl."

Since it appeared in 1976, *A Very Young Dancer* has remained a favorite with readers, and Krementz has followed it with an entire series of books, including *A*

The first book in Krementz's "A Very Young...." series, *A Very Young Dancer* explores the efforts of a ten-year-old girl to master the art of ballet. (Photograph by Krementz.)

Krementz interviewed a number of young people who had lost a parent for *How It Feels When a Parent Dies*. (Photograph by Krementz.)

Very Young Rider and *A Very Young Gymnast*. Creating the books was not always easy. To photograph the dancer at work Krementz attended all the rehearsals, plus twenty-two performances, of a production of the *Nutcracker* ballet. To depict the rider Krementz woke up at 4 a.m. to reach the girl's horse shows. And, as Krementz told *Contemporary Authors,* "For *A Very Young Gymnast* I went with the gym team to Germany, so I ended up being the chaperone for a dozen little ten-year-olds who were all homesick!"

"In doing the 'A Very Young' series, I'd seen children being put on the fast track at a very early age," Krementz continued. "I thought it would be nice to do a book showing children doing something that is family oriented and involves sharing." This led her into new, more relaxed children's books, beginning with *The Fun of Cooking,* which shows young cooks in the family kitchen. Krementz also saw the need for a much different kind of book, which would help children through some of the pains and anxieties of life. Her volume *How It Feels When A Parent Dies* was inspired when she attended the funeral of a friend and saw the dead woman's young son stoically enduring his grief. For the book she interviewed several young people who had lost a parent, then accompanied their narratives

with her photographic portraits. "This lovely book has relevance for readers of all ages," wrote Hilma Wolitzer in the *New York Times Book Review,* "but it should offer particular solace and reassurance to those young people who cannot articulate their grief and who are confused and terrified by what has befallen them." After the success of *How It Feels When a Parent Dies,* Krementz created a number of similar books, including *How It Feels When Parents Divorce* and *How It Feels to Be Adopted.* The divorce and adoption books offered her a study in contrast: while children of divorce seemed deeply wounded by their experience, children of adoption were often quite comfortable with their lot, particularly if the adoption was handled frankly and openly. Writing in *Washington Post Book World,* Alice Digilio called *How It Feels to Be Adopted* "a beautiful book and an honest one" and concluded: "In her photographs Krementz makes sure these children look real, not precious, and what they say rings with sincerity."

"I keep in touch with the children in *all* of my books," Krementz told *Contemporary Authors.* Moreover, she added, "I have a special relationship with all the kids in *How It Feels to Be Adopted.*" Not long after Krementz finished work on the book, she and her husband

Children spoke openly and honestly with Krementz about their experiences as adoptees in *How It Feels to Be Adopted*. (Photograph by Krementz.)

Vivi Malloy and her pony Ready Penny share a quiet moment in *A Very Young Rider*. (Photograph by Krementz.)

adopted a daughter—Lily—who eventually became the star of another Krementz photo story, *Lily Goes to the Playground*. And the adopted kids Krementz already knew? "They figured I must have a pretty high opinion of them," she declared, "if I'd go out and adopt my own child."

WORKS CITED:

Arond, Miriam, "Krementz in Control," *Writer's Digest,* January, 1981, p. 14.

Barnes, Clive, review of *A Very Young Dancer, New York Times Book Review,* December 26, 1976, p. 11.

Contemporary Authors New Revision Series, Volume 23, Gale, 1988, pp. 227-232.

Digilio, Alice, review of *How It Feels to Be Adopted, Washington Post Book World,* January 9, 1983, p. 10.

Mahoney, Lawrence, "Jill Krementz: Getting the Picture Is the Focus of Her Life," *Miami Herald,* April 4, 1975.

Mead, Margaret, introduction to *Sweet Pea: A Black Girl Growing Up in the Rural South,* Harcourt, 1969.

Rosenberg, Ira, "Jill Krementz: 'Camera Nut,'" *Detroit Free Press,* December 25, 1974.

Wolitzer, Hilma, "Children in Mourning," *New York Times Book Review,* July 19, 1981, p. 8.

FOR MORE INFORMATION SEE:

BOOKS

Authors in the News, Gale, Volume 1, 1976, p. 289, Volume 2, 1976, p. 169.

Children's Literature Review, Volume 5, Gale, 1983, pp. 150-56.

Something about the Author Autobiography Series, Volume 8, Gale, 1989.

PERIODICALS

Los Angeles Times Book Review, December 5, 1982, p. 10; May 4, 1986, p. 11; October 22, 1989, p. 11.

New York Times Book Review, December 8, 1985, p. 21; January 12, 1986, p. 25; November 12, 1989, p. 29.

Washington Post Book World, June 14, 1987, p. 8.*

—Sketch by Thomas Kozikowski

L

LANSING, Karen E. 1954-

PERSONAL: Born February 27, 1954, in Greenville, SC; daughter of Harold (a minister) and Joyce (a homemaker; maiden name, Teeslink) Vander Ploeg; married Micheal Alan Lansing (a U.S. Army officer), August 30, 1975; children: Micheal Alan, Christopher Ryan, Jonathan Derrick. *Education:* Wheaton College, B.A. (literature), 1976. *Religion:* Protestant.

ADDRESSES: Office—c/o Herald Press, 616 Walnut Ave., Scottdale, PA 15683.

CAREER: Freelance writer of children's articles and books, 1986—.

WRITINGS:

Time to Fly, Herald Press, 1991.
Time to Be a Friend, Herald Press, 1993.

WORK IN PROGRESS: The Real Jenna, a juvenile fiction in the religious market for 8-12 year olds.

SIDELIGHTS: "The writing bug took hold of me at a very early age," Karen E. Lansing told *SATA.* "I would always encourage parents of young 'story-tellers' to listen and ask questions and provide opportunities to write down their imaginative tales. I even began sending stories to magazines in the fifth or sixth grade. I never had anything published *then,* but I did receive many wonderful handwritten rejection letters. I'm thankful for those sensitive editors who took the time to turn me down gently. Now that I'm a 'grown-up' I realize just how nice they were—as a standard form letter rejection is the norm.

"In college I majored in literature but filled my electives with as many writing courses as I could manage. Soon after graduating I married, and then moved to Germany. Aside from some journal entries and poetry, writing was not a major part of my life. In 1986 I was back in the States and by that time had three sons. I decided to do something I'd wanted to do for a long time—I took a children's magazine writing course. I learned that if I prepared a manuscript for publishing properly, the possibility for publication was much better.

"I wrote for all ages, but most of the stories that sold quickly were the ones for teens. For some reason, this age in my own life stuck with me; I can feel and remember the confusion and changing morals of the young teen.

"Late in 1989 I took a follow-up children's book writing course and my novel *Time to Fly* was the result. I found it exciting to create characters and plots that could be expanded to a book-length project rather than trying to fit it—or crop it—for a short story. The main character's house in *Time to Fly* was a house taken partiallly from my memories of a house I lived in when I was six. I never told anyone about it, but it was gratifying that both my mother and sister recognized it from the

KAREN E. LANSING

description. My second book is a sequel to *Time to Fly*. It deals with child abuse and the differing friendships of a 13-year-old.

"It's important for me to deal with contemporary issues from a Christian perspective. But I want my readers to identify positively with the characters. They are not goody-goodies but real teens with problems like anyone else. But they have a base (a belief in God) and caring friends and parents to turn to."

*   *   *

LAROCHE, Giles 1956-

PERSONAL: Born July 1, 1956, in Berlin, NH; son of Romeo and Claire (Huot) Laroche. *Education:* Attended Montserrat College of Art, 1977-81.

ADDRESSES: Home and office—41 Dearborn St., Salem, MA 01970.

CAREER: Artist and illustrator of children's books, with studios in Salem, MA, and Washington, NH. Paintings, drawings and illustrations have been exhibited nationally, including Dimensional Illustrator's Awards Show, New York, NY.

MEMBER: Society of Children's Book Writers.

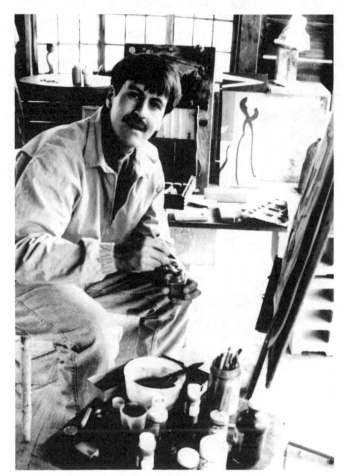

GILES LAROCHE

ILLUSTRATOR:

Lois Lenski, *Sing a Song of People,* Little, Brown, 1987.
Rachel Field, *General Store,* Little, Brown, 1988.
Rachel Field, *A Road Might Lead to Anywhere,* Little, Brown, 1990.
Dayle Ann Dodds, *The Color Box,* Little, Brown, 1992.

SIDELIGHTS: Giles Laroche writes, "I grew up in a town in the White mountains of New Hampshire. My family lived on the second floor of a triple-decker, which is a three story three family house surrounded by long porches. There are many triple-deckers in New England. A great aunt lived below us and on the third floor was another family. In the triple-decker next door were three more families. Our porches faced each other and I remember many of the people (especially the other children). It was a paper manufacturing town, and our neighborhood was filled with the sounds of the mills, the five o'clock whistle, and endless freight trains. Huge piles of lumber seemed to reach as high as the White Mountains.

"We were mostly of French-Canadian descent, and we attended L'Ecole de L'Ange Guardian. It was a bilingual parochial school and my first memory of art occured there. My first grade teacher had the marvelous ability to hold a book in one hand, which she read from, and to create wonderful illustrations of the story she read in colored chalks. How I yearned to have my very own blackboard and colored chalks. Crayons and a pad of drawing paper from Woolworth's had to suffice. I loved sketching the surrounding mountains and the summer houses we sometimes drove by in the neighboring towns of Shelburne and Randolph. Another art memory from this time is of my second grade class viewing the entries for the eighth grade student's model making competition of the Christmas nativity scene. One of them was a 'Lincoln log' creche with figures made from models cut out of a Sears catalog and glued onto Popsicle sticks. Another used figures made from a flour and water paste dyed with food coloring. I couldn't wait for my chance to participate. Drawing and bicycling became my favorite activities and both are still very much a part of me.

"In the fifth grade I left L'Ecole de L'Ange Guardian to attend a public school in another part of town. This was a difficult transition for me, and I was going to miss my friends (not to mention the eighth grade Christmas competition). However, my experiences at the new school (Brown School) made the transition smoother. In the sixth grade my teacher, who was a Sunday painter, devoted our Friday afternoons to drawing with crayons, mostly from nature (including the view from our classroom of the Mahoosuc Range and the snow-capped Mt. Goose Eye). What that teacher could do with crayons fascinated me, and I still think of some of his tricks in my pastel work today. Through high school my interest in art remained, and I became aware that art could be more than a pastime. My high school art teacher was a sculptor with endless energy and ideas. I became very interested in sculpture and drawing and studied with various sculptors and artists during the summers of 1977-1979 in Jefferson, New Hampshire.

"At about this time, my two brothers were married and had children with whom I enjoyed sharing books, particularly picture books. This made me realize that children's book illustration had evolved dramatically since my childhood, and suddenly an artist's role in the illustration and design of a book became very appealing to me. In 1977 I enrolled at Montserrat College of Art in Beverly, Massachusetts and studied all disciplines of fine and commercial art for four years. I became very interested in abstact painting while I was there and also in illustration. My illustration instructor, who was a master in many fields of illustration, had a great enthusiasm for her work and made the life of an illutrator seem both exciting and rewarding. In 1982 I found a part-time position as an office assistant in a very large architectural firm in Cambridge Massachusetts. At about the same time I found at the edge of a meadow in the hills of Washington, New Hampshire, a 200 year-old barn which I slowly converted into one of my studios where I now work on my children's book illustrations and paintings.

"In 1984 I moved to Salem, Massachusetts, into a house where I also spend a great deal of creative time. While working at the architectural firm I developed a strong interest in buildings and building styles, and my work reflected this fascination. I had always enjoyed the collage process, and I began creating collages depicting scenes of medieval towns and colonial villages. In time my collages became more dimensional, and I found myself hand-coloring my own cut-out collage elements. Then I remembered children's books, and I thought that perhaps my collages (paper reliefs) would lend themselves well as book illustrations if they could be lit and photographed in an interesting and dramatic way. I went to Little, Brown & Co. in Boston with my portfolio of paper reliefs. Later an editor there sent me five poems in the mail. I read them all, but the one which excited me the most was Lois Lenski's 'Sing a Song of People.' It was written in 1965 and it described day to day life in the city. I decided I would set the illustrations to the poem in Boston, since it was the city I knew best. I was able to include in my illustrations many buildings and even people I had encountered in my countless errands for the architectural firm.

"In 1988 I found Rachel Field's poem 'General Store' in her book entitled *Taxis and Toadstools.* I thought it would be interesting to create pictures of an old-fashioned store so that today's children might have a sense of what shopping was like for their great-grandparents. My hometown in New Hampshire had many wonderful corner grocery stores which I used as inspiration.

"'General Store' introduced me to the many wonderful poems and stories of Rachel Field, including 'A Road Might Lead to Anywhere,' which I translated into a children's picture book in 1990. It was an enormous pleasure to work on 'A Road Might Lead To Anywhere,' since I could use in my illustrations scenes of many of my favorite places, including the mountains I grew up in, trees, and architecture. One of the illustrations (by Miss Pim's the milliner's) shows Salem's famed House of the Seven Gables in the guise of a hat shop.

"In the spring of 1992 a new book entitled *The Color Box* will be released. It was written by Dale Ann Dodds and is about a monkey who discovers color after entering a funny-looking box. The book will have the added dimension of having die-cut holes which Alexander (the monkey) will enter in his color adventure.

"I'm also just beginning a new book which will be a poetry anthology picture book. Someday I would like to write and illustrate a book about life in a northern New England mill town or a book about hiking and the many things one sees on a hike; from the forest floor to the birds to the spectacular views from mountain summits.

"I have travelled extensively in Europe from Istanbul to the French countryside, and I especially enjoyed hiking in the Alps. I'd like to someday write and illustrate a book depicting the pleasures and drama of hiking from hut to hut in the German and Austrian Alps."

*   *   *

LEHR, Norma 1930-

PERSONAL: Born June 21, 1930, in San Francisco, CA; daughter of Peter (an inventor) and Elizabeth (Hoffman) Kurle; married Deward Lashley, 1949 (divorced, 1968); married Mel Lehr (in electronics research and development), April 1, 1972; children: (first marriage) Mark, Ramona, Brian, Heather. *Education:* Attended University of Utah, and Utah State University.

ADDRESSES: Agent—James Allen, 538 East Harford, Milford, PA 18337.

NORMA LEHR

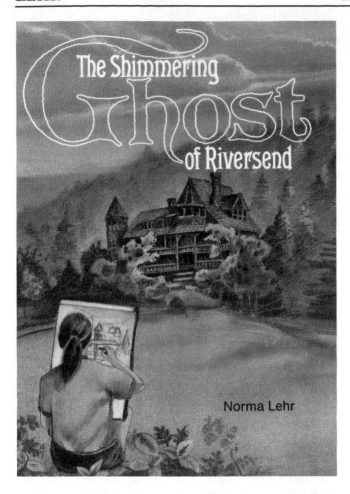

Lehr was inspired to write her novel about ghostly happenings in a spooky mansion after reading about hauntings at a dinner house in California. (Cover illustration by Aldo Abelliera.)

CAREER: Author.

MEMBER: Society of Children's Book Writers, California Writers.

WRITINGS:

The Shimmering Ghost of Riversend, Lerner, 1991.

WORK IN PROGRESS: The Secret of the Floating Phantom, the second book in a series featuring Kathy Wicklow, the heroine of *The Shimmering Ghost of Riversend.*

SIDELIGHTS: Norma Lehr writes, "My first awareness of an audience for my writing came in elementary school. A teacher, after reading one of my poems to the class, called my mother for permission to send the poem to the school district office to be put on display for a teacher's conference. I recall the admiration in my teachers's eyes, and I also remember how proud my mother was that my poetry would be honored.

"In Junior High School, I started writing essays and short, short stories and received the same enthusiastic support from my teachers. I recall wondering back then,

what all the fuss was about for something that came easily to me.

"High School English was harder. Diagraming sentences in my freshman year didn't come easy at all. In spite of my struggle, when I handed in a class assigned story, I was often commended for my imaginative plot. Midway through my Junior Year my English teacher, Miss Nell Madsen, asked me one day to stay after class. I did, and she seriously spoke to me that afternoon, stressing the importance of my talent as a god-given gift and encouraged me to never give that gift up—regardless!

"There have been years in my life when having the time to write was impossible. But the dream never died. When occasionally I did find the time to write an article or an essay, I yearned to write fiction. The time finally came when I could, and now, after spending the last nine years as a serious fiction writer, I have completed two unpublished adult novels. I am currently with an agent and have published my first children's novel for eight to twelve-year olds.

"I switched from writing adult fiction to writing children's fiction in December of 1987, when Betty Ren Wright, a retired editor-turned author from Scholastic Books, spoke at our town library. Something happened at that meeting to inspire me. I do believe it was being there, surrounded by enthusiastic children scrunched in beside me as they clutched their books and waited impatiently for Ms. Wright to sign them. It was then I decided that this was the audience I wanted to write for.

"A couple of weeks later I was invited to dinner at the Vineyard House in Marshall Gold Discovery State Park, Coloma, California, a dinner house that has the reputation of being haunted. I heard stories there that night about past and recent ghostly happenings from the staff. On our way out, I read a newspaper article tacked on the wall about ghostly happenings from overnight guests who had stayed at the Inn. On the drive back home, I made contact with my child within and wondered, 'what if...' and *The Shimmering Ghost of Riversend* was born. I started the book that month; the setting, the California Gold Country. When I was two-thirds finished, I started planning the series, setting the second book on the Monterey Peninsula and the third in Four Corners, New Mexico.

"Writing for children is enormously fun and satisfying for me. I really work at trying to inform as well as entertain, and I love signing books. I guess what I'm saying is, I'm just crazy about kids. I have four of my own and two grandchildren. Life is good."

*   *   *

LISSON, Deborah 1941-

PERSONAL: Born October 9, 1941, in Croydon, England; daughter of James Oliver (a writer) and Enid Betty (a homemaker; maiden name, Wade) Cornes; married Richard John Lisson (a technical college lecturer), November 1, 1963; children: Andrew, Peter, Christina, Malcolm, Roderick, Alan (died, 1977). *Education:* Attended Edith Cowan University, Bunbury campus. *Politics:* "A little left of centre." *Religion:* Catholic.

ADDRESSES: Home and office—20 Floreat St., Bunbury, Western Australia 6230, Australia. *Agent*—Walter McVitty, 27 Hereford St., Sydney, New South Wales 2037, Australia.

CAREER: Foyles Bookshop, London, England, telephonist, 1959-60; British Market Research Bureau, London, telephonist, 1960-62; New South Wales Health Department, Sydney, Australia, mobile x-ray unit operator, 1963; writer. Volunteer for Palliative Care Association, 1988—.

MEMBER: Society of Women Writers.

AWARDS, HONORS: Western Australia Premier's Award and shortlisted, Children's Book of the Year Award, both 1991, both for *The Devil's Own.*

WRITINGS:

The Devil's Own, Holiday House, 1991.

WORK IN PROGRESS: The Warrigal (tentative title), a children's novel, publication expected in 1992. Research on the plight of Italian internees in Western Australia during World War II; also research for a biographical novel on the life and death of the Inca warrior Chalcuchima.

SIDELIGHTS: Deborah Lisson told *SATA:* "I was born in Croydon, England, in 1941. My Dad was away at the war—I didn't see him till I was three and a half—and, during the war years, I lived with my mother and twin sister, in Brentwood, Essex. After my father came home, we moved to the country, living in many parts of England before settling in East Anglia when I was eight. My eldest brother was born when I was four and after that babies seemed to come along at regular intervals until, eventually, there were ten of us—seven girls and three boys.

"My father was a writer—a very successful one, for he managed to feed and clothe us all on his earnings from short stories and, later, picture scripts for children's comics: *Wizard, Rover, Hotspur,* etc. We were very proud of him—it was great to be able to show the comics to all the kids at school and say casually: 'My Dad wrote that.'

"Dad was the person who, more than any other, encouraged me and fired my own dreams of becoming a writer. It is one of my greatest joys that he has lived long enough to see my first book in print. One of the first series of stories he ever wrote was called 'Sergeant Blake of the Ironfists' and I always vowed that my first book would be dedicated to 'Sergeant Blake.'

"Creative writing was not taught much in schools in my day, but I was fortunate that in my last year of primary (elementary) school I had a wonderful teacher who

DEBORAH LISSON

encouraged all his class to write stories. We had half an hour a week for 'composition' and I would use this time to write long exciting serial stories—one chapter a week. Looking back now, I believe this was the most valuable part of my entire education. It taught me how to construct stories (I became adept at cliff-hanger chapter endings), how to research stories, and how to study other writers to see how they resolved their plots and manipulated their characters. I just lived for that precious half hour of writing time and I started writing in my spare time also. Sadly, once I got to high school all this came to an end, as the high school curriculum of my day simply didn't cater to creative writers. I started churning out history essays and geography essays and all the wonderful adventure stories went back into my head to be taken out, rehearsed and experienced in bed at night—or whenever I could find, or make, myself enough quiet time. I was notorious throughout the school for my 'daydreaming.'

"After a fairly undistinguished school career, I went out into the workforce without any real idea of what I wanted to do with my life. I spent a couple of years in London, working as a telephonist and being a beatnik in my spare time. Then, in 1962, I migrated to Australia, telling everyone I was a refugee from the English weather. Within weeks of arriving in Sydney I met the man who was to become my husband and moved with him to Perth, where we were married. Soon after this I discovered the joy of babies (Andrew in 1963, Peter in 1964, Christina in 1965, Malcolm in 1966, Roderick in 1970). When Roderick was six, my husband, a technical college lecturer, was transferred to Kalgoorie. We spent two years here and during that time adopted another little boy, Alan, whom we had already been fostering for eighteen months. Alan was an unexpected gift from God and for two years filled our hearts and our home with his very special love. Tragically, he suffered from congenital heart disease, and died in my arms on the Flying Doctor aircraft three months before what would have been his third birthday. At the time I believed I would never recover, but now, fourteen years later, I remember him only with love and happiness and an overwhelming sense of gratitude that of all the people in the world, we, with five children of our own, should have been given this very special and unlooked-for gift.

"In 1979 we moved to Bunbury, where we still live. By this time my family was demanding less of my attention and I began to think about putting some of my 'daydreams' down on paper and calling them books. I was very nervous and uncertain of my ability, but in 1983 I won a state-wide poetry competition from over twelve thousand other entrants and this gave me enormous encouragement. I needed it, as it was to be another six years before my first manuscript was accepted.

"*The Devil's Own* is my third book—the first two are still languishing in a drawer of my desk but I have not lost hope for them. I have since completed another manuscript—a fantasy set thousands of years into the future—which should be published in 1992, and I am busy researching a further one. In my spare time (ha ha) I am also studying part-time for a bachelor's degree in English literature."

M

MARIS, Ron

PERSONAL: Married; three sons.

ADDRESSES: Home—Yorkshire, England.

CAREER: Author and illustrator of children's books. Huddlesfield Polytechnic, West Yorkshire, England, senior lecturer in art and design.

AWARDS, HONORS: Kate Greenaway Medal (runner up), for *My Book.*

WRITINGS:

JUVENILE; SELF-ILLUSTRATED

Better Move On, Frog!, Greenwillow Books, 1982.
My Book, MacRae, 1983.
The Punch and Judy Book, Gollancz, 1984.
Are You There, Bear?, Greenwillow Books, 1985.
Is Anyone Home?, Greenwillow Books, 1986.
I Wish I Could Fly, Greenwillow Books, 1987.
In My Garden, Greenwillow Books, 1988.
Runaway Rabbit, Delacorte, 1989.
Hold Tight, Bear!, Delacorte, 1989.

My book

In Ron Maris's self-illustrated *My Book,* a little boy takes readers on a special tour of his home.

OTHER

(Illustrator) Eileen Colwell, compiler, *Humblepuppy and Other Stories for Telling,* Bodley Head, 1981.
Social Problems, Wadsworth, 1988.
(Editor) *Suicide and Its Prevention: The Role of Attitudes in Suicidal Behavior,* Brill, 1989.

SIDELIGHTS: Ron Maris is best known for his colorful and imaginative books that help introduce young children to reading. His most popular works, such as *Are You There, Bear?* and *My Book,* have been praised for both their design and text. *Are You There, Bear?* takes place in a child's bedroom, where a group of toys looks for a lost teddy bear; eventually, Bear is found behind a chair reading a book. Tanya Harrod, writing in the *Times Literary Supplement,* terms the story "ingeniously handled," and "full of lots of details." In *My Book,* a little boy points out some of the important things in his house. "A nice selection to share with preschoolers at bedtime," notes a reviewer for *Booklist.* "The full-color illustrations are comfortably literal and depict a homey, lived-in house." In a review of *Runaway Rabbit* for *School Library Journal,* Virginia Opacensky praises Maris for his ability to create "read it again, please" texts. "The presentation is totally successful," she notes, "right on target for the intended age group."

WORKS CITED:

Harrod, Tanya, review of *Are You There, Bear?, Times Literary Supplement,* November 30, 1984.
Review of *My Book, Booklist,* July, 1984, p. 1550.
Opacensky, Virginia, review of *Runaway Rabbit, School Library Journal,* December, 1989, pp. 85-86.

FOR MORE INFORMATION SEE:

PERIODICALS

Horn Book, July/August, 1983, p. 483; September/October, 1987, p. 601.
New York Times Book Review, February 19, 1984, p. 29.
Publishers Weekly, December 23, 1988, p. 80.
School Library Journal, April, 1985, p. 81.*

* * *

MARRIOTT, Alice Lee 1910-1992

OBITUARY NOTICE—See index for *SATA* sketch: Born January 8, 1910, in Wilmette, IL; died of heart failure, March 18, 1992, in Oklahoma City, OK. Librarian, anthropologist, and author. Marriott, the first woman to receive a Ph.D. in anthropology at the University of Oklahoma, was noted for promoting a wider understanding of various Native American cultures with her books. Originally a librarian, Marriott's interest in Indians was aroused while indexing local history books in the library she worked in Oklahoma, propelling her to study anthropology. While still in graduate school, Marriott went on a field trip to Oregon to interview the Modoc Indians. Later, she stayed with the Kiowa Indians in Oklahoma and worked with the Plains Indian in time to know some of the last buffalo hunters. In the 1940s, she helped organize two impor-

tant exhibits of Indian art. Her early books, *The Ten Grandmothers* and *Maria, the Potter of San Ildefonso,* written in the 1940s, received accolades from reviewers for their sensitivity in portraying the unique cultures of their subjects. Among her other books, written for both children and adults, are *Sequoyah: Leader of the Cherokees, Oklahoma: Its Past and Its Present, First Comers: Indians of America's Dawn,* and, with Carol K. Rachlin, *Plains Indian Mythology.*

OBITUARIES AND OTHER SOURCES:

BOOKS

Authors of Books for Young People, 3rd edition, Scarecrow, 1990.

PERIODICALS

New York Times, March 21, 1992, p. 11.

* * *

MATTHEWS, Downs 1925-

PERSONAL: Born March 24, 1925, in Waco, TX; son of Harold (a sociologist) and Grace (a teacher; maiden name, Downs) Matthews; married Mary Byers, 1948 (divorced, 1971); married Marianne Reeder (an editor), November 22, 1972; children: Mark, Lisa Lambdin. *Education:* Attended Southwestern University; University of Texas at Austin, B.J., 1947. *Politics:* Independent. *Religion:* Protestant. *Hobbies and other interests:* Photography, orchids, sailing, reading, and travel.

ADDRESSES: Home and office—3501 Underwood, Houston, TX 77025.

CAREER: Houston Chronicle, Houston, TX, reporter, 1945; Schlumberger Well Services, Houston, manager of employee communication, 1948-1968; Exxon Company, U.S.A., Houston, editor of *Exxon U.S.A.* magazine, 1968-1986; freelance editor and writer, 1986—; Nature Ventures (a calendar publishing company), co-owner, 1988—. Accredited business communicator and fellow, International Association of Business Communicators; communications consultant, University of Houston.

MEMBER: Travel Journalists Guild, North American Mycological Association, Outdoor Writers Association of America, American Orchid Society (chairman of publications committee, 1989-90).

AWARDS, HONORS: Matthews has received 128 awards for achievement in corporate communications; Reading Magic Award, *Parenting* magazine, 1989, for *Polar Bear Cubs.*

WRITINGS:

How to Manage Company Publications, Williams Company, 1986.
Polar Bear Cubs, photographs by Dan Guravich, Simon & Schuster, 1989.
Skimmers, photographs by Guravich, Simon & Schuster, 1990.

DOWNS MATTHEWS

Contributor of several hundred feature articles and essays to periodicals.

WORK IN PROGRESS: An adult book about polar bears; two books for children on the Arctic ecology and Arctic animals.

SIDELIGHTS: Downs Matthews told *SATA:* "My children's books are created in partnership with Dr. Dan Guravich, a Canadian living in Greenville, Mississippi. The texts couple good science simply told in narrative form with extraordinary photographs. Using the techniques of fiction, I describe the life cycle of an animal from conception to near maturity. The biology is technically sound; the events and circumstances are derived from personal observation, often over a period of years. The stories entertain and inform, but they also address the role of the parent as teacher and the child's need to learn how to live. (In nature, the heedless offspring seldom reaches maturity.)

"The subjects of our books are not anthropomorphic comic-strip characters with cute names who talk and think like people. In fact, we resist the urge to turn animals into human beings. It isn't necessary. There is nothing more beautiful or more charming than a polar bear cub or a skimmer chick [a baby marine bird]. Our animals are real. They do as animals do. While we don't highlight 'Nature, red in tooth and claw,' our animals don't eat lasagne, either.

"It makes sense for parents to give children the basis for an objective understanding of other life forms and their needs so that sensible environmental conservation can succeed.

"For most of my working life, I have written about the people and technologies of organizations involved in some aspect of the petroleum business. As a student of the earth sciences, I was able to indulge a penchant for travel and a fascination with the great outdoors. Today, as a free lance, I have been able to direct these interests into natural science and far-off places. The wildlife of the Arctic, particularly polar bears, has captured my attention in recent years."

* * *

McDANIEL, Lurlene 1944-

PERSONAL: Born April 5, 1944, in Philadelphia, PA: daughter of James (a chief petty officer in the U.S. Navy) and Bebe (a homemaker; maiden name, Donaldson) Gallagher; married Joe McDaniel, March 12, 1966 (divorced, 1987); children: Sean Clifford, Erik James. *Education:* University of Florida, B.A., 1965. *Politics:* Republican. *Religion:* Presbyterian Church of America.

ADDRESSES: Home—Chattanooga, TN. *Agent*—Meg Ruley/Jane Rotrosen, 318 East 51st St., New York, NY 10022.

CAREER: Writer. Frequent speaker and lecturer at writers' conferences.

MEMBER: Romance Writers of America, East Tennessee Romance Writers of America.

AWARDS, HONORS: Six Months to Live was placed in a literacy time capsule in the Library of Congress in November, 1990; *Too Young to Die* and *Goodbye*

LURLENE McDANIEL

Doesn't Mean Forever were selected Children's Choice books by the International Reader's Association.

WRITINGS:

PRE-TEEN BOOKS

What's It Like to Be a Star?, Willowisp Press/School Book Fairs, 1982.
I'm a Cover Girl Now, Willowisp Press/School Book Fairs, 1982.
Head over Heels, Willowisp Press/School Book Fairs, 1983.
If I Should Die before I Wake, Willowisp Press/School Book Fairs, 1983.
Sometimes Love Just Isn't Enough, Willowisp Press/School Book Fairs, 1984.
Three's a Crowd, Willowisp Press/School Book Fairs, 1984.
Six Months to Live, Willowisp Press/School Book Fairs, 1985.
The Secret Life of Steffie Martin, Willowisp Press/School Book Fairs, 1985.
Why Did She Have to Die?, Willowisp Press/School Book Fairs, 1986.
I Want to Live, Willowisp Press/School Book Fairs, 1987.
More than Just a Smart Girl, Willowisp Press/School Book Fairs, 1987.
My Secret Boyfriend, Willowisp Press/School Book Fairs, 1988.
Mother, Please Don't Die, Willowisp Press/School Book Fairs, 1988.
So Much to Live For, Willowisp Press/School Book Fairs, 1991.

INTERMEDIATE BOOKS

The Pony Nobody Wanted, Willowisp Press/School Book Fairs, 1982.
The Battle of Zorn, Willowisp Press/School Book Fairs, 1983.
Peanut Butter for Supper Again, Willowisp Press/School Book Fairs, 1985.
A Horse for Mandy, Willowisp Press/School Book Fairs, 1981.

YOUNG ADULT NOVELS

Too Young to Die, Bantam, 1989.
Goodbye Doesn't Mean Forever, Bantam, 1989.
Somewhere between Life and Death, Bantam, 1991.
Time to Let Go, Bantam, 1991.
Now I Lay Me Down to Sleep, Bantam, 1991.
When Happily Ever After Ends, Bantam, 1992.
A Time to Die, Bantam, 1992.
Mourning Song, Bantam, 1992.

Fiction editor, *Faith'n'Stuff, the Magazine for Kids.*

McDaniel's books have been translated into German, Norwegian, and Dutch.

WORK IN PROGRESS: A limited series of books for Bantam; research on medical ethics, dying, and grieving.

SIDELIGHTS: Lurlene McDaniel told *SATA:* "I can't remember a time when I didn't love to write and tell stories. My earliest childhood memories were of crawling up on my favorite uncle's lap and demanding that he 'read the book.' I started writing poems and stories in the first grade and by third grade had written a play that was performed by my classmates. By high school I was editor of the school newspaper and yearbook, and in college I was coeditor of the yearbook.

"However, I never dreamed that I would actually become a full-time novelist. I sought a more practical application for my talents. In college, I took my degree in English, but had a minor in advertising and public relations. Upon graduation, I worked for television stations in Tampa, Florida and Lansing, Michigan, where I wrote promotional ads and public service announcements. Yet the desire to write creatively—to write stories with engaging characters—never left me.

"In 1973, when my son Sean was three, he became critically ill and almost died. The diagnosis, juvenile diabetes, changed all our lives forever. He became wedded to twice-daily insulin shots, diet management, and regular exercise while I became intent on learning how to best manage his illness. I dedicated many years to his well-being, remaining at home and becoming a free-lance copywriter for numerous ad agencies to earn extra income. His brother Erik also came along in 1973. I would not have another such eventful year until 1987, when I divorced and started my career as a full-time writer.

"In 1980, I was given the opportunity to present a book manuscript to School Book Fairs, a then fledgling company that marketed children's books to school systems. In the years and books that followed with this publisher, I was able to build my reputation and my reading public. One of my first books (about a thirteen-year-old ballerina who gets diabetes) sold so well that the publisher asked for another of a similar kind—with a character overcoming a major medical handicap. In 1985 they published *Six Months to Live,* which has gone on to sell well over a half million copies through book fairs and book clubs. *Six Months to Live* has been twice nominated for Ohio's Buckeye Children's Book Award and in November, 1990, was placed in a literacy time capsule with forty-seven other titles at the Library of Congress and sealed for 100 years. A traveling display of the capsule will be on tour of the United States for two years before returning to the Library for a permanent berth.

"When I struck out to be a full-time writer in 1987, I acquired an agent who sold my first retail contract to Bantam Books. Since that time, I have written eight titles for Bantam and am currently writing six more. My readership has grown steadily and my reader mail load is heavy. Unwittingly, I seem to have struck a chord in the hearts of girls ten to sixteen years old. My novels deal with characters facing, through no fault of their own, a life-altering event—usually medical in nature—and overcoming the event. Sometimes my characters

In books such as *Goodbye Doesn't Mean Forever,* McDaniel explores sensitive issues like death and loss from a teen perspective.

actually die in the book, but this leads readers to tell me, 'It was like real life.' The ultimate message I want to send my audience is simply that no one can control what life dishes out. What you can control is how you respond to it.

"Since I am a deeply committed Christian, my novels reflect a Biblical ethic. My characters face death with the strength and courage that comes from a belief in God and a hope for eternal life. This message is implied and never dogmatic. One of the things that concerns me, and that I write about, is the advent of a medical technology that our culture is not ethically prepared to administrate. Without a strong ethical foundation, without moral absolutes, we are troubled as a society. Some of my books attempt to present this dilemma and help the reader to see that what one believes determines how one will act when faced with life's difficulties. Often suffering and pain breeds character and hope—not defeatism.

"Today, I reside in Chattanooga, Tennessee, and both my sons are grown. Sean helped put himself through college with soccer scholarships (all that exercise to help his diabetes paid off), and Erik is also attending college on a soccer scholarship (what big brother did, little brother wanted to do too).

"My days are filled with writing. I write daily in my home office on a word processor. I consider writing both my joy and my business, so I am as professional as possible in my work schedule. I love to travel and often speak and teach at conferences and seminars. I am also fiction editor on a children's magazine and write occasional short stories to sell.

"I wouldn't trade my lifestyle for anything. Mail from my readers brightens my days as each letter reminds me that a real live kid is reading and being affected by my work. I have many touching letters that I share during speaking engagements to encourage others. I remind my readers that good things can come out of bad things. To wit—my entire novel-writing career came out of my son's diagnosis of diabetes. The doors of life are always opening and presenting challenges. And even when the challenges seem insurmountable, with the help of a divine, loving creator, we can find deep satisfaction and joy through serving him and doing good for others."

FOR MORE INFORMATION SEE:

PERIODICALS

Publishers Weekly, April 6, 1992, p. 23.

*   *   *

MEEKER, Richard
See BROWN, Fornan

*   *   *

MICHAELS, Steve 1955-

PERSONAL: Born February 13, 1955, in Germany; son of Herman John (a career army officer) and Rita (Hughes) Michaels; married Helen Moore, May 27, 1978; children: Stephanie Marguerite. *Education:* East Carolina University, B.F.A., 1978. *Politics:* Democrat. *Religion:* Episcopalian.

ADDRESSES: Home—1391 Osceola Ave., St. Paul, MN 55105.

CAREER: Paul Brink Associates, Minneapolis, MN, staff artist, 1978-83; Financial Timing Publications, Minneapolis, art director, 1984-88; free-lance artist, 1988—. Volunteer elementary school teacher; Sunday school teacher.

ILLUSTRATOR:

Jeri Ferris, *What Do You Mean? A Story about Noah Webster,* Carolrhoda, 1988.
Jim Haskins, *Count Your Way through Canada,* Carolrhoda, 1989.
Emily Crofford, *Healing Warrior: A Story about Sister Elizabeth Kenny,* Carolrhoda, 1989.
David R. Collins, *Pioneer Plowmaker: A Story about John Deere,* Carolrhoda, 1990.
Jonni Kincher, *Psychology for Kids: Forty Fun Tests That Help You Learn about Yourself,* Free Spirit, 1990.
Barbara A. Lewis, *Kid's Guide to Social Action: How to Solve the Social Problems You Choose and Turn Creative Thinking into Positive Action,* Free Spirit, 1991.

WORK IN PROGRESS: The Green de Soto, a humorous depiction of the life of a military family in Europe with a big car, written and illustrated by Michaels.

SIDELIGHTS: Steve Michaels told *SATA:* "I was greatly influenced by the art of the Disney studio and read many comic books drawn by Carl Barks. (Being raised in a military family in Europe this was a chief form of entertainment.) I was also inspired by Classics Illus-

Erin tries to deal with the death of her younger sister, severe, unexplained headaches, and an annoying young man in *Time to Let Go*. (Cover illustration by Ben Stahl.)

trated, and in later years by the works of N. C. Wyeth. Wyeth's paintings have so much 'soul' and move me deeply. I was also influenced by Dr. Seuss."

*   *   *

MIRANDA, Anne 1954-

PERSONAL: Born July 6, 1954, in Cleveland, OH; daughter of Allen Shields (a violist) and Mary Jane (a managing editor; maiden name, Evans) Martin; married Saturnino L. Miranda (an engineer), July 29, 1978; children: Evan Michael, Tyler Martin. *Education:* Attended University of Massachusetts. *Religion:* Christian.

ADDRESSES: Home and office—33 Glen Devin, Amesbury, MA 01913.   *Agent*—Liza Pulitzer Voges, Kirchoff/Wohlberg, Inc., 866 U.N. Plaza, New York, NY 10017.

CAREER: Boston Education Research, Boston, MA, staff writer, 1974-75; free-lance writer, 1978—.

WRITINGS:

Baby Talk, Dutton, 1987.
Baby Walk, Dutton, 1988.
Baby-Sit, Joy Street Books, 1990.
(Self-illustrated) *Night Songs,* Bradbury, in press.

SIDELIGHTS: Anne Miranda told *SATA:* "I always wanted to be an artist. I remember when I was about four, my mother sat me down with a set of pastels and a glass of warm milk. She told me to dip the pastels in the warm milk so the chalk would stick to the paper and the colors would be brighter. We made beautiful vases of colorful flowers. It was heavenly!

ANNE MIRANDA

"When I was eight or nine, I saw a touring Van Gogh exhibit at the Cleveland Art Museum. I marveled at vases of colorful flowers, beautiful countrysides, and a dark table where a family sat down to a meal of potatoes. I was sure then that I wanted to spend my life painting. But many things in my life got in the way of that dream.

"When I was about twenty-one, I became a writer. Actually, I was nudged into writing by my mother, Mary Jane Martin. I was between colleges, working in a dead-end job. My mother suggested, very strongly, that I write some controlled vocabulary stories for a reading program she was working on at Boston Educational Research. So I did. I was hired as a staff writer. I found writing another way to put the pictures in my head down on paper, with words instead of colors. It was a very satisfying alternative.

"I've worked on many projects with my mother since then. She has taught me everything I know. I owe my writing career to her. And now I have to thank her for my new career as an illustrator. She suggested, very strongly, that I illustrate a poetry book I had written. So I did. Bradbury Press liked it so much, they are publishing it! The book, *Night Songs,* will be on their Spring of 1993 list.

"Sometimes dreams do come true."

*   *   *

MOSS, Marissa 1959-

PERSONAL: Born September 29, 1959, in Jeanette, PA; daughter of Robert (an aerospace engineer) and Harriet (a homemaker) Moss; married Harvey Stahl (a professor), April, 1985; children: Simon, Elias. *Education:* University of California at Berkeley, B.A., graduate study in art history. Studied illustration at California College of Arts & Crafts, and at a workshop with Uri Shulevitz.

ADDRESSES: Agent—Barbara Kouts, P.O. Box 558, Bellport, NY 11713.

CAREER: Free-lance graphic designer, Berkeley, CA, 1981-86; Oakland Public School System, Oakland, CA, elementary school art teacher, 1986-88; University of California, Berkeley, instructor in children's book illustration, 1988—.

MEMBER: Society of Children's Book Writers.

AWARDS, HONORS: Book of the Year designation, National Council of Teachers of Social Studies, 1991, for *Regina's Big Mistake.*

WRITINGS:

SELF-ILLUSTRATED

Who Was It?, Houghton, 1989.
Want to Play?, Houghton, 1990.
Regina's Big Mistake, Houghton, 1990.

After School Monster, Lothrop, 1991.
But Not Kate, Lothrop, 1992.
Knick Knack Paddywack, Houghton, 1992.

ILLUSTRATOR

Catherine Gray, *One, Two, Three and Four. No More?,* Houghton, 1988.
Dr. Hickey, *Mother Goose and More,* Additions Press, 1990.

WORK IN PROGRESS: A book about family members who emigrated from Eastern Europe to America.

SIDELIGHTS: Writer and illustrator Marissa Moss grew up in a home where reading was a central part of daily life. "We went to the library every week and came home each with our own pile of books," Moss told *SATA.* "Nobody directed my choices and I read widely, whatever I chanced upon, from Dr. Seuss to Roald Dahl to Ray Bradbury. Once I opened a book I felt compelled to finish it. I was drawn into a world and I had to know what would happen, how it would end." Even with her great love of books and talent for telling stories, Moss never actively pursued becoming a "writer." Although she has gone on to write several popular children's books, illuminating both her own stories and those of other authors with her endearing watercolor illustrations, Moss still defines herself as primarily an artist and a storyteller. "As far back as I can remember, I drew pictures and made up stories to go with them, entertaining myself, my brothers and sisters, and my friends at school. The art always came first. I spun the words around the images, the narrative suggested already in the picture."

As a college student, Moss studied fine arts, but found the experience frustrating. "As an art major I was constantly resisting the draw that narrative has for me, trying for a 'higher,' more abstract aesthetic and failing miserably. Finally I changed my major to art history— the story of art—but that didn't satisfy my need to create visual narrative, only the need to see and understand it. I quit graduate school in art history to concentrate on my art, on how I wanted to draw. What kept coming out were humorous watercolors that were stories in themselves. I realized I was making single-page children's books and that I wanted to tell stories."

Moss finds the ideas for her books within the memories of dreams and situations from her own childhood: "My books arise out of a single image or visual idea. The story opens out from it like rings that ripple the surface of water when a stone is thrown in a pool." She explained the source of *Regina's Big Mistake,* telling *SATA* that it "grew out of my own sense of the enormity of starting a drawing, of transforming a piece of blank paper into a world." Although Moss's book *After School Monster* relates to many of the fears of latchkey children, she explained that the story "reflects a recurring nightmare I had, even though my mother stayed home."

Although many of the ideas of her books are autobiographical in nature, Moss does not model her characters after herself. Instead, she approaches each new character by allowing her drawing pencil to make the introductions. "I start by drawing sketches of [the story's characters] with different expressions and positions, and the drawings tell *me* who they are. From them I learn what the characters wear, what kind of cereal they like for breakfast, what games they play. They're independent personalities and I enter their worlds much as I enter the worlds of books."

FOR MORE INFORMATION SEE:

PERIODICALS

School Library Journal, December, 1989, p. 86; July, 1990, p. 63.

Marissa Moss addresses the the fears of latchkey children in her self-illustrated *After School Monster.*

MURPHY, Shirley Rousseau 1928-

PERSONAL: Born May 20, 1928, in Oakland, CA; daughter of Otto Francis (a horse trainer) and Helen (an artist; maiden name, Hoffman) Rousseau; married Patrick J. Murphy (a U.S. probation officer), August 5, 1951. *Education:* California School of Fine Arts (now San Francisco Art Institute), A.A., 1951. *Hobbies and other interests:* "Swimming, kayaking on our lake, occasional horse riding. I take long walks with the neighbors' dogs, and like to watch the wild animals around our lake. I love impressionist painting, and love listening to Dixieland jazz, but can get dangerously lost in either, and distracted from my own work. I also like to remodel houses."

ADDRESSES: Home—1977 Upper Grandview Rd., Jasper, GA 30143. *Agent*—Elaine Markson Agency, 44 Greenwich Ave., New York, NY 10011.

CAREER: Sam Kweller (designer), Los Angeles, CA, packaging designer, 1952-53; Bullock's (department store), Los Angeles, interior decorator, 1953-55; San Bernardino Valley College, San Bernardino, CA, teacher of mosaics, 1953-61; Canal Zone Library-Museum, Canal Zone, Panama, documents assistant, 1964-67; writer, painter, and sculptor. *Exhibitions:* Dual show with mother, Helen Rousseau, at Instituto Panameno de Arte, 1964, and numerous one-woman shows in California, 1957-63; paintings, drawing, and sculpture also exhibited at group and juried shows in California, Arizona, and Nevada, and with traveling exhibits.

MEMBER: Society of Children's Book Writers, Authors Guild.

AWARDS, HONORS: Received eight awards for sculpture and four for painting at San Francisco Museum and other exhibitions, 1959-62; Dixie Council of Authors and Journalists' Award, 1977, for *The Ring of Fire* and *Silver Woven in My Hair,* 1979, for *The Flight of the Fox,* 1981, for *Mrs. Tortino's Return to the Sun,* 1986, for *Nightpool,* and 1988, for *The Ivory Lyre.*

WRITINGS:

The Sand Ponies, illustrations by Erika Weihs, Viking, 1967.
White Ghost Summer, illustrations by Barbara McGee, Viking, 1967.
Elmo Doolan and the Search for the Golden Mouse, illustrations by Fritz Kredel, Viking, 1970.
(With husband, Patrick J. Murphy) *Carlos Charles,* Viking, 1971.
Poor Jenny, Bright as a Penny, Viking, 1974.
The Grass Tower, illustrations by Charles Robinson, Atheneum, 1976.
The Ring of Fire, Atheneum, 1977.
Silver Woven in My Hair, illustrations by Alan Tiegreen, Atheneum, 1977.
The Flight of the Fox, illustrations by Don Sibley, Atheneum, 1978.

SHIRLEY ROUSSEAU MURPHY

The Pig Who Could Conjure the Wind, illustrations by Mark Lefkowitz, Atheneum, 1978.
Soonie and the Dragon, illustrations by Susan Vaeth, Atheneum, 1979.
The Wolf Bell, Atheneum, 1979.
The Castle of Hape, Atheneum, 1980.
Caves of Fire and Ice, Atheneum, 1980.
(With P. J. Murphy) *Mrs. Tortino's Return to the Sun,* illustrations by Susan Russo, Lothrop, 1980.
The Joining of the Stone, Atheneum, 1981.
Tattie's River Journey, illustrations by Tomie de Paola, Dial, 1983.
Valentine for a Dragon, illustrations by Kay Chorao, Atheneum, 1984.
Nightpool (first book in "Dragonbards" trilogy), Harper, 1985.
The Ivory Lyre (second book in "Dragonbards" trilogy), Harper, 1987.
The Dragonbards (third book in "Dragonbards" trilogy), Harper, 1988.
(With Welch Suggs) *Medallion of the Black Hound,* Harper, 1989.
The Song of the Christmas Mouse, illustrations by Donna Diamond, Harper, 1990.
The Catswold Portal (adult fantasy), Roc, 1992.
Wind Child, illustrations by Leo and Diane Dillon, Harper, 1993.

Contributor to anthologies, including *Anywhere, Anywhen,* edited by Sylvia Engdahl, Atheneum, 1976; *The Unicorn Treasury,* edited by Bruce Coville, Doubleday, 1988; and *Herds of Thunder, Manes of Gold,* edited by B. Coville, Doubleday, 1989. Also contributor to periodicals, including *Advocate* and *Writer.* Murphy's manuscripts are held by the de Grummond Collection at the University of Southern Mississippi.

ADAPTATIONS: Tattie's River Journey was recorded on videotape by Listening Library, 1984.

WORK IN PROGRESS: Working on *The White Otter* and *The Dragon Flute,* prequels to the "Dragonbard" trilogy but written for younger readers, and sequels to *The Dragonbards* and *The Catswold Portal.*

SIDELIGHTS: In Shirley Rousseau Murphy's complex, richly imagined fantasies for young adults, animals join with children to battle the forces of evil and darkness that lurk in detailed imaginary landscapes. Murphy's created worlds contain all the intricacies and peculiarities of the real world, but the talking otters, clairvoyant dragons, and characters who jump across the barriers of time make her stories thoroughly fantastic. Murphy's books are full of detail, and more than one critic has complained that the abundance of characters and plot twists is confusing. But the complexity is balanced by episodes that Ruth M. McConnell, reviewing *The Castle of Hape* in *School Library Journal,* calls "magnificently imagined," and by animals that, according to Jane Anne Hannigan in *Twentieth-Century Children's Writers,* are described "with such beauty and sensitivity that the reader is forced to believe in their intelligence and their contribution to the good."

In Murphy's *The Flight of the Fox,* a boy joins forces with a kangaroo rat and a pet lemming to convert a scrapped model airplane into a real flying machine. (Cover illustration by Richard Cuffari.)

Murphy was born in California in 1928, the daughter of a horse trainer and an artist. She once told *SATA* that she attributed her adult habits—hard work interspersed with flights of imagination—to the divergent vocations of her parents: from her father she learned the discipline of training horses; from her mother she learned the joys of painting and sculpting. Murphy commented that her "childhood was a life of opposites: the solitary make-believe world and a world where I was expected to exact unquestioning discipline of myself and over whatever horse I might be working with." When training a horse, she continued, "each situation must be brought to a successful conclusion to avoid destroying many months of careful training. I think this experience has been valuable to me both as a fine artist and as a writer."

Murphy pursued a career in the fine arts in the late 1950s and early 1960s, but when she moved to Panama with her husband Patrick and got a job in the Canal Zone Library she turned her artistic talents to writing. "My first books were realistic, first about horses, and then about the side of life my husband sees in his work" as a probation officer, she told *SATA.* For instance, *Poor Jenny, Bright as a Penny* tells the story of an imaginative girl who grows up in a filthy part of the city with a drunken mother who continually abuses her. Despite having the odds stacked against her, Jenny sticks to her writing and eventually finds happiness with the family that adopts her. Alix Nelson, writing in the *New York Times Book Review,* recommends the book for any "young person who is convinced he or she is always getting a raw deal. When you see what giant obstacles Jenny has to scale, what strength and inner resources she must throw into the effort, life for the rest of us seems suddenly to be lived on Easy Street."

Despite her success at these early writings, Murphy vowed that one day she would write fantasy. With over a dozen fantasies to her credit, she seems to have reached that goal. Murphy describes her writing process in *The Writer:* "My ... approach is rather haphazard. I sort through bits and pieces I've collected, through images that have stayed in my mind, through quickly written sketches, snatches of conversation, and notes from scattered reading." In writing *The Dragonbards* she began with three unconnected images—dragons, otters, and green islands scattered on a blue sea. These images stayed in her mind for some time when, she recounts, "suddenly I saw [the islands] from the back of a winging dragon, and saw the progress of history in vision created by [the dragon.] The otters were a natural part of the island world. Now the images had joined, and I was ready to shape the story." Once Murphy had joined the images for her story, she could set about creating the world in which her story would take place: she drew maps, and developed a geography and geology and a history of its peoples.

The next stage in Murphy's writing process is the act of construction, "a quicksilver time of restlessness.... I write unrelated scenes and conversations not knowing, often, where they came from or where they are going. I let each character speak as he will," she says in *Writer.*

The magic of the Christmas season comes to life in Murphy's tale of a boy who tries to rescue an orphaned field mouse. (Cover illustration for Murphy's *Song of the Christmas Mouse* by Donna Diamond.)

When the world of her story is fully shaped, Murphy begins "to write seriously, working usually ten hours a day. My habit is to write quickly, but turning back every morning to edit what I did the day before." Upon finishing her work, she lets it "cool," saying: "I want to come back to the final polishing as if it were the work of a stranger, when new discovery is heightened."

Murphy, who tries to write every day, uses her trade to recover some of the magic she saw in the world as a young girl. "As a little girl alone on horseback in the woods and fields," she remembers in *SATA*, "I moved in a world of such wonders and beauty that its discovery, every day, was almost a physical pain. A world that, in its intensity and clarity, seemed to be beyond this world; a world washed with what C. S. Lewis called 'Joy.' Perhaps it is that world so sharply seen that I try to recapture in some small way, perhaps in writing fantasy I am trying to touch again that 'other' universe that spoke to me then." And, she vows, "I will never stop writing fantasy."

WORKS CITED:

Hannigan, Jane Anne, sketch in *Twentieth-Century Children's Writers,* 3rd edition, St. James Press, 1989, pp. 706-07.
McConnell, Ruth M., review of *The Castle of Hape, School Library Journal,* May, 1980, p. 79.
Murphy, Shirley Rousseau, "Fantasy for Young Readers," *Writer,* September, 1989, pp. 19-20, 33.
Nelson, Alix, review of *Poor Jenny, Bright as a Penny, New York Times Book Review,* September 15, 1974, p. 8-9.
Something about the Author, Volume 36, Gale, 1984, pp. 142-45.

FOR MORE INFORMATION SEE:

BOOKS

Rasmusen, H., and A. Grant, *Sculpture from Junk,* Reinhold, 1967.

PERIODICALS

Publishers Weekly, February 3, 1992.
School Library Journal, October, 1977, p. 116; January, 1979, p. 56; March, 1981, p. 158; February, 1982, p. 91; December, 1985, p. 104; March, 1988, pp. 215-16; July, 1990, p. 23.

*   *   *

MYERS, Walter Dean 1937-
(Walter M. Myers)

PERSONAL: Given name Walter Milton Myers; born August 12, 1937, in Martinsburg, WV; son of George Ambrose and Mary (Green) Myers; raised from age three by Herbert Julius (a shipping clerk) and Florence (a factory worker) Dean; married second wife, Constance Brendel, June 19, 1973; children: (first marriage) Karen, Michael Dean; (second marriage) Christopher.

WALTER DEAN MYERS

Education: Attended City College of the City University of New York; Empire State College, B.A., 1984.

ADDRESSES: Home—2543 Kennedy Blvd., Jersey City, NJ 07304.

CAREER: New York State Department of Labor, New York City, employment supervisor, 1966-70; Bobbs-Merrill Co., Inc. (publisher), New York City, senior trade books editor, 1970-77; full-time writer, 1977—. Teacher of creative writing and black history on a part-time basis in New York City, 1974-75; worked variously as a post-office clerk, inter-office messenger, and a interviewer at a factory. *Military service:* U.S. Army, 1954-57.

MEMBER: PEN, Harlem Writers Guild.

AWARDS, HONORS: Council on Interracial Books for Children Award, 1968, for the manuscript of *Where Does the Day Go?; The Dancers* was selected one of Child Study Association of America's children's books of the year, 1972; American Library Association (ALA) notable book citations, 1975, for *Fast Sam, Cool Clyde, and Stuff,* 1978, for *It Ain't All for Nothin',* 1979, for *The Young Landlords,* and 1988, for *Scorpions* and *Me, Mop, and the Moondance Kid;* Woodward Park School Annual Book Award, 1976, for *Fast Sam, Cool Clyde, and Stuff;* ALA best books for young adults citation, 1978, for *It Ain't All for Nothin',* 1979, for *The Young Landlords,* 1981, for *The Legend of Tarik,* 1982, for *Hoops,* and 1988, for *Fallen Angels* and *Scorpions;* Coretta Scott King Awards for fiction, 1980, for *The Young Landlords,* 1985, for *Motown and Didi,* and 1988, for *Fallen Angels,* and for nonfiction, 1992, for *Now Is Your Time: The African-American Struggle for Freedom;* Notable Children's Trade Book in the Field of Social Studies from the National Council for Social Studies and the Children's Book Council, 1982, for *The Legend of Tarik;* Edgar Allan Poe Award runner-up, 1982, for *Hoops; Parents' Choice* Award from the Parents' Choice Foundation, 1982, for *Won't Know Till I Get There,* 1984, for *The Outside Shot,* and 1988, for *Fallen Angels;* New Jersey Institute of Technology Authors Award, 1983, for *Tales of a Dead King; Adventure in Granada* was selected one of Child Study Association of America's children's books of the year, 1987; Newbery Honor Book, 1989, for *Scorpions; Boston Globe/Horn Book* Honor Book, 1992, for *Somewhere in the Darkness.*

WRITINGS:

PICTURE BOOKS

(Under name Walter M. Myers) *Where Does the Day Go?,* illustrated by Leo Carty, Parents Magazine Press, 1969.
The Dragon Takes a Wife, illustrated by Ann Grifalconi, Bobbs-Merrill, 1972.
The Dancers, illustrated by Anne Rockwell, Parents Magazine Press, 1972.
Fly, Jimmy, Fly!, illustrated by Moneta Barnett, Putnam, 1974.

In addition to the universal problems of adolescence, the characters in *Scorpions* must also confront the obstacles presented by inner city life.

The Black Pearl and the Ghost; or, One Mystery after Another, illustrated by Robert Quackenbush, Viking, 1980.
Mr. Monkey and the Gotcha Bird, illustrated by Leslie Morrill, Delacorte, 1984.

NOVELS; FOR CHILDREN AND YOUNG ADULTS

Fast Sam, Cool Clyde, and Stuff, Viking, 1975.
Brainstorm, photographs by Chuck Freedman, F. Watts, 1977.
Mojo and the Russians, Viking, 1977.
Victory for Jamie, Scholastic, 1977.
It Ain't All for Nothin', Viking, 1978.
The Young Landlords, Viking, 1979.
The Golden Serpent, illustrated by Alice Provensen and Martin Provensen, Viking, 1980.
Hoops, Delacorte, 1981.
The Legend of Tarik, Viking, 1981.
Won't Know Till I Get There, Viking, 1982.
The Nicholas Factor, Viking, 1983.
Tales of a Dead King, Morrow, 1983.
Motown and Didi: A Love Story, Viking, 1984.
The Outside Shot, Delacorte, 1984.
Sweet Illusions, Teachers & Writers Collaborative, 1986.
Crystal, Viking, 1987.
Scorpions, Harper, 1988.

Me, Mop, and the Moondance Kid, illustrated by Rodney Pate, Delacorte, 1988.

Fallen Angels, Scholastic, 1988.

The Mouse Rap, HarperCollins, 1990.

Somewhere in the Darkness, Scholastic, 1992.

Mop, Moondance, and the Nagasaki Knights, Delacorte, 1992.

The Righteous Revenge of Artemis Bonner, HarperCollins, 1992.

Also editor of the "18 Pine St." series of young adult novels featuring African-American characters, Bantam Books, 1992—.

"THE ARROW" SERIES

Adventure in Granada, Viking, 1985.

The Hidden Shrine, Viking, 1985.

Duel in the Desert, Viking, 1986.

Ambush in the Amazon, Viking, 1986.

OTHER

The World of Work: A Guide to Choosing a Career (nonfiction), Bobbs-Merrill, 1975.

Social Welfare (nonfiction), F. Watts, 1976.

Malcolm X: By Any Means Necessary, Scholastic, 1993.

Work represented in anthologies, including *What We Must See: Young Black Storytellers,* Dodd, 1971, and *We Be Word Sorcerers: Twenty-five Stories by Black Americans.* Contributor of articles and fiction to periodicals, including *Black Creation, Black World, Scholastic, McCall's, Espionage, Alfred Hitchcock Mystery Magazine, Essence, Ebony, Jr.!,* and *Boy's Life.*

ADAPTATIONS: The Young Landlords was adapted as a film by Topol Productions.

SIDELIGHTS: Award-winning author Walter Dean Myers has secured a reputation as a versatile creator of fiction for children and young adults. His works include picture books, science fiction, fantasy, nonfiction, and mystery-adventure stories. Myers is perhaps best known, however, as the author of young adult novels that focus on the experience of black teenagers living in the New York City district of Harlem, such as *Fast Sam, Cool Clyde, and Stuff; The Young Landlords; Motown and Didi; Scorpions;* and *The Mouse Rap.* In these books, Myers's protagonists confront the obstacles presented by inner-city life in addition to facing the universal problems of adolescence. Though Myers addresses serious topics such as teen pregnancy, suicide, adoption, and parental neglect in his works, his tone is often optimistic. In *Shadow and Substance: Afro-American Experience in Contemporary Children's Fiction,* Rudine Sims remarked that "Myers's work focuses on the love and laughter that is part of the Afro-American experience," and added that his books emphasize community support as well as "the individual strengths and the inner resources that enable us to cope and to survive."

Born in Martinsburg, West Virginia, Myers was adopted by family friends after the death of his mother. His foster parents, Florence and Herbert Dean, settled in Harlem when Myers was about three years old. "I loved Harlem," Myers recalled in his *Something about the Author Autobiography Series (SAAS)* essay. "I lived in an exciting corner of the renowned Black capital and in an exciting era. The people I met there, the things I did, have left a permanent impression on me."

From an early age Myers showed an interest in reading and writing. He learned to read at age four, and by age five he read the daily newspaper to his foster mother while she did household chores. The author remarked in a *Contemporary Authors New Revision Series (CANR)* interview that he "wrote fiction on a regular basis from the time I was ten or eleven, filling up notebooks." Myers did not intend to pursue a career as a writer, however, because, as he related in the *CANR* interview, he "never knew writing was a job. When I was a kid, my people didn't think of being a writer as legitimate kind of work." As a teenager Myers won contests for his poetry and essays, but since his parents did not consider writing a practical pursuit they did not encourage him to cultivate his talent. Myers also began to realize that although he possessed intelligence he was limited by his economic status—he couldn't afford college—and, as he

Each chapter of *Sweet Illusions*—a book about teen pregnancy told from varying perspectives—ends with blank pages for reader response. (Cover illustration by Louise Hamlin.)

wrote in *SAAS,* was "defined more by my race than my abilities."

Although he did not consider writing a possible occupation, Myers continued to read voraciously and to write stories and poems. He joined the U.S. Army as a seventeen-year-old and spent three years in the service. After he was discharged in 1957 Myers worked variously as a mail clerk, messenger, and interviewer at a factory. Dissatisfied with the direction of his career, Myers recalled in *SAAS* that "I decided that what I wanted to do with myself was to become a writer and live what I imagined would be the life of the writer, whatever that might be."

In the late 1960s Myers entered a writing contest sponsored by the Council on Interracial Books for Children. "When I entered a contest for picture book writers," he explained in *SAAS,* "it was more because I wanted to write *anything* than because I wanted to write a picture book." Myers won the contest with the manuscript of *Where Does the Day Go?,* which was published in 1969. In the story, which was illustrated by Leo Carty, an ethnically-diverse group of children and a sensitive father explore the concepts of night and day. Encouraged by the publication of *Where Does the Day Go?,* Myers created texts for other picture books, including *The Dragon Takes a Wife, The Dancers,* and *Fly, Jimmy, Fly!*

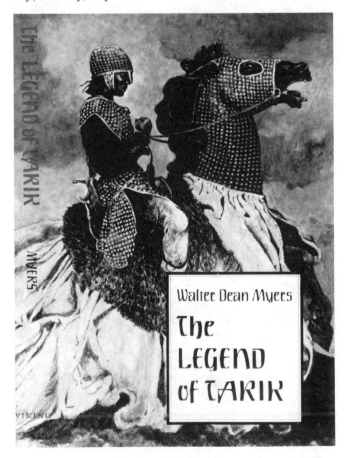

Myers turns from teenage problems to exotic adventure in *The Legend of Tarik.*

Myers published his first novel for young adults, *Fast Sam, Cool Clyde, and Stuff,* in 1975. The book is narrated by eighteen-year-old Stuff, who nostalgically recalls his experiences as a thirteen-year-old living in Harlem. Stuff and his friends form a gang called the Good People in order to cope with their world of broken homes, police encounters, street fights, sex, and drugs. In *Dictionary of Literary Biography,* Carmen Subryan observed that "because of the bonding which occurs among the members of the group, the reader realizes that each individual's potential for survival has increased." Reviewers considered *Fast Sam, Cool Clyde, and Stuff* to be humorous and engrossing, and praised Myers for his natural dialogue and positive portrayal of inner-city youth. Writing in *English Journal,* Alleen Pace Nilsen commented that "one of the nicest things about the book is that it is so hopeful. The kids live near drugs and welfare checks but the reader finishes the book buoyed up instead of depressed."

Over the years, Myers has created a number of upbeat novels concerning urban life. In *The Young Landlords* a group of teenagers become the owners of a run-down apartment house and in the course of their adventures learn about the complexities of relationships between landlords and tenants as well as those between friends. Set in Chicago, *Me, Mop, and the Moondance Kid* introduces two young boys who have recently been adopted. They hope to have a winning Little League season as well as help their friend from the orphanage, Mop, become adopted by the baseball coach. In *The Mouse Rap,* each chapter begins with a rap verse provided by Mouse, whose summer activities include avoiding his father, entering a dance contest, and searching for a dead mobster's hidden loot. Critics praised these works, noting that Myers presents endearing, often eccentric characters, humorous dialogue, and optimistic plot resolutions. In a *Horn Book* review of *The Young Landlords,* Kate M. Flanagan asserted that Myers "has once again demonstrated his keen sensitivity to the joys and frustrations of adolescence."

Myers has also written novels that focus on the often grim realities that inner-city teenagers must confront, works that reviewers have recommended for their poignancy, compassion, and honesty. In *It Ain't All for Nothin'* Tippy must live with his abusive father—an ex-con who makes a living by stealing—when his grandmother is admitted to a nursing home. Myers presents Tippy's fear, loneliness, and pain in a book that "pretties up nothing; not the language, not the circumstances, not the despair," wrote *Interracial Books for Children Bulletin* contributor Ashley Jane Pennington. *Sweet Illusions* addresses the issue of teen pregnancy by presenting the perspectives of unwed mothers, fathers, and their friends and families. Readers are invited to imagine themselves in the situations of the narrators; blank pages are reserved at the end of each chapter for recording readers' responses. And in *Scorpions,* twelve-year-old Jamal and his best friend Tito are pressured to join the drug-running gang that Jamal's older brother Randy, now imprisoned for murder, used to lead. Writing in *Horn Book,* Margaret Bush observed that

A versatile author, Myers wrote two comic mysteries for 1980's *The Black Pearl and The Ghost; or, One Mystery after Another,* illustrated by Robert Quackenbush.

Jamal and Tito's "predicament is an evocative reflection on the awful web of poverty, drugs, gangs, and guns."

Myers is recognized for providing quality fiction both for and about black young adults. He pointed out in *SAAS* that during his childhood the image of blacks in film, television, and literature was "disturbing. Blacks were portrayed as nonserious people. Perhaps we were sports figures, or hustlers, or comedians, but we were still nonserious." The author continued, "As my books for teenagers gained in popularity I sensed that my soul-searching for my place in the artistic world was taking on an added dimension. As a Black writer I had not only the personal desire to find myself, but the obligation to use my abilities to fill a void." Writing for black children, Myers found, meant more than simply including black characters in his books or having them live in rough, inner-city neighborhoods. The author explained in the *New York Times Book Review* that "it meant understanding the nuances of value, of religion, of dreams. It meant capturing the subtle rhythms of language and movement and weaving it all, the sound and the gesture, the sweat and the prayers, into the recognizable fabric of black life."

In addition to novels that focus on the lives of black teenagers, Myers has penned adventure stories set in exotic locales, such as *The Legend of Tarik, The Hidden Shrine,* and *Ambush in the Amazon,* and nonfiction works such as *The World of Work: A Guide to Choosing a Career* and *Social Welfare.* According to Subryan, "whether he is writing about the ghettos of New York, the remote countries of Africa, or social institutions, Myers captures the essence of the developing experiences of youth. His tone can be funny or serious, but his concern for young people is clearly demonstrated in the basic themes of each work." Critics have affirmed that Myers's books provide valuable messages as well as entertainment for readers of all backgrounds. The author remarked in the *New York Times Book Review* that he especially enjoys writing for young people: "I'm drawn to the eternal promise of childhood, and the flair of the young for capturing the essence of life."

WORKS CITED:

Bush, Margaret, review of *Scorpions, Horn Book,* July/August, 1988, p. 504.
Contemporary Authors New Revisions Series, Volume 20, Gale, 1987, pp. 325-30.
Dictionary of Literary Biography, Volume 33: *Afro-American Fiction Writers after 1955,* Gale, 1984, pp. 199-202.
Flanagan, Kate M., review of *The Young Landlords, Horn Book,* October, 1979, p. 535.
Myers, Walter Dean, "I Actually Thought We Would Revolutionize the Industry," *New York Times Book Review,* November 9, 1986, p. 50.
Myers, Walter Dean, article in *Something about the Author Autobiography Series,* Volume 2, Gale, 1986, pp. 143-56.
Nilsen, Alleen Pace, "Love and the Teenage Reader," *English Journal,* March, 1976, pp. 90-92.
Pennington, Ashley Jane, "Bookshelf: 'It Ain't All for Nothin'," *Interracial Books for Children Bulletin,* No. 4, 1979, p. 18.
Sims, Rudine, "The Image-Makers," *Shadow and Substance: Afro-American Experience in Contemporary Children's Fiction,* National Council of Teachers of English, 1982, pp. 79-102.

FOR MORE INFORMATION SEE:

BOOKS

Children's Literature Review, Gale, Volume 4, 1982, pp. 155-60, Volume 16, 1989, pp. 134-44.

PERIODICALS

New York Times Book Review, September 13, 1987, p. 48; January 22, 1989, p. 29; May 20, 1990, p. 44.
Publishers Weekly, May 13, 1988, p. 277.
Washington Post Book World, July 9, 1989, p. 10.

—Sketch by Michelle M. Motowski

*   *   *

MYERS, Walter M.
See MYERS, Walter Dean

N–O

NEWMAN, Leslea 1955-

PERSONAL: Given name is pronounced "Les-*lee*-a"; born November 5, 1955, in Brooklyn, NY. *Education:* University of Vermont, B.S. (education), 1977; Naropa Institute, certificate in poetics, 1980. *Religion:* Jewish.

ADDRESSES: Office—Write From the Heart, P.O. Box 815, Northampton, MA 01061. *Agent*—Charlotte Raymond, 32 Bradlee Road, Marblehead, MA 01945.

CAREER: Mademoiselle and *Redbook,* New York City, magazine reader, 1982; *Valley Advocate,* Hatfield, MA, journalist and book reviewer, 1983-87; Mount Holyoke College, South Hadley, MA, summer program for high school women, director and teacher of creative writing, 1986-88; Write From the Heart: Writing Workshops for Women, Northampton, MA, founder and director, 1986—. Lectures and conducts creative writing work-

LESLEA NEWMAN

shops at colleges and universities, including Amherst College, Smith College, Swarthmore College, Trinity College, and Yale University.

MEMBER: Society of Children's Book Writers, Authors League of America, Poets and Writers, Feminist Writers Guild, Publishing Triangle, Academy of American Poets.

AWARDS, HONORS: Massachusetts Artists fellowship, 1989.

WRITINGS:

FOR YOUNG PEOPLE

Heather Has Two Mommies, illustrated by Diana Souza, In Other Words/Inland, 1989.
Gloria Goes to Gay Pride, Alyson, 1991.
Belinda's Bouquet, Alyson, 1991.

FOR ADULTS

Just Looking for My Shoes (poetry), Back Door Press, 1980.
Good Enough to Eat (novel), Firebrand Books, 1986.
Love Me Like You Mean It (poetry), HerBooks, 1987.
A Letter to Harvey Milk, Firebrand Books, 1988.
Secrets (short stories), New Victoria, 1990.
Sweet Dark Places (poetry), Herbooks, 1991.
Somebody to Love: A Guide to Loving the Body You Have, Third Side Press, 1991.
In Every Laugh A Tear (novel), New Victoria Publishers, 1992.

Contributor to magazines, including *Backbone, Common Lives, Conditions, Heresies, Sinister Wisdom,* and *Sojourner.*

WORK IN PROGRESS: Fat Chance, a young-adult novel; *Too Far Away to Touch, Close Enough to See,* a picture book about AIDS; *Write from the Heart: A Book for Women Who Want to Write.*

SIDELIGHTS: Leslea Newman is an author, poet, and teacher of creative writing who is strongly motivated by

Heather gives one of her parents a helping hand in Newman's *Heather Has Two Mommies*. (Illustration by Diana Souza.)

her feminist values and strong Jewish heritage. Newman once commented: "Writing continues to teach me, surprise me, and inform me in new and exciting ways." One avenue that she has explored with great success is writing for young children. Newman realized there was a need for books to help lesbian couples who chose to become parents deal with questions common to all children, especially the universal "Where did I come from?" Responding to this need, she has written several books that provide both lesbian parents and the offspring of such non-traditional families books and stories that portray their unique circumstances in a sensitive and informed manner.

Heather Has Two Mommies answers a little girl's questions about where she came from and why she has no "Daddy." Heather's "mommies" describe her conception and birth and provide young Heather with a basic biological understanding of how she came to be, doing so in a loving and sympathetic manner. A reviewer for *Bulletin of the Center for Children's Books* describes the book as "a positive, if idealized, portrait of a loving lesbian family, and it preaches a respect for all kinds of families." As Newman writes in *Heather Has Two Mommies,* "The most important thing about a family is that all the people in it love each other."

WORKS CITED:

Bulletin of the Center for Children's Books, February, 1990, p. 144.
Newman, Leslea, *Heather Has Two Mommies,* In Other Words/Inland, 1989.

NIKOLA-LISA, W. 1951-

PERSONAL: Born June 15, 1951, in Jersey City, NJ; son of William Henry (an engineer) and Dorothy Ethel (a nurse; maiden name, Wormann) Nikola-lisa; married Joan Nikola-lisa, June 6, 1975 (divorced); married Barbara Cooper (a sculptor), August 12, 1988; children: (first marriage) Ylla, Larissa. *Education:* University of Florida, B.A. (religion), 1974, M.Ed., 1976; Montana State University, Ed.D., 1986. *Politics:* Independent. *Religion:* Agnostic.

ADDRESSES: Home—2045 West Farragut St., Chicago, IL 60625. *Office*—National-Louis University, 2840 Sheridan Road, Evanston, IL 60201-1796.

CAREER: World Family School, Bozeman, MT, head teacher, 1976-78; Irving Elementary School, Bozeman, second grade teacher, 1978-82; National-Louis University, Evanston, IL, associate professor, 1986—.

MEMBER: Children's Literature Association, National Council of Teachers of English, Society of Children's Book Writers, Chicago Reading Round Table.

WRITINGS:

Night Is Coming, illustrated by Jamichael Henterly, Dutton, 1991.
1, 2, 3, Thanksgiving, illustrated by Robin Kramer, Albert Whitman, 1991.
Storm, Atheneum, in press.
Tangletalk, Dutton, in press.

W. NIKOLA-LISA

SIDELIGHTS: W. Nikola-lisa told *SATA:* "*Night is Coming* surprised me! I thought at first I was writing about my experiences living in Montana as an adult, but the more I wrote (and revised) the deeper my source became—it was during the time I lived in Texas as a child that became the real source and inspiration for this nostalgic reminiscence.

"*1, 2, 3, Thanksgiving* is pure joy and celebration. Although it went through significant revisions, once I had the entire concept down it was easy to write.... When I look at both books, and other writings similar to them, I see a common thread—I like writing about human relationships in the context of both everyday life and special occasions. I think my strongest writing comes when I allow myself to sink way down into my feelings and explore the world when I was young. There's something intensely intimate about those moments, few and far between as they sometimes are."

FOR MORE INFORMATION SEE:

PERIODICALS

Los Angeles Times Book Review, May 26, 1991, p. 7.
School Library Journal, April, 1991, p. 100.
Smithsonian, November 1991, p. 183.

*   *   *

O'TOOLE, Thomas 1941-

PERSONAL: Born September 10, 1941, in Adrian, MN; son of Philip J. (an electrician) and Dorothy A. (Trautt) O'Toole; married Ann Squier Gates (an administrative assistant), June 10, 1967; children: Rachel Sarah, Phillip Gates. *Education:* St. Mary's College, B.A. (cum laude), 1963; University of Minnesota, M.A., 1967, C.Ph., 1972; Carnegie-Mellon University, Doctor of Arts, 1976. *Politics:* Democratic. *Religion:* Roman Catholic.

ADDRESSES: Home—3223 37th Ave. S., Minneapolis, MN 55406. *Office*—Department of Interdisciplinary Studies, St. Cloud State University, St. Cloud, MN 56301.

CAREER: University of Minnesota General College, Minneapolis, instructor, 1968-72; Western Carolina University, Cullowhee, NC, associate professor, 1972-82; University of Minnesota, director, studies in international development, 1982-84; St. Cloud State University, St. Cloud, MN, director, social studies and African studies, 1985—. University of Bangui, Bangui, Central African Republic, Fulbright Professor, 1979-80; Minnesota International Health Volunteers, Haiti, 1986; Student Project for Amity among Nations, Zimbabwe, 1990; University of Pittsburgh, semester at sea, 1992.

MEMBER: African Studies Association, National Council for the Social Studies, Fulbright Alumni Association (board member, 1989-91).

AWARDS, HONORS: Distinguished Teacher of the Year Award, St. Cloud State University, 1988.

WRITINGS:

The Central African Republic: The Continent's Hidden Heart, Westview Press, 1986.
Historical Dictionary of Guinea (Republic of Guinea/Conakry), second edition, Scarecrow Press, 1987.
(Translator) *Historical Dictionary of the Central African Republic,* second edition, Scarecrow Press, 1992.

"ECONOMICS FOR TODAY" SERIES

The Economic History of the United States, Lerner Publications, 1990.
Global Economics, Lerner Publications, 1991.

"VISUAL GEOGRAPHY" SERIES

Malawi in Pictures, revised edition, Lerner Publications, 1988.
Zimbabwe in Pictures (revision of *Rhodesia in Pictures* by Bernardine Bailey, Sterling, 1974), Lerner Publications, 1988.
Central African Republic in Pictures, revised edition, Lerner Publications, 1989.
Botswana in Pictures, revised edition, Lerner Publications, 1989.
Mali in Pictures, revised edition, Lerner Publications, 1990.

O'Toole also contributed to *Understanding Contemporary Africa,* edited by Gordon and Gordon, Lynne Rienner, 1992; author of "Guinea" entry in *Encyclopedia Britannica.*

WORK IN PROGRESS: Research on the diaspora communities in Africa.

SIDELIGHTS: Thomas O'Toole has revised several volumes in the "Visual Geography" series—books about the countries that make up the continent of

THOMAS O'TOOLE

Africa—which have been noted for both their thoroughness and readability. O'Toole's shift in focus from the white colonial settlers in the original edition of *Zimbabwe in Pictures* to concentrate upon the black majority in his revision volume has pleased critics and educators alike. Reviewer Nancy J. Schmidt calls the book a "straightforward, clearly organized, and balanced presentation of colonial and post-independence history" in her review for *School Library Journal.*

O'Toole has actively studied the ethnohistory of Africa and "third world" nations and supervised academic internships into this region of the world. He told *SATA:* "The opportunities for a working-class person to travel to and work in Africa, afforded [me] by the Peace Corps and Fulbright scholarship, initiated and sustained my whole adult lifetime interest in Africa and African studies."

WORKS CITED:

Schmidt, Nancy J., review of *Zimbabwe in Pictures,* *School Library Journal,* June, 1988, p. 129.

P

PARKER, Mary Jessie 1948-

PERSONAL: Full name, Mary Elizabeth Parker; born December 25, 1948, in Kankakee, IL; daughter of James Greenfield (an Episcopal priest) and Ida Jennie (a teacher; maiden name, Collins) Parker. *Education:* Illinois State University, B.S., 1971; University of Illinois, M.A. (library and information science), 1985. *Politics:* Independent. *Religion:* Episcopal.

MARY JESSIE PARKER

ADDRESSES: Home—1933-C North Bowman Ave., Danville, IL 61832. *Office*—Garfield School, 1101 North Gilbert, Danville, IL 61832.

CAREER: Cissna Park Grade School, Cissna Park, IL, primary teacher, 1971-73; Danville School District 118, Danville, IL, primary teacher, 1973—. Museum of Science and Industry, Chicago, IL, book review committee member, 1991—. Active in local organizations, including Reading is Fundamental (Danville chapter), Illinois State Young Authors (state and local chapters), and Friends of the Danville Public Library.

MEMBER: Society of Children's Book Writers, National Education Association, National Congress of Parents and Teachers, Illinois Reading Council, Chicago Reading Round Table, Delta Kappa Gamma Society International.

WRITINGS:

Night Fire!, illustrated by Lynne Dennis, Scholastic Inc., 1989.
City Storm, illustrated by Dennis, Scholastic Inc., 1990.

Also contributor to *Pennywhistle Press* and *The Volunteer Fireman.*

SIDELIGHTS: Mary Jessie Parker's experience as an elementary school teacher has supplied her with an ever-growing familiarity with children's literature. Coupled with the fact that she was raised in a large family with three older brothers and sisters, Parker's childhood love of writing and the active imaginations of the children who constantly surround her in her classrooms continue to provide her with an endless supply of ideas for books for young readers.

Parker told *SATA:* "Most of my writing goes through a long, arduous 'buried seed' stage. Something I scribble down as notes one day may well stay in that 'seed' form for many months, or even years. Then something I see, hear, do, read, or maybe just think about connects, clicks, or bursts, bringing the idea to the forefront of my thoughts again. Only then does it feel right to work on the story. Rarely do I abandon the idea at that stage.

"I write my versions and revisions—as many as it takes—with a pencil on lined paper. Only I can decipher those messy pages! Eventually I type a rough draft to visualize the story's form, and I practice reading it out loud. It must sound right, too. When it is as good as I can make it, I type the final copy to send to a publisher. There is a feeling of relief and joy when it is completed, but also one of apprehension. Will anyone else like it?"

Parker's first picture book, *Night Fire!*, grew out of the experiences of two of her second-grade students with fires in their homes. Intended as a springboard for class or family discussion of what to do during a house-fire, Parker wrote the book in a simple noun/verb format to make it more easily understood by younger children. *City Storm,* about a storm passing over a city and how it interrupts an outing of school girls, is drawn from Parker's personal recollection of storms during her own childhood.

*   *   *

PARKINSON, Kathy 1954-

PERSONAL: Full name, Kathryn N. Parkinson; born December 2, 1954, in Los Gatos, CA; daughter of William Evan (a doctor) and Joan (a housewife; maiden name, Peterson) Nunn; married Thomas W. Parkinson

They pulled and they pulled and they pulled,

Kathy Parkinson's interest in folk tales resulted in *The Enormous Turnip,* the tale of a giant—and very stubborn—garden vegetable. (Illustration by the author.)

(a consultant), July 15, 1978; children: John Thomas, Sarah Joan, Emily Kathryn. *Education:* University of California, Davis, B.S., 1976; University of California, Los Angeles, M.A. (design), 1979.

ADDRESSES: Home and office—83 Bow Road, Belmont, MA 02178.

CAREER: Free-lance illustrator and designer, 1980—.

MEMBER: Society of Children's Book Writers, Massachusetts Society of Children's Book Writers, Cambridge Illustrators Group.

WRITINGS:

(Reteller; self-illustrated) *The Enormous Turnip,* Albert Whitman, 1985.

ILLUSTRATOR

Sandra Guzzo, *Fox and Heggie,* Albert Whitman, 1983.
E. W. Hildick, *The Case of the Vanishing Ventriloquist,* Macmillan, 1985.
The Farmer in the Dell, Albert Whitman, 1988.
Abby Levine, editor, *Too Much Mush!,* Albert Whitman, 1989.

WORK IN PROGRESS: Writing and illustrating books for children; designing a line of greeting cards.

SIDELIGHTS: Kathy Parkinson once commented: "Primarily I am an illustrator. It was my interest in folk tales that led me to retell and illustrate *The Enormous Turnip.* Although at present writing is secondary to my illustration work, I hope to write more as time goes on." Parkinson enjoys the opportunity that children's picture books provide for showcasing her artistic technique: "I try to capture the feeling and the action of the moment being illustrated. My style tends to be loose so as to give the work a fresh, lively quality."

*   *   *

PINKNEY, Jerry 1939-

PERSONAL: Born December 22, 1939, in Philadelphia, PA; son of James H. (a carpenter) and Williemae (a housewife) Pinkney; married Gloria Maultsby, 1960; children: Troy Bernadette, Jerry Brian, Scott Cannon, Myles Carter. *Education:* Attended Philadelphia Museum College of Art (now University of the Arts), 1957-59. *Hobbies and other interests:* "I am a lover of music, with a large music collection. I enjoy all kinds of music: jazz, classical, rock and pop."

ADDRESSES: Home—41 Furnace Rock Rd., Croton-on-Hudson, NY 10520. *Office*—Department of Art, University of Delaware, Newark, DE 19716.

CAREER: Worked as a designer/illustrator for Rustcraft Greeting Card Co., Dedham, MA, and Barker-Black Studio, Boston, MA, and helped found the Kaleidoscope Studio before opening his own studio, Jerry Pinkney, Inc., Croton-on-Hudson, NY, in 1971. Rhode Island

School of Design, visiting critic, 1969-70, member of visiting committee, 1991; Pratt Institute, Brooklyn, NY, associate professor of illustration, 1986-87; University of Delaware, distinguished visiting professor, 1986-88, associate professor of art, 1988—; University of Buffalo, NY, visiting artist, 1989; Syracuse University, NY, guest faculty, 1989; Fashion Institute of Technology, NY, art mentor, 1989; State University of New York at Buffalo, visiting professor, 1991; guest lecturer at numerous schools and universities; served on judging committees for numerous art and illustration shows. United States Postal Service, Stamp Advisory Committee, 1982—, Quality Assurance Committee, 1986—; served on the NASA Artist Team for the space shuttle Columbia. Designer of commemorative stamps for the United States Postal Service "Black Heritage" series and the "Honey Bee" commemorative envelope. *Exhibitions:* Pinkney has exhibited his works at numerous group and one-man shows throughout the U.S. and in Japan and Italy, including shows at the Brooklyn Museum, the National Center of Afro-American Artists, Boston, the Air and Space Museum, Washington, D.C., and the Boston Museum of Fine Arts.

MEMBER: Society of Illustrators, Graphic Artists Guild, Society of Children's Book Writers.

AWARDS, HONORS: Numerous awards for illustration from the Society of Illustrators; New Jersey Institute of Technology award, 1969, for *Babushka and the Pig;* Council on Interracial Books for Children Award, 1973, Children's Book Showcase selection, 1976, and Jane Addams Book Group Award, 1976, all for *Song of the Trees;* Newbery Medal, *Boston Globe-Horn Book* Honor Book, Jane Addams Book Group Award, and National Book Award finalist, all 1977, and Young Readers Choice award, 1979, all for *Roll of Thunder, Hear My Cry; Childtimes: A Three-Generation Memoir* and

JERRY PINKNEY

Tonweya and the Eagles, and Other Lakota Indian Tales were both American Institute of Graphic Arts Book Show selections, 1980; *Boston Globe/Horn Book* Award, and Carter G. Woodson Award, both 1980, both for *Childtimes: A Three-Generation Memoir;* Outstanding Science Book Award, National Association of Science Teachers, 1980, Carter G. Woodson Award, and Coretta Scott King Award runner-up, both for *Count on Your Fingers African Style;* Christopher Award and Coretta Scott King Award, both 1986, both for *The Patchwork Quilt; Redbook* Award, 1987, for *Strange Animals of the Sea;* Coretta Scott King Award, 1987, for *Half a Moon and One Whole Star;* Coretta Scott King Award, 1988, and Caldecott Honor Book, 1989, both for *Mirandy and Brother Wind;* Caldecott Honor Book, and Coretta Scott King honor book, both 1990, and Golden Sower Award, 1992, all for *The Talking Eggs;* Golden Kite Award, Society of Children's Book Writers, 1990, for *Home Place;* citation for children's literature from Drexel University, 1992; Phladelphia College of Art and Design Alumni Award, 1992; David McCord Children's Literature Citation from Framingham State College, 1992.

ILLUSTRATOR:

Joyce Cooper Arkhurst, reteller, *The Adventures of Spider: West African Folk Tales,* Little, Brown, 1964.

Adeline McCall, *This Is Music,* Allyn & Bacon, 1965.

V. Mikhailovich Garshin, *The Traveling Frog,* McGraw, 1966.

Lila Green, compiler, *Folktales and Fairytales of Africa,* Silver Burdett, 1967.

Ken Sobol, *The Clock Museum,* McGraw, 1967.

Harold J. Saleh, *Even Tiny Ants Must Sleep,* McGraw, 1967.

John W. Spellman, editor, *The Beautiful Blue Jay, and Other Tales of India,* Little, Brown, 1967.

Ralph Dale, *Shoes, Pennies, and Rockets,* L. W. Singer, 1968.

Traudl (pseudonym of Traudl Flaxman), *Kostas the Rooster,* Lothrop, 1968.

Cora Annett, *Homerhenry,* Addison-Wesley, 1969.

Irv Phillips, *The Twin Witches of Fingle Fu,* L. W. Singer, 1969.

Fern Powell, *The Porcupine and the Tiger,* Lothrop, 1969.

Ann Trofimuk, *Babushka and the Pig,* Houghton, 1969.

Thelma Shaw, *Juano and the Wonderful Fresh Fish,* Addison-Wesley, 1969.

K. Sobol, *Sizes and Shapes,* McGraw, 1969.

Francine Jacobs, adapter, *The King's Ditch: A Hawaiian Tale,* Coward, 1971.

(Cover illustration) Virginia Hamilton, *The Planet of Junior Brown,* Macmillan, 1971.

J. C. Arkhurst, *More Adventures of Spider,* Scholastic Book Services, 1972.

Adjai Robinson, *Femi and Old Grandaddie,* Coward, 1972.

Mari Evans, *JD,* Doubleday, 1973.

A. Robinson, *Kasho and the Twin Flutes,* Coward, 1973.

Berniece Freschet, *Prince Littlefoot,* Cheshire, 1974.

Beth P. Wilson, *The Great Minu,* Follett, 1974.

Mildred D. Taylor, *Song of the Trees,* Dial, 1975.

Cruz Martel, *Yagua Days,* Dial, 1976.

Taylor, *Roll of Thunder, Hear My Cry,* Dial, 1976.

Phyllis Green, *Mildred Murphy, How Does Your Garden Grow?,* Addison-Wesley, 1977.

Eloise Greenfield, *Mary McLeod Bethune* (biography), Crowell, 1977.

Verna Aardema, *Ji-Nongo-Nongo Means Riddles,* Four Winds Press, 1978.

L. Green, reteller, *Tales from Africa,* Silver Burdett, 1979.

Rosebud Yellow Robe, reteller, *Tonweya and the Eagles, and Other Lakota Indian Tales,* Dial, 1979.

E. Greenfield and Lessie Jones Little, *Childtimes: A Three-Generation Memoir,* Crowell, 1979.

V. Hamilton, *Jahdu,* Greenwillow, 1980.

Claudia Zaslavsky, *Count on Your Fingers African Style,* Crowell, 1980.

William Wise, *Monster Myths of Ancient Greece,* Putnam, 1981.

Barbara Michels and Bettye White, editors, *Apples on a Stick: The Folklore of Black Children,* Coward, 1983.

Valerie Flournoy, *The Patchwork Quilt,* Dial, 1985.

Crescent Dragonwagon, *Half a Moon and One Whole Star,* Macmillan, 1986.

Barbara Gibson, *Creatures of the Desert World and Strange Animals of the Sea,* edited by Donald J. Crump, National Geographic Society, 1987.

Nancy White Carlstrom, *Wild, Wild Sunflower Child Anna,* Macmillan, 1987.

Julius Lester, *The Tales of Uncle Remus,* Dial, 1988.

J. Lester, *More Tales of Uncle Remus: Further Adventures of Brer Rabbit, His Friends, Enemies and Others,* Dial, 1988.

Julia Fields, *The Green Lion of Zion Street,* Macmillan, 1988.

Pat McKissack, *Mirandy and Brother Wind,* Knopf, 1988.

V. Aardema, *Rabbit Makes a Monkey of Lion,* Dial, 1989.

Robert D. San Souci, *The Talking Eggs,* Dial, 1989.

Marilyn Singer, *Turtle in July,* Macmillan, 1989.

C. Dragonwagon, *Home Place,* Macmillan, 1990.

Jean Marzollo, *Pretend You're a Cat,* Dial, 1990.

J. Lester, *Further Tales of Uncle Remus: The Misadventures of Brer Rabbit, Brer Fox, Brer Wolf, the Doodang, and All the Other Creatures,* Dial, 1990.

Arnold Adoff, *In for Winter, Out for Spring,* Harcourt, 1991.

Zora Neale Hurston, *Their Eyes Were Watching God,* University of Illinois Press, 1991.

The Man with His Heart in a Bucket, Dial, 1991.

Gloria Jean Pinkney, *Back Home,* Dial, 1992.

V. Hamilton, *Drylongso,* Harcourt, 1992.

Contributor of illustrations to textbooks and magazines, including *Boys' Life, Contact, Essence, Post,* and *Seventeen.* Also illustrator of Helen Fletcher's *The Year Around Book,* and of a series of limited edition books for adults published by Franklin Library that includes *Wuthering Heights, The Winthrop Covenant, Early Autumn, Rabbit Run, Gulliver's Travels, Selected Plays,*

Pinkney's illustrations for Pat McKissack's *Mirandy and Brother Wind* have been praised for harmonizing with the book's folk language and rural setting.

Tom Jones, The Flowering of New England, These Thirteen, The Covenant, Lolita, Rabbit Redux, and *The Education of Henry Adams.*

ADAPTATIONS: The Patchwork Quilt, Half a Moon and One Whole Star and *Yagua Days* were presented on *Reading Rainbow,* PBS-TV.

SIDELIGHTS: From the day he began copying drawings from comic books and photo magazines, illustrator Jerry Pinkney pushed himself to be the best artist he could be. Pinkney's drive has made him, some four decades later, a nationally-recognized illustrator of children's books, as well as a gifted designer and illustrator of stamps, posters, calendars, and books for adults. Much of his work pays tribute to his African-American heritage, but the artist has illustrated books about Hispanic-Americans and Native Americans as well. Expressing his commitment to multi-cultural works in his autobiographical essay in *Something about the Author Autobiography Series* (*SAAS*), Pinkney says "these books are needed and are my contribution in terms of my concern for this country and the issue of racism."

Pinkney was born in 1939 to a large family living on an all-black block in the Germantown section of Philadelphia, Pennsylvania. His neighborhood and extended family provided the young Pinkney with all the entertainment he needed, for the children were always involved in the many family projects, ranging from all-day barbecues to summer-long house raising ventures. He discovered drawing at an early age, however, and remembers in *SAAS* that "I was always caught in the middle between the thing that I wanted to do, which would be to sit and draw, and the other side of me that really wanted to be more social; and yet, being social was more work for me." Pinkney's artistic urges were rewarded in school, where his teachers and fellow students admired and encouraged his work, but he also remembers that "somehow I hooked into that competitive mode so that it became very important that I succeed." This "competitive mode" drove his performance throughout the rest of his schooling, and though Pinkney received consistently high marks in his classes, he was plagued by doubts about his abilities and his intelligence. He says in *SAAS* that he was "unable to make a connection between what I thought about myself and how others felt about my achievements."

Pinkney's mother actively encouraged his study of art, and his father, though skeptical, supported his decision to continue pursuing art studies into high school as well. Dobbins Vocational High School had an excellent program in commercial art, and Pinkney received encouragement and guidance from his teachers and peers. Upon graduation, he applied for and received a four-year scholarship to the Philadelphia Museum College of Art, becoming the first in his family to go to college. There he met and married his wife, Gloria, and established a network of contacts that would support him throughout his artistic career, as well as land him his first job with a greeting card company near Boston.

In Boston, Pinkney was involved in the expanding civil rights movement, and as a result of the wide variety of people he met through these activities, Pinkney says in *SAAS* that "I worked toward being a well-rounded artist and I chose not to focus on one style or put all my energies into one visual discipline."

Pinkney's commitment to expanding his artistic range left him frustrated with his job, so with some friends he founded the Kaleidoscope Studio, where he worked for a little over two years before starting a studio of his own—the Jerry Pinkney Studio. Though he kept busy doing advertising and textbook illustration, Pinkney most loved doing illustrations for books and tried to do at least one or two a year. "The marriage of typography and illustration was always very important to me and the picture-book area provided me with the opportunity to illustrate and design," he comments in his autobiographical sketch. Fredrick Woodard, interviewed by Donnarae MacCann and Olga Richard in *Wilson Library Bulletin,* notes that in *Mirandy and Brother Wind* the "stunning color and movement [of Pinkney's illustrations] are in perfect harmony with the beauty of the book's folk language." The book, which won the the Coretta Scott King Award and was named a Caldecott Honor Book, tells the story of a young girl convinced that she will dance with the wind at an upcoming dance. Valerie Wilson Wesley, reviewing the book in the *New York Times Book Review,* says that the combination of text and pictures "captures the texture of rural life and culture 40 years after the end of slavery."

Soon Pinkney had even more book illustration offers because, he explains in *SAAS,* "the late sixties and early seventies brought an awareness of black writers. Publishers sought out black artists to illustrate black subject matter and the work of black writers. And there I was—it was almost like a setup." Pinkney was soon creating illustrations for a wide variety of projects, including African-American historical calendars, a number of limited-edition books for Franklin Library and, in 1983, a set of stamps for the U.S. Postal Service's Black Heritage series that would include Harriet Tubman, Martin Luther King, Jr., Scott Joplin, and Jackie Robinson. Pinkney comments in *SAAS:* "I was trying to use these projects as vehicles to address the issues of being an African-American and the importance of African-American contributions to society.... I wanted to show that an African-American artist could certainly make it in this country on a national level in the visual graphic arts. And I wanted to show my children the possibilities that lay ahead for them. That was very important. I wanted to be a strong role model for my family and for other African-Americans."

During this period, Pinkney got involved with a number of book projects that brought him a great deal of critical attention. *The Patchwork Quilt,* written by Valerie Flournoy, tells of a wonderful relationship between a grandmother and a granddaughter and celebrates the strength of the black family. Pinkney found people to model the relationships described in the book, and he created his drawings from these modeling sessions. The

Using a mixture of soft colors and finely-drawn images, Pinkney depicts the world of a sleepy little girl. (Illustration from

Susan lies in bed, not sleeping.
Not yet sleeping, but does she doze,
Blinking as the curtain blows?
Yes, yes, yes, she does, sleep, Susan, sleep.

Half a Moon and One Whole Star by Crescent Dragonwagon.)

book won a number of awards, including two that were very important to the illustrator: the Christopher Award and the Coretta Scott King Award. Pinkney carried his live model concept further in crafting the illustrations for Julius Lester's retelling of *The Tales of Uncle Remus.* "After a number of preliminary drawings, I realized that the answer was for me to model and pose as the animals," he says in *SAAS.* "And that's what I did. I got dressed up in vests and baggy pants and I took on the posture and attitude of whatever that animal might be." June Jordan, reviewing the book in *New York Times Book Review,* comments that "every single illustration ... is fastidious, inspired and a marvel of delightful imagination."

Although Pinkney is now an accomplished artist and teaches art to others at numerous universities, he has not lost the drive to improve that launched his career. He tells *SAAS* that his future goals are "to have my work continually grow and to have something artistic to put back into the pot. Another goal is to continue acting as a role model, sharing my time with young artists and children. As for the work itself, my interest is in doing more multi-cultural projects."

WORKS CITED:

Jordan, June, "A Truly Bad Rabbit," *New York Times Book Review,* May 17, 1987, p. 32.
McCann, Donnarae and Olga Richard, interview with Fredrick Woodard, "Picture Books for Children," *Wilson Library Bulletin,* April, 1989, pp. 92-93.
Pinkney, Jerry, essay in *Something about the Author Autobiography Series,* Volume 12, Gale, 1991, pp. 249-266.
Wesley, Valerie Wilson, review of *Mirandy and Brother Wind, New York Times Book Review,* November 20, 1988.

FOR MORE INFORMATION SEE:

BOOKS

Cederholm, Theresa Dickason, compiler and editor, *Afro-American Artists: A Bibliographical Directory,* Boston Public Library, 1973.
Kingman, Lee and others, compilers, *Illustrators of Children's Books: 1957-1966,* Horn Book, 1968.
Rollock, Barbara, *Black Authors and Illustrators of Children's Books,* Garland, 1988.
Twelve Black Artists from Boston, Brandeis University, 1969.

PERIODICALS

American Artist, May/June, 1982.
Communication Art, May/June, 1975.
Horn Book, March/April, 1988.
New York Times, February 26, 1978; December 13, 1988.

—*Sketch by Tom Pendergast*

PITTMAN, Helena Clare 1945-

PERSONAL: Born January 26, 1945, in Brooklyn, NY; daughter of Jacob (a scholar and teacher) and Florence (a librarian; maiden name, Bailenson) Steinberg; children: Theo (daughter), Galen (son). *Education:* Pratt Institute, B.F.A., 1969; attended Parsons School of Design. *Religion:* "Jewish/Catholic."

ADDRESSES: Home—45 Hemlock Ave., Huntington, NY 11743. *Agent*—Edythea Ginis Selman, 14 Washington Pl., New York, NY 10003.

CAREER: Author and illustrator. State University of New York, Farmingdale, assistant professor, 1983—; Parsons School of Design, New York City, instructor, 1984—. Teacher with Huntington Township Art League; guest speaker at libraries and schools.

MEMBER: Jean Fritz Writers Workshop.

AWARDS, HONORS: Chicago Book Clinic Award for Design and Illustration, and Children's Choice List, both 1988, for *The Gift of the Willows.*

WRITINGS:

Once When I Was Scared, Dutton, 1988.
Uncle Phil's Diner, Carolrhoda, in press.

SELF-ILLUSTRATED

A Grain of Rice, Hastings House, 1986.
Martha and the Nightbird, Caedmon, 1986.
The Gift of the Willows, Carolrhoda, 1988.
Miss Hindy's Cats, Carolrhoda, 1990.
Gerald-Not-Practical, Carolrhoda, 1990.
A Dinosaur for Gerald, Carolrhoda, 1990.
Counting Jennie, Carolrhoda, in press.

HELENA CLARE PITTMAN

Pittman's interest in mixing colorful illustrations with classic folk themes is evident in her self-illustrated *The Gift of the Willows*.

ILLUSTRATOR

Milly Jane Limmer, *Where Will You Swim Tonight?*, Albert Whitman, 1991.

ADAPTATIONS: Once When I Was Scared was made into a video for the McGraw-Hill Library series.

WORK IN PROGRESS: The Shadow Dog, a story about the loss of a dog; *The Call of the Dove,* the story of a young Buddhist disciple in Tibet; *A Birthday for Ruthie; Agatha Upside Down;* and *One Quiet Morning.*

SIDELIGHTS: Helena Clare Pittman told *SATA:* "I was an artist from childhood. My father was amazed at the pictures I drew, sometimes on the paper he brought home for me from the school where he taught, or on the paper napkins at the dinner table. Because I loved and admired my father, his respect for my drawings awed me and filled me with a sense of discovery. The affirmation from my father woke me up to the gift I had."

Pittman's artistic ability was evident to teachers and friends who called upon her to create posters, stage sets, and other illustrations. "By that time I had begun to experience a very clear sense that I would have to live my life as an artist or I would not be happy," Pittman said. As time went on she met other artists and explored new and different art forms; she also discovered museums. "This was a very exciting time in my life," Pittman explained, "because it was then that I discovered the French impressionists and post-impressionists at the Metropolitan Museum of Art, and later the American painters of the Ash Can School, particularly Edward Hopper, at the Museum of Modern Art and the Whitney. I studied the work of other painters, not by reading about them, but by looking very closely at their brush strokes, and even the eraser marks in their drawings."

Despite her father's early encouragement, Pittman encountered resistance from her parents when she decided to pursue art as a career. "Looking back, I can see how worried my parents were about me," Pittman related. "Life can be very confusing particularly when a young person is trying to figure out who they are! But my parents' caution which seemed an obstacle at the time was guidance that has helped my life greatly." She agreed to study art education along with painting so she would have an easier time finding work. "Teaching has provided a much-needed balance to the solitary studio life that being an artist entails, and the vigorous interchange with students is very enriching," Pittman noted. She teaches drawing, design, color theory, painting, and illustration at the Parsons School of Design, the State University of New York, and the Huntington Township Art League, an association of artists on Long Island.

Pittman credits the birth of her son for her newfound understanding of childhood. "I was very young when I had my first child, my daughter," Pittman related. "Thirteen years passed until the birth of my son. Paradoxically, by that time I was ready to reopen the doors of childhood and explore." When her son was born, "a very surprising and exciting thing happened," Pittman said. "I put aside my work for several years and happened into a magical world of being with my son and experiencing the world through the eyes of a child.... It was a way to share his wonder. When I picked up my paints again it was to paint him and scenes of stories that I had told and made up about him." The experience led her to create her first children's book, *A Grain of Rice.*

Pittman still enjoys and seeks out the perspective of youngsters. "Though my own children are now grown, happily the stories I've written have kept me in touch with many children, since I present my work at schools, camps, and libraries," Pittman commented. "Reading my stories to children is one of my deepest pleasures. It makes working in the quiet of my studio, writing and painting pictures sometimes into the wee hours of the morning when my eyes are bleary, most definitely worthwhile. It is then that my spirit, the deepest self I know, is free to speak, and how I love to speak this way to children! Children are the ones in whom imagination lives unfettered."

*   *   *

PLACE, Robin (Mary) 1926-

PERSONAL: Born May 29, 1926, in Blackheath, London, England; daughter of John Alexander (an accountant) and Gladys Marie (an education editor; maiden name, Biddle) Place; married Denis Kenward (an aeronautical engineer), July 22, 1950; children: Robert Denis de Vitre, Rachel Evelyn Mary. *Education:* Newnham College, Cambridge, M.A. (with first-class honors), 1947. *Politics:* Liberal. *Religion:* Church of England. *Hobbies and other interests:* Gardening, painting, playing bridge.

ADDRESSES: Home—Little Sharps, Piltdown, Uckfield, East Sussex TN22 3XG, England.

CAREER: Writer of archaeology books, 1949—. Ministry of Agriculture and Fisheries, London, England, assistant principal, 1947-48; St.-George-in-the-East, East London, teacher, 1948; Horniman Museum, London, first education officer, 1949-52. Lecturer in adult education on various archaeological subjects for LCC, University of London, University of Sussex, United States International University (Sussex campus), and Local Authorities in Wimbledon (London), Richmond, and Kingston, Surrey, 1947-89; assistant director of two archaeological excavations in Wiltshire and Oxfordshire, England, for the Ministry of Works/Department of the Environment in the 1960s and 1970s.

MEMBER: Kingston upon Thames Archaeological Society (president, 1970-79; honorary vice-president, 1980—), Society of Antiquaries of London (fellow), London Prehistoric Society (council member, 1968-71), Lewes Archaeology Group (chairman, 1979-82), Sussex Archaeological Society (council member, 1980-89).

AWARDS, HONORS: Medieval Britain was listed among the Book Trust Children's Books of the Year of 1990.

WRITINGS:

Britain before History, Rockliffe, 1951.
Our First Homes, Rockliffe, 1951.
Down to Earth (also see below), Rockliffe, 1955.
Finding Fossil Man, Rockliffe, 1957.
Prehistoric Britain, Longman, 1959.
(Co-translator) K. Jazdzewski, *Poland,* Thames & Hudson, 1965.

ROBIN PLACE

Introduction to Archaeology, Newnes-Butterworth, 1968.
(Editor) *Young Archaeologist Series,* Hart-Davis, 1968-71.
A Long Time Ago (twelve booklets), Ginn, 1970.
The Celts, Macdonald Educational, 1977.
The Vikings, Longman, 1980.
Search for the Past (eight booklets), Ginn, 1985.
Vikings—Fact and Fiction, Cambridge University Press, 1985.
Romans—Fact and Fiction, Cambridge University Press, 1988.
Medieval Britain, Wayland, 1989.
Saxon Villages, Wayland, 1989.
Adventure and Encounter, Ginn, 1991.
Exploration and Encounters, Ginn, 1991.
Clues from the Past, Wayland, 1993.

Also author of scripts for British Broadcasting Corporation Schools Television and filmstrips based on her books. Contributor to *Nature,* edited by James Fisher, Julian Huxley, and J. Bronowski, Macdonald, 1960; *Concise Encyclopaedia of Archaeology,* edited by Leonard Cottrell, Hutchinson, 1960; *The Emergence of Man,* Low, Marston, 1976; and *Ancient Civilizations,* Low, Marston, 1978. Contributor of articles and book reviews to periodicals, including *Amateur Historian, Antiquity, Guide, Guider, History Today, Man, Manchester Guardian, Pictorial Education, Practical Junior Teacher, Preparatory Schools Review, Schoolmaster, Tablet,* and *Times Educational Supplement. Down to Earth* has also been published in Braille.

WORK IN PROGRESS: "Am planning to write magazine articles on archaeology or any books that may come my way. I have reported on human bones from excavations for the Department of the Environment for some years and am still doing this intermittently."

SIDELIGHTS: Robin Place told *SATA:* "My mother started my interest in archaeology by taking me to the British Museum when I was very young. I loved the Egyptian room with the mummies. She also took me to the Horniman Museum, where one day I was to become Education Officer and show parties of children all the exciting things there." Place studied archaeology at Cambridge University and said she enjoyed it "so much that I have tried to pass it on to those who did not have the opportunity to study there, through adult education lecturing, for forty-one years.... It is a challenge to try to express complex material for adult students or schoolchildren to understand."

"I feel that the development of ancient humans and civilisation should be a more basic part of school education," Place continued. "It is tragic that so many sites have been lost in town and country through lack of funds for excavation before development."

Place discovered a surprising coincidence when she met her future husband, Denis Kenward. "I was fascinated by his having been born at Piltdown, in Sussex," she said. "The notorious Piltdown Man was found on his grandfather's land at Barkham Manor." Piltdown Man, at first thought to be a genuine archaeological find dating from the early Pleistocene, was later proven to be a hoax. After she and Kenward married, Place began writing books for children about archaeology. They moved to Piltdown in 1979 and took up residence in the house where her husband's aunt had lived until her death at age 91. "She well remembered the discovery of Piltdown Man," Place said. "When it was discovered to be a fake, she appeared in a television programme."

Besides writing, Place's interests include keeping a garden. "We work very hard gardening," she said. "We keep bees and grow a lot of our own fruit and vegetables. I fit weeding and freezing in with my writing. It is very hard shutting myself in my study with my typewriter when the sun is shining and there is weeding to be done. But I have to be firm with myself." She also enjoys visiting schools to talk with students and hear their reactions to her stories in progress. In addition, she presents lectures on subjects of archaeological interest, such as Stonehenge, and participates in village activities with her husband. "It's strange how getting older seems to mean finding more than ever to do," Place commented. "But most of all I enjoy writing. It's such a challenge trying to put a complicated archaeological subject into simple words so that children and people who don't know anything about archaeology can understand it. I hope my readers enjoy finding out about the past as much as I do."

*   *   *

POPPEL, Hans 1942-

PERSONAL: Born March 7, 1942, in Kempten, Germany; son of Christian Robert Hans (a civil engineer) and Sigrid (a housewife; maiden name, von Cancrin) Poppel; married Ann Ketzner, June 18, 1969 (divorced October 31, 1987); married Stephanie Roeder (a psy-chologist), January 9, 1988; children: (first marriage) Felix. *Education:* Attended Academy of Fine Arts, Munich, Germany, three years. *Religion:* Protestant. *Hobbies and other interests:* Jazz piano.

ADDRESSES: Home—861 Barrett's Mill Rd., Concord, MA 01742.

CAREER: Bavarian State Opera, Munich, Germany, assistant stage designer, 1959-62; Municipal Theatre, Heidelberg, Germany, stage and costume designer, 1962-63; Hessian State Theatre, Wiesbaden, Germany, stage and costume designer, 1963-66; Municipal Theatre, St. Gallen, Switzerland, stage designer, 1969-70; illustrator of books for children, 1978—. Has worked as a jazz pianist. Active in citizens' initiative groups, 1971-74. *Exhibitions:* Poppel's work has appeared in group exhibitions, including Annual '84, Illustrators of Children's Books, International Children's Book Fair, Bologna, Italy, 1984; Exhibition of International Children's Book Illustrators, Otani Memorial Art Museum, Nishinomija City, Japan, 1984; Exhibition of Original Pictures of International Children's Picture Books, Shiko-Sha Co. Ltd./Maruzen Co. Ltd., Tokyo, Japan, 1984; Biennale d'Illustrations (BIB), Bratislava, Czechoslovakia, 1985; Annual Exhibition of Picture Book Illustrations, Museum der Stadt Troisdorf, Germany, 1986-87; Tenth Original Art Exhibition Celebrating the Fine Art of Children's Book Illustration, Society of Illustrators, Museum of American Illustration, New York, 1990; and First Wonders: The Fine Art of Illustrating Books for Children, Park Avenue Atrium, New York, 1991.

MEMBER: New England Authors and Illustrators of Children's Books, Association for Copyright Protection of Authors and Artists (Germany).

AWARDS, HONORS: Book of the Month award from the German Academy of Children's Literature, 1983,

HANS POPPEL

for *Erklaer mir die Musik,* 1986, for *Zauberbuehne Oper,* 1987, for *Die Geschichte von den Feigen,* and 1990, for *Ein wunderlicher Rat;* Honour List, German Children's Literature Prize, 1985, for *Scheint der Mond hell auf das Haus,* and 1986, for *Zauberbuehne Oper;* Honour List, Hans Christian Andersen Award, International Board on Books for Young People, 1986, for *Scheint der Mond hell auf das Haus;* Best Latin-American Publications award, Banco del Libro, Venezuela, 1990, for *Que Ruido!* (Spanish translation of *Ein Wunderlicher Rat*).

ILLUSTRATOR:

Eberhard Spangenberg, *So einfach ist Theater* (title means "So Simple Is Theater"), Ellermann, 1979.

Luise Rinser, *Das Geheimnis des Brunnens,* Thienemann, 1979.

Eveline Hasler, *Hexe Lakritze,* Rowohlt, 1981.

Dorothee Kreusch-Jacob, *Das Liedmobil,* Ellermann, 1981.

(With Helmut Lesch and Katrin Behrend) *Erklaer mir die Musik,* R. Piper & Co. Verlag, 1982, new edition published as *Musik Musik Musik,* Arena, 1989.

Margarete Kubelka, *Ich werde Oma fragen,* Ellermann, 1983, published in English as *Abracadabra!,* Hutchinson, 1983.

Kubelka, *Mein Freund Fuechslein,* Ellermann, 1984.

Illona Bodden, *Scheint der Mond hell auf das Haus,* Ellermann, 1984, translation by Robert and Rita

Kimber published as *When the Moon Shines Brightly on the House,* Barron's, 1985.

Kreusch-Jacob, *Zauberbuehne Oper,* Ellermann, 1985.

Siegfried Aust, *Frei wie ein Vogel—Von Ikarus zum Weltraumgleiter,* Carl Ueberreuter, 1986, translation by Amy Gelman published as *Flight! Free as a Bird,* Lerner Publications, 1991.

Renate Welsh, *Ein Geburtstag fuer Kitty,* Deutscher Taschenbuch Verlag, 1986.

Aliana Brodmann, *Die Geschichte von den Feigen,* Ellermann, 1987.

Kreusch-Jacob, *Da huepft der Frosch den Berg hinauf,* Ellermann, 1987.

Christl Pfister, *Schrumpelhexe Warzenschoen,* Rowohlt, 1988.

Brodmann, *Ein wunderlicher Rat,* Ellermann, 1989, translation by Brodmann and David Fillingham published as *Such a Noise!,* Kane/Miller, 1989.

Dirk Walbrecker, *Bennys Hut,* Thienemann, 1990, translation by Linda Wagner Tyler published as *Benny's Hat,* Atomium Books, 1990.

Karen Glennon, *Miss Eva and the Red Balloon,* Simon & Schuster, 1990, textbook edition, Harcourt, 1991.

Elke Kahlert, *Einmal Wolkenkuckucksheim und zurueck,* Rowohlt, 1991.

Nortrud Boge-Erli and Kreusch-Jacob, *Potifar mit Wuschelhaar,* Ellermann, 1991.

Joan W. Blos, *A Seed a Flower a Minute an Hour,* Simon & Schuster, 1992.

WORK IN PROGRESS: Illustrations for several children's books.

SIDELIGHTS: Hans Poppel told *SATA:* "At age four I began to draw. Everything that moved interested me: horses, trains, dogs, automobiles, birds, witches, Punch and Judy characters, clouds and people. I drew on little pieces of paper. Sometimes I cut out the figures and built a tiny puppet theater. For hours, I played with the paper cut-outs. I had such a longing to be as little as those figures, preferably to crawl inside them.

"At age eight I began to play the piano. I was lucky to have a piano teacher who was very patient with me. When I made mistakes, I didn't stop playing. I simply continued on, improvising as I went. She would say, 'It was very nice, what you just played, but it was not Mozart.' These lessons were very important because they led me to a deeper understanding of improvisation. I learned to relate to ideas and forms in a free and playful way. My heart opened up to Jazz.

"At seventeen I met my mentor, Helmut Juergens, who would decisively influence my artistic development. He was the head of stage design for the Bavarian State Opera in Munich as well as a professor at the Academy of Fine Arts. I began to explore the magical world of opera and experience for myself what went on in front of and behind the scenes. Seeing, listening, experiencing, creating—the magic stage would become the playground of my wishes and dreams. I became a stage designer and worked for theaters in Germany and Switzerland. The world of theater—of lights, colors,

Max tries to hide from his neighbor Mr. Smith, an intimidating man with a bad temper. (Illustration by Poppel from *Abracadabra!,* written by Margarete Kubelka.)

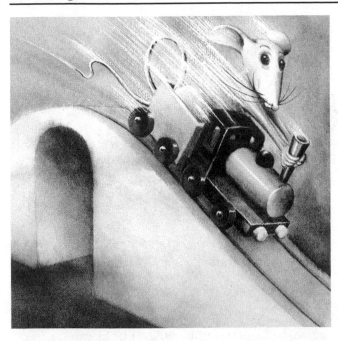

Magic and mayhem are the key themes behind Poppel's illustrations for Illona Bodden's *When the Moon Shines Brightly on the House.*

movement and space—is closely related to the imaginative world of children's toys and books.

"*So Simple Is Theatre* by Eberhard Spangenberg was the first children's book that I designed and illustrated when I was 37 years old. I thought it should be made like stage flats—out of wood, cloth, cardboard, tin and so on. My publisher, Christa Spangenberg, threw up her hands, saying, 'We're talking about a *book* here!' I heard her. What followed was a real book. Many others came after. It was the beginning of a lively collaboration and a friendship which has continued to this day.

"Throughout my life, my father had watched my career as an artist with some concern. One day, when he was quite old, I told him that, in creating children's books, I had found my life's work. He stared at me and, after a long pause, said, 'Children's books? Son, when will you ever grow up?' This question of my father's has often given me pause to think. Strangely, perhaps within his question lies the secret—how to grow up without being a grown-up. The older I grow, the more this becomes my task."

R

READER, Dennis 1929-

PERSONAL: Born May 28, 1929, in Peterborough, Cambridgeshire, England; son of George William (a furniture maker) and Eva Mary (a milliner; maiden name, Colls) Reader; married Anita Helen Edgley (a tax inspector). *Education:* All Souls' Catholic Convent School, England. *Politics:* "I would not put my faith in any politician or political party. They all betray one's trust!" *Religion:* "*Not* Catholic, but a degree of sympathy with their religion as I have with many religions. I have a someways private but solid belief in God." *Hobbies and other interests:* "Creating and planting a garden. Walking and gazing at the beauty of the English Lake District. Music from Mozart to Art Tatum. Getting excited about football!"

ADDRESSES: Home—Kiln House, The Paddock, Woodnewton, county of Northamptonshire, near Peterborough, Cambridgeshire PE8 5EL, England.

CAREER: Author and illustrator of children's books. Apprentice in general and newspaper printing to the Sharman Group, 1944-50; children's comic strip artist, 1950-53; graphic designer, illustrator, and studio manager, Perkins Diesel Engines Group, 1953-80.

WRITINGS:

SELF-ILLUSTRATED

A Lovely Bunch of Coconuts, Ideals, 1989.
I Want One!, Ideals, 1990.
Butterfingers, Houghton, 1991.
Fed Up!, HarperCollins, 1991.
Joe Useless, HarperCollins, 1993.
Into the Jungle, HarperCollins, 1993.

ILLUSTRATOR

Diana Webb, *The Monster Pot Plant,* Hodder & Stoughton, 1989.

ADAPTATIONS: A Lovely Bunch of Coconuts was presented by British Independent Television in picture format with narration for children's program *Cue George,* 1990; *I Want One!* was presented by the British Broadcasting Company (BBC-TV) for children's picture book program *Harum Scarum,* 1991.

SIDELIGHTS: Dennis Reader told *SATA:* "I was hauled screaming and complaining to school at the age of five." At first frightened at the prospect of attending a Catholic school, he soon found that it provided just the right atmosphere to encourage curiosity. "As schools should, All Souls awakened my enquiring mind," Reader commented. "I began with wondering what sort of hair, what colour, lay beneath the Nuns' huge seagull-winged hats, hats which incidentally I still remember would painfully prod me in the ear and eye when they

DENNIS READER

There was once a boy called Boris who had nearly everything. His mother and father gave him

nearly everything, because whenever Boris wanted anything he screamed very loudly until he got it.

Reader's self-illustrated tale about a selfish child was adapted by the British Broadcasting Company's picture book program *Harum Scarum*. (Illustration from *I Want One*.)

leaned over me to suggest that my spelling left a lot to be desired."

Reader's mother sparked his interest in art through her work with watercolors. "Seeing her at work in her every spare minute convinced me that that was what everybody did so I should do it too," he said. "So a way of life it became."

True to his name, Reader read "quite hefty tomes" early on. His grandfather was blind and Reader read to him, often not comprehending the books, but as he said, "it taught me all those mile-long words." He discovered an interest in America when he read one of his all-time favorite books, *Gone with the Wind,* around age eight. "I think that *Gone with the Wind,* even at that early age, transported my imagination into other worlds, across an ocean, into another era, as nothing else had . . . . It was *GWTW,* because it was so wondrously entertaining, that encouraged me to read and read." Around the same time, another American influence came along that, like *Gone with the Wind,* was to have a lasting effect on Reader. The "Sunday Supplement Comic Pages," which arrived in England from the United States periodically, included the work of "the marvelous 'Krazy Kat's' George Herriman and the vastly underrated Cliff Sterrett of 'Polly and Her Pals,' two giants of their craft," Reader noted. The comics shaped Reader's ideas of "mass-market art," a concept he embraced. "There is a too-popular belief that if a picture or a book is loved and

enjoyed by all it cannot be any good. It is a snobbery built on envy," Reader declared.

His career as an author and illustrator of children's books began when Reader was fifty-one. He had worked as a graphic designer for almost thirty years, but was laid off during the recession in 1980. When he found himself suddenly unemployed, Reader decided to act on his life-long wish to create children's books. "I had always wanted to produce books for children, a world of colour and imagination with no real boundaries," he said. *A Lovely Bunch of Coconuts* was his first success. Since then he has continued to produce children's books based on his early influences. "*GWTW* and the Sunday Comic Supplements [have] successfully come together," Reader noted. "I want to be as bright, as bouncy, as entertaining as they have been. An odd partnership but I am sure they are the dreams, the influences that have stayed with me, spurred me on through disappointments and rejections, the blocks of creativity."

*   *   *

RELF, Patricia 1954-

PERSONAL: Born July 28, 1954, in Caracas, Venezuela; daughter of George O. (a geologist and oil company executive) and Hannah (a homemaker; maiden name, Moseley) Relf; married William F. Hanavan (a physician), March 28, 1981; children: Louise, Emily. *Educa-*

tion: Cornell University, A.B., 1976; Western Michigan University, 1990—.

ADDRESSES: Home—6301 Winding Lane, Richland, MI 49083.

CAREER: Random House Books for Young Readers, New York City, editorial trainee, 1976-78; *Sesame Street* magazine, Children's Television Workshop, New York City, associate editor, 1978-79; free-lance writer, 1979—.

WRITINGS:

Show and Tell, Western Publishing/Sesame Street Books, 1980.
That New Baby, Western Publishing, 1980.
Muppet Manners, Random House, 1981.
The First Day of School, Western Publishing, 1981.
The Adventures of Superman, Western Publishing, 1982.
Follow the Zookeeper, Western Publishing, 1984.
Big Work Machines, Western Publishing, 1984.
The Big Golden Book of Boats and Ships, Western Publishing, 1991.

Also author of educational computer games for Scholastic, Inc., National Audubon Society, and Tom Snyder Productions; author of workbooks for Scholastic, Inc.

WORK IN PROGRESS: Farm Animals, a Golden Tell-a-Tale Book; *The Barnyard Mystery;* and *Hurry, Hurry!,* a Little Golden Sound Book.

SIDELIGHTS: Patricia Relf told *SATA:* "Our family moved a lot when my brother and I were young—Houston, Pittsburgh, and five years each in London, England, and Calgary, Alberta [Canada]. We traveled all over, saw lots of interesting things, and learned to be curious. That's what makes writing nonfiction so much fun—the chance to learn about a subject that is completely new to you."

*　　*　　*

RHUE, Morton
See STRASSER, Todd

*　　*　　*

RICKARD, Graham 1949-

PERSONAL: Born February 7, 1949, in Cornwall, England; son of Albany (in grocery sales) and Muriel (in accounts; maiden name, Bate) Rickard; divorced; children: Daniel. *Education:* University College, Cardiff, B.A.; postgraduate diploma. *Politics:* "Leftish." *Religion:* Pantheist. *Hobbies and other interests:* Photography.

ADDRESSES: Home—19 Long Park Corner, Ditchling, East Sussex BN6 8UX, England.

CAREER: Writer. Has worked as an archaeologist, photographer, fisherman, postman, farmer, driver, building laborer, decorator, fairground worker, musician, and stage-set builder. Currently training local schoolchildren in cycling proficiency.

MEMBER: Canon Professional Services.

AWARDS, HONORS: The Chernobyl Catastrophe was nominated for the Book Trust Book of the Year for Children award in 1989.

WRITINGS:

Famous Names in Popular Music, Wayland, 1980.
A Day with a Racing Driver, Wayland, 1981.
A Day with a T.V. Producer, Wayland, 1981.
Great Press Barons, Wayland, 1981.
A Day with a Dancer, Wayland, 1983.
A Day with a Postman, Wayland, 1984.
A Day with a Musician, Wayland, 1984.
The Electricity Showroom, Wayland, 1984.
How Places Got Their Names, Young Library, c. 1985.
Working for a Garage, photographs by Tim Humphrey, Wayland, 1985.
(And illustrator) *Working for Yourself,* Wayland, 1985.
Robots, Wayland, 1985.
Spacecraft, Wayland, 1985.
Airports, Wayland, 1986.
Bridges, Bookwright, 1986.
Helicopters, Wayland, 1986.
Focus on Rice, Wayland, 1986.
Focus on Silver, Wayland, 1987.
Prisons and Punishment, Wayland, 1987.
Canals, Wayland, 1987.
Focus on Diamonds, Wayland, 1987.

GRAHAM RICKARD

Tunnels, Wayland, 1988.
Building Homes, Wayland, 1988.
The Chernobyl Catastrophe, illustrated by Peter Bull, Wayland, 1989.
Mobile Homes, Lerner Publications, 1989.
Farming, Wayland, 1989.
Homes in Space, Wayland, 1989.
Focus on Cocoa, Wayland, 1989.
Let's Look at Tractors, illustrated by Clifford Meadway, Wayland, 1989.
Focus on Building Materials, Wayland, 1989.
Let's Look at Volcanoes, illustrated by Carolyn Scrace, Wayland, 1989.
Norman Castles, illustrated by Michael Bragg, Wayland, 1989.
Water Energy, Wayland, 1990.
Wind Energy, Wayland, 1991.
Geothermal Energy, Wayland, 1991.
Oil, Wayland, 1992.
Bricks, Wayland, in press.

Also author of *Focus on Glass* and *Solar Energy* for Wayland. Photographer for *Miss Cole Is a Policewoman,* Young Library, 1987. Contributor of articles and photographs to magazines.

WORK IN PROGRESS: Government information pamphlets; an Army recruitment brochure.

SIDELIGHTS: Graham Rickard told *SATA:* "I consider myself a writer rather than an author, because all of my work to date has been strictly factual—writing educational books on many different subjects for children of all age groups." Rickard says he never intended to be a writer, and fell into his profession as the result of another of his interests: photography. After completing several photo assignments for a friend who was a children's book editor, Rickard learned of a project for which his friend had been unable to find an author. He volunteered and became the author of *Famous Names in Popular Music.* "They were fairly dubious" at first, Rickard notes, "but after submitting a specimen chapter they gave me the contract.... I have been writing children's books, on and off, ever since."

"I usually prefer subjects which I know nothing about," Rickard says, "because then I have the same approach to the topic as the children who will eventually read the book."

*   *   *

RINGGOLD, Faith 1930-

PERSONAL: Born October 8, 1930, in New York, NY; daughter of Andrew Louis Jones, Sr. and Willi (Posey) Jones; married Robert Earl Wallace, 1950 (divorced, 1956); married Burdette Ringgold, 1962; children: (first marriage) Barbara, Michele. *Education:* City College of the City University of New York, B.S., 1955, M.A., 1959.

ADDRESSES: Home—La Jolla, CA and New York, NY. *Agent*—(literary) Marie Brown Associates, Room 902, 625 Broadway, New York, NY 10012.

CAREER: Painter, mixed media sculptor, performance artist, and writer. Professor of art, University of California, San Diego, 1984—. Art teacher in public schools, New York City, 1955-73. In 1960s, after trip to Europe, completed first political paintings and held first one-person show. In 1972, began making paintings framed in cloth (called tankas), soft sculptures, costumes, and masks, later using these media in masked performances of the early and mid 1970s. In 1980, produced first painted quilt and in 1983, created first story quilt. Performances include appearances at various colleges, universities, and museums, including Purdue University, 1977, University of Massachusetts, 1980, Rutgers University, 1981, Occidental College, 1984, Long Island University, 1986, Baltimore Museum of Art, 1988, De Pauw University, 1989, and Washington and Lee University, 1991. Visiting lecturer and artist at art centers, universities, and museums, including Mills College, 1987, Museum of Modern Art, 1988, University of West Florida, 1989, San Diego Museum, 1990, Museum of African American Art, 1991, and Atlantic Center for the Arts, 1992.

EXHIBITIONS: Artwork has been nationally exhibited in many museums and numerous galleries as well as in Europe, Asia, South America, and Africa. Artwork has been featured in many one person shows, including shows at the Spectrum Gallery, New York City, 1967, 1970, and the Bernice Steinbaum Gallery, 1987, 1989, 1992. Artwork is in many public and private collections, including Boston Museum of Fine Art, Chase Manhattan Bank Collection, Clark Museum, Guggenheim Museum, High Museum, Metropolitan Museum of Art, Museum of Modern Art, Newark Museum, Phillip Morris Collection, and Studio Museum in Harlem. "Faith Ringgold: A 25 Year Survey," a nationally touring retrospective exhibition, curated by the Fine Arts Museum of Long Island, 1990-93.

AWARDS, HONORS: Coretta Scott King Illustrator Award and Caldecott Honor Book Award, both 1992, both for *Tar Beach.* Artwork has received numerous awards, including Creative Artists Public Service Award, 1971; American Association of University Women Award for travel to Africa, 1976; National Endowment for the Arts Awards, 1978, for sculpture, 1989, for painting; John Simon Guggenheim Memorial Foundation fellowship, 1987, for painting; New York Foundation for the Arts Award, 1988, for painting; and Henry Clews Foundation Award, 1990, for painting in the south of France. Honorary Doctor of Fine Arts degrees from Moore College of Art, 1986, College of Wooster, 1987, Massachusetts College of Art, 1991, City College of the City University of New York, 1991, and Brockport State University, 1992.

WRITINGS:

(Contributor) Amiri Baraka and Amina Baraka, editors, *Confirmation: An Anthology of African American Women,* Morrow, 1983.

Faith Ringgold: A 25 Year Survey (catalog), Fine Arts Museum of Long Island, 1990.

(Self-illustrated) *Tar Beach* (for children of all ages), Crown, 1991.

Aunt Harriet's Underground Railroad in the Sky, Crown, 1993.

Also author of articles, essays, and short stories to numerous periodicals, including *Artpaper, Heresies: A Feminist Publication on Art and Politics, Women's Art Journal, Women's Artists News, Feminist Art Journal, Arts Magazine,* and *Art Gallery Guide.*

Work represented in catalogs, including *Faith Ringgold Change: Painted Story Quilts,* Bernice Steinbaum Gallery, 1987, and *The French Collection,* B MOW Press, 1992.

SIDELIGHTS: Faith Ringgold is a widely respected and accomplished painter, mixed media sculptor, performance artist, college professor, and author. Considered by many critics to be the leading black woman artist in America today, Ringgold is perhaps best known for her beautifully created and intricately designed story quilts that piece together Ringgold's past, present, and future. When asked to define her art, Ringgold told Eleanor Flomenhaft in *Faith Ringgold: A 25 Year Survey:* "I'm a painter who works in the quilt medium; and that I sew on my painting doesn't make it less of a painting; and that it's made into a quilt does not make it not a painting. It's still a painting." Recently, Ringgold successfully bridged another art form when she wrote and illustrated her award-winning book for children, *Tar Beach.*

Possessing enormous talent, dedication, and perseverance, Ringgold seems to be a success at almost every venture she undertakes. Her professional life is full of demanding projects: teaching art at the University of California, San Diego, developing artwork that graces the permanent collections housed in many prestigious galleries and museums, and sharing her vision of art in interpretative performances across the country and abroad. In addition, Ringgold is also generally considered to be a savvy political activist, frequently speaking out on political issues that effect her role as an African-American woman artist living and working in contemporary America. With such a schedule one might marvel at the fact that Ringgold has added producing children's books to her list of accomplishments. While very successful, Ringgold has worked hard for everything she has achieved in her professional life.

As a young child growing up in New York City during the Great Depression of the 1930s and 40s, Ringgold was the youngest of three children born to Andrew Louis Jones, Sr., a sanitation department truck driver, and Willi Posey Jones, a housewife who became a

FAITH RINGGOLD

dressmaker and fashion designer in the 1940s. Ringgold enthusiastically described her childhood in an interview with *Something about the Author (SATA):* "Life for me was quite wonderful! While I had asthma and was home sick a lot, I got a chance to do a lot of things with my mother. When I was recuperating my mother would take me to see live performances of people like Duke Ellington and Jimmy Lunceford and Count Basie. Actually those people were my first stars—my first artists. Part of my being with my mother a lot was that I was the youngest in the family. So when the other kids were in school she would take me to the museums. Also because I would be home with asthma, she would teach me and give me crayons and paper so I could draw. My mother would also give me pieces of fabric since she was a dressmaker. Later on, my mother became a fashion designer but at the time she was just making clothes for my family. She learned the skill from her mother and her mother learned from her mother and so on, and I learned from my mother.

"So I had a very protected life because I had asthma which a lot of children today have. It affected everything about my life. What it also gave me was a lot of quality time with my father that my other siblings didn't have. I would go out with my father on his day off and my siblings did not because they'd be in school. My childhood [years] were the best years of my life, I guess.

I mean for good stories and wonderful connections with people and inspirations and positive affirmation. My childhood was the best aside from the fact that I was sick."

Except for her periodical bouts with asthma, Ringgold's childhood was very much like that of her friends and neighbors. She attended the local public elementary and high schools, played with her friends, listened to music, and lived the life of the average New York City child. Ringgold also learned to work with fabrics at her mother's side, and often visited the many great museums located in New York City. As she remembers: "I was always the class artist. I drew and painted constantly. That was a natural thing to me—making pictures and pieces of art. I cannot remember a time I did not do that. Still, I had no idea that I would be an artist when I grew up. I did know, however, that I would go to college because we had been told all of our lives that we would go to college."

In 1948 after her graduation from high school, Ringgold enrolled at the City College of the City University of New York. She was told that she was required to choose a field of study to matriculate in college. So, Ringgold declared a major in art. She recalled: "When I was asked: 'What do you want to major in?' I said 'If I have to say one thing that I want my life's work to be than it's going to be art because I can't picture my life without it.' But I had no idea what it was to be an artist. I had no idea of the difficulties involved for an African American woman in the field of visual art."

Studying at City College Ringgold learned a great deal about her chosen field of study and her talents as an artist began to develop and shine. While her instructors provided a very sound technical education, Ringgold searched for her own voice and hungered for more information and insight on African-American art and artists. Looking back on her education, Ringgold explained to Flomenhaft in *Faith Ringgold: A 25 Year Study:* "When I went on to City College they taught art in a traditional way. We copied Greek busts; we copied Cezanne and Degas; we copied the Eupropean masters. It was generally thought that we weren't experienced enough to be original; and if we were original we were sometimes up for ridicule."

With a desire to create work that reflected what she felt as an African-American woman artist, Ringgold set out on her own to learn more about this area of art. "African art and African-American artists are interests that I had to pursue on my own after I had my degrees," Ringgold recounted to *SATA.* "I researched African—my own art, the classical art form of Black people—on my own. I really taught myself because there were no courses being taught on African Art and artists. Even today there aren't very many courses taught on African Art. I had to get my education [and] then I had to get my reeducation which was what I gave myself."

Ringgold's personal life took a detour during college. In 1950, she eloped with her childhood sweetheart, a jazz pianist who lived in the apartment house next to her parent's house in Harlem. Within a year, Ringgold gave birth to two daughters, but the marriage began to fall apart because of her husband's addiction to drugs. Devastating as this situation was to her, Rinngold told Teresa Annas of the *Virginian-Pilot* that this experience "positively affected the entire rest of my life." Annas explained Ringgold's thoughts as "thinking of the lack of control [her former husband] had over his life," caused her to leave him and file for divorce.

Ringgold contined with her studies and graduated in 1955. After graduation, Ringgold took a job as an art teacher in the New York public school system and spent much of her spare time on her own art projects. "I love teaching children," Ringgold told *SATA*. "I learned a lot because kids are so gifted. They paint so beautifully and have this wonderful facility with form and space and color that is art. So I would paint with them and notice that my paintings were not as free and wonderful as their paintings were . . . . I really attribute a lot of my painting skills to my young students. Because I had to go through this massive relearning process to go from Picasso and all the great artists I had to copy in college. I had to go from them to me via African art. I wanted to find a way of creating American art out of my experiences as an African-American. So the children really helped me to do that—they showed me what it is to be free, to be able to express yourself directly."

After teaching for several years and spending only part of her time on her own artwork, Ringgold made a decision that would drastically alter the course of her personal and professional life. Determined to find out if she had what it took to become a full-time artist and a major force in the art world, Ringgold packed up her two young daughters and her mother and set off to see the great art works on display in the famous museums in Europe. Ringgold identified the details behind her decision: "'Let me go and see some of these things that I've studied because most people really never really see the Mona Lisa—they just look at it in a book'. So I wanted to go to the Louvre in Paris, France and look at it, stand in front of it, and see if I couldn't understand some of the aura of creating a work of art that could last 400 years. A work of art that people could want to look at for that long. Could I possibly be an artist of any magnitude? I wanted to go to the place where those works of art that I had been told were Masters were made—Europe. I came back feeling that I would be an artist, that I could be, and that I should be an artist."

So after returning home from her trip to Europe, Ringgold went about the task of making her art known to art collectors, galleries, colleges, and institutions across America. Ringgold worked tirelessly arranging exhibits, sending her work across the country, and calling agents and galleries. As she recounted to Leigh Fenly in the *San Diego Union:* "I went to towns where the airport was like a little hut, almost. But you should realize that it's all important. As long as people are there and people are appreciating you work, it's valid. It doesn't have to be New York." Soon people were

Daddy said that the George Washington Bridge is the
longest and most beautiful bridge in the world and that it
opened in 1931, on the very day I was born.

Daddy worked on that bridge, hoisting cables. Since then,
I've wanted that bridge to be mine.

In her self-illustrated *Tar Beach*, Ringgold tells the story of eight-year-old Cassie, who experiences a tremendous feeling of freedom when she realizes that she can fly.

learning about Ringgold's art and her work began to receive critical recognition.

Ringgold's early pieces were paintings done in oil on stretch canvas. Many of these paintings were political though traditional in technique. By the end of the 1960s, Ringgold's work began to reflect her passion for African art and her desire to more accurately express her ethnicity. Both influenced by and involved in the growing civil rights movement during this period, Ringgold began to vigorously explore the burning political issues of the day—race, class, and gender and her work started mirroring her rising social and political consciousness. "Since the early sixties Faith Ringgold's art has been a stage for her ideas," noted Thalia Gouma-Peterson in *Faith Ringgold Change: Painted Story Quilts,* "an expression of her capacity to speak, to voice a specifically Black and female perspective in a dominant male and White art world . . . . She developed and articulated a personal formal language, her artistic voice, both female and Black." And a reviewer for *Journal and Guide* described Ringgold in this manner: "As a black feminist, she unselfconsciously comments on political and social concerns in America. As a prolific writer, she produces art in which narrative and images interweave in works at times ironic, sometimes magical or art historical and always poetic."

In 1972, Ringgold's art underwent another major change in focus: from painting in oils on stretch canvas to creating paintings on canvas that were framed in fabric and quilted. On a trip to Amsterdam, Holland, Ringgold visited museums where she was introduced to Tibetan Napalan tankas—paintings framed in cloth—dating back to the 14th century. Ringgold remarked to *SATA:* "I was amazed that those works were not always framed under glass but had been framed in fabric in beautiful brocade. I decided I wanted to work that way because I could do my pictures, frame them in cloth, and them I could roll them up and transport them anywhere I wanted to. I thought that was a great idea because one of the problems that I had was getting an audience, having people see my work."

"Artists do not, contrary to popular thought, work in a garret in isolation away from people so that no one ever sees their work. You take the work that's done and communicate it to other people because that's what art is, it's a form of communication . . . . You have human eyes looking at your work and responding to it, that is your audience. Even if your audience hates what you do at least there is an emotion about it that brings life to that work. And so I had to have an audience and in order for my work to have an audience it had to be able to travel to college and university campuses and galleries where they were interested in seeing what I was doing. If the work was going to be heavy and under glass and in heavy crates, I would not be able to do it but if I could take all my work and roll it up and fold it up and put it in the trunk and send it...."

So coupling her desire to bring her art to greater numbers of people with her fascination with the tankas she saw in Amsterdam, Ringgold began experimenting with this new art medium. She collaborated with her mother who used her sewing skills as a dressmaker to create the tankas. Ringgold turned her focus toward painting on canvas that her mother framed in cloth, thereby producing her own tankas, in the 1970s what would become quilts in the 1980s.

These early quilts developed into the art form that Ringgold is now internationally famous for—story quilts. While similar to her early tankas, Ringgold added written text along the borders to more fully elaborate the concept or theme of each particular piece. Dina Stein described Ringgold's unique Story Quilt art form in *Alumnus City College:* "What Faith Ringgold is best known for today is a very special art form known as The Story Quilt. The central part of the quilt is done on canvas while the borders are done in the traditional pieced fabric method. The story text is frequently written directly on the quilt. For the most part, these quilts address political and social issues. For example, *Flag Story Quilt* is about a disabled Vietnam vet; *Slave Rape Story* is about a young slave girl on a South Carolina plantation; and *Street Story Quilt* is a pictorial narrative of urban American life."

In a *New York Times* article praising Ringgold's use of "vivid colors" and acknowledging her gift for "melding elements of fantasy and autobiography in a manner reminiscent of early Chagall," Roberta Smith wrote glowingly of Ringgold's story quilts and pointed out that Ringgold "juxtaposes the solitary, traditionally male activity of painting with the collective, traditionally female one of quilting, while fusing their different visual effects into a single work of art."

"In 1983, I started writing what I call picture story quilts," Ringgold told *SATA.* "I had already done the tankas—many of which had words on them—a little story—so it was a natural progression. I really felt that writing was very important. It helped to develop the work in the minds of other people in a way that just a picture could not, that the words could go places that pictures could not go.... I had very specific things I wanted to say and I wanted to get those things published and I couldn't count on getting a publisher to do it for me. So I would write the words on the quilts and as the quilts were published, the words would be too."

After viewing a showing of the eight story quilts that make up part of her "French Collection," Ellen Handy observed in *ARTS* magazine: "Ringgold's simple and effective style is agreeably folksy, the quilt reference a reminder of the craft tradition: women's work in all its glory and subordination. But the main thing is that her work is so impressive in its conviction. Big, colorful, and loquaciously articulate, this art allows no ambiguity

concerning questions of race, gender, art, and power. These subjects, couched as stories, have the joy, sorrow, and continuity of individual experience.... These paintings are vivid with life triumphant over both adversity and dogma."

After seeing one of Ringgold's story quilts from her "A Woman on a Bridge" series, Andrea Cascardi, an editor at Crown Publishers approached Ringgold about making "Tar Beach" into a illustrated book for children. At first, Ringgold could not envision this work, depicting an eight-year-old girl lying on the tarpaper rooftop of a Harlem apartment building dreaming of flying, as possible subject material for children literature. Ringgold admitted to *SATA:* "The editor saw that this was a children's book and I never saw it. I was just doing my work. I was doing [the] 'A Woman on a Bridge' series and I did 'Tar Beach' because it comes out of my childhood."

Elaborating on the idea from the original story quilt, the book *Tar Beach* is the story of the hopes and dreams of the eight-year-old girl, Cassie, who dreams about traveling wherever she wants, whenever she wants. One night, while lying on the rooftop—"Tar Beach"—Cassie is lifted up by the stars and soars above the clouds of her Harlem apartment building. As her family, neighbors, and friends play cards on the rooftop below, the young girl glides through the dark sky and is treated to a dazzling "world of living color" that gives her a tremendous sense of freedom and joy. "Anyone can fly," young Cassie proclaims in *Tar Beach.* "All you need is somewhere to go that you can't get to any other way. The next thing you know, you're flying among the stars."

"Few picture books are as visually dazzling or as poetically immediate as this story about the summer nights when Cassie's family would picnic, party, and sleep on 'Tar Beach'—their apartment house roof," Michele Landsberg stated in *Entertainment Weekly.* "Ringgold's narrative of a child's self-affirmation and love of family is fresh, direct, and poignant. Her full-page paintings vibrate with ravishing colors: the nighttime sky spangled with stars and city lights and the bright hues of the family's home life.... *Tar Beach,* Ringgold's first book, is an exhilarating celebration of a child's life in the city."

Corky Pollan remarked in *New York* magazine that "in *Tar Beach,* Faith Ringgold has woven black history with autobiography and fiction; but, more important, she has created a children's book that is magical and inspiring.... *Tar Beach* explodes with the artist's exuberant pictures." And Rosellen Brown wrote of *Tar Beach* in *New York Times Book Review:* "It's hard to imagine a child who wouldn't willingly imagine something—a place, a tough spot, a hard life or a high ambition—worth flying out of or into. There's an air of triumph, not the downfall of Icarus but perhaps the swooping power of the eagle or the phoenix, only domesticated in perfect detail, in Ms. Ringgold's vision. Fortunately it's not exclusive: it's not only for African-Americans, or girls, or even—I'll testify—for children."

Ringgold explained to *SATA* her thoughts behind creating *Tar Beach:* "I did this story because it comes out of my childhood. It is not autobiographical but it was a very warm, wonderful period in my life growing up in Harlem in which we went on the roof. We went up to 'Tar Beach' and we could see the George Washington Bridge. I wanted to put those two together because I'm fascinated with bridges and I'm also fascinated with the 30s so I put them together. My daughter, writer Michele Wallace, told me that when you're writing you have to have an unique voice.... It's just like in art you have to have an unique vision. You have to express your vision like no one else. So writing is the same way. You have to speak in a clear voice that's coming from you. So if I'm writing a children's story I have to connect with the child in me and let that child speak those words. So that's what I did. You have to speak through the child as a child. So *Tar Beach* turned out to be a children's story book."

Because of the success of *Tar Beach*, Ringgold sees more children's books in her future as a writer. "Writing for children is important to me. There is no doubt about it .... I can't believe that I have been directed to a new career that is so supportive of my original one in that I can do children's books—and I do it well because that's the way I write my story quilts. I've done thirty-five stories on my story quilts and the same way in which I write for adults on the story quilts, I can write for children. It's a very no-frills way of writing, in which something has to happen in each sentence. My story quilts might be thought of as children's books for adults."

As Carol Davala once noted in *Quilt World:* "Over the years, Faith Ringgold has proven herself to be an artist of remarkable talent and vision. She struck out on a path which set her apart as an artist with great sensitivity to images of blackness and femaleness in American life. Faith and her art will continue to grow and change as she finds more and more ways to translate her unique artistic vision."

WORKS CITED:

Annas, Teresa, "The Fabric of Freedom," *Virginian-Pilot,* July 19, 1991, pp. B1, B4.
Brown, Rosellen, "Children's Books," *New York Times Book Review,* February 24, 1991, p. 30.
Davala, Carol, "The Quilt Lady," *Quilt World,* February/March, 1991, pp. 22-24.
Fenly, Leigh, "Artist Lets Dreams of Freedom Take Wing," *San Diego Union,* February 16, 1991, pp. C1, C3.
Flomenhaft, Eleanor, "Interviewing Faith Ringgold/A Contemporary Heroine," *Faith Ringgold: A 25 Year Survey,* Fine Arts Museum of Long Island, 1990, pp. 7-15. Amended by Faith Ringgold.

Gouma-Peterson, Thalia, *Faith Ringgold Change: Painted Story Quilts,* Bernice Steinbaum Gallery, 1989. Amended by F. Ringgold.
Handy, Ellen, review of collection "The French Collection," *ARTS,* Volume 66, number 8, April, 1992, p. 88.
Landsberg, Michele, "Up on the Roof and on to the 'Beach'," *Entertainment Weekly,* February 8, 1991, pp. 68-69.
Pollan, Corky, "'Tar' Quality," *New York,* February 18, 1991, p. 56.
"Portsmouth Art Museum to Display New York Artist," *Journal and Guide,* June 12-18, 1991, p. 3.
Ringgold, Faith, from an interview with Margaret Mazurkiewicz for *Something about the Author,* April 27, 1992.
Ringgold, Faith, *Tar Beach,* Crown, 1991.
Smith, Roberta, "Art in Review," *New York Times,* February 14, 1992.
Stein, Dina, "Faith Ringgold and the Story Quilt," *Alumnus City College,* winter, 1990, pp. 8-9.

FOR MORE INFORMATION SEE:

BOOKS

Chadwick, Whitney, *Women, Art, and Society,* Thames and Hudson, 1990.
Contemporary American Women Artists, Cedco Publishing, 1991.
Davis, Marianna W., *Contributions of Black Women to America: The Arts,* Kenday, 1982.
Miller, Lynn, and Sally S. Swenson, *Lives and Works: Talks with Women Artists,* Simon & Schuster, 1981.
Munro, Eleanor, *Originals: American Women Artists,* Simon & Schuster, 1979, pp. 409-416.
Sills, Leslie, *Inspirations: Stories of Women Artists for Children,* A. Whitman, 1988, pp. 40-51.
Slatkin, Wendy, *Women Artists in History: From Antiquity to the Twentieth Century,* 2nd edition, Prentice-Hall, 1990, pp. 190-92.
Witzling, Mara R., editor, *Writings in Voicing Our Visions: Writings by Women Artists,* Universe, 1991.

PERIODICALS

Artweek, February 13, 1992, pp. 10-11.
Atlanta Constitution, July 30, 1990, pp. E1-E5.
Black American Literary Forum, spring, 1985, pp. 12-13.
Essence, May, 1990, p. 78.
Gallerie Women's Art, Volume 6, 1989, pp. 40-43.
Horn Book, May, 1991, p. 322.
Los Angeles Times Book Review, February 24, 1991, p. 8.
New York Times, July 29, 1984, pp. 24-25.
Publishers Weekly, February 15, 1991, pp. 61-62.
School Arts, May, 1989, pp. 23-26.

—Sketch by Margaret Mazurkiewicz

ROCKWELL, Anne F. 1934-

PERSONAL: Born February 8, 1934, in Memphis, TN; daughter of Emerson (an advertising executive) and Sabina (Fromhold) Foote; married Harlow Rockwell (a writer and artist), March 16, 1955; children: Hannah, Elizabeth (Lizzy), Oliver Penn. *Education:* Attended Sculpture Center and Pratt Graphic Arts Center. *Politics:* "Liberal Democrat." *Religion:* Episcopalian.

ADDRESSES: Home—4 Raymond St., Old Greenwich, CT 06870.

CAREER: Author and illustrator. Silver Burdett Publishers, Morristown, NJ, member of production department, 1952; Young and Rubicam (advertising agency), art-buying secretary, 1953; Goldwater Memorial Hospital, New York City, assistant recreation leader, 1954-56.

MEMBER: Authors Guild.

AWARDS, HONORS: Boys Club Junior Book Award certificate, 1968, for *The Minstrel and the Mountain: A Tale of Peace;* American Institute of Graphic Arts selection for children's book show, 1971-72, for *The Toolbox,* 1973-74, for *Head to Toe, Games (and How to Play Them), The Awful Mess,* and *Paul and Arthur and the Little Explorer;* Children's Book Showcase selection, 1973, for *Toad,* and 1975, for *Befana: A Christmas Story; No More Work* and *Poor Goose: A French Folktale* were selected as children's books of the year by the Child Study Association, 1976; *In Our House* was named a *Redbook* top ten children's picture book of 1985.

WRITINGS:

SELF-ILLUSTRATED, EXCEPT WHERE INDICATED

Paul and Arthur Search for the Egg, Doubleday, 1964.

ANNE F. ROCKWELL

Gypsy Girl's Best Shoes, Parents Magazine Press, 1966.
Sally's Caterpillar, illustrated by husband, Harlow Rockwell, Parents Magazine Press, 1966.
Filippo's Dome: Brunelleschi and the Cathedral of Florence, Atheneum, 1967.
The Stolen Necklace: A Picture Story from India, World, 1968.
Glass, Stones and Crown: The Abbe Suger and the Building of St. Denis, Atheneum, 1968.
The Good Llama: A Picture Story from Peru, World, 1968.
Temple on the Hill: The Building of the Parthenon, Atheneum, 1969.
The Wonderful Eggs of Furicchia: A Picture Story from Italy, World, 1969.
(Compiler) *Savez-vous planter les choux? and Other French Songs,* World, 1969.
When the Drum Sang: An African Folktale, Parents Magazine Press, 1970.
(Adapter) *The Monkey's Whiskers: A Brazilian Folktale,* Parents Magazine Press, 1971.
El toro pinto and Other Songs in Spanish, Macmillan, 1971.
Paintbrush and Peacepipe: The Story of George Catlin, Atheneum, 1971.
Tuhurahura and the Whale, Parents Magazine Press, 1971.
What Bobolino Knew, McCall Publishing, 1971.
The Dancing Stars: An Iroquois Legend, Crowell, 1972.
Paul and Arthur and the Little Explorer, Parents Magazine Press, 1972.
The Awful Mess, Parents Magazine Press, 1973.
The Boy Who Drew Sheep, Atheneum, 1973.
Games (and How to Play Them), Crowell, 1973.
(Reteller) *The Wolf Who Had a Wonderful Dream: A French Folktale,* Crowell, 1973.
Befana: A Christmas Story, Atheneum, 1974.
Gift for a Gift, Parents Magazine Press, 1974.
The Gollywhopper Egg, Macmillan, 1974.
The Story Snail, Macmillan, 1974.
(Reteller) *The Three Bears and Fifteen Other Stories,* Crowell, 1975.
Big Boss, Macmillan, 1975.
(Reteller) *Poor Goose: A French Folktale,* Crowell, 1976.
No More Work, Greenwillow, 1976.
I Like the Library, Dutton, 1977.
A Bear, a Bobcat, and Three Ghosts, Macmillan, 1977.
Albert B. Cub and Zebra: An Alphabet Storybook, Crowell, 1977.
Willy Runs Away, Dutton, 1978.
Timothy Todd's Good Things Are Gone, Macmillan, 1978.
Gogo's Pay Day, Doubleday, 1978.
Gogo's Car Breaks Down, illustrated by H. Rockwell, Doubleday, 1978.
Buster and the Bogeyman, Four Winds, 1978.
(Reteller) *The Old Woman and Her Pig and Ten Other Stories,* Crowell, 1979.
The Girl with a Donkey Tail, Dutton, 1979.
The Bump in the Night, Greenwillow, 1979.
Walking Shoes, Doubleday, 1980.
Honk Honk!, Dutton, 1980.
Henry the Cat and the Big Sneeze, Greenwillow, 1980.

King Louis VII of France weeps at his first sight of Jerusalem, the Holy City, in Rockwell's self-illustrated *Glass, Stones, and Crown.*

Gray Goose and Gander and Other Mother Goose Rhymes, Crowell, 1980.
When We Grow Up, Dutton, 1981.
Up a Tall Tree, illustrated by Jim Arnosky, Doubleday, 1981.
Thump Thump Thump!, Dutton, 1981.
Boats, Dutton, 1982.
(Reteller) Hans Christian Andersen, *The Emperor's New Clothes,* Crowell, 1982.
Big Bad Goat, Dutton, 1982.
The Mother Goose Cookie-Candy Book, Random House, 1983.
Cars, Dutton, 1984.
Trucks, Dutton, 1984.
In Our House, Crowell, 1985.
Planes, Dutton, 1985.
First Comes Spring, Crowell, 1985.
The Three Sillies and Ten Other Stories to Read Aloud, Harper, 1986.
Big Wheels, Dutton, 1986.
Fire Engines, Dutton, 1986.
Things That Go, Dutton, 1986.
At Night, Crowell, 1986.
At the Playground, Crowell, 1986.
In the Morning, Crowell, 1986.
In the Rain, Crowell, 1986.
Come to Town, Crowell, 1987.
Bear Child's Book of Hours, Crowell, 1987.

Bikes, Dutton, 1987.
Handy Hank Will Fix It, Holt Rinehart, 1988.
Hugo at the Window, Macmillan, 1988.
Things to Play With, Macmillan, 1988.
Puss in Boots and Other Stories, Macmillan, 1988.
Trains, Dutton, 1988.
My Spring Robin, illustrated by H. Rockwell and Lizzy Rockwell, Macmillan, 1989.
On Our Vacation, Dutton, 1989.
Apples and Pumpkins, illustrated by L. Rockwell, Macmillan, 1989.
Bear Child's Book of Special Days, Dutton, 1989.
Willy Can Count, Arcade Publishing, 1989.
Root-a-Toot-Toot, Macmillan, 1991.

WITH HUSBAND, HARLOW ROCKWELL; SELF-ILLUSTRATED

Olly's Polliwogs, Doubleday, 1970.
Molly's Woodland Garden, Doubleday, 1971.
The Toolbox, Macmillan, 1971.
Machines, Macmillan, 1972.
Thruway, Macmillan, 1972.
Toad, Doubleday, 1972.
Head to Toe, Doubleday, 1973.
Blackout, Macmillan, 1979.
The Supermarket, Macmillan, 1979.
Out to Sea, Macmillan, 1980.
My Barber, Macmillan, 1981.
Happy Birthday to Me, Macmillan, 1981.
I Play in My Room, Macmillan, 1981.
Can I Help?, Macmillan, 1982.
How My Garden Grew, Macmillan, 1982.
I Love My Pets, Macmillan, 1982.
Sick in Bed, Macmillan, 1982.
The Night We Slept Outside, Macmillan, 1983.
My Back Yard, Macmillan, 1984.
Our Garage Sale, Greenwillow, 1984.
When I Go Visiting, Macmillan, 1984.
Nice and Clean, Macmillan, 1984.
My Baby-Sitter, Collier Books, 1985.
The Emergency Room, Collier Books, 1985, published in England as *Going to Casualty,* Hamish Hamilton, 1987.
At the Beach, Macmillan, 1987.
The First Snowfall, Macmillan, 1987.

ILLUSTRATOR

Majorie Hopkins, *The Three Visitors,* Parents Magazine Press, 1967.
Jane Yolen, *The Minstrel and the Mountain: A Tale of Peace,* World, 1967.
Lillian Bason, *Eric and the Little Canal Boat,* Parents Magazine Press, 1967.
M. Hopkins, *The Glass Valentine,* Parents Magazine Press, 1968.
Paul Showers, *What Happens to a Hamburger,* Crowell, 1970.
Kathryn Hitte, *Mexacali Soup,* Parents Magazine Press, 1970.
Joseph Jacobs, *Munacher and Manacher: An Irish Story,* Crowell, 1970.
Anne Petry, *Legends of the Saints,* Crowell, 1970.
J. Jacobs, *Master of All Masters,* Grosset, 1972.

M. Hopkins, *A Gift for Tolum,* Parents Magazine Press, 1972.

Walter Dean Myers, *The Dancers,* Parents Magazine Press, 1972.

Barbara Brenner, *Cunningham's Rooster,* Parents Magazine Press, 1975.

Barbara Williams, *Never Hit a Porcupine,* Dutton, 1977.

Gerda Mantinband, *Bing Bong Band and Fiddle Dee Dee,* Doubleday, 1979.

Clyde Robert Bulla, *The Stubborn Old Woman,* Crowell, 1980.

Patricia Plante and David Bergman, retellers, *The Turtle and the Two Ducks and Ten Other Animal Fables Freely Retold from La Fontaine,* Methuen, 1980.

Steven Kroll, *Toot! Toot!,* Holiday House, 1983.

ADAPTATIONS: The Stolen Necklace: A Picture Story from India, was adapted as a film by Paramount/Oxford, 1971; *The Toolbox* and *Machines* were adapted as filmstrips, Threshold Filmstrips, 1974.

SIDELIGHTS: Anne Rockwell is a prolific author and illustrator of children's books with more than eighty titles of her own, close to thirty collaborative efforts with her husband, Harlow Rockwell, and artwork cred-

its for nearly twenty works by other authors. During a career which has spanned several decades, Rockwell has gradually decreased the age of her target audience. Initially producing works for middle-graders, she has turned to books for preschool and beginning readers.

Rockwell was born in Memphis, Tennessee, but also spent time in the Midwest and Southwest while growing up. Although she attended both the Sculpture Center and Pratt Graphic Arts Center, the artist relied mainly on self-teaching to learn her trade. She worked at an advertising agency before marrying another artist, Harlow Rockwell. After the couple had their first child, Rockwell realized that she wanted to produce children's books to share the joy of reading she had first experienced as a youngster.

Rockwell believes that for very young readers pictures can communicate better than words. Her drawings feature animated subjects and backgrounds with numerous details. Rockwell attributes her success as an author and illustrator of children's books to the fact that she can remember what it is like to be a child and is able look at the world from that viewpoint. Having children, Rockwell added, strengthened this ability.

Weighed down by his bag of rocks, the greedy fox sinks to the bottom of a deep pool in Rockwell's retelling of "The Cock and the Mouse and the Little Red Hen." (Illustration by the author from *The Three Bears and Fifteen Other Stories.*)

Some of Rockwell's early self-illustrated publications, including *The Dancing Stars: An Iroquois Legend, The Good Llama: A Picture Story from Peru,* and *The Stolen Necklace: A Picture Story from India,* introduce readers to folktales from different cultures. In the late 1970s, however, she changed her focus to informative works for children just learning to read. With works such as *I Like the Library, Walking Shoes,* and *When We Grow Up,* Rockwell provides simple text and detailed and attention-grabbing pictures.

Books such as these earned praise as straightforward presentations of everyday objects and occurrences. Kimberly Olson Fakih, writing in *Publishers Weekly,* highlighted editor Ann Durrell's comment that Rockwell shows genius in her nonfiction works. "In [Rockwell's] books, kids can see what's meaningful to them and what's around them," Durrell stated. An example of her nonfiction work is Rockwell's series of picture books explaining various types of transportation. These books, including *Boats, Cars, Planes, Trucks, Trains,* and *Bikes,* feature lively watercolor illustrations—with animals operating the machinery—and easy-to-understand prose.

Rockwell has also written and illustrated numerous books with her husband, Harlow Rockwell. *Out to Sea* tells of a the unintended maritime adventure involving a brother and sister. Another work, *The Emergency Room,* describes a protagonist's trip to the hospital after spraining his ankle. P. Susan Gerrity, writing in *New York Times Book Review,* remarked that the book "provides excellent background information" and will reassure children afraid of visiting the emergency room.

Rockwell collaborated with her husband Harlow on the text for many books, including her self-illustrated *My Barber.*

Nearly thirty years after publishing her first story, Rockwell has continued her string of successful, eye-pleasing, and educational works. In her 1990 book *Willy Can Count,* the author presents a counting game played by mother and son during a walk. In her illustrations, Rockwell provides plenty of objects to count, prompting Joanna G. Jones of *School Library Journal* to remark that *Willy Can Count* is "bound to become a favorite."

While grateful for the recognition her works receive, Rockwell prefers not to comment about them. In *Illustrators of Children's Books: 1967-76,* Rockwell mentioned that she believes her "books are a more eloquent statement" about her art than any remarks she could add.

WORKS CITED:

Fakih, Kimberly Olson, "The News is Nonfiction," *Publishers Weekly,* February 26, 1988, pp. 108-111.
Gerrity, P. Susan, review of *The Emergency Room, New York Times Book Review,* April 21, 1985, p. 18.
Illustrators of Children's Books: 1967-76, Horn Book, 1978, p. 392.
Jones, Joanna G., review of *Willy Can Count, School Library Journal,* January 1990, p. 89.

FOR MORE INFORMATION SEE:

PERIODICALS

Books for Keeps, May 1990, p. 12.
Horn Book, November, 1987, p. 731; November, 1989, p. 764.
School Library Journal, August, 1989, p. 131; January, 1991, p. 37.
Times Literary Supplement, October 9, 1987, p. 1120.*

The detailed background and animated subjects in Rockwell's illustration from *The Old Woman and Her Pig and Ten Other Stories* are typical of her work.

ROSE, Deborah Lee 1955-

PERSONAL: Born October 24, 1955, in Philadelphia, PA; daughter of Bernard and Helen Rose; married; children: one daughter. *Education:* Cornell University, B.A., 1977.

ADDRESSES: c/o Publicity Director, Albert Whitman & Co., 6340 Oakton, Morton Grove, IL 60053; c/o Roberts Rinehart Inc., P.O. Box 666, Niwot, CO 80544-0666.

CAREER: Time-Life Books, Alexandria, VA, editorial researcher, 1977-82; Council for the Advancement of Science Writing, national science writing fellow, 1983-84; University of California at Berkeley, Berkeley, CA, science writer and speech writer, 1984-91.

MEMBER: Society of Children's Book Writers, Northern California Science Writers Association.

AWARDS, HONORS: Jane Addams Children's Peace Book Award recommended list, 1990, for *The People Who Hugged the Trees;* First Prize for Juvenile Trade Books, Chicago Women in Publishing, 1991, for *Meredith's Mother Takes the Train.*

WRITINGS:

The People Who Hugged the Trees, illustrated by Birgitta Saeflund, Roberts Rinehart, 1990.
Meredith's Mother Takes the Train, illustrated by Irene Trivas, Albert Whitman, 1991.

The People Who Hugged the Trees has also been published in German translation.

WORK IN PROGRESS: "Historical fiction with a Jewish theme."

SIDELIGHTS: Deborah Lee Rose told *SATA:* "*The People Who Hugged the Trees* is an environmental folktale, based on a three-hundred-year-old story from Rajasthan, India. I was particularly struck by this story of a young girl who grows up to lead her entire village in saving a forest. I hope, as my daughter grows up, she will also feel strongly about making the world a better place in some way." *Meredith's Mother Takes the Train* was based on a girl Rose knows who must face being

DEBORAH LEE ROSE

separated from her mother every workday. The girl's mother commutes by train to her workplace. If read aloud at a quick pace, the story captures the rhythm of the train. Other elements of the story are drawn from Rose's own experiences as the working mother of a preschool-age child.

"Since I began writing children's books, I have been rereading my childhood favorites," Rose commented. "The character I admire most is Charlotte, the spider in *Charlotte's Web.* Not only does she love words and take the time to explain them, she understands that words can be very powerful. They can teach, surprise, entertain, convince, and even save a life."

S

SAXBY, H. M.
See SAXBY, (Henry) Maurice

*   *   *

SAXBY, (Henry) Maurice 1924-
(H. M. Saxby)

PERSONAL: Born December 26, 1924, in Australia; son of Maurice Henry (a civil servant) and Nettie (Thompson) Saxby; married Norma Jean Bateson (an executive officer in medical education), December 14, 1972 (died October 24, 1990); children: Hil. *Education:* Sydney University, B.A., 1954, M.Ed., 1967. *Politics:* Liberal. *Religion:* Anglican.

ADDRESSES: Home—50 Carnarvon Rd., East Roseville, NSW 2069, Australia.

CAREER: New South Wales Department of Education, Australia, teacher, 1950-56; New South Wales State Teachers' Colleges, Australia, lecturer, 1957-72; Kuringgai College of Advanced Education, New South Wales, Australia, professor and head of English department, 1973-85. Consultant to Penguin Books of Australia and Macmillan Company of Australia. *Military service:* Australian Imperial Forces, 1943-46, served in Papua, New Guinea; became sergeant.

MEMBER: Children's Book Council of Australia (formerly first national president; trustee of New South Wales branch, 1980—; life membership recognition, 1991; currently vice-president).

AWARDS, HONORS: Dromkeen Medal for Services to Children's Literature, 1983; Rotary International Award for Vocational Excellence, 1986; Lady Cutler Award for Services to Children's Literature, 1989; Australian School Library Association citation, 1991.

WRITINGS:

A History of Australian Children's Literature 1841-1941, Wentworth, 1969.

A History of Australian Children's Literature 1941-1970, Wentworth, 1971.

Teaching the New English in Primary Schools, Novak, 1974.

Through Folklore to Literature, International Board on Books for Young People, 1977.

When Johnny and Judy Don't Read, Primary English Teaching Association, 1978.

Children and Literature, University of Sydney Press, 1978.

(Editor with Gordon Winch) *Give Them Wings: The Experience of Children's Literature,* Macmillan, 1987.

MAURICE SAXBY

(Editor with Glenys Smith) *Dimensions,* eighteen volumes, Methuen, 1988-89.

The Great Deeds of Superheroes, illustrated by Robert Ingpen, Millennium, 1989, Peter Bedrick, 1990.

The Great Deeds of Heroic Women, illustrated by Ingpen, Millennium, 1990.

Russell and the Star Shell, illustrated by Astra Lacis, Margaret Hamilton Books, 1990.

First Choice: A Guide to the Best in Children's Fiction, Oxford, 1990.

The Proof of the Puddin': Australian Children's Literature 1970-1990, Ashton Scholastic, 1992.

Russell and the Highwayman, Margaret Hamilton Books, in press.

Contributor of reviews to *Literature Base, Magpies, Papers, Reading Time,* and other periodicals.

WORK IN PROGRESS: A series of folk and fairy tale retellings; *Fables, Myths, and Legends,* for Macmillan Australia.

SIDELIGHTS: Maurice Saxby told *SATA:* "Although I learned to read before I started school, I grew into books in the isolated silver-mining town of Broken Hill in the western desert of New South Wales, Australia. There I was fortunate enough to have a teacher who introduced me to the great body of traditional literature—folk and fairy tales, epic, myth, and legend. This was to become a lifelong passion."

As a lecturer and instructor in English, Saxby worked to institute courses in children's literature in the Commonwealth of Australia and the state of New South Wales, and developed Australia's first master's program in children's literature and reading. During his career in education, Saxby focused on writing *about* children's literature; it wasn't until after his retirement that he began writing *for* children. Beginning with the editing of a series of anthologies of children's literature, Saxby soon found himself writing "hero tales." These stories became the companion volumes *The Great Deeds of Superheroes* and *The Great Deeds of Heroic Women.*

"Having had a taste of writing for children rather than about them and their literature, I felt the urge to take the further step and try my hand at the text for a picture story book," Saxby related. The result, *Russell and the Star Shell,* is a "fond portrait of my own grandparents," based on memories of childhood visits with them, Saxby said. *Russell and the Highwayman* followed, again inspired by an episode in the life of one of Saxby's grandfathers. "Children need continuity with the past and I believe loving grandparents can help provide this," Saxby noted.

*   *   *

SCHWARTZ, Alvin 1927-1992

OBITUARY NOTICE—See index for *SATA* sketch: Born April 25, 1927, in Brooklyn, NY; died of lymphoma, March 14, 1992, in Princeton, NJ. Journalist and author. Schwartz, the author of many best-selling books for children, was noted for his appealing use of folklore, his humor, a sense of absurdity, and also for some frightening characters in his books. Schwartz, who knew early in life that he wanted to write, studied journalism in college and worked as a newspaper reporter and professional writer during the 1950s. In the 1960s he became a free-lance writer and went on to publish more than fifty books. Many of his most popular books are compilations of folk tales, ghost stories, tongue-twisters, jokes, riddles, and superstitions, but he also wrote nonfiction about such institutions as fatherhood, workers' unions, stores, museums, universities, and the government. Although much of Schwartz's work is funny and lighthearted, the witches, ghosts, and zombies in books such as *In a Dark, Dark Room and Other Scary Stories, Ghosts,* and *Scary Stories 3,* were considered by some parents and teachers to be too frightening for youthful readers. Polls, however, have shown Schwartz to be a favorite among students. Schwartz's children's books include *Tomfoolery: Trickery and Foolery with Words, Kickle Snifters and Other Fearsome Critters, Central City/Spread City: The Metropolitan Regions Where More and More of Us Spend Our Lives,* and *Stores.*

OBITUARIES AND OTHER SOURCES:

BOOKS

Authors of Books for Young People, 3rd edition, Scarecrow, 1990.

PERIODICALS

Chicago Tribune, March 16, 1992, section 1, p. 13; April 22, 1992, section 2, p. 6.
Los Angeles Tribune, March 17, 1992, p. A18.
Washington Post, March 18, 1992, p. C7.

*   *   *

SEELEY, Laura L. 1958-

PERSONAL: Born July 9, 1958, in Boston, MA; daughter of Clinton B. (a radiologist) and Gail Ruth (Robyn) Seeley. *Education:* Rochester Institute of Technology, B.F.A., 1980.

ADDRESSES: Home—2125 Fairhaven Cir., Atlanta, GA 30305.

CAREER: Writer and illustrator of children's books. Instructor of illustration, Atlanta College of Art, 1991—.

AWARDS, HONORS: Georgia Author of the Year Award for literature for children, 1990, for illustrating *The Book of Shadowboxes: A Story of the ABC's.*

WRITINGS:

(Self-illustrated) *The Book of Shadowboxes: A Story of the ABC's,* Peachtree, 1990.

(Self-illustrated) *The Magical Moonballs,* Peachtree, 1992.

LAURA L. SEELEY

ILLUSTRATOR

Tom T. Hall, *Christmas and the Old House,* Peachtree,
    1989.
Carmen Deedy, *Agatha's Featherbed,* Peachtree, 1991.

Also illustrator of book covers for *Heart of a Distant
Forest,* by Phil Williams, *Helping the Child Who Doesn't
Fit In,* by Stephen Nowicki and Marshall P. Duke, and
After Eli, by Terry Kay.

WORK IN PROGRESS: Creating illustrations for Tom
T. Hall's *Christmas and the Old Cave.*

SIDELIGHTS: Laura L. Seeley told *SATA:* "I enjoy
turning my thoughts into shape and color for others to
enjoy. It's a very fulfilling way to communicate.

"Ever since I was a kid, along with my brothers and
sister, I have loved to draw. Mom and Dad always kept
us in full supply of paper, paints, colored pencils, and we
even got an art lesson on occasion.

"*The Book of Shadowboxes* came to be through my
interest in collecting miniatures. (Since I was six, and I
got a little yellow submarine from a Cracker Jacks box.)
I keep my miniatures in shadowboxes on the walls.
Chances are if you think of something, I'll probably
have it in miniature. There was also my fascination of
words and the alphabet. I pretty much read the dictionary for this ABC book picking out the 'fun' words. And
I enjoy writing in verse. It's a great feeling to express
thoughts and simultaneously make it work in rhyme and
rhythm. The character 'Shadow' in the book came from

a little character I created when I was nine. He has since
gone through a metamorphosis, having grown arms, legs
and a nose. I am hoping he will appear in future books.

"My own illustration has taken on a metamorphosis as
well . . . . *The Magical Moonballs,* also in verse, has a lot
of color and animation, like *Shadowboxes,* but the lines
have softened, and my art has more of a loose flow. It's
the same old cliche—'An artist's best piece is the next
one.'

"Detail will always be important to me. I like to tuck
little surprises throughout a scene so that the longer the
viewer looks the more he discovers.

"As a newcomer in this business, I still have much to
learn, but it's exciting to learn through doing—to keep
growing and getting better with each new book."

*   *   *

SHARPE, Susan 1946-

PERSONAL: Born April 10, 1946, in Albany, NY;
daughter of William Walker (a professor of English) and
Nancy (Close) Gibson; married Maitland Sharpe (asso-
ciate executive director, Izaak Walton League), 1976;
children: Katherine, Alison. *Education:* Swarthmore
College, B.A. (with distinction), 1968; Yale University,
M.A.T. in English, 1969; University of Massachusetts,
Ph.D., 1974. *Politics:* Democrat.

SUSAN SHARPE

ADDRESSES: Office—Department of English, North Virginia Community College, Annandale, VA 22003.

CAREER: Northern Virginia Community College, 1974—, began as member of English faculty, Manassas Campus, became associate professor of English, Annandale Campus, 1992.

MEMBER: Society of Children's Book Writers, Chesapeake Bay Foundation.

AWARDS, HONORS: Book of the year award, Child Study Book Committee of Bank Street College, 1991, for *Spirit Quest; Waterman's Boy* was named to South Carolina's Children's and Young Adult Book Award master list for 1992-93.

WRITINGS:

BOOKS FOR CHILDREN

Waterman's Boy, Bradbury, 1990, published as *Trouble at Marsh Harbor,* Viking, 1991.
Spirit Quest, illustrated by daughters Katherine Sharpe and Alison Sharpe, Bradbury, 1991.
Chicken Bucks, Bradbury, 1992.

OTHER

Voice Audience Content: A Reader for Writers, Longman, 1979.

Contributor of articles to *Northern Virginia Review, College Composition and Communication,* and *Gypsy Scholar;* also contributor of essays to *Cricket, Washington Post, Baltimore Sun,* and *Christian Science Monitor.*

SIDELIGHTS: Susan Sharpe told *SATA:* "Although I was born in Albany, I grew up in western Massachusetts, where my father was a professor at Amherst College, and we lived in an old New England farmhouse, with a garden and occasional livestock. It was a lovely place in which to be a little girl, but sometimes lonely. But I took the initiative. I used to visit a reclusive poet, Robert Francis (now of moderate fame), who lived a quarter mile down the road, and made me feel important. He fed me obscure homemade teas, and introduced me to his stone man and his garden and his bird friends. He had a naturalist's interest in praying mantises, which he sometimes brought into the house; you had to be careful not to sit on one.

"At home I had an older brother, exciting and dangerous, and a mother who believed that children should not be supervised or organized too much, and should get plenty of fresh air. I was always (it seemed then) being pushed away from a good book to 'go play outside.' Now that I am an adult I can't tell which is better, the book or the outside, so I write books about the outside.

"When my own children came of reading age I seemed to remember that when I was a child I had wanted to write children's books. We began going as a family to Chincoteague, VA (location of Marguerite Henry's popular book for children, *Misty of Chincoteague*), which is now primarily devoted to tourists but had an active

Sharpe's interest in Northwest mythology and love of nature formed the inspiration for *Spirit Quest*. (Cover photograph by the author; cover illustration by Katherine Sharpe.)

fishery only a short while ago. We also visited places where crabbing and oystering are still big business, like Crisfield, MD, and Smith Island. It seemed to me to be a better place to be a kid than the suburbs in at least one important way: children can see their fathers at work, and even work with them at very young ages. Ben Warren (from *Water's Boy*) came to my imagination as a boy who would be unusually close to his father. The environmental theme comes from my husband but also from just seeing what is apparent to the most casual observation—the Chesapeake Bay does not support the old levels of harvesting, even as more and more city people (like us) want to vacation there, adding to the environmental stresses.

"*Spirit Quest* began with a trip to visit my brother-in-law in Seattle. Two trips, actually; one before we had children, when we hiked a long way down the coast from LaPush, and a second one, with children, when I knew something about the book I wanted to write. The book comes from a collection of different experiences: the mysticism of my own childhood, experiences of nature, my reading of Northwest mythology (which sometimes seems to correspond to the mysticism), and the experience of trying to make friends, as a child, across a

In *Chicken Bucks,* two young entrepreneurs learn about the day-to-day workings of a busy farm. (Cover illustration by Karen L. Schmidt.)

cultural gap. But I wanted, besides, an adventure, as I had in *Waterman's Boy.* The feminist movement gave us girl heroes who are strong and wonderful, which is a fine thing. And it gave us boy protagonists who are warm and sensitive, which was a good antidote. But everyone wants a good plot, a little action, and I didn't want to see it getting left out of boys' books.

"*Chicken Bucks...* has many of the same interests. It starts with a wonderful place, a farm where, again, the children understand very well the work that adults do. The hero is a boy who wants to be a farmer, though this time I have added a major girl character, too. Again, the livelihood is threatened, this time in more complicated ways, financial as well as environmental. I did a lot of reading about 'sustainable agriculture,' which is an attempt to use less in the way of chemical inputs, to conserve soil, and to guard water quality. In some ways, sustainable agriculture may be able to help farmers who are overburdened with debt; in any case, one of its principles is diversity—more different kinds of livestock, more different crops. Any kid would figure that a diverse farm is more interesting than 1,000 acres of corn.

"The greatest fun of this book was, again, the research. It turned out that one of my friends had grown up in a

town on the Minnesota/Iowa border, where many of her relatives are still farming. She hadn't been back for fifteen years, so we went together. We flew out and rented a car, feeling bold at having left children and husbands behind, and we stayed at several farms, all engaged in different kinds of operations. People were incredibly hospitable, rode me around in tractors and talked to me about what they raised and why and what the problems were. Children told me about driving tractors and 4H and expectations. One second grader still writes to me and sends me his pictures of tractors. I'd like to put them up on the refrigerator but my own eight-year-old gets too jealous."

* * *

SHAW, Nancy 1946-

PERSONAL: Born April 27, 1946, in Pittsburgh, PA; daughter of Walter Mark (a graphic-arts purchasing agent and accountant) and Dorothy L. (a medical secretary; maiden name, Douthitt) Shaw; married D. Scott Shaw (an engineer), November 11, 1972; children: Allison, Daniel. *Education:* University of Michigan, A.B. (with high distinction), 1968; Harvard University, M.A.T., 1970. *Hobbies and other interests:* Gardening.

ADDRESSES: Office—c/o Houghton Mifflin Co., 2 Park St., Boston, MA 02108.

CAREER: Children's author and homemaker. Author of radio scripts for "Senior Sounds," University of Michigan Institute of Gerontology, Ann Arbor, MI, 1978-81; free-lance writer, 1982—.

MEMBER: Authors Guild, Authors League of America, American Association of University Women, Society of Children's Book Writers, Phi Beta Kappa, Herb Study (Ann Arbor, MI).

AWARDS, HONORS: Jules and Avery Hopwood Award, University of Michigan, 1968; "Fanfare 1987" citation, *Horn Book,* 1987, for *Sheep in a Jeep;* "Best Books for 1991" citation, *School Library Journal,* 1991, for *Sheep in a Shop;* Reading Magic Award, *Parenting* magazine, 1991, for *Sheep in a Shop.*

WRITINGS:

ILLUSTRATED BY MARGOT APPLE

Sheep in a Jeep, Houghton, 1986.
Sheep on a Ship, Houghton, 1989.
Sheep in a Shop, Houghton, 1991.
Sheep Out to Eat, Houghton, 1992.

ADAPTATIONS: Sheep in a Jeep and *Sheep on a Ship* have been produced as school readers; *Sheep in a Jeep* also appears as a book-and-cassette package.

SIDELIGHTS: Nancy Shaw told *SATA* that a boring car trip inspired her first book, *Sheep in a Jeep.* "I have a long history of getting bored on trips, going back to my childhood. We used to take very long ones to my grandparents' house," Shaw said in an interview for

SATA. "One time, when my kids were fairly young, we were on a trip to their grandparents' house and we had been reading a rhyming book. I tried making more rhymes and once I hit upon 'sheep' and 'Jeep,' I felt I wanted to extend that and see what else went with it. Pretty soon a fair amount did go with it." From those first rhymes Shaw created *Sheep in a Jeep,* working off and on for two-and-a-half years. During that time Shaw discovered one of the challenges of writing children's books—to tell her story in very few words, and, in her case, words that rhyme. "A lot of it is a process of putting the words together and then stripping away what doesn't belong," she said.

Shaw had had ideas for children's books before *Sheep in a Jeep,* but "I just had not had one that I pursued as doggedly as I did this," she said. She began by reading books on how to write and sell picture books, then gathered publishers' addresses from *Writers' Market* and *Literary Marketplace.* In choosing companies, "I just thought about the different publishers that I enjoyed," Shaw said. "I read a whole lot of books to my children so I chose publishers who I thought would have views similar to mine or who had published books I liked a lot." Two years passed while Shaw sent the book to various publishers, received several rejection notices, and finally found "a very, very good editor at Houghton Mifflin who helped me make the story just a little bit more coherent."

NANCY SHAW

Houghton assigned the *Sheep in a Jeep* manuscript to illustrator Margot Apple, creating a successful partnership that has continued through each of the later "Sheep" books. "I'm very pleased with what's come of it," Shaw commented. "I love the way she counterpoints the text." While Apple was responsible for the drawings in *Sheep in a Jeep,* Shaw noted that she also had ideas about the illustrations for the book. "It's not unusual for me to make up a dummy copy of a book" with her ideas of what the pictures should be and where they should be placed, Shaw said. "In fact, I did that with the first three 'Sheep' books, and finally got lazy on the fourth." As she writes, Shaw keeps in mind the need for balanced pacing and "drawable" scenes in her stories. She said she creates dummy copies because "I have to see that the story is proceeding at the right pace. There has to be so much text per page turned; if the text is a little bit skimpy on a certain action, it might be possible for a picture to fill in for it. On the other hand, it can't be too skimpy; you can't ask pictures to do things that aren't there."

Shaw explained her method of creating rhyme sequences for her books. "I don't like it if a book maintains the same rhythm in a sing-song fashion. I prefer to switch from very short couplets to longer ones," she said. Shaw noted that it takes more than simple rhymes to make her books work. "A lot of what I'm doing in writing is following sounds as well as following meaning," she continued. "I find that it's often quite stiff if I just take an idea and go looking for the rhymes for it. I have to do that, too, but the best rhymes seem to come together with a strong sound component. With *Sheep in a Jeep* I was just challenging myself to see if I could get all the sounds to work together and make something, so it's a little bit choppier. In the later books, the actions are a little more complex. And the sheep start learning how to *solve* problems, thank goodness!"

Kids in her Ann Arbor, Michigan, neighborhood help Shaw write books that are challenging but not beyond a child's comprehension. She often creates a draft of each book, "and then I'll usually send it around to some of my neighbors and let them read it to their younger children and see how well the kids follow it." This technique was especially helpful with *Sheep on a Ship,* in which Shaw introduced somewhat sophisticated sailing terms.

Many authors and artists have influenced Shaw, including Graham Oakley, and James Stevenson "for his artwork as well as his whimsy as a writer." "I have strong reactions to certain artistic styles," Shaw commented. "I love Beatrix Potter's work. There is an English school of watercolors that I have always enjoyed. A lot of the picture books I've enjoyed are the ones that my kids enjoyed."

"I have strong memories of stories I read as a child," Shaw related. "We didn't get a television until I was nine. Now, I'm glad I didn't have it to entertain me when I was little. Most of the time, I'd rather read than

Sheep find blocks.
Sheep wind clocks.

Sheep try trains. Sheep fly planes.

The third book in Shaw's popular "Sheep" series, *Sheep in a Shop* highlights the sheep's problem-solving and shopping skills. (Illustration by Margot Apple.)

watch TV. I remember *Half Magic, Ellen Tebbits, The Twenty-One Balloons,* and *Mrs. Piggle-Wiggle.* 'Uncle Scrooge' comics were a treasure. They were funny; they taught me about the Abominable Snowman, the Philosopher's Stone, and all sorts of exotic lands and legends—and Huey, Louie, and Dewey were always getting their elders out of a jam."

During college Shaw worked at the Ann Arbor Public Library, and became interested in Maurice Sendak's work while shelving children's books. She went on to write an essay about him that earned her the University of Michigan's Hopwood Award. Now she often finds herself back in the library, sometimes to read her books to children. She also visits elementary schools. "I tell kids about publishing from start to finish and show them how sloppy a book looks at first," she said. "I explain how I think about the material over a period of time and put it away, then bring it back out and think about it some more." She enjoys showing actual printing materials from various stages of the publishing process, from first draft to galley. "I think everybody is fascinated by the way the colors go together," Shaw noted. Her audiences especially enjoy seeing a book's color separations: sheets from the printing press, one for each color, that will combine to create a full-color image. "It's a little hard to picture how a book would look if only the yellow part showed up," Shaw said.

Shaw noted several elements she considers important to writing children's books. "I don't like preachy books, but I think a good book has some kind of a lesson in life as its core," Shaw commented. "The lesson in the 'Sheep' books is, 'Look before you leap.' Also, I think that there is a very important place for slapstick and silliness in helping very small children sort out what's sensible and what isn't. There is a strong place for humor in kids' books." After they learned to read and

began selecting their own stories, "I was fascinated by the way my kids always came back to the silly books," Shaw recalled. "They'd reach for the slapstick books over and over again. So when I got bored silly— literally—in the car and searched for sheep rhymes, I must have known there was something to this slapstick idea. I kept at it until the story for *Sheep in a Jeep* came together. I had the basic idea in less than half an hour, but I played around with the words for days, then months, then finally years, before it became a book. Now I play around with ideas in my study, surrounded by books and toy sheep. Or I might just get bored in the car again."

WORKS CITED:

Shaw, Nancy, interview with Deborah A. Stanley for *Something about the Author,* May 4, 1992.

FOR MORE INFORMATION SEE:

PERIODICALS

Detroit Free Press, July 9, 1991, p. 1E, 2E.
Wall Street Journal, November 21, 1991, p. 1.

—*Sketch by Deborah A. Stanley*

*   *   *

SHERLOCK, Patti

PERSONAL: Married George Grimes (an engineer); children: Matt and Shane (twins), Mary.

ADDRESSES: Home—5655 Aurora Dr., Idaho Falls, ID 83402. *Agent*—Jean Naggar Literary Agency, 216 East 75th St., New York, NY 10021.

PATTI SHERLOCK

CAREER: Writer of books for children. Has worked with Community Food Bank and Regional Council of Christian Ministry. 4-H Livestock leader.

MEMBER: Western Writers of America, Pacific Northwest Writers, Toastmasters.

AWARDS, HONORS: First place award, Pacific Northwest Writers, 1988; Spur Award for best juvenile fiction runner-up, Western Writers of America, 1991, for *Four of a Kind.*

WRITINGS:

Alone on the Mountain, Doubleday, 1978.
Four of a Kind, Holiday House, 1991.
Some Fine Dog, Holiday House, 1992.

Contributor of fiction and non-fiction to numerous periodicals.

WORK IN PROGRESS: Animal fantasy book.

SIDELIGHTS: Patti Sherlock told *SATA:* "When I was a little girl, my neighbor owned an elderly Palomino horse named Star. I hung around the neighbor's a lot—brushing Star and trying to attract the attention of people in the house. Eventually, someone would notice me, and come out and saddle Star. Away I would ride, the happiest child on the planet.

"Star would run under low branches to brush me off, or next to fences to scrape me off, but that didn't stop me from worshipping her.

"One Saturday morning I looked out my upstairs window, and saw a stranger leading Star into a horse trailer. I dashed outside to find out what was going on. It turned out that Star's owner, a young mother with small children, had sold the horse because she had no time to ride. Maybe the new owner was someone who wanted a saddle horse, but old horses often have a much worse fate.

"Even without knowing that, I was crushed. I refused breakfast, went to my attic room, and spent the entire morning writing a maudlin story about a girl who lost the horse she loved. I can only guess how overdramatic and terrible the story was. But, looking backing, I can see that episode showed how I would handle pain. I would write about it. And, of course, not just pain.

"When I was in sixth grade I wrote a comedy play, and my teacher helped me produce it for the class. In seventh grade, I wrote silly commercials for the school talent show, and got a lot of laughs. That encouraged me.

"In high school, I wrote for the paper, an excellent excuse to get out of class. 'Mrs. Smith, I need to go do a story on construction of the new wing for the school. May I be excused?' Teachers, amazingly, trusted me,

In *Four of a Kind,* Sherlock tells the tale of a young boy's adventures in the rough-and-tumble West. (Cover illustration by Ronald Himler.)

SOME FINE DOG

Patti Sherlock

Sherlock's border collie, Duncan, served as the inspiration for *Some Fine Dog.* (Cover illustration by Himler.)

and I met my friends in the rest room to gossip and laugh. Once, though, I wrote a satire for the front page, and an English teacher took me aside and said solemnly, 'Please go to college and become a writer.'

"In college journalism classes, I learned little. (Perhaps I didn't pay attention.) Later, working on newspapers under tough editors, I learned much. I loved my job. For the first time in my life, my social life took a back seat to work. If a promising assignment came up, I would stand up friends or dates so I could do the story.

"When I was expecting my first child, I practiced cartooning four hours a day. I had decided cartooning was the career I wanted to try next. I gave birth to twins and the next year was very busy. I found that when I did have a few minutes to my self, I didn't cartoon. I wrote. That told me something.

"My first book, *Along on the Mountain,* came to me out of the blue. An editor at Doubleday saw a magazine story I'd written about sheepherders. He suggested expanding the idea into a book about the life of sheepherders, and framing it with the verses from the twenty-third Psalm.

"When I watched powerful draft horses pull at the Eastern Idaho State Fair in Blackfoot, I knew I wanted to do a book on the subject. The unpublished manuscript won first place in the Pacific Northwest Writer's juvenile novel category, and that led to my getting an agent and, later, publishing with Holiday House.

"Our border collie, Duncan, was the inspiration for *Some Fine Dog.* Duncan is brilliant, and invaluable help when we are moving our sheep. Often it has hit me how unhappy Duncan would be if he couldn't do what his instinct and breeding tell him to—work sheep. I decided to do a book about a boy who lives in a town and owns a border collie. Serious problems arise because the dog is not able to work sheep.

"Currently I am working on an animal fantasy. The main character is a dairy heifer. My daughter's 4-H project is the inspiration. A picture book for young children is at my agent's.

"Recently, at an autographing, I was signing a copy of *Four of a Kind* for a woman. She had bought the book for her son, who is interested in horses. It struck me, suddenly, how satisfying it is to write books for children. What I mean is, when you're busy writing a story you want to tell, you don't envision the people the story is intended for. But when you're autographing a book for a person with a name and individual interests, well, that is exciting. Creating a story is a joy, but knowing it will be read by a child is an extra happiness."

* * *

SHINE, Deborah 1932-
(Debby Slier; pseudonyms: Edith Adams, Sarah Bright, Robin Harris)

PERSONAL: Born April 18, 1932, in Johannesburg, South Africa; came to the United States in 1964; daughter of Jack and Sara (Altuskia) Slier.

ADDRESSES: Home—Riverside Dr., New York, NY 10032. *Office*—Checkerboard Press, Inc., 30 Vesey St., New York, NY 10007.

CAREER: Fashion designer in Johannesburg, South Africa, and London, England, 1953-58; The Owl and the Pussycat Children's Bookstore, Lexington, KY, owner, 1968-78; Random House, Inc., New York City, children's book editor, 1981-85; Checkerboard Press, Inc., New York City, editor, 1986—. Author of children's books.

MEMBER: Author's Guild.

WRITINGS:

Little Puppy's New Name, illustrated by Denise Fleming, Random House, 1985.
The Little Engine that Could, illustrated by Christina Ong, Putnam, 1988.
The Pudgy I Love You Book, illustrated by Katherine D. Coville, Putnam, 1988.

Three puppies lived with their
mother in a cozy basket in the kitchen.
Two of the puppies were named
Spotty and Brownie. But the third
puppy was so small that everyone
just called him Little Puppy.

In *Little Puppy's New Name,* **Deborah Shine presents the comical adventures of a very small dog trying to adjust to a very big world.** (Illustration by Denise Fleming.)

The Pudgy Noisy Book, illustrated by Kathleen G. McCord, Putnam, 1988.

(Editor) *Make a Joyful Sound: Poems for Children by African-American Poets,* illustrated by Cornelius Van Wright and Ying-Hwa Hu, Checkerboard Press, 1989.

(Editor) *We Can Do It!,* illustrated with photographs by Laura Dwight, Checkerboard Press, 1991.

UNDER NAME DEBBY SLIER

Teddy Beddy Bear's Bedtime Book, illustrated by Nancy Herndon, Random House, 1985.

Teddy Beddy Bear's Bedtime Adventure, illustrated by Betty Reichmeier, Random House, 1985.

What Do Babies Do, Random House, 1985.

What Do Toddlers Do, Random House, 1985.

Mr. Potato Head's New Tool Set, illustrated by Renzo Barto, Random House, 1985.

Mrs. Potato Head's New Hat, illustrated by Barto, Random House, 1985.

Whose Baby Are You?, Random House, 1987.

What Goes With This?, Random House, 1987.

Baby's Words, Random House, 1988.

Busy Baby, Checkerboard Press, 1988.

Hello Baby, Checkerboard Press, 1988.

Santa's Special Gift, illustrated by Kit Wray, Checkerboard Press, 1988.

(Adaptor) *The Gingerbread Boy,* illustrated by Jill Dubin, Checkerboard Press, 1988.

Elsie's Clean Day, illustrated by Kitty Diamantis, Checkerboard Press, 1988.

Alf on the Move, illustrated by Ted Enik, Checkerboard Press, 1988.

Farm Animals, Checkerboard Press, 1988.

Baby Places, Checkerboard Press, 1989.

(Adaptor) *The Brementown Musicians,* illustrated by Heidi Petach, Checkerboard Press, 1989.

Brothers and Sisters, Checkerboard Press, 1989.

Little Animals, Checkerboard Press, 1989.

Little Babies, Checkerboard Press, 1989.

Words I Know, Checkerboard Press, 1989.

(Editor) *Animal Noises,* illustrated by Cathy Beylon, Checkerboard Press, 1990.

Hello School, illustrated with photographs by Dwight, Checkerboard Press, 1990.

(Editor) *I Can Do It!,* illustrated with photographs by Dwight, Checkerboard Press, 1990.

(Editor) *Me and My Dad,* illustrated with photographs by Dwight, Checkerboard Press, 1990.

(Editor) *Me and My Mom,* illustrated with photographs by Dwight, Checkerboard Press, 1990.

My First ABC, illustrated by Louise Bates, McClanahan, 1990.

(Editor) *My Noisy Book,* Checkerboard Press, 1990.

(Editor) *When You Were a Baby,* illustrated by Barbara Steadman, 1990.

(Editor) *Baby's Games,* illustrated by Pat Schories, Checkerboard Press, 1990.

(Editor) *Where's the Baby?,* illustrated with photographs by Dwight, Checkerboard Press, 1991.

(Editor) *Where's the Kitten?,* illustrated with photographs by Dwight, Checkerboard Press, 1991.

(Editor) *Where's the Puppy?,* illustrated with photographs by Dwight, Checkerboard Press, 1991.

UNDER PSEUDONYM EDITH ADAMS

The Charmkins Discover Big World, illustrated by Denise Fleming, Random House, 1983.

The Noisy Book Starring Yakey Yak, illustrated by Richard Hefter, Random House, 1983.

My Little Pony and the New Friends, illustrated by Beylon, Random House, 1984.

Santa's Christmas Surprise, illustrated by Pat Susetendal, Random House, 1985.

UNDER PSEUDONYM SARAH BRIGHT

Hello Kitty's Bedtime Search, illustrated by Scott Sullivan, Random House, 1982.

Hello Kitty's Paper Kiss, illustrated by Bruce McGowin, Random House, 1982.

My Melody's Good-Night Book, Random House, 1982.

Hello Kitty's Happy Christmas, illustrated by J. M. L. Gray, Random House, 1984.

Hello Kitty's Early Day, illustrated by Gray, Random House, 1984.

Hello Kitty's Special Present, illustrated by Gray, Random House, 1984.

UNDER PSEUDONYM ROBIN HARRIS

Hello Kitty Sleeps Over, illustrated by Gray, Random House, 1982.

My Melody's New Bike, illustrated by Carolyn Bracken, Random House, 1982.

OTHER

Also author of activity books for children. Contributor of poetry to numerous poetry collections.

SIDELIGHTS: Deborah Shine writes *SATA:* "I'm interested in the world of the small child—the marvelous age of discovery when they notice the world around them, and are eager to explore it." Shine opened the first children's bookstore in the United States—The Owl and the Pussycat Children's Bookstore—in Lexington, Kentucky, in 1968.

* * *

SLIER, Debby
See SHINE, Deborah

* * *

SPINELLI, Jerry 1941-

PERSONAL: Born February 1, 1941, in Norristown, PA; son of Louis A. (a printer) and Lorna Mae (Bigler) Spinelli; married Eileen Mesi (a writer), May 21, 1977;

children: Kevin, Barbara, Lana, Jeffrey, Molly, Sean, Ben. *Education:* Gettysburg College, A.B., 1963; Johns Hopkins University, M.A., 1964; atttended Temple University, 1964.

ADDRESSES: Home—331 Melvin Rd. Phoenixville, PA 19460. *Agent*—Ms. Ray Lincoln, Ray Lincoln Literary Agency, 4 Surrey Rd., Melrose Park, PA 19126.

CAREER: Chilton Company (magazine publishers), Radnor, PA, editor, 1966-89; writer. *Military service:* U.S. Naval Reserve, 1966-72.

MEMBER: Philadelphia Writers Organization.

AWARDS, HONORS: Boston Globe/Horn Book Award, 1990, Newbery Medal, American Library Association, 1991, and D.C. Fisher Award, 1992, all for *Maniac Magee.*

WRITINGS:

Space Station Seventh Grade, Little, Brown, 1982.
Who Put That Hair in My Toothbrush?, Little, Brown, 1984.
Night of the Whale, Little, Brown, 1985.
Jason and Marceline, Little, Brown, 1986.
Dump Days, Little, Brown, 1988.
Maniac Magee, Little, Brown, 1990.
The Bathwater Gang, illustrated by Meredith Johnson, Little, Brown, 1990.
There's a Girl in My Hammerlock, Simon & Schuster, 1991.
Fourth Grade Rats, Scholastic, 1991.

Contributor to books, including *Our Roots Grow Deeper Than We Know: Pennsylvania Writers—Pennsylvania Life,* edited by Lee Gutkind, University of Pittsburgh Press, 1985, and *Noble Pursuits,* edited by Virginia A.

JERRY SPINELLI

Arnold and Carl B. Smith, Macmillan, 1988. Work represented in anthologies, including *Best Sports Stories of 1982,* Dutton.

SIDELIGHTS: Best known for his Newbery-Award-winning book *Maniac Magee,* Jerry Spinelli's entire body of work is distinguished by his accurate and humorous depictions of adolescent life. *Washington Post Book World* contributor Deborah Churchman deemed Spinelli "a master of those embarrassing, gloppy, painful and suddenly wonderful things that happen on the razor's edge between childhood and full-fledged adolescence." While some parents may cringe at his characters' ribald jokes and risque topics of conversation, this approach has earned the author both the respect and loyal following of young readers. Critics maintain that Spinelli is popular because he accepts kids for what they are. The author "neither judges nor berates but shakes everyone up in his own bag of tricks and watches to see what will spill out," according to Ethel R. Twichell in a *Horn Book* review of Spinelli's book *Dump Days.*

Spinelli grew up in Norristown, Pennsylvania, and his first claim to fame was that a local paper published a poem he wrote about a hometown team's football victory. This experience left him eager to continue writing, and the author tried to match this success as an adult. Spinelli thought that because he was older he had to write about issues important to grownups. Publishers, however, were not interested in these topics. Spinelli found his narrative voice after he married. One of his children's feats—eating food that the author had been saving for a snack—inspired him to write, and this incident became the part of his first novel, *Space Station Seventh Grade.* Spinelli once remarked that when he started writing about youngsters he began "to see that in my own memories and in the kids around me, I had all the material I needed for a schoolbagful of books. I saw that each kid is a population unto him- or herself, and that a child's bedroom is as much a window to the universe as an orbiting telescope or a philosopher's study."

Space Station Seventh Grade recounts the everyday adventures of Jason Herkimer, a junior high school student. With seemingly mundane events—such as masterminding classroom pranks and chasing after girls—the author traces Jason's awkward entrance into adolescence. Although Jason seems impulsive and has a penchant for getting into trouble because he speaks before he thinks, he must also contend with more serious issues, including coping with divorced parents and accepting a stepfather. Some critics disapproved of the crude humor Spinelli's characters continually use, but judged that the author accurately represents the adolescent milieu. *Voice of Youth Advocates* contributor James J. McPeak called the story "first-rate," and Twichell, writing in *Horn Book,* deemed *Space Station Seventh Grade* a "truly funny book."

Spinelli followed *Space Station Seventh Grade* with *Who Put That Hair in My Toothbrush?* In this book, the

Friendships become strained when a number of clubs fight for membership in *The Bathwater Gang.* (Illustration by Meredith Johnson.)

chapters alternate between the first-person narration of Megin and Greg, a sister and brother two years apart with vastly different personalities. Greg is preoccupied with a possible romance, while sports-crazy Megin secretly befriends an elderly woman confined to a nursing home. The pair fights constantly, but when a crisis nearly erupts, they join forces. Critics appreciated Spinelli's humorous depiction of sibling rivalry mixed with his inclusion of weighty themes. In a review for *Horn Book,* Karen Jameyson credited the author with a "sure ear for adolescent dialogue" and called the book "hilarious."

Jason and Marceline, published in 1986, serves as a sequel to *Space Station Seventh Grade.* Now a ninth grader, Jason again copes with the daily trials of adolescence, including attempting romance with Marceline, a trombone player who once beat him up. Marceline initially rejects Jason's advances because he tries to impress her the same bravado and macho behavior that his friends employ in their romantic conquests. When he shows his caring side in a heroic lunchroom incident,

Spinelli's Newbery-award-winning tale about a runaway orphan addressed a number of social issues, including poverty, alcoholism, and race relations.

however, Marceline forgives Jason's antics and their relationship progresses. With *Jason and Marceline,* Spinelli earned praise for pointing out that respect and friendship are necessary in a loving relationship between people of any age. Writing again in *Horn Book,* Twichell noted Spinelli's that Jason "truly sounds like a teenager."

Maniac Magee, Spinelli's book that won the prestigious Newbery Medal, is a folktale involving an athletically gifted boy who accomplishments ignite legends about him. Jeffrey Magee, a caucasian boy nicknamed Maniac, is an orphan who has run away from his foster home. His search for a loving household to become a part of is problematic in the racially divided town of Two Mills. Maniac's first stay is with a black family, but after racist graffiti is spray-painted on their house, he leaves. He spends several happy months with an old man in a park equipment room before the man dies. Maniac then moves into a white family's house, filled with roaches, alcohol, and cursing. The sons are gang members and the entire family is racist. Maniac then tries his greatest feat—to initiate better relations between blacks and whites in Two Mills.

Although some critics felt that Spinelli diluted his message about the absurdity of racism by presenting

Maniac Magee as a fable, others believed the author's focus on such an incident was noteworthy. Alison Teal, in her *New York Times Book Review* appraisal, judged that "Spinelli grapples ... with a racial tension rarely addressed in fiction for children in the middle grades." And *Washington Post Book World* contributor Claudia Logan lauded Spinelli's "colorful writing and originality."

Spinelli produced both *There's a Girl in My Hammerlock* and *Fourth Grade Rats* in 1991. *There's a Girl in My Hammerlock* chronicles the adventures of Maisie Potter, an eighth-grade girl who tries out for her school's wrestling team. The school allows her to participate, but Maisie encounters various roadblocks, including her teammates' jealousy about the media attention she receives. *Fourth Grade Rats* focuses on peer pressure and growing up too fast. The main characters are Suds and Joey, two friends who decide they have to become tough and mean now that they are entering fourth grade. Nice-guy Suds initially balks at the plan, but Joey's relentless needling persuades him to reconsider. The experiment is short-lived, however, as both boys are

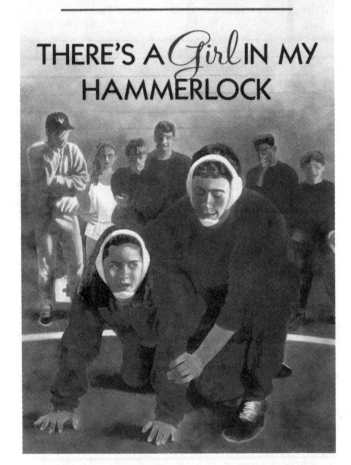

Maisie Potter encounters a number of roadblocks when she tries out for her school's wrestling team, including her teammates' jealousy about the media attention she receives. (Cover illustration by Peter Catalanotto.)

forced—and relieved—to resume their normal behavior.

Spinelli continues to create witty, refreshing books for young readers and it appears there will be no shortage of ideas for future volumes. In his Newbery Award acceptance speech excerpted in *Horn Book,* the author recounted his conversation with a group of schoolchildren. When they asked him where he gets his ideas, the author replied, "from you." Spinelli continued, "You're the funny ones. You're the fascinating ones. You're the elusive and inspiring and promising and heroic and maddening ones."

WORKS CITED:

Churchman, Deborah, "Tales of the Awkward Age," *Washington Post Book World,* January 13, 1985, p. 8.
Jameyson, Karen, review of *Who Put That Hair in My Toothbrush?, Horn Book,* June, 1984, pp. 343-344.
Logan, Claudia, review of *Fourth Grade Rats, Washington Post Book World,* August 11, 1991, p. 11.
McPeak, James J., review of *Space Station Seventh Grade, Voice of Youth Advocates,* April, 1983, p. 42.
Spinelli, Jerry, "Newbery Medal Acceptance," *Horn Book,* July/August, 1991, pp. 426-432.
Teal, Alison, review of *Maniac Magee, New York Times Book Review,* April 21, 1991, p. 33.
Twichell, Ethel R., review of *Space Station Seventh Grade, Horn Book,* February, 1983, p. 54.
Twichell, Ethel R., review of *Jason and Marceline, Horn Book,* March, 1987, p. 217.
Twichell, Ethel R., review of *Dump Days, Horn Book,* May, 1988, p. 355.

FOR MORE INFORMATION SEE:

BOOKS

PERIODICALS

Horn Book, July/August 1991, pp. 433-436.
School Library Journal, June, 1990, p. 138.

* * *

SPIRES, Elizabeth 1952-

PERSONAL: Born May 28, 1952, in Lancaster, OH; daughter of Richard C. (in grounds maintenance) and Sue (a real estate broker; maiden name, Wagner) Spires; married Madison Smartt Bell (a novelist), June 15, 1985; children: Celia Dovell Bell. *Education:* Vassar College, B.A., 1974; Johns Hopkins University, M.A., 1979.

ADDRESSES: Home—6208 Pinehurst Rd., Baltimore, MD 21212. *Office*—Department of English, Goucher College, Towson, MD 21204.

CAREER: Charles E. Merrill Publishing Co., Columbus, OH, assistant editor, 1976-77; free-lance writer, 1977-81; Washington College, Chestertown, MD, visiting assistant professor of English, 1981; Loyola College, Baltimore, MD, adjunct assistant professor of English,

1981-82; Johns Hopkins University, Baltimore, visiting associate professor in writing seminars, 1984-85, 1988-92; Goucher College, Towson, MD, writer in residence, 1985-86, 1988-92.

AWARDS, HONORS: W. K. Rose fellowship, Vassar College, 1976; Pushcart Prize, 1981, for "Blame"; Ingram Merrill Foundation award, 1981; National Endowment for the Arts fellowship, 1981, 1992; Amy Lowell Travelling Poetry scholarship, 1986-87; Sara Teasdale Poetry Prize, 1990; Guggenheim fellowship, 1992.

WRITINGS:

Broadwalk (poems), Bits Press, 1980.
Globe (poems), Wesleyan University Press, 1981.
The Falling Star (juvenile), illustrated by Carlo A. Michelini, C. E. Merrill, 1981.
Count with Me (juvenile), C. E. Merrill, 1981.
The Wheels Go Round (juvenile), C. E. Merrill, 1981.
Simon's Adventure (juvenile), illustrated by Judy Hand, Antioch Publishing, 1982.
Top Bananas (juvenile), Antioch Publishing, 1982.
Things That Go Fast (juvenile), illustrated by Jean Rudegeair, Antioch Publishing, 1982.
Swan's Island (poems), Holt, 1985.
Annonciade (poems), Viking, 1989.

Contributor of poems to anthologies, including *Best American Poems, 1989, 1990, 1991,* and *1992,* and to periodicals, including *New Yorker, Mademoiselle, Poetry, American Poetry Review, Yale Review, Partisan Review, New Criterion,* and *Paris Review.*

WORK IN PROGRESS: A book of poems; *The Tree of Heaven,* a picture book for children.

ELIZABETH SPIRES

SIDELIGHTS: Elizabeth Spires writes *SATA:* "I think by the time I was twelve, I knew I would be a writer, though at the time I thought I would write short stories, not poetry (I was under the influence of Flannery O'Connor at the time).... I'm an Anglophile by nature, particularly interested in English literature and literary landmarks. I certainly feel that living in England has given me a different perspective on the U.S. and allowed me to see a 'fresher' way. Being outside my native country has pushed me toward thinking more about global problems, such as the ever-present threat of war, and about cultural differences and idiosyncrasies. I've also been thinking a lot about the future, what life ten or twenty or thirty years from now will be like, both for myself as an individual, and for society as a whole. My new book of poems is concerned, in part, with the birth of my daughter, Celia, and larger questions concerning the soul's physical existence in the world.

"My poetry has been influenced by my close reading, and love, of the poetry of John Donne, Elizabeth Bishop, Robert Lowell, John Berryman, W. D. Snodgrass, C. K. Williams, and Robert Frost. That's not an exhaustive list at all, though. Currently, I'm working on a fourth collection of poems and hope this year to finish one or two picture books for children which veer away from the 'realistic' towards something concerned with magic, the motif of transformation in everyday life."

*   *   *

STEVENSON, James 1929-

PERSONAL: Born in 1929 in New York, NY; son of Harvey (an architect) and Winifred (Worcester) Stevenson; married Jane Walker, 1953; children: five sons, four daughters. *Education:* Yale University, B.A., 1951.

ADDRESSES: Agent—c/o Greenwillow Books, 1350 Avenue of the Americas, New York, NY 10019.

CAREER: Life, New York City, reporter, 1954-56; *New Yorker,* New York City, cartoonist and writer for "Talk of the Town" (comic strip), 1956-1963. Creator of "Capitol Games" (syndicated political comic strip). Writer and illustrator, 1962—. *Military service:* U.S. Marine Corps, 1951-53.

AWARDS, HONORS: New York Times Outstanding Children's Book of the Year and *School Library Journal* Best Books for Spring honor, both 1977, for *"Could Be Worse!";* American Library Association (ALA) Notable Book designation, 1978, for *The Sea View Hotel,* 1979, for *Fast Friends: Two Stories,* 1980, for *That Terrible Halloween Night; School Library Journal* Best Books for Spring honor, 1979, for *Monty;* Children's Choice Award, International Reading Association, 1979, for *The Worst Person in the World,* 1980, for *That Terrible Halloween Night,* 1982, for *The Night after Christmas,* 1989, for *The Supreme Souvenir Factory,* and 1990, for *Oh No, It's Waylon's Birthday!;* Best Illustrated Book and Outstanding Book honors, both *New York Times,* 1980, for *Howard; School Library Journal* Best Books of 1981 honor, for *The Wish Card Ran Out!; Boston*

Globe/Horn Book honor list, 1981, for *The Night after Christmas;* Christopher Award, 1982, for *We Can't Sleep;* Parents Choice Award, 1982, for *Oliver, Clarence, and Violet;* Boston *Globe/Horn Book* honor list, ALA Notable Book designation, *School Library Journal* Best Books of 1983 honor, all 1983, for *What's under My Bed?;* Garden State Children's Book Award, New Jersey Library Association, 1983, for *Clams Can't Sing;* ALA Notable Book designation, 1986, for *When I Was Nine; Redbook* award, 1987, for *Higher on the Door.*

WRITINGS:

Do Yourself a Favor, Kid (novel), Macmillan, 1962.
The Summer Houses, Macmillan, 1963.
Sorry, Lady, This Beach Is Private! (cartoons), Macmillan, 1963.
Sometimes, But Not Always (autobiographical novel), Little, Brown, 1967.
Something Marvelous Is About to Happen (humor), Harper, 1971.
Cool Jack and the Beanstalk, Penguin, 1976.
Let's Boogie! (cartoons), Dodd, 1978.
Uptown Local, Downtown Express, Viking, 1983.

FOR CHILDREN; SELF-ILLUSTRATED, EXCEPT AS INDICATED

Walker, the Witch, and the Striped Flying Saucer, Little, Brown, 1969.
The Bear Who Had No Place to Go, Harper, 1972.
Here Comes Herb's Hurricane!, Harper, 1973.
"Could be Worse!," Greenwillow, 1977.
Wilfred the Rat, Greenwillow, 1977.
(With daughter, Edwina Stevenson) *"Help!" Yelled Maxwell,* Greenwillow, 1978.
The Sea View Hotel, Greenwillow, 1978.
Winston, Newton, Elton, and Ed, Greenwillow, 1978.
The Worst Person in the World, Greenwillow, 1978.
Fast Friends: Two Stories, Greenwillow, 1979.

JAMES STEVENSON

A cantankerous curmudgeon terrorizes other vacationers while on seaside holiday in Stevenson's self-illustrated *The Worst Person in the World at Crab Beach.*

Monty, Greenwillow, 1979.
Howard, Greenwillow, 1980.
That Terrible Halloween Night, Greenwillow, 1980.
Clams Can't Sing, Greenwillow, 1980.
The Night after Christmas, Greenwillow, 1981.
The Wish Card Ran Out!, Greenwillow, 1981.
The Whale Tale, Random House, 1981.
Oliver, Clarence, and Violet, Greenwillow, 1982.
We Can't Sleep, Greenwillow, 1982.
What's under My Bed?, Greenwillow, 1983.
The Great Big Especially Beautiful Easter Egg, Green-
    willow, 1983.
Barbara's Birthday, Greenwillow, 1983.
Grandpa's Great City Tour: An Alphabet Book, Green-
    willow, 1983.
Worse Than Willy!, Greenwillow, 1984.
Yuck!, Greenwillow, 1984.
Emma, Greenwillow, 1985.
Are We Almost There?, Greenwillow, 1985.
That Dreadful Day, Greenwillow, 1985.
Fried Feathers for Thanksgiving, Greenwillow, 1986.

No Friends, Greenwillow, 1986.
There's Nothing To Do!, Greenwillow, 1986.
When I Was Nine (autobiographical), Greenwillow,
    1986.
Happy Valentine's Day, Emma!, Greenwillow, 1987.
Higher on the Door (sequel to *When I Was Nine*),
    Greenwillow, 1987.
No Need for Monty, Greenwillow, 1987.
Will You Please Feed Our Cat?, Greenwillow, 1987.
The Supreme Souvenir Factory, Greenwillow, 1988.
We Hate Rain!, Greenwillow, 1988.
The Worst Person in the World at Crab Beach, Greenwil-
    low, 1988.
Grandpa's Too-Good Garden, Greenwillow, 1989.
Oh No, It's Waylon's Birthday!, Greenwillow, 1989.
Un-Happy New Year, Emma!, Greenwillow, 1989.
Emma at the Beach, Greenwillow, 1990.
July, Greenwillow, 1990.
National Worm Day, Greenwillow, 1990.
Quick! Turn the Page!, Greenwillow, 1990.
The Stowaway, Greenwillow, 1990.

Which One Is Whitney?, Greenwillow, 1990.
Mr. Hacker, illustrated by Frank Modell, Greenwillow, 1990.
Brrr!, Greenwillow, 1991.
That's Exactly the Way It Wasn't, Greenwillow, 1991.
The Worst Person's Christmas, Greenwillow, 1991.
Rolling Rose, Greenwillow, 1991.
Don't You Know There's a War On?, Greenwillow, 1992.
And Then What?, Greenwillow, 1992.
The Flying Acorns, Greenwillow, 1993.

ILLUSTRATOR

William K. Zinsser, *Weekend Guests: From "We're So Glad You Could Come" to "We're So Sorry You Have to Go," and Vice-Versa* (adult), Harper, 1963.
James Walker Stevenson (son), *If I Owned a Candy Factory*, Little, Brown, 1968.
Eric Stevenson, *Tony and the Toll Collector*, Little, Brown, 1969.
Lavinia Ross, *Alec's Sand Castle*, Harper, 1972.
Alan Arkin, *Tony's Hard Work Day*, Harper, 1972.
Sara D. Gilbert, *What's a Father For?: A Father's Guide to the Pleasures and Problems of Parenthood with Advice from the Experts*, Parents Magazine Press, 1975.
John Donovan, *Good Old James*, Harper, 1975.
Janet Schulman, *Jack the Bum and the Halloween Handout*, Greenwillow, 1977.
Schulman, *Jack the Bum and the Haunted House*, Greenwillow, 1977.
Schulman, *Jack the Bum and the UFO*, Greenwillow, 1978.
Charlotte Zolotow, *Say It!* (ALA Notable Book), Greenwillow, 1980.
Jack Prelutsky, *The Baby Uggs Are Hatching* (poetry), Greenwillow, 1982.
Louis Phillips, *How Do You Get a Horse Out of the Bathtub?: Profound Answers to Preposterous Questions*, Viking, 1983.
Wilson Gage (pseudonym of Mary Q. Steele), *Cully Cully and the Bear*, Greenwillow, 1983.
Zolotow, *I Know a Lady*, Greenwillow, 1984.
Prelutsky, *The New Kid on the Block* (poems), Greenwillow, 1984.
John Thorn, editor, *The Armchair Book of Baseball*, Macmillan, 1985.
Franz Brandenberg, *Otto Is Different*, Greenwillow, 1985.
Phillips, *Brain Busters: Just How Smart Are You, Anyway?*, Viking, 1985.
Helen V. Griffith, *Georgia Music*, Greenwillow, 1986.
Cynthia Rylant, *Henry and Mudge*, Bradbury, 1987.
Rylant, *Henry and Mudge in Puddle Trouble*, Bradbury, 1987.
Griffith, *Grandaddy's Place*, Greenwillow, 1987.
Dr. Seuss (pseudonym of Theodor Seuss Geisel), *I Am Not Going to Get up Today!*, Random House, 1987.
Phillips, *How Do You Lift a Walrus with One Hand?: More Profound Answers to Preposterous Questions*, Viking, 1988.
Else Holmelund Minarik, *Percy and the Five Houses*, Greenwillow, 1989.

Prelutsky, *Something Big Has Been Here* (poetry), Greenwillow, 1990.
Rupert Matthews, *Explorer*, Random House, 1991.
Barbara Dugan, *Loop the Loop*, Greenwillow, 1992.
Griffith, *Grandaddy and Janetta*, Greenwillow, 1993.

OTHER

Also author of plays and television sketches. Contributor of articles to *New Yorker*.

ADAPTATIONS: Many of Stevenson's books have been adapted for filmstrip or audio cassette, including: *Fast Friends*, Educational Enrichment Materials, 1981; *"Could Be Worse!"* and *That Terrible Halloween Night*, both Educational Enrichment Materials, 1982; *What's under My Bed?*, Weston Woods, 1984; *We Can't Sleep*, Random House, 1984, re-released on videocassette, 1988. *Howard* was adapted for film as *New Friends*, Made-to-Order Library Products. *"Could Be Worse!"* and *What's under My Bed?* were highlighted on *Reading Rainbow*, PBS-TV.

SIDELIGHTS: James Stevenson, a prolific author and illustrator of books for children, is noted for gently humorous, animated stories that depict the world of childhood with understanding and wit. Stevenson chooses sibling rivalry, nighttime fears, boredom, and other concerns of family life as subjects for his stories, and approaches them from a child's point of view. Incorporating a subtle moral message into his books, Stevenson carries an upbeat view of life throughout his stories and illustrations, always ending on an optimistic note. His sketchy, high-spirited drawings have also illustrated the books of such notable children's authors as Dr. Seuss, Else Holmelund Minarik, Charlotte Zolotow, and Franz Brandenberg.

Stevenson was born in New York City, and was raised in small towns throughout New York state. He credits his public school education with having a great impact on his life: "[One school I went to] had a kind of policy of telling you that everybody could do everything. Everybody could sing, dance, act, play musical instruments, write stories, make pictures and change the world," he recalled to Kimberly Olson Fakih in *Publishers Weekly*. Stevenson continued his education at Yale University, majoring in English with the intention of becoming a writer. His first success was with art rather than writing, however; he was selling ideas for cartoons to the *New Yorker* magazine while still a student at Yale. After graduating in 1951, Stevenson spent two years in the U.S. Marine Corps Officer Training Program, followed by another two years as a *Life* reporter. In 1956, Stevenson moved to the *New Yorker* art department full-time, developing cartoon ideas for staff artists. During this period he continued to pursue his goal of becoming a writer. In 1960, Stevenson graduated to working as a *New Yorker* reporter while writing a series of three adult novels as well as a book of original cartoons. Stevenson's novels, as well as the many cartoons he has created for the *New Yorker*, are full of social and political satire, poking fun at suburban living, the media, and other aspects of the "establishment."

Gradually Stevenson's focus shifted away from current issues, and he adopted a more nostalgic approach in his art. He became interested in subjects of concern to children and eventually began creating books for a younger audience. His first involvement with picture books was with his eight-year-old son James. Stevenson recalled to Fakih, "[I said to James,] 'Tell me a story and we'll make a book.' He stood at my desk and narrated a story; I wrote it down and then did the pictures. It was a collaboration, and it was published. We split the royalties." The book that resulted was *If I Owned a Candy Factory*, published in 1968.

The first picture book that Stevenson both wrote and illustrated was *Walker, the Witch, and the Striped Flying Saucer*, published the following year. A few years later, *"Could Be Worse!"* firmly established him as a writer of children's books, as well being the first story to introduce the character "Grandpa," Stevenson's "alter-ego." "A more engaging character than Grandpa has not emerged in recent picture books," commented Gertrude Herman in *Horn Book*. A master of the incredibly tall tale, Grandpa responds to grandchildren Mary Ann and Louie's concern that his life is boring by recounting a recent—and totally unbelievable—adventure. In later books, Grandpa helps his grandchildren deal with

various problems by concocting suitable tall tales he claims are from his past. Grandpa's whoppers console Mary Ann and Louie when they come home from a terrible first day of school (*That Dreadful Day*), help them deal with the move to a new neighborhood (*No Friends*), and calm their fear of the dark (*What's Under My Bed?*). Stevenson combines verbal nonsense with humorous drawings of Grandpa and his younger brother, Uncle Wainwright, as mustachioed children to appeal directly to children's love of the silly and absurd. Louie and Mary Ann, together with Stevenson's young readers, can count on the fact that, whatever their problem, Grandpa has probably had one like it, but so much worse that theirs don't seem as bad by comparison.

Stevenson has featured Mary Ann, Louie, and Grandpa in several popular books. In *That Terrible Halloween Night*, the two children are busy attempting to frighten Grandpa: "'Something not *too* scary,' said Mary Ann. 'Grandpa's pretty old.'" No matter what they try, Grandpa remains unruffled behind his newspaper, claiming "I don't get very scared anymore—not since that terrible Halloween night." The dapper old gentleman goes on to tell his grandchildren a scary story about what happened to him on a Halloween long ago,

In Stevenson's self-illustrated story *Brrr!*, Grandpa makes a humorous point about how cold it was when he and his brother were children.

Mary Ann and her brother Louie try to frighten Grandpa in *The Terrible Halloween Night.* (Illustration by Stevenson.)

complete with pumpkins, a haunted house, spiders, and lots of yucky green stuff. Grandpa's story ends on a typically Stevensonian note, with a quiet chuckle and a warm smile.

Stevenson has expanded his cast of characters throughout his career as a children's author. Several books, including *Emma* and *Un-happy New Year, Emma!,* are about a good-natured young witch/apprentice named Emma who triumphs over the efforts of two older sorceresses, Dolores and Lavinia, to undermine her attempts at magic. Then there are the "worst" books. The worst is a crotchety old gentleman: "The worst person in the world didn't like anything anybody else liked. He didn't like springtime, or music, or dessert, or laughing, or people who were friendly." The worst disguises his need for companionship by grumbling and complaining where the most people will hear him. In *The Worst Person's Christmas,* the old curmudgeon relishes the spirit of the holiday season: "That night the worst put a chair by his front window so that, when the carol singers came, he could tell them to get off his property and go away." As in Stevenson's other "worst" books, *The Worst Person in the World* and *The Worst Person in the World at Crab Beach,* a series of mishaps occur that don't exactly make the worst any nicer, but by story's end he isn't the worst person in the whole *entire* world anymore either.

Stevenson began writing and drawing as a boy and was encouraged by his father who was a watercolorist. He says he was influenced by movies and comics rather

than any of the children's books he read as a child. "I think that my experience and creative mind have been formed much more by movies and comic books. I like the idea of a storyboard and I like the idea of a movie and all the different angles from which things can be viewed," he once told an interviewer.

Stevenson's books are often illustrated in comic-book or cartoon style. The intermix of story line with dialogue "balloons" and graffiti adds energy and dimension to his humorously-drawn tales. The use of pencil as an artistic medium in drawing his appealing, scruffy characters brings an air of informality and spontaneity to his stories. Stevenson adds a wash of soft color to his drawings, avoiding the vivid contrasts of the traditional comic book in favor of a more subtle effect.

"I have no ideas until I sit here with the paper in front of me," Stevenson told Fakih from his office at the *New Yorker.* "I never think of cartoon ideas until I'm here. For children's books, it's a different desk. One of the problems of working is that you try to stay fresh. You can't do it unless you just stop and do something else." To his young audience, Stevenson has continued to provide a fresh, lively view of things. As Karla Kuskin wrote in the *New York Times Book Review,* "Whether writing or drawing, Mr. Stevenson understands perfectly the strength of a simple understated line and a quiet laugh."

WORKS CITED:

Fakih, Kimberly Olsen, "James Stevenson," *Publishers Weekly,* February 27, 1987, pp. 148-149.
Herman, Gertrude, "A Picture Is Worth Several Hundred Words," *Horn Book,* September-October, 1985, p. 605.
Kuskin, Karla, "The Art of Picture Books," *New York Times Book Review,* November 15, 1981, p. 57.
Stevenson, James, *That Terrible Halloween Night,* Greenwillow, 1980.
Stevenson, James, *The Worst Person's Christmas,* Greenwillow, 1991.

FOR MORE INFORMATION SEE:

BOOKS

Children's Literature Review, Volume 17, Gale, 1989, pp. 148-168.
Kingman, Lee, and others, compilers, *Illustrators of Children's Books: 1967-1976,* Horn Book, 1978.
Twentieth Century Children's Writers, third edition, St. James Press, 1989, pp. 919-920.

PERIODICALS

Atlantic, July, 1963.
Best Sellers, August 15, 1967.
Books for Your Children, autumn-winter, 1985, p. 25.
Chicago Tribune Book World, October 5, 1980; April 10, 1983.
Christian Science Monitor, November 6, 1969; November 10, 1980.
Commonweal, November 11, 1977.
Horn Book, August, 1977, pp. 432-433.
Junior Bookshelf, December, 1971, p. 367.
Los Angeles Times Book Review, August 14, 1983.
National Observer, July 24, 1967.
Newsweek, April 8, 1963; July 14, 1969; December 29, 1971; December 11, 1978; December 18, 1978; December 7, 1981.
New Yorker, July 20, 1963; August 5, 1967; December 11, 1971; December 2, 1972; December 6, 1982.
New York Times, August 4, 1972.
New York Times Book Review, July 23, 1967; August 7, 1977; November 13, 1977; April 30, 1978; June 17, 1979; October 7, 1979; April 27, 1980; October 26, 1980; April 26, 1981; April 25, 1982; November 14, 1982; March 27, 1983; April 24, 1983; May 20, 1984.
Saturday Review/World, December 4, 1973.
Spectator, November 13, 1971.
Time, August 4, 1967.
Times Educational Supplement, October 21, 1977; December 14, 1979; March 27, 1981; February 18, 1983, p. 30.
Village Voice, December 11, 1978.
Washington Post Book World, October 26, 1969; April 13, 1980; October 12, 1980; December 13, 1981; May 13, 1984.

—Sketch by Pamela L. Shelton

STOLZ, Mary (Slattery) 1920-

PERSONAL: Born March 24, 1920, in Boston, MA; daughter of Thomas Francis and Mary Margaret (a nurse; maiden name, Burgey) Slattery; married Stanley Burr Stolz (a civil engineer), January, 1940 (divorced, 1956); married Thomas C. Jaleski (a physician), June, 1965; children: (first marriage) William. *Education:* Attended Birch Wathen School, Columbia University Teacher's College, 1936-38, and Katharine Gibbs School, 1938-39. *Politics:* "Liberal Northern Democrat." *Hobbies and other interests:* Social and environmental issues, ballet, baseball, cats, hard games of Scrabble, bird-watching, reading.

ADDRESSES: Home—P.O. Box 82, Longboat Key, FL 34228. *Agent*—Roslyn Targ Literary Agency, 105 West 13th St., Suite 15E, New York, NY 10011.

CAREER: Writer of books for children and young adults. Worked variously as a bookstore clerk and secretary.

MEMBER: Authors League of America.

AWARDS, HONORS: Notable Book citation, American Library Association (ALA), 1951, for *The Sea Gulls Woke Me;* Children's Book Award, Child Study Children's Book Committee at Bank Street College, 1953, for *In a Mirror;* Spring Book Festival Older Honor Award, *New York Herald Tribune,* 1953, for *Ready or Not,* 1956, for *The Day and the Way We Met,* and 1957, for *Because of Madeline;* ALA Notable Book citation, 1961, for *Belling the Tiger;* Newbery Award Honor Book, 1962, for *Belling the Tiger,* and 1966, for *The Noonday Friends;* Junior Book Award, Boys' Club of America, 1964, for *The Bully of Barkham Street;* Honor List citation, *Boston Globe/Horn Book,* and National Book Award finalist, Association of American Publish-

MARY STOLZ

ers, both 1975, for *The Edge of Next Year;* Recognition of Merit award, George G. Stone Center for Children's Books, 1982, for entire body of work; ALA Notable Book citation, 1985, for *Quentin Corn;* Children's Science Book Younger Honor Award, New York Academy of Sciences, 1986, for *Night of Ghosts and Hermits: Nocturnal Life on the Seashore;* German Youth Festival Award; ALA Notable Book citation, and Notable Children's Trade Books in Social Studies, Children's Book Council, both 1988, and Teacher's Choice citation, International Reading Association, 1989, all for *Storm in the Night;* numerous other ALA Notable Book citations.

WRITINGS:

FOR YOUNG ADULTS

To Tell Your Love, Harper, 1950.
The Organdy Cupcakes, Harper, 1951.
The Sea Gulls Woke Me, Harper, 1951.
In a Mirror, Harper, 1953.
Ready or Not, Harper, 1953.
Pray Love, Remember, Harper, 1954.
Two by Two, Houghton, 1954, revised edition published as *A Love, or a Season,* Harper, 1964.
Rosemary, Harper, 1955.
Hospital Zone, Harper, 1956.
The Day and the Way We Met, Harper, 1956.
Good-by My Shadow, Harper, 1957.
Because of Madeline, Harper, 1957.
And Love Replied, Harper, 1958.
Second Nature, Harper, 1958.
Some Merry-Go-Round Music, Harper, 1959.
The Beautiful Friend and Other Stories, Harper, 1960.
Wait for Me, Michael, Harper, 1961.
Who Wants Music on Monday?, Harper, 1963.
By the Highway Home, Harper, 1971.
Leap before You Look, Harper, 1972.
The Edge of Next Year, Harper, 1974.
Cat in the Mirror, Harper, 1975.
Ferris Wheel, Harper, 1977.
Cider Days, Harper, 1978.
Go and Catch a Flying Fish, Harper, 1979.
What Time of Night Is It?, Harper, 1981.
Ivy Larkin: A Novel, Harcourt, 1986.

FOR CHILDREN

The Leftover Elf, illustrated by Peggy Bacon, Harper, 1952.
Emmett's Pig, illustrated by Garth Williams, Harper, 1959.
A Dog on Barkham Street (also see below), illustrated by Leonard Shortall, Harper, 1960.
Belling the Tiger, illustrated by Beni Montresor, Harper, 1961.
The Great Rebellion (also see below), illustrated by Montresor, Harper, 1961.
Fredou, illustrated by Tomi Ungerer, Harper, 1962.
Pigeon Flight, illustrated by Murray Tinkelman, Harper, 1962.
Siri, the Conquistador (also see below), illustrated by Montresor, Harper, 1963.

The Bully of Barkham Street (also see below), illustrated by Shortall, Harper, 1963.
The Mystery of the Woods, illustrated by Uri Shulevitz, Harper, 1964.
The Noonday Friends, illustrated by Louis S. Glanzman, Harper, 1965.
Maximilian's World (also see below), illustrated by Shulevitz, Harper, 1966.
A Wonderful, Terrible Time, illustrated by Glanzman, Harper, 1967.
Say Something, illustrated by Edward Frascino, Harper, 1968, revised edition illustrated by Alexander Koshkin, 1993.
The Story of a Singular Hen and Her Peculiar Children, illustrated by Frascino, Harper, 1969.
The Dragons of the Queen, illustrated by Frascino, Harper, 1969.
Juan, illustrated by Glanzman, Harper, 1970.
Land's End, illustrated by Dennis Hermanson, Harper, 1973.
Cat Walk, illustrated by Erik Blegvad, Harper, 1983.
Quentin Corn, illustrated by Pamela Johnson, David Godine, 1985.
The Explorer of Barkham Street (also see below), illustrated by Emily Arnold McCully, Harper, 1985.
Night of Ghosts and Hermits: Nocturnal Life on the Seashore (nonfiction), illustrated by Susan Gallagher, Harcourt, 1985.
The Cuckoo Clock, illustrated by Johnson, David Godine, 1986.
The Scarecrows and Their Child, illustrated by Amy Schwartz, Harper, 1987.
Zekmet, the Stone Carver: A Tale of Ancient Egypt, illustrated by Deborah Nourse Lattimore, Harcourt, 1988.
Storm in the Night, illustrated by Pat Cummings, Harper, 1988.
Pangur Ban, illustrated by Johnson, Harper, 1988.
Barkham Street Trilogy (contains *A Dog on Barkham Street, The Bully of Barkham Street,* and *The Explorer of Barkham Street*), Harper, 1989.
Bartholomew Fair, Greenwillow, 1990.
Tales at the Mousehole (contains revised versions of *The Great Rebellion, Maximilian's World,* and *Siri, the Conquistador*), illustrated by Johnson, David Godine, 1990.
Deputy Shep, illustrated by Johnson, HarperCollins, 1991.
King Emmett the Second, illustrated by Williams, Greenwillow, 1991.
Go Fish, illustrated by Cummings, HarperCollins, 1991.
Stealing Home, HarperCollins, 1992.
The Weeds and the Weather, Greenwillow, in press.

OTHER

Truth and Consequence (adult novel), Harper, 1953.

Stolz has also contributed short stories to periodicals, including *Cosmopolitan, Cricket, Good Housekeeping, Ladies' Home Journal, McCall's, Redbook, Seventeen, Woman's Day,* and *The Writer.* Her books have been published in over twenty-five languages; several have been made available in Braille editions. Stolz's manuscripts are included in the Kerlan Collection at the University of Minnesota, Minneapolis.

ADAPTATIONS: "Baby Blue Expression" (short story; first published in *McCall's*) was adapted for television by Alfred Hitchcock. *The Noonday Friends* was recorded by Miller-Brody, 1976.

WORK IN PROGRESS: Cezanne Pinto, Cowboy, a book about Thomas's ancestor, a runaway slave who eventually became a cowboy.

SIDELIGHTS: Mary Stolz is the author of numerous novels and short stories for both children and young adults. Noted for her eloquence and sensitivity to the everyday events that shape the lives of her characters, her books for teen-age girls were among the first to be recognized for their accurate representation of the emotional concerns of adolescence. Stolz creates realistic characters to inhabit the vivid settings of her novels and incorporates a boy/girl relationship into many of her plots. She has written on such subjects as divorce, family relationships, social problems, and the growth towards adulthood, all with a characteristic respect for the sensitivity and maturity of her young readers. Stolz's novels are especially noted for their dynamic young female protagonists: intelligent and ambitious young

Stolz tells the story of two young girls who must assume some very adult responsibilities in *The Noonday Friends*. (Cover art by Louis S. Glanzman.)

women interested in the arts, curious about the world around them, and desirous of its betterment.

Stolz was born in Boston, Massachusetts, into a family of strong Irish traditions. Together with her sister Eileen and cousin Peg, she moved to New York City where the three girls were raised. Stolz developed a love for books early in her childhood, and was encouraged in her reading by her Uncle Bill. He bought her volumes of literature over the years, including works by such authors as A. A. Milne, Kenneth Grahame, Ernest Thompson Seton, Emily Dickinson, Jane Austen, and John Keats. "They instructed—without scaring me witless—amused, saddened, puzzled, delighted, enriched. Opened worlds, lighted corners. They sustained me," she wrote in *Children's Book Council: 1975*. Her love of reading has oftentimes extended into the lives of her characters and much of her writing is interspersed with literary allusion.

"As a girl I was flighty, flirtatious, impulsive, self-involved and not very thoughtful," Stolz once told *SATA*. "Then I read *Pride and Prejudice* and fell in love with Elizabeth Bennet. To me, she's the loveliest female in fiction, as Rochester is the most captivating male. I used to think they should have married each other. Anyway, I tried to model myself after Elizabeth Bennet, so you can see how much the book affected me. It worked, too. Sort of. My manners improved, even my deportment changed. I think I became more considerate. And *Little Women* ... I don't know if anyone still reads it. I hope so. The book has such warmth and closeness—the closeness of family and friends. The death of Beth March was devastating to me. I used to go back and start over again, actually almost thinking that the next time it would turn out differently. But that book showed how a family faced a loss so great, and survived it, and went on, and even knew happiness again. Quite a lesson to learn from a book."

Stolz's love of reading soon transformed itself into a love of writing, using words to compose the stories of her own imagination. Stolz's prolific outpouring of stories extended into her teenage years, and she wrote constantly while a student at the Birch Wathen School in New York City. The unstructured academic environment of this progressive school allowed her the freedom to both read and write material of her own choosing. Stolz recalled in *Something about the Author Autobiography Series* (*SAAS*), "I always wanted to be a writer, a real, published writer—the way other girls at school wanted to become actresses. A few of them did become actresses, and here am I, a writer."

Stolz went on to study at Columbia University Teacher's College, followed by a year at the Katharine Gibbs School, where she attained typing skills which allowed her to get a secretarial position at Columbia as well as aiding her in her own writing efforts. When she was eighteen years old, Stolz left her job and married Stanley Burr Stolz. She and her husband had a son, William, who kept her busy and away from writing for several years. However, in 1950, after suffering a great deal of physical pain which necessitated her undergoing an operation, Stolz found herself confined to her home during her recovery. Her physician, Dr. Thomas Jaleski (who later was to become her second husband), encouraged her to occupy herself with something during her recuperation. As she recalled in *SAAS:* "I told him that when I was in school (not so awfully far in the past) I'd liked to write. 'Well, that's excellent,' he said. 'My advice is that you write something that will take you a long time. Write a novel.'" She got a secondhand typewriter, a ream of yellow paper, and started writing. Her efforts paid off when the manuscript was accepted by the first publisher she sent it to. *To Tell Your Love* was published in 1950.

"It is sometimes said that the first novel is written some ten years back in a writer's life," the author remembered in *SAAS*. "This probably isn't a rule, but I followed it, writing about a fifteen-year-old girl who falls in love and loses her love, which probably should, or anyway does, happen to most fifteen-year-old girls. It had happened to me, and it was easy to recall the disbelief, the *pain* of having to accept that a boy who had seemed to love me, who had *said* he loved me, no longer did. Creating a family, adding some relatives, putting in my cat, July, I simply wrote my own story and sent the book to Harper's."

Stolz developed a strong relationship with her editor at Harper's over the many years since she began her writing career, and told *SATA:* "The matchless Ursula Nordstrom supported, inspired, and *put up* with me over many, many years. When she died in 1988, I wrote an essay in her memory, in her honor.... She was the finest children's book editor ever, the trail blazer, and all her artists and writers would say the same. When I finish a book, or when working on one, I actually ache, knowing she will not see it."

Much of Stolz's writing is a patchwork of memories of people, places, and circumstances from her own life. *Ready or Not* is the story of the Connor family, who live in a low-income housing project in New York City and try to get by on a small income. The book centers around the eldest daughter, Morgan Connor, and her efforts to help sustain the family through their rough times with her warmth and mature wisdom. *Ivy Larkin: A Novel,* published in 1986, is also set in New York City, and takes place during the Depression era when Stolz herself was a young girl. The protagonist, fourteen-year-old Ivy, faces the isolation of being a scholarship student from a poor family at an exclusive private school catering to the children of wealthy parents. The book tells how Ivy overcomes her fear of being an outsider, her worries when her father loses his job, and her resentments of the snobbishness of the other students.

Although Stolz began her career writing primarily for teenage girls, she soon varied her audience by writing for pre-teens and younger children as well. When her son, Billy, was old enough to be read aloud to, he wanted his mother to write stories that he would enjoy. His insistence inspired her first book for young children,

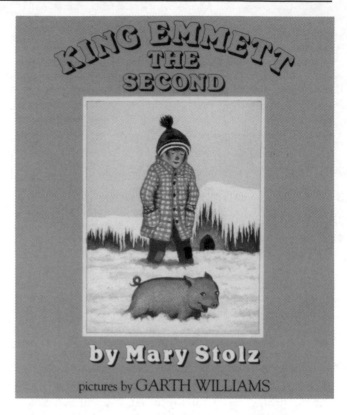

Emmett learns to adjust to change, including the death of his pet pig, in Stolz's book *King Emmett the Second.* (Cover art by Garth Williams.)

The Leftover Elf, which has been followed by many notable children's books, including *Belling the Tiger, The Bully of Barkham Street,* and *Emmett's Pig.* As with her books for teenagers, Stolz's stories for younger readers have emotional depth, as well as entertainment value. *King Emmett the Second,* the sequel to *Emmett's Pig,* deals with the adjustments that young Emmett must make, not only in moving from the city out to a new home in the country, but with the death of his beloved pet pig. Emmett learns to cope with loss and change and by story's end is able to accept a new pet, as well as a new home, into both his life and his heart. *The Noonday Friends,* designated as a Newbery Honor Book in 1966, is written for the junior high school reader. The book tells the story of Franny Davis, whose father is an out-of-work artist and whose mother must work to keep the family together. Eleven-year-old Franny develops a close friendship with Simone, a Puerto Rican girl she is only able to meet during school lunch period. The two friends have a great deal in common: they have to give up their social life for the responsibilities of baby-sitting for younger brothers and sisters and keeping house for their working mothers. Franny and Simone feel overwhelmed by their household chores but their friendship helps each girl learn to accept her family situation.

Stolz credits the daily experience of life with providing the inspiration for her writing. Asked where the ideas from her stories come from, she replied to *SATA:* "From living, and looking, and being curious, and eavesdropping, and caring about nearly everything. From reading." Stolz is adamant about the importance of books to the developing writer: "Reading has been my university, my way of living in history, prehistory, the present, the future. I mean that reading has made me know and understand more people than one person ever could know, or possibly understand, in seven lifetimes. I mean that to me, and to most writers, I think, reading has been as necessary as taking nourishment, sleeping, loving. I mean that to me a life without books would not be worth living." She discussed the development of her characters: "Fictional characters are an amalgam of the real, the imagined, the dreamed-of. They are mosaics—bits of a nephew, a stranger, a beloved poet, a character in someone else's fiction (I think that I put a little of Elizabeth Bennet in my heroines). All these, and more, are put together, pulled apart, shuffled, and altered until, on paper, there is someone not to be recognized as that nephew, that woman seen on a subway and never seen again, that reclusive poet, *or* Jane Austen's perfect young lady."

In an article in *The Writer,* Stolz commented: "On the whole, it is my belief—and I have written from that belief—that after infancy there develops between children and adults (especially parents) an uneasiness, a withdrawal, a perplexity, sometimes hostility. In some cases, the feelings persist until the children are adults. Sometimes, between parents and children, it simply never stops. This tension, this loving and hating, this bafflement and struggle to understand is, in my opinion, the underpinning of all I've written."

Stolz's books are highly regarded as quality literature for young adult readers. *New York Times Book Review* critic Ellen Lewis Buell commented on the "wit, originality and a rare maturity," contained within Stolz's books. "Mary Stolz's remarkable empathy with the characters in her books is particularly important in her stories about older boys and girls," Ruth Hill Viguers agreed in *Margin for Surprise: About Books, Children, and Librarians.* "At a time when many teen-age stories are misleading, she always plays fair. The people of her books are alive, their world is the contemporary world, and their stories are told with truth and dignity." Stolz's more recent young-adult novels have been criticized by some as not "relevant" to today's teen-age reader; that her method of dealing with social problems faced by young people has not kept pace with changing times. Stolz agrees that today's high school student is more sophisticated than when she began writing. "I have not dealt with the drug scene. My characters ... are not battered, they are not criminals, they are not homeless on the road," Stolz commented in *The Writer.* "I know that many writers today ... handle all these themes in their books.... But a writer can write only as he can write." Stolz recognizes her limitations in reflecting the issues of modern young people: "I don't understand the drug culture of today," she told Linda Giuca in the *Hartford Courant.* "You can't write about what you don't know." In more recent books, Stolz has shifted her energies to writing for younger children who still seem to grow up in much the same fashion as they did thirty years ago.

Stolz told *SATA:* "Many people who think they want to write want, actually, to have written something. This is not the same as writing, which is very disciplined work, and there are a lot of things to be doing that are simpler and, perhaps, more fun. So—reading, reading, reading ... writing, writing, writing. When I say this sort of thing to groups of children, I can feel them thinking, 'Then what does she *do:* she reads things, and then she goes and writes something.' I had one child tell me right out that it sounded like a funny way to go about it. I tried to explain that, to me, the reading, in addition to everything else it is, is a form of going to school. It's not imitating, it's learning.

"There are books in which you lose yourself and there are books in which you find yourself. There's a place for both. Detective stories, for instance, are fine for getting lost in. But the great books are those in which you find yourself. And a great book needn't be a classic. It just needs to be the right book at the right time for the person who's reading it."

Today, Stolz lives with her second husband, Thomas Jaleski, in Florida. "We live a shell's throw from the Gulf of Mexico, with nothing between us and the ocean but pale sand and sea oats," she told *SAAS.* "Sunrise, sunset, seabirds, shorebirds, and the mockingbird who comes in early spring bringing us the songs of the north. It is not New England, and we shall always miss New England, but in its way this hurricane-threatened island where we live has us in thrall."

Stolz has always been very concerned about the role human beings have played in the custodianship of the earth. Quoting from her acceptance speech for the George C. Stone recognition of merit in *SAAS,* Stolz said: "Perhaps the animals are planning some fine benign surprise for us. Maybe the whales and elephants with their massive brains are conspiring ... with the eagles ... and, of course, our pets, to lead us blunderers into respect for this small, shared planet. We seem unlikely to arrive at such an attitude on our own, but without it we won't need to wait for a cosmic finale to the earthly drama. We'll arrange one ourselves." Stolz considers young people best able to look ahead, to change the course of society: "Children do a lot of thinking. They continue to ask the simple-hard questions: What's the world about? Life about? What am I about? Or you? What's worth something? What's worth everything? Who *am* I and who are all these others and what are we going to do about *that?* From my mail, I know that there are many children still looking for answers in books. I used to, as a child. I still think something reassuring is to be found in them. If we read hard enough they can offer us at least part of a perspective.... Even with that ... we could, possibly, still save our world. It's a hope." Stolz's faith and optimism in the possibilities of childhood have inspired her as a children's writer. "[Children] are, at present, all we can hope through. Which is why I write for them."

WORKS CITED:

Buell, Ellen Lewis, review of *Ready or Not, New York Times Book Review,* March 22, 1953, p. 24.

Giuca, Linda, "Add Talent to Volumes of Reading, Writing," *Hartford Courant,* June 2, 1974.

Stolz, Mary, "American Bicentennial Reading," *Children's Book Council: 1975,* 1975.

Stolz, Mary, "Believe What You Write About," *The Writer,* October, 1980, pp. 22-23.

Stolz, Mary, essay in *Something about the Author Autobiography Series,* Volume 3, Gale, 1986, pp. 281-92.

Viguers, Ruth Hill, *Margin for Surprise: About Books, Children, and Librarians,* Little, Brown, 1964, p. 107.

FOR MORE INFORMATION SEE:

BOOKS

Contemporary Literary Criticism, Volume 12, Gale, 1980.

Eakin, Mary K., *Good Books for Children,* 3rd edition, University of Chicago Press, 1966, pp. 318-19.

Fisher, Margerie, *Who's Who in Children's Books,* Holt, 1975.

Fuller, Muriel, editor, *More Junior Authors,* H. W. Wilson, 1963, pp. 195-96.

Hopkins, Lee Bennett, *More Books by More People: Interviews with Sixty-five Authors of Books for Children,* Citation, 1974.

Twentieth Century Children's Writers, 3rd edition, St. James Press, 1989, pp. 921-23.

PERIODICALS

Atlantic Monthly, December, 1953.

Booklist, September 15, 1974; January 1, 1976, p. 628; November 1, 1988.

Bulletin of the Center for Children's Books, November, 1965, pp. 50-51; May, 1969; December, 1969; July, 1979; July, 1981; July, 1983; October, 1985; May, 1988.

Chicago Sunday Tribune, August 23, 1953; November 6, 1960, p. 49.

Christian Science Monitor, November 11, 1971, p. B5.

Cricket, September, 1974.

English Journal, September, 1952; September, 1955; April, 1975; October, 1975.

Horn Book, December, 1953, pp. 469-70; April, 1957, p. 141; October, 1957, pp. 406-07; October, 1965; October, 1971; October, 1974; December, 1975, p. 598; April, 1981; November, 1985; January, 1986, p. 61.

Kirkus Review, October 15, 1974, pp. 111-12.

Los Angeles Times Book Review, July 28, 1985; April 20, 1986; May 3, 1987.

New York Herald Tribune Book Review, October 28, 1951; December 13, 1953; November 14, 1954; November 28, 1954; November 13, 1955; December 30, 1956.

New York Times Book Review, May 13, 1951; August 30, 1953, p. 15; September 26, 1954; April 22, 1956; May 18, 1958; November 13, 1960, p. 28; May 14,

1961; November 12, 1961; October 24, 1971, p. 81; September 3, 1972.

Psychology Today, July, 1975.

Publishers Weekly, July 12, 1985; August 9, 1985; September 20, 1985; September 26, 1986; October 9, 1987; January 15, 1988; February 12, 1988; August 26, 1988; August 31, 1990.

School Library Journal, April, 1964; September, 1985; November, 1985; January, 1986; December, 1986; April, 1987; January, 1988; November, 1990.

Times Literary Supplement, November 26, 1954.

Washington Post Book World, May 10, 1987; February 10, 1991.

Wilson Library Bulletin, September, 1953.

—Sketch by Pamela L. Shelton

* * *

STRASSER, Todd 1950-
(Morton Rhue)

PERSONAL: Born May 5, 1950, in New York, NY; son of Chester S. (a manufacturer of dresses) and Sheila (a copy editor; maiden name, Reisner) Strasser; married Pamela Older (a businesswoman), July 2, 1981; children: Lia, Geoff. *Education:* Beloit College, B.A., 1974.

ADDRESSES: Agent—Ellen Levine, 432 Park Ave. S., New York, NY 10016.

CAREER: Free-lance writer, 1975—. Beloit College, Beloit, WI, worked in public relations, 1973-74; *Times Herald Record* (newspaper), Middletown, NY, reporter,

TODD STRASSER

1974-76; Compton Advertising, New York City, copywriter, 1976-77; *Esquire,* New York City, researcher, 1977-78; Toggle, Inc., (fortune cookie company), New York City, owner, 1978-89. Speaker at teachers' and librarians' conferences, middle schools, and at junior and senior high schools. Lectures and conducts writing workshops for adults and teenagers.

MEMBER: International Reading Association, Writers Guild of America, Authors Guild, Freedom to Read Foundation, PEN.

AWARDS, HONORS: American Library Association's Best Books for Young Adults citations, 1981, for *Friends Till the End,* and 1982, for *Rock 'n' Roll Nights;* New York Public Library's Books for the Teen Age citations, 1981, for *Angel Dust Blues,* 1982, for *The Wave* and *Friends Till the End,* 1983, for *Rock 'n' Roll Nights,* and 1984, for *Workin' for Peanuts; Friends Till the End* was chosen a Notable Children's Trade Book in the Field of Social Studies by the National Council for Social Studies and the Children's Book Council, 1982; *Rock 'n' Roll Nights* was chosen for the Acton Public Library's CRABbery Award List, 1983; Young Reader Medal nomination from the California Reading Association, 1983, for *Friends Till the End;* Book Award from the Federation of Children's Books (Great Britain), 1983, for *The Wave,* and 1984, for *Turn It Up!;* Outstanding Book Award from the Iowa Books for Young Adult Program, 1985, for *Turn It Up!;* Colorado Blue Spruce Award nomination, 1987, for *Angel Dust Blues;* Edgar Award nomination from Mystery Writers of America, for *The Accident.*

WRITINGS:

YOUNG ADULT FICTION

Angel Dust Blues, Coward, 1979.
Friends Till the End: A Novel, Delacorte, 1981.
(Under pseudonym Morton Rhue) *The Wave* (novelization based on the television drama of the same title by Johnny Dawkins), Delacorte, 1981.
Rock 'n' Roll Nights: A Novel, Delacorte, 1982.
Workin' for Peanuts, Delacorte, 1983.
Turn It Up! (sequel to *Rock 'n' Roll Nights*), Delacorte, 1984.
A Very Touchy Subject, Delacorte, 1985.
Ferris Bueller's Day Off (novelization based on feature film of the same title by John Hughes), New American Library, 1986.
Wildlife (sequel to *Turn It Up!*), Delacorte, 1987.
Rock It to the Top, Delacorte, 1987.
The Accident, Delacorte, 1988.
Cookie (novelization based on feature film of the same title by Nora Ephron), New American Library, 1989.
Moving Target, Fawcett, 1989.
Beyond the Reef, illustrated by Debbie Heller, Delacorte, 1989.
Home Alone (novelization), Scholastic, 1991.
The Diving Bell, illusrated by Heller, Scholastic, 1992.

In Strasser's *The Complete Computer Popularity Program,* the issue of nuclear power serves as a backdrop for a young boy's struggle to remain loyal to his family and friends. (Cover illustration by Stephanie Gerber.)

OTHER

The Complete Computer Popularity Program, Delacorte, 1984.
The Mall from Outer Space, Scholastic, 1987.
The Family Man (adult novel), St. Martin's, 1988.
Over the Limit (teleplay based on *The Accident*), ABC Afterschool Special, ABC-TV, 1990.

Teacher's guides are available for *Angel Dust Blues* and *The Wave.* Also contributor to periodicals, including *New Yorker, Esquire, New York Times,* and *Village Voice.*

ADAPTATIONS: Workin' for Peanuts was broadcast on Home Box Office "Family Showcase," 1985; *Can a Guy Say No?,* based on *A Very Touchy Subject,* was shown as an "ABC Afterschool Special," February, 1986.

WORK IN PROGRESS: Young Adult novels about the importance of the play *Anne Frank: Diary of a Young Girl,* and about a New York teenager's adventure in Alaska; novelizations of screenplays *Honey I Blew Up the Baby* and *Home Alone Again.*

SIDELIGHTS: Todd Strasser writes critically recognized realistic fiction for preteens and teenagers. In works ranging from *Friends Till the End,* the story of a young man stricken with leukemia, to *Wildlife,* a study of the breakup of a successful rock group, Strasser mixes humor and romance with timely subjects to address concerns of teens: drugs, sex, illness, and music. His understanding of the feelings of youth and adolescents has made his works popular with young people.

Strasser was born in New York City, but he grew up on Long Island. "Looking back," he states in *Authors and Artists for Young Adults (AAYA),* "I had a fine childhood in a very nice suburban setting. Like any kid I had my insecurities, but I also had a stable family life, attended good public schools and went to summer camp. Scholastically I was an underachiever and had a particularly tough time with reading and spelling. In general I did minimal amounts of homework, but if a subject excited me I would immerse myself in it. Those subjects included dinosaurs, sea shells and James Bond novels."

"Even in the midst of conflict and turmoil, we could usually share a laugh. I think this came from my grandfather, who profited from every loss by turning it

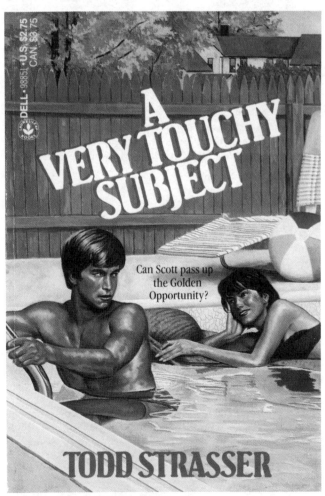

Scott tries to adjust to new feelings—as well as a changing body—with humor and honesty in Strasser's humorous and thoughtful novel.

into a humorous anecdote. For instance, he used to tell the story of when I was three and he took me clamming near his summer home in Bayville. Leaving me in the boat, he hopped into the shoulder-deep water and began digging the clams with a rake and throwing them into a bushel basket in the boat. As fast as he threw clams in, I dropped them back over the side. He dug in the same spot for almost an hour, amazed at how plentiful the clams were. Of course, when he climbed back into the boat and found an empty basket, he realized what had happened. I guess it's no surprise that my characters sometimes turn to humor in a tough moment. When I think of Tony facing a new school in *The Complete Computer Popularity Program,* and Scott facing new hormones in *A Very Touchy Subject,* I know my grandfather would be proud."

During his teen years Strasser exhibited the "anti-establishment" feelings characteristic of the 1960s. "I grew my hair long, listened to Led Zeppelin and rode my motorcycle to the Woodstock festival," he remembers in *AAYA.* "The Establishment said the war in Viet Nam was good and the counter culture (long hair, rock music, drugs) was bad, and in retrospect they were mostly wrong on the first count and sometimes right (especially concerning drugs) on the second. At the time they appeared to be dead wrong on both counts and I was about as countercultural as they came. Sometimes I think I write YA books because I'm still trying to resolve the conflicts of my own youth. When I say that I hope that each of my books shows an example of a young adult who learns good judgment, I sometimes want to add, 'because I wish I had when I was a teen.'"

After high school Strasser enrolled at New York University. He began to write poetry and some short fiction, but regarded it only as a hobby and did not expect to be published. A few years later he dropped out. During the next two years he hitchhiked around most of Europe and the United States, taking odd jobs whenever money ran low. He was a street musician in France and Germany, worked on a ship in Denmark, lived on a commune in Virginia, worked in a health food store in New York and was kidnapped briefly by religious fanatics in South Bend, Indiana.

During these wandering years Strasser continued to write, documenting his travels in journals and letters. "Finally it occurred to me that perhaps I should give writing a try as a student and, possibly, some sort of profession," he recalls in *AAYA.* "I enrolled at Beloit College and began taking literature and writing courses." Strasser told Jim Roginski in *Behind the Covers,* "I guess my becoming a writer was really a process of elimination. I tried a variety of things in college. Medicine, law. Nothing worked. My family felt I had to be a business person, or if I was lucky, a doctor or a lawyer. I never really thought I would be a writer."

After graduation, Strasser worked temporarily for the public relations department at Beloit, wrote for two years for the *Times Herald-Record,* a Middletown, NY, newspaper, and then became an advertising copywriter

After surviving a drunk driving accident, a high school swimming star tries to uncover what really happened the night of the crash.

for Compton Advertising in New York City as well as a researcher for *Esquire* magazine. "When I sold my first novel I quit my advertising job," he told Roginski. "And then I went the route of the poor struggling novelist. I used to do things like cut my own hair." After *Angel Dust Blues,* Strasser's first novel, was accepted for publication, Strasser used the three-thousand dollar advance to start a business of his own. "I . . . realized that [the money] wasn't going to last me very long," he told Roginski. "Since I come from a business family, I had some idea of what to do. I just happened to start with fortune cookies."

Strasser found the cookie business more successful than he expected. "It started as a way to come up with a little extra cash while I did my serious writing," he tells Roy Sorrels in *Writer's Digest.* "In October, 1978, I started with 5,000 cookies hoping to sell them all by Christmas. I sold 100,000!" "To get it going," Strasser continues, "I wore out a pair of shoes hiking from store to store in a seventy-block area of Manhattan. About thirty stores agreed to stock my cookies. They were immediately popular and before long I had sales reps around the city and all over the country." "I recently dropped into one of the shops down the street that sells my fortune

cookies," he concludes, "and asked the proprietor how they were moving. He said, 'They're my bestseller!' So I thought—my first bestseller is a one-line manuscript wrapped in cookie dough!" Strasser also found that the business complimented his writing. "It's good to get up from my typewriter and put my real work aside once in a while. And it's a way to supplement my serious writing. I must admit it's fun. When I look around at other friends who are waiting tables or driving cabs, it makes grinding out fortune cookie messages much more palatable. And I'll never be a starving writer. I can always eat my cookies."

Angel Dust Blues appeared in 1979 and won Strasser critical acclaim. The story itself is about, Strasser tells Nina Piwoz in *Media and Methods,* "a group of fairly well-to-do, suburban teenagers who get into trouble with drugs." It was based on actual events Strasser had witnessed when he was growing up. Two years later, he published another young-adult novel, again based on his own experiences. "My second book, *Friends Till the End,* is about a healthy teenager who has a friend who becomes extremely ill with leukemia," he explains to Piwoz. "When I moved to New York, I had a roommate . . . an old friend of mine. Within a few weeks, he became very ill. I spent a year visiting him in the hospital, not knowing whether he was going to live or die." The same year he also married Pamela Older, a production manager of *Esquire* magazine, and did a novelization (using the pseudonym Morton Rhue) of the teleplay *The Wave,* the story of how a teacher's experiment with Nazi-like socialization methods failed disastrously.

Rock 'n' Roll Nights, Strasser's third novel under his own name, was a change of pace from the serious themes of his first two works. "It's about a teenage rock and roll band—something with which I had absolutely no direct experience," he tells Piwoz. "However, I grew up in the 1960s when rock and roll was really our 'national anthem.' I relate much better to rock stars than to politicians. I always wanted to be in a rock band, as did just about everybody I knew." "I think the kind of music teens listen to may change, or what they wear may change," Strasser continues, "but dealing with being popular, friends or the opposite sex, or questions of morality and decency... [I don't think] those things really ever change. I hate to say this, but I think authors tell the same stories—just in today's language and in today's settings." Strasser continued the story of the band "Coming Attractions" in two sequels, *Turn It Up!* and *Wildlife.*

In his more recent works, Strasser continues to write hard-hitting, realistic stories about teenagers and their problems. For example, *The Accident,* which Strasser adapted for ABC TV's "Afterschool Special" series under the title *Over the Edge,* deals with a drunken driving incident in which three of four high school swimming stars are killed. The surviving teen commits himself to understanding what actually happened the night of the accident. *Beyond the Reef* has many of the trappings of a traditional boys' adventure story: at first glance, it seems to be about exploration for sunken treasure in the Florida Keys. However, Strasser focusses not so much on the treasure hunting itself as on the father's obsession with it, which threatens to break up the family. *The Complete Computer Popularity Program* deals with questions of the morality of nuclear power; a young boy, whose father is the new security engineer at a local nuclear power plant, must confront the community's hostility with his only friend, a "computer nerd." Strasser has also produced several lighter-hearted books for younger readers: *The Mall from Outer Space,* for instance, is about extraterrestrial aliens who have chosen, for mysterious reasons of their own, to construct shopping centers on Earth.

"Over the years," Strasser writes in *Horn Book,* "I had often complained to my wife that I wished that there were some easier way to do research on teenagers, especially in New York where, except for a few weeks each spring and fall, they seem particularly hard to find. Then ... we had our first child, a daughter. Shortly after we brought her home from the hospital, my wife turned to me and said, 'Just think, in thirteen years you won't have to leave the house at all to do your research.' Perhaps that's the best solution: grow your own."

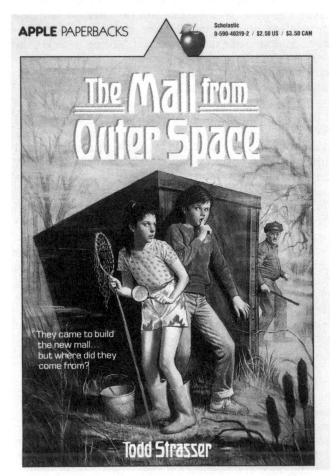

For very mysterious reasons, extraterrestrials decide to build shopping centers on Earth in Strasser's light-hearted novel.

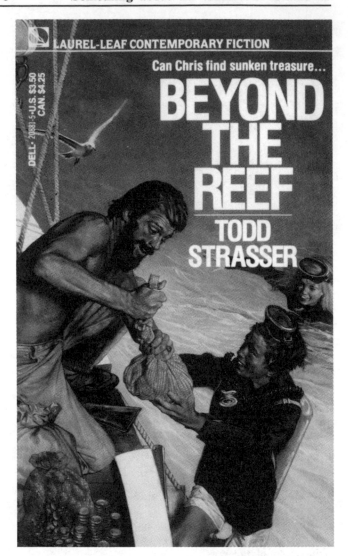

While searching for sunken treasure off the Florida Keys, Chris faces both deep-sea dangers and painful family conflicts.

WORKS CITED:

Authors and Artists for Young Adults, Volume 2, Gale, 1989, pp. 211-21.

Piwoz, Nina, "The Writers Are Writing: I Was a Teenage Boy—An Interview with Todd Strasser," *Media & Methods,* February, 1983.

Roginski, Jim, *Behind the Covers: Interviews with Authors and Illustrators of Books for Children and Young Adults,* Libraries Unlimited, 1985.

Sorrels, Roy, "The Writing Life: Cookie Funster," *Writer's Digest,* December, 1979.

Strasser, Todd, "Young Adult Books: Stalking the Teen," *Horn Book,* March/April, 1986.

FOR MORE INFORMATION SEE:

BOOKS

Children's Literature Review, Volume 11, Gale, 1986.

Holtze, Sally Holmes, *Sixth Book of Junior Authors and Illustrators,* H. W. Wilson, 1989.

Nilsen, Alleen Pace, and Kenneth L. Donelson, *Literature for Today's Young Adults,* second edition, Scott, Foresman, 1985.

PERIODICALS

Best Sellers, May, 1983, p. 75; June, 1984, p. 118.
Bulletin of the Center for Children's Books, February, 1980, p. 120.
English Journal, September, 1982, p. 87; January, 1985; December, 1985; December, 1986; November, 1987, p. 93; March, 1988, p. 85.
Horn Book, April, 1980, p. 178; April, 1983, p. 175; May-June, 1985, p. 321; January, 1990, p. 90.
Journal of Youth Services in Libraries, fall, 1988, pp. 64-70.
Library Journal, January, 1988, p. 100.

New Yorker, January 24, 1977, p. 28.
New York Times, January 4, 1976, travel section; October 2, 1983; June 19, 1985.
Publishers Weekly, November 27, 1981, p. 88; April 24, 1987, p. 73; December 4, 1987, p. 63.
School Library Journal, January, 1980, p. 81; March, 1982, p. 160; August, 1983, p. 80; August, 1984, p. 87; April, 1985, p. 100; February, 1988, p. 75; June/July, 1988, p. 59; September, 1989, p. 278.
Variety, March 22, 1990, p. 14.
Voice of Youth Advocates, June, 1981, p. 32; December, 1982, p. 36; October, 1983, p. 209; June, 1984, p. 98; June, 1985, p. 136; December, 1986; December, 1988, p. 242; October, 1989, p. 217.
Wilson Library Bulletin, May, 1981, p. 691; April, 1983, p. 692; March, 1985, p. 485.

T

TAHA, Karen T(erry) 1942-

PERSONAL: Born January 10, 1942, in Mena, AR; daughter of Alvin R. (a banker) and Catherine (in business; maiden name, Carver) Terry; married Hamdy A. Taha (a professor of engineering), May 12, 1965; children: Tarek (son), Sharif (son), Maisa (daughter). *Education:* Arizona State University, B.A., 1963; University of Oklahoma, M.S. (Spanish), 1970; University of Arkansas, M.S. (instructional resources), 1981.

KAREN T. TAHA

ADDRESSES: Home—Springdale, AR. *Office*—Elmdale Elementary School, 420 North West End, Springdale, AR 72764.

CAREER: Tempe High School, Tempe, AR, teacher of Spanish, 1963-64; Centro de Estudios Norteamericanos, Valencia, Spain, English teacher, 1964-65; Amun School, Suez, Egypt, English teacher, 1965-66; worked variously as Spanish tutor and free-lance translator, 1969-78; Springdale Public Schools, Springdale, AR, library media specialist, 1980—.

MEMBER: Society of Children's Book Writers, American Library Association, Arkansas Library Association.

WRITINGS:

A Gift for Tia Rosa (juvenile), illustrated by Dee DeRosa, Dillon, 1986.
(With Janet Greeson) *Name That Book!: Questions and Answers on Outstanding Children's Books,* Scarecrow, 1986.
Marshmallow Muscles, Banana Brainstorms, Harcourt, 1988.

Contributor to children's magazines, including *Ebony, Jr., Story Friends,* and *Friend.*

WORK IN PROGRESS: Bugs, Bananas, and Birthday Cake, a middle grade novel.

SIDELIGHTS: Karen T. Taha wrote *SATA:* "Working as a library media specialist in an elementary school keeps me in touch with the two most important criteria for authors of juvenile literature—children and books. I've incorporated my travel experiences into many of my stories, having lived in Spain, Egypt, Mexico, and Kuwait. I am fluent in Spanish and speak some French and Arabic. My stories hopefully lead to greater understanding of other cultures by showing the universality of human emotions."

A young girl learns some important lessons about life, love, and growing old in Taha's *A Gift for Tia Rosa*. (Illustration by Dee deRosa.)

TUERK, Hanne 1951-

PERSONAL: Born October 11, 1951, in Mauthen, Austria; daughter of Hans and Elfriede (Toergler) Tuerk. *Education:* Attended Academy of Art, Vienna, Austria, 1971-72, and Academy of Art, Paris, France, 1974-78. *Religion:* Buddhist.

ADDRESSES: c/o Neugebauer Press, Aignerstrasse 127, A-5026 Salzburg, Austria.

CAREER: Free-lance illustrator and writer, 1980—.

WRITINGS:

Who Is Afraid of . . . ?, Neugebauer Press, 1980.
(Self-illustrated) *Hieronymus*, Neugebauer Press, 1981.

"MAX THE MOUSE" PICTURE BOOK SERIES; SELF-ILLUSTRATED

A Surprise for Max, Neugebauer Press, 1982.
The Rope Skips Max, Neugebauer Press, 1982.
Max Versus the Cube, Neugebauer Press, 1982.
Rainy Day Max, Neugebauer Press, 1983.
Goodnight, Max, Neugebauer Press, 1983.
A Lesson for Max, Neugebauer Press, 1983.
Max the Art Lover, Neugebauer Press, 1983.
Merry Christmas, Max, Neugebauer Press, 1983.
Raking Leaves With Max, Neugebauer Press, 1983.
Happy Birthday, Max!, Neugebauer Press, 1984.
Max Packs, Neugebauer Press, 1984.
Snapshot Max, Neugebauer Press, 1984.

Butterfly Max, Neugebauer Press, 1984.
Good Sport Max, Neugebauer Press, 1984.
Friendship Max, Neugebauer Press, 1985.
Chocolate Max, Neugebauer Press, 1985.
Robinson Max, Neugebauer Press, 1985.

ILLUSTRATOR

Norbert Landa, *Rabbit and Chicken Count Eggs*, Morrow, 1992.
Landa, *Rabbit and Chicken Find the Right Box*, Morrow, 1992.
Landa, *Rabbit and Chicken Look at Colors*, Morrow, 1992.
Landa, *Rabbit and Chicken Play Hide and Seek*, Morrow, 1992.

WORK IN PROGRESS: Additional "Max the Mouse" books; "Max the Mouse" cards, posters, and calendars.

SIDELIGHTS: Hanne Tuerk is best known for her ongoing "Max the Mouse" picture book series, which has earned widespread acclaim. Featured in Tuerk's original creation is a whimsical mouse named Max, who maneuvers his way through one adventure after another demonstrating his problem-solving ability in a manner that some critics have described as ingenious and charming. In *Max Versus the Cube*, for instance, the winsome mouse buys a Rubik's Cube and proceeds to master its complexities. Unable to restore the puzzle to its original state, Max resolves the dilemma by painting each side its correct color. Successive stories pose new situations and difficulties over which the tiny character triumphs.

Max's amusing escapades are generally suggested for children aged three years and older, and are noted for having charmed people of all ages and nationalities. The

Hanne Tuerk's "Max the Mouse" picture book series highlights the adventures of a whimsical rodent as he maneuvers his way through a number of adventures.

books appear in several countries, including the United States, France, Italy, Germany, Spain, Greece, and Japan, as well as Tuerk's native Austria.

Tuerk writes: "I illustrate mostly for children because my imagination is full of dreams and wishes, and I am trying to convey my feelings to the children."

*   *   *

TURNER, Glennette Tilley 1933-

PERSONAL: Born November 23, 1933, in Raleigh, NC; daughter of John Lee (a theologian, college president, and civil rights leader) and Phyllis Geraldine (a nursery school teacher and parent educator; maiden name, Jones) Tilley; married Albert W. Turner (a postal administrator), April 1, 1956; children: Albert, Cyril. *Education:* Lake Forest College, B.A., 1955; Goddard College, M.A., 1979. *Politics:* Independent. *Religion:* Unitarian-Universalist.

ADDRESSES: Home—P.O. Box 461, Glen Ellyn, IL. 60138.

CAREER: Charles A. Stevens & Co., Chicago, IL, advertising copywriter, 1955-56; primary teacher at public schools in Chicago, 1962-66, Maywood, IL, 1966-68, 1970-88, and Wheaton, IL, 1968-69; Ginn & Co., Boston, MA, staff writer, 1969-70; National Louis University, Evanston, IL, teacher of minority education classes and student teacher supervisor, 1988—. Writer in residence, Longfellow School. Instructor, 1991 Taste of Chicago Writers Conference, Saint Xavier College.

Turner's work in recounting the lives of notable African Americans includes this full-length biography of the nineteenth-century inventor whose work helped bring about the widespread use of electric lighting.

Member of Illinois Language Arts and Teacher Assessment Committees, READ Illinois Committee, and Northern Illinois University Children's Literature Conference; member of board of directors, Graue Mill Museum and DuPage County Historical Board; member of Wheaton Cable Commission. Lecturer. Consultant to numerous groups, including Naper Settlement.

MEMBER: American Society of Journalists and Authors, Authors Guild, Society of Children's Book Writers, Afro-American Historical and Genealogical Society, Black Caucus of the American Library Association, Midland Authors, Afro-American Genealogical and Historical Society of Chicago, Children's Reading Roundtable of Chicago (president, 1983-84), Chicago Women in Publishing, Independent Writers of Chicago, Off Campus Writers Association for the Study of Afro-American Life and History, Black Literary Umbrella (president, 1986), Patricia Liddell Researchers, Phi Beta Kappa, Delta Kappa Gamma (vice-president, Epsilon chapter, 1983).

GLENNETTE TILLEY TURNER

AWARDS, HONORS: Honored in a resolution from Illinois State Legislature, 1988; grant from American Association of University Women.

WRITINGS:

Surprise for Mrs. Burns, Albert Whitman, 1971.
The Underground Railroad in DuPage County, Illinois, Newman Educational Publishers, 1980, revised edition, 1986.
Take a Walk in Their Shoes (for children), Dutton, 1989.
Lewis Howard Latimer, Silver Burdett, 1990.

Work represented in anthologies. Author of "Tips for Parents," a regular feature in *Black Child Journal,* and "Take a Walk in Their Shoes," in *Ebony, Jr.* Chief researcher for *Martin, the Emancipator,* broadcast on WGN-TV.

WORK IN PROGRESS: Follow in Their Footsteps; Aunt Leanna's Hands; Escape.

SIDELIGHTS: Glennette Tilley Turner told *SATA:* "Research and writing have given me a greater appreciation of how interconnected all aspects of life and learning are. I hope I can convey to children their sense of relatedness and wonder."

WALKER, David Harry 1911-1992

OBITUARY NOTICE—See index for *SATA* sketch: Born February 11, 1911, in Dundee, Scotland; died March 5, 1992, in St. Andrews, New Brunswick, Canada. Soldier, comptroller to the viceroy of India, and writer. Walker authored twenty novels for adults and children, marked by their outdoor adventures and masculine values. A soldier in the Black Watch of the British Army for sixteen years beginning in 1931, Walker served in Sudan, India, and Canada before World War II. During the war, he was captured by the Germans and held in prisoner of war camps for five years. After his release, and a brief term as comptroller to the Viceroy of India, Walker began a new life as a writer in Canada, writing such books as *Harry Black,* a novel about his experiences in prison camp, and his best known novel, *Geordie,* the story of a young Scottish athlete who makes it to the Olympics. A popular film adaptation called *Wee Geordie* was made in 1956. Appreciating the art of survival, Walker frequently traveled to rough environments. His novel *Where the High Winds Blow* portrays his adventures on a dog sled trip across the Arctic, and his autobiography, *Lean, Wind, Lean* provides an overview of his eventful life. Walker also wrote children's books, including *Big Ben* and *Pirate Rock.*

OBITUARIES AND OTHER SOURCES:

BOOKS

Who's Who in America, 46th edition, Marquis, 1990.

PERIODICALS

Times (London), March 20, 1992, p. 19.

*   *   *

WALTER, Francis V. 1923-

PERSONAL: Born April 21, 1923, in Ordway, CO; daughter of Harry J. (a shovel operator) and Golda (a homemaker; maiden name, Gentner) Lane; married Ralph N. Walter (a minister), November 20, 1945; children: Carol, Gavin, Brian, Lorrie, Melodie. *Educa-*

tion: Arizona Bible College, bible school degree; Oklahoma University, linguistic degree. *Religion:* Baptist.

ADDRESSES: Home—170 Green Brook Rd., Green Brook, NJ 08812.

CAREER: Montgomery Wards, Denver, CO, typist and personnel manager, 1942-43; public school system, Middlesex, NJ, substitute teacher, 1957-83; full-time teacher at private school in Green Brook, NJ, 1984-86. Also worked as a secretary and bookkeeper for office in Middlesex.

WRITINGS:

Eager Beaver Primary Course (twelve-book set), Accent Books, 1966.
(With Violet T. Pearson) *Here's Benjie: A Child's Animal Story Book,* Accent Books, 1976.

FRANCIS V. WALTER

(With Pearson) *Benjie and His Friends,* Accent Books, 1977.

(With Pearson) *Benjie and the Flood,* Accent Books, 1978.

Also author of television and radio scripts.

SIDELIGHTS: Frances V. Walter told *SATA:* "If I have a gift, I feel it is the gift of teaching. I always used my writing and art in connection with my teaching." Walter gained a lot of her writing experience as a child. Because her family moved around a great deal, she became adept at writing letters and keeping diaries about her family's travels. In high school, Walter liked to read works by Milton, Chaucer, and Shakespeare. "It was then I dreamed of writing an epic," she recalled. While the epic never took shape, Walter did write a number of stories, "typical 'girl meets boy' stories with which teenagers could identify."

After getting married in 1945, Walter started a Sunday school with her husband (she wrote all the lessons and taught weekly classes). Some time after starting a special summer Bible course, Walters was contacted by Accent Books. "They were interested in a three-year course for primary age children. It took me three years, but I wrote twelve books for them," she noted. Later, some of these books became a reading series featuring a little beaver called Benjie. Over time, the series began to drain Walter; eventually, she started to devote more time to church activities, confining her writing to family newsletters. "I am back to writing for fun," Walter related to *SATA.* "I continue to teach school, and can express my talents this way, and use my art and writing as well."

*   *   *

WILKON, Jozef 1930-

PERSONAL: Born February 12, 1930, in Bogucice, Poland; son of Piotr (an artist) and Karolina (Olech) Wilkon; married Malgorzata Jagoszewska, December 22, 1955; children: Piotr. *Education:* Jagiellonian University, Cracow, Poland, M.A. (history of art), 1954; Academy of Fine Arts, Cracow, Poland, M.A. (painting), 1955. *Religion:* Roman Catholic.

ADDRESSES: Home—Hoza 39, Apt. 79, 00-681 Warsaw, Poland. *Agent*—Agencja Autorska, ul Hipoteczna 2, 00-950 Warsaw, Poland.

CAREER: Illustrator. Wydawnictwo Arkady (publisher), Warsaw, Poland, art director, 1979-82. W. Horzyca Theatre, Torun, Poland, stage designer, 1978; S. Wyspianski Cooperative, Cracow, Poland, tapestry designer, 1980.

EXHIBITIONS: Solo shows at MDM Gallery, Poland, 1960; Society of Arts Friends, Cracow, Poland, 1961; Galerie in der Biberstrasse, Vienna, Austria, 1964; Lublin, Chelm, and Torun, Poland, 1967-68; Manchester, England, 1969; Kordegarda Warszawa, Poland, 1970 and 1988; Herder Gallerie, West Berlin, (now Berlin), 1971; Herder Gallerie, Cologne, West Germany (now Germany), 1973; Slupsk, 1975; Philharmonia, Rzeszow, Poland, 1976; Polish Museum of America, Chicago, 1976; Bialystok, Torun, and Poznan, Poland, 1979; Academy of Fine Arts, Katowice, Poland, 1980; MAG Gallery, Zurich, Switzerland, 1980; Pulawy, Poland, 1988; Centrum Pompidou, Paris, 1989; Klingspor Museum, Offenbach am Main, West Germany (now Germany), 1990; Galeria Plakatu, Warsaw, 1990; Tokyo, 1990 and 1992; Nijmegen, Arnhem, Netherlands, 1992.

Group shows in Rzeszow, 1955; Leipzig, East Germany (now Germany), 1959 and 1965; Nancy, France, 1959; London, 1960 and 1967; Warsaw, 1961-64, 1966-67, 1969, 1973, and 1984; Moscow, U.S.S.R. (now Russia), 1964, 1974-75, and 1979; Berlin, 1964, 1970, and 1980; Buenos Aires, 1965; Bologna, Italy, 1966, 1969-70, 1974, 1984, and 1988; Tokyo, 1966, 1968, 1970, and 1982; Brussels and Ghent, Belgium, 1968; Baghdad, Iraq, 1968; Mexico, 1968; Hannover, West Germany (now Germany), 1969; Poznan, 1973 and 1976; Bratislava, Czechoslovakia, 1973 and 1984-85; Paris, 1977 and 1983; Sofia, Bulgaria, 1977 and 1983; Prague, 1979; Vienna, 1980 and 1988; Zamosc, Poland, 1981 and 1983-84; Cairo, 1984; Denmark, 1984; Prado, Madrid, Spain, 1986; Metropolitan Museum, New York City, 1986; Havana, Cuba, 1987; Barcelona, Spain, 1987.

MEMBER: Union of Polish Artists and Designers, Society of Authors.

AWARDS, HONORS: Prizes from Polish Publishers Association for "The Most Beautiful Book of the Year" in 1959 for *Iv i Finetta* and *Pawie wiersze,* in 1961 for

JOZEF WILKON

Beowulf, in 1964 for *Zaczarowana jagoda,* in 1970 for *Maciupinka,* in 1973 for *Pan Tadeusz* and *Grajmy,* and in 1974 for *Kraina sto piatej tajemnicy* and *Od gor do morza;* Gold Medal, International Exhibition of Editing Art, Leipzig, 1959; second place award at "Polish Visual Art in Fifteen Years of the Polish People's Republic: The Book and Illustration Exhibition," Minister of Culture and Art, 1962; first prize in competition for illustrations for *Pan Tadeusz,* Museum of Literature, 1963; Prize of Honour in competition for illustrations for *Don Quixote,* 1965 (Buenos Aires, Argentina); Deutscher Jugendbuchpreis fuer Graphische Gestaltung, Duesseldorf, West Germany (now Germany), and Premio Europeo Citta di Caorle, 1966, both for *Herr Minkepatt und seine Freunde;* third degree award, Minister of Culture and Art, and State's Award, both for achievements in the field of book illustration, 1967; Gold Medal, International Illustration Biennale, Bratislava, 1969, for *W nieparyzu i gdzie indziej;* Silver Goats, Biennale of Arts for Children, Poznan, 1970, for *Piesn o Cydzie,* and 1973, for *Siedem ksiezycow;* Prize of Honour, International Illustration Biennale, Bratislava, 1973; third award, book illustration exhibition, Warsaw, 1973; Medal of National Education Committee for artistic activity for children, 1973; distinction award, International Illustration Biennale, Bratislava, and Premio Europeo, both 1974, for *List do Warszawy;* Premio Grafico, International Exhibition of the Children's Book Illustrations, Bologna, 1974; Award of the Chairman of the Ministers' Council and Prime Minister's Prize, both for production of children's books, 1974; Gold Medal, International Book Exhibition, Moscow, 1975, for illustrations for *Pan Tadeusz;* Premio Europeo, 1975, for *Nasze podworko;* Golden Goats, Biennale of Arts for Children, Poznan, 1977; "Loisirs Jeunes" diploma for best illustrated foreign book, Paris, 1980, for *Waldkonzert;* Owl Prize for illustrations, Tokyo, 1984, for *Die Geschichte vom guten Wolf;* Great Award of the Polish Publishers' Association, Warsaw, 1987, for the whole artistic output; Premio Grafico, Bologna, 1991, for *Rosalind, das Katzenkind;* Totem for illustrations, Salon du Livre de Jeunesse, 1991, for *Les Quatre Fils de la terre;* many other awards for illustration.

WRITINGS:

SELF-ILLUSTRATED; TRANSLATED WORKS

Little Tom and the Big Cats, Dent, 1978 (originally published in Japan as *Little Tom and the Big Cat,* Shiko-Sha, 1976).

The Horse and the Huge Hippopotamus, Dent, 1984.

Jozef Wilkon: Book Illustration/Ilustracja ksiazkowa, Centre Georges Pompidou, 1989.

(With Hermann Moers) *Lullaby for a Newborn King: A Christmas Story,* translation by Rosemary Lanning, North-South, 1991 (originally published as *Das allererste Weihnachtslied,* Nord-Sued, 1991).

SELF-ILLUSTRATED; UNTRANSLATED WORKS

Minka, Parabel, 1978.

ILLUSTRATOR; TRANSLATED WORKS

Paul Schaaf, *The Crane with One Leg,* Warne, 1964.

Wilkon's bold and dreamlike illustrations evoke the wonder of Jesus' birth in *Lullaby for a Newborn King: A Christmas Story,* written with Hermann Moers.

Ursula Valentin, *Herr Minkepatt and His Friends,* Dobson, 1965 (also published as *Herr Minkepatt und seine Freunde,* Middelhauve, 1965).

Paul Buxil, *The Adventures of Three Little Lions* (based on a story by Wilkon), World Distributors, 1969 (originally published as *L'Escapade des trois lionceaux,* Coqe d'Or, 1967).

Paul Buxil, *The Panther and the Chimpanzee,* World Distributors, 1969 (originally published as *La Panthere et le chimpanze,* Coqe d'Or, 1967).

Uwe Friesel, *Tim, the Peacemaker* (based on a story by Wilkon), Scroll Press, 1970 (also published as *Der kleine Herr Timm und die Zauberfloete,* Middelhauve, 1970).

Daniel Defoe, *Robinson Crusoe,* Loewes, 1973.

Vladimir Mayakovski, *Lions Are Not Elephants,* verse adaptation by Karl Dedecius, Hodder & Stoughton, 1978 (originally published as *Ein Loewe ist kein Elefant,* Middelhauve, 1975).

Irina Korschunow, *Timothy, an Extraordinary Tiger* (based on a story by Wilkon), translation by Gwen Marsh, Dent, 1979 (originally published as *Jussuf will ein Tiger sein,* Parabel, 1978).

Kurt Baumann, *The Concert of the Birds* (based on a story by Wilkon), Hutchinson, 1980 (originally published as *Waldkonzert,* Bohem Press, 1979).

Mateusz Siuchninski, *An Illustrated History of Poland,* translation by Stanislaw Tarnowski, Interpress,

1979 (also published as *Ilustrowane dzieje Polski,* Interpress, 1979).

Mark Twain, *Tom Sawyer,* Loewes, 1979.

Desanka Maksimovic, *The Shaggy Little Dog,* Faber & Faber, 1983 (originally published as *Der kleine Hund,* Nord-Sued, 1981).

Max Bolliger, *Three Little Bears,* translation by Gabriella Modan, Adama Books, 1987 (originally published as *Der Baerenberg,* Bohem Press, 1982).

Peter Nickl, *The Story of the Kind Wolf* (based on a story by Wilkon), Faber, 1982 (also published as *Die Geschichte vom guten Wolf,* Nord-Sued, 1982).

Rosemary Lanning, *No Room at the Inn: A Version of the Christmas Story,* Abelard, 1983 (also published as *Die Herberge zu Bethlehem,* Nord-Sued, 1983).

Shyusaku Endo, *A Visitor from the Paradise,* Atelier Muze, 1985.

Josef Guggenmos, *Hippety, Hoppety, Hop,* North-South, 1985 (also published as *Hase hopp hopp hopp,* Nord-Sued, 1985).

Konrad Richter, *Wipe Your Feet, Santa Claus!,* translation by Rosemary Lanning, North-South, 1985 (also published as *Sankt Nikolaus kommt,* Nord-Sued, 1985).

Mischa Damjan, *The Clown Said No,* translation by Anthea Bell, North-South, 1986 (also published as *Der Clown sagte nein,* Nord-Sued, 1986).

Hermann Moers, *Hugo the Baby Lion,* translation by Rosemary Lanning, North-South, 1986 (also published as *Hugo der Babyloewe,* Nord-Sued, 1986).

Mischa Damjan, *The Fake Flamingos,* translation by Anthea Bell, North-South, 1987 (also published as *Die falschen Flamingos,* Nord-Sued, 1987).

Annaliese Lussert, *The Farmer and the Moon,* translation by Anthea Bell, North-South, 1987 (also published as *Die sieben Mondtaler,* Nord-Sued, 1987).

Slawomir Wolski, *Tiger Cat* (based on a story by Wilkon), translation by Elizabeth D. Crawford, North-South, 1988 (originally published as *Mister Braun Katze,* Nord-Sued, 1987).

Gerda Marie Scheidl, *Flowers for the Snowman,* translation by Rosemary Lanning, North-South, 1988 (also published as *Lieber Schneemann wohin willst du?,* Nord-Sued, 1988).

Hermann Moers, *Tonio the Great,* North-South, 1990 (originally published as *Tonio auf dem Hochseil* [title means "Tonio on a Trapeze"], Nord-Sued, 1989).

Siegfried P. Rupprecht, *The Tale of the Vanishing Rainbow,* translation by Naomi Lewis, North-South, 1989 (also published as *Der Streit um den Regenbogen* and as *Baerenland,* both Nord-Sued, 1989).

Piotr Wilkon, *Cats,* Green Peace, 1989.

Piotr Wilkon, *Rosie the Cool Cat,* Viking, 1991 (originally published as *Rosalind, das Katzenkind,* Bohem Press, 1989).

Piotr Wilkon, *The Brave Little Kittens,* translation by Helen Graves, North-South, 1991 (originally published as *Katzenausflug,* Nord-Sued, 1990).

Hermann Moers, *Hugo's Baby Brother,* translation by Rosemary Lanning from the original German, *Hugo wird grosser Bruder,* North-South, 1991.

Piotr Wilkon, *Noah's Ark,* North-South, 1992.

ILLUSTRATOR; UNTRANSLATED WORKS

Helena Bechlerowa, *O kotku, ktory szukal czarnego mleka,* Nasza Ksiegarnia, 1959.

Natalia Galczynska, *Iv i Finetta* (title means "Iv and Finetta"), Ruch, 1959.

Tadeusz Kubiak, *Pawie wiersze* (based on a story by Wilkon; title means "Peacock's Poems"), Nasza Ksiegarnia, 1959.

Stanislaw Szydlowski, *Przygoda pewnego pawia* (based on a story by Wilkon), Ruch, 1960.

Beowulf, Nasza Ksiegarnia, 1961.

Leopold Staff, *Szum drzew,* Nasza Ksiegarnia, 1961.

Wiktor Woroszylski, *Duzo smiechu, troche smutku . . . ,* Czytelnik, 1961.

Czeslaw Janczarski, *Tygrys o zlotym sercu* (based on a story by Wilkon), Nasza Ksiegarnia, 1963.

Henry de Monfreid, *L'Esclave du batteur d'or,* Flammarion, 1963.

Ogden Nash, *Envers et contre tous,* Seghers, 1963.

Denise Basdevant, *Des monts en mervilles,* Flammarion, 1964.

Mieczyslawa Buczkowna, *Zaczarowana jagoda* (title means "Magic Berry"), Czytelnik, 1964.

A portrait in opaque watercolors and pastels, this illustration by Wilkon from Jozef Ratajczak's *Wlazt Kotek na plotek* is one of the artist's favorites.

Eleanor Farjeon, *Marcin spod dzikiej jabloni* (translation of *Martin Pippin in the Apple Orchard*), Nasza Ksiegarnia, 1964.

Rainer Maria Rilke, *Sonety do Orfeusza*, Literackie, 1964.

Mieczyslawa Buczkowna, *Nad jeziorem*, Ruch, 1965.

Anna Milska, *O ksieciu Ibrahimie i pieknej Sinedhur*, Ruch, 1965.

Jerzy Ficowski, *Lustro i promyk*, Ruch, 1966.

Hanna Januszewska, *Szesc grubych ryb*, Nasza Ksiegarnia, 1966.

H. Morsztyn, *Fraszki*, Ruch, 1966.

Ewa Zarembina, *Pozegnanie ogrodu*, Literackie, 1966.

Anna Kamienska, *W nieparyzu i gdzie indziej* (title means "Not in Paris and Elsewhere"), Nasza Ksiegarnia, 1967.

Jan Sztaudynger, *Zwrotki dla Dorotki*, Nasza Ksiegarnia, 1968.

Czeslawa Niemysky-Raczaszkowa, *Przyjaciele*, Nasza Ksiegarnia, 1969.

Robert Wolfgang Schnell, *Bonko* (based on a story by Wilkon), Dobson, 1969, Scroll Press, 1970 (also published by Middelhauve, 1969).

Wanda Chotomska, *Siedem ksiezycow* (title means "Seven Moons"), Ruch, 1970.

Marek Dubas, *Tu mieszka murzynek*, Ruch, 1970.

Jerzy Ficowski, *Maciupinka*, Ruch, 1970.

Francesco Petrarch, *Piesn o Cydzie*, Literackie, 1970.

Henryk Sienkiewicz, *Basnie i legendy*, Ludowa, 1970.

Helena Bobinska, *O krolu sloncu i jego czterech corkach*, Nasza Ksiegarnia, 1971.

Robert Louis Stevenson, *Die Schatzinsel* (title means "Treasure Island"), Loewes, 1971.

James Joyce, *Utwory poetyckie*, Literackie, 1972.

Eveline Hasler, *Ein Baum fuer Filippo*, Atlantis, 1973.

Hanna Januszewska, *Grajmy* (title means "Let's Play"), Ruch, 1973.

Adam Mickiewicz, *Pan Tadeusz*, Arkady, 1973.

Jerzy Kierst, *Od gor do morza* (title means "From Mountains to the Sea"), Ruch, 1974.

Tadeusz Kubiak, *List do Warszawy* (title means "Letter to Warsaw"), Nasza Ksiegarnia, 1974.

Guenter Spang, *Kossik* (based on a story by Wilkon), Parabel, 1974.

Marta Tomaszewska, *Wyprawa Tapatikow* (title means "The Tapatikos Expedition"), KAW, 1974.

Zbigniew Zakiewicz, *Kraina sto piatej tajemnicy* (title means "Country of 105 Mysteries"), Czytelnik, 1974.

Calderon de la Barca, *Dramaty*, Literackie, 1975.

Konstanty Ildefons Galczynski, *Noctes Aninenses*, Czytelnik, 1975.

Andrzej Hausbrandt, *Pantomima Tomaszewskiego*, Interpress, 1975.

Ludwik Jerzy Kern, *Nasze podworko* (title means "Our Backyard"), Nasza Ksiegarnia, 1975.

Francesco Petrarka, *Sonety do Laury*, Literackie, 1975.

Guenter Spang, *Wolfskinder* (title means "Children of Wolf"; based on a story by Wilkon), Parabel, 1975.

Ira Joswiakowski, *Chantecler*, Kinderbuchverlag, 1976.

Marta Tomaszewska, *Tapatiki na Ziemi*, Krajowa, 1976.

Miguel de Cervantes, *Intermedia*, Literackie, 1977.

Konstanty Ildefons Galczynski, *Dziela*, Czytelnik, 1979.

Fredrik Vahle, *Wem gibt der Elefant die Hand* (title means "With Whom the Elephant Shakes Hands"; based on a story by Wilkon), Middelhauve, 1982.

Zbigniew Zakiewicz, *Pan Tip-Top*, Nasza Ksiegarnia, 1982.

Polakow portret wlasny, Arkady, 1983.

Kurt Baumann, *Das Pferd am Nil* (based on a story by Wilkon), Bohem Press, 1983.

Josef Guggenmos, *Mein neuer Ball* (based on a story by Wilkon), Nord-Sued, 1984.

Josef Guggenmos, *Baeren im Schnee* (based on a story by Wilkon), Nord-Sued, 1984.

Jozef Ratajczak, *Wlazt kotek na plotek*, [Warsaw], 1984.

Josef Guggenmos, *Ich rieche Honig* (based on a story by Wilkon), Nord-Sued, 1985.

Eveline Hasler, *Die Pipistrellis* (based on a story by Wilkon), Bohem Press, 1985.

Rudolf Otto Wiemer, *Warum der Buer sich wecken liess* (based on a story by Wilkon), Patmos, 1985.

W zakletym borze (anthology of Russian poetry; title means "The Magic Forest"), Nasza Ksiegarnia, 1985.

Jozef Ratajczak, *Idzie wiosna* (title means "Spring Is Coming"), Nasza Ksiegarnia, 1986.

Rudolf Otto Wiemer, *Thomas und die Taube* (based on a story by Wilkon), Patmos, 1987.

John Wilson, *Der kleinste Elefant der Welt*, Bohem Press, 1987.

Lene Mayer-Skumanz, *Der kleine Hirte und der grosse Raeuber*, Patmos, 1988.

Josef Guggenmos, *Was bin ich?*, Bohem Press, 1989.

Mischa Damjan, *Atuk*, Nord-Sued, 1990.

Ave Maria, *Zdeptana kotka*, Green Peace, 1990.

Piotr Wilkon, *Leopanther*, Patmos, 1991.

Jacques Cassabois, *Les Quatre Fils de la terre*, Messidor, 1991.

Piotr Wilkon, *Die Arche Noach*, Nord-Sued, 1992.

WORK IN PROGRESS: Three books, tentatively titled *Anthology of Animal Fables, Animal Portraits,* and *Don Kichot.*

SIDELIGHTS: For more than thirty years Jozef Wilkon's art has graced books for both children and adults. In his native Poland and abroad he has won acclaim for his ability to evoke wonder in his illustrations, earning numerous awards throughout Europe and beyond. Observed Naomi Lewis in a commentary for his book *Jozef Wilkon: Book Illustration/Ilustracja ksiazkowa,* "Wilkon's pictures are unmistakable: bold yet dreamlike, strange, exciting, child-angled yet by no means as simple as they seem." His work encompasses both straightforward narrative art and more symbolic approaches, and his media vary as well, including pastel, watercolor, gouache, and ink. In another commentary in *Jozef Wilkon,* Danuta Wroblewska remarked that Wilkon "does not care about uniformity of style or technique because his style is openness onto the world."

Illustrator of more than one hundred books for others, Wilkon has also written and illustrated books of his own. In 1991, for example, he collaborated with Her-

Wilkon uses light, form, color, and composition to prompt a child's imagination. (Illustration from *Herr Minkepatt and His Friends,* written by Ursula Valentin.)

mann Moers on *Lullaby for a Newborn King: A Christmas Story,* about a poor shepherd boy's encounter with Jesus Christ. The story describes the sudden appearance of a bright star, signifying the birth of a long-awaited king, in a poor rural community. Following the star to Bethlehem, everyone brings a gift except young Simon, who has only his flute. Yet his flute playing proves a worthy gift when it lulls the crying baby Jesus to sleep. Matching the simplicity of the story, Wilkon's soft pastel pictures sketch out the village's little thatched huts, snow-covered hills, and bare trees in muted tones and radiate the warm glow of the star. Colored backgrounds add drama and richness to his uncluttered compositions.

Wilkon's art is "saturated with the warmth of intensely emotional perception of the world," noted Wroblewska. Playing with light, form, color, and composition, he is a "conjurer of form, but his art is by no means a cool manipulation with matter since it evokes our feelings," the writer continued. As Wilkon revealed in dust-jacket notes for *Jozef Wilkon,* he thinks of a book illustration as "something personal and dear that a child has close at hand.... It should prompt the child's imagination." Believing that children need to be aware of opposites and contrasts, he does not shy away from drama in his illustrations. His approach seems to succeed; in her commentary Lewis declared that Wilkon's picture books "make immediate rapport with children in all countries."

WORKS CITED:

Lewis, Naomi, commentary in *Jozef Wilkon: Book Illustration/Ilustracja ksiazkowa,* Centre Georges Pompidou, 1989, p. 5.
Wilkon, Jozef, dust jacket notes for *Jozef Wilkon: Book Illustration/Ilustracja ksiazkowa,* Centre Georges Pompidou, 1989.
Wroblewska, Danuta, commentary in *Jozef Wilkon: Book Illustration/Ilustracja ksiazkowa,* Centre Georges Pompidou, 1989, p. 10.

FOR MORE INFORMATION SEE:

PERIODICALS

Esse, February, 1990, p. 152.
Moe, September, 1990, p. 143.
New Statesman, November 3, 1978, p. 593; November 9, 1979, p. 732.
Observer (London), August 5, 1979, p. 37.
Projekt, January, 1968; January, 1979.
Publishers Weekly, December 7, 1990, p. 80.

*　　*　　*

WILLARD, Nancy 1936-

PERSONAL: Born June 26, 1936, in Ann Arbor, MI; daughter of Hobart Hurd (a chemistry professor) and Marge (Sheppard) Willard; married Eric Lindbloom (a logician and photographer), August 15, 1964; children: James Anatole. *Education:* University of Michigan, B.A., 1958, Ph.D., 1963; Stanford University, M.A.,

1960; studied art in Paris, France, and Oslo, Norway. *Hobbies and other interests:* Painting, sculpture, sewing, cooking, crafts.

ADDRESSES: Home—133 College Ave., Poughkeepsie, NY 12603. *Office*—Department of English, Vassar College, Poughkeepsie, NY 12601. *Agent*—Jean V. Naggar Literary Agency, 336 East 73rd St., Suite C, New York, NY 10021.

CAREER: Writer. Vassar College, Poughkeepsie, NY, lecturer in English, 1965—; Bread Loaf Writers' Conference, teacher, summers, 1975—.

AWARDS, HONORS: Five Jules and Avery Hopwood awards for poetry and essays, University of Michigan, including one in 1958; Woodrow Wilson fellowship, 1960; Devins Memorial Award, 1967, for *Skin of Grace;* O. Henry Award, best short story, 1970, for "Theo's Girl"; *Sailing to Cythera and Other Anatole Stories* was selected as one of the Fifty Books of the Year by the American Institute of Graphic Arts, 1974; grants, National Endowment for the Arts, 1976 and 1987; Creative Artists' Public Service Award, 1977, for poetry; Lewis Carroll Shelf awards, 1977, for *Sailing to Cythera and Other Anatole Stories,* and 1979, for *The Island of the Grass King: The Further Adventures of Anatole;* Art Books for Children citation from Brooklyn Museum and Brooklyn Public Library, 1978, for *Simple Pictures Are Best; The Marzipan Moon* was named a *New York Times* Outstanding Book, 1981; Golden Kite fiction honor book, 1981, and Newbery Medal, *Boston Globe/Horn Book* Award for Illustration, and American Book Award nomination, children's picture book, Asso-

NANCY WILLARD

ciation of American Publishers, all 1982, all for *A Visit to William Blake's Inn: Poems for Innocent and Experienced Travelers;* National Book Critics Circle Award nomination, 1989, for *Water Walker.*

WRITINGS:

FICTION FOR CHILDREN

Sailing to Cythera and Other Anatole Stories, illustrated by David McPhail, Harcourt, 1974.

The Snow Rabbit, illustrated by Laura Lydecker, Putnam, 1975.

Shoes without Leather, illustrated by Lydecker, Putnam, 1976.

The Well-Mannered Balloon, illustrated by Haig Shekerjian and Regina Shekerjian, Harcourt, 1976.

Simple Pictures Are Best, illustrated by Tomie de Paola, Harcourt, 1977.

Strangers' Bread, illustrated by McPhail, Harcourt, 1977.

The Highest Hit, illustrated by Emily McCully, Harcourt, 1978.

The Island of the Grass King: The Further Adventures of Anatole, illustrated by McPhail, Harcourt, 1979.

Papa's Panda, illustrated by Lillian Hoban, Harcourt, 1979.

The Marzipan Moon, illustrated by Marcia Sewall, Harcourt, 1981.

Uncle Terrible: More Adventures of Anatole, illustrated by McPhail, Harcourt, 1982.

The Nightgown of the Sullen Moon, illustrated by McPhail, Harcourt, 1983.

The Mountains of Quilt, illustrated by de Paola, Harcourt, 1987.

Firebrat, illustrated by David Wiesner, Knopf, 1988.

The High Rise Glorious Skittle Skat Roarious Sky Pie Angel Food Cake, illustrated by Richard Jesse Watson, Harcourt, 1990.

Pish Posh, Said Hieronymus Bosch, illustrated by Leo Dillon and Diane Dillon, Harcourt, 1992.

POETRY FOR CHILDREN

The Merry History of a Christmas Pie: With a Delicious Description of a Christmas Soup, illustrated by H. Shekerjian and R. Shekerjian, Putnam, 1974.

All on a May Morning, illustrated by H. Shekerjian and R. Shekerjian, Putnam, 1975.

A Visit to William Blake's Inn: Poems for Innocent and Experienced Travelers, illustrated by Alice Provensen and Martin Provensen, Harcourt, 1981.

Night Story, illustrated by Ilse Plume, Harcourt, 1986.

The Voyage of the Ludgate Hill: A Journey with Robert Louis Stevenson, illustrated by A. Provensen and M. Provensen, Harcourt, 1987.

The Ballad of Biddy Early, illustrated by Barry Moser, Knopf, 1989.

FOR ADULTS

In His Country: Poems, Generation (Ann Arbor, MI), 1966.

Skin of Grace (poetry), University of Missouri Press, 1967.

In *Sailing to Cythera,* Willard chronicles the adventures of young Anatole and his visits to a magical and mysterious secret world. (Illustration by David McPhail.)

A New Herball: Poems, Ferdinand-Roter Gallerias, 1968.

The Lively Anatomy of God (short stories), Eakins, 1968.

Testimony of the Invisible Man: William Carlos Williams, Francis Ponge, Rainer Maria Rilke, Pablo Neruda (criticism), University of Missouri Press, 1970.

Nineteen Masks for the Naked Poet: Poems (also see below), Kayak, 1971.

Childhood of the Magician (short stories), Liveright, 1973.

The Carpenter of the Sun: Poems (includes poems from *Nineteen Masks for the Naked Poet*), Liveright, 1974.

Household Tales of Moon and Water (poetry), Harcourt, 1982.

Angel in the Parlor: Five Stories and Eight Essays, Harcourt, 1983.

Things Invisible to See (novel), Knopf, 1984.

Water Walker (poetry), Knopf, 1989.

Sister Water (novel), Knopf, in press.

ILLUSTRATOR

John Kater, *The Letter of John to James,* Seabury, 1981.

J. Kater, *Another Letter of John to James,* Seabury, 1982.

Robert Pack, *The Octopus Who Wanted to Juggle,* Galileo, 1990.

OTHER

East of the Sun, West of the Moon (play), illustrated by Barry Moser, Harcourt, 1989.

A Nancy Willard Reader: Selected Poetry and Prose, edited by Robert Pack and Jay Parini, University Press of New England, 1991.

Beauty and the Beast, illustrated by Moser, Harcourt, 1992.

Contributor to periodicals, including *Antioch Review, Cricket, Esquire, Horn Book, Massachusetts Review, Michigan Quarterly Review, New Yorker, Redbook,* and *Writer.*

Willard's papers are housed in the special collection at the University of Michigan Library and the Kerlan Collection at the University of Minnesota.

ADAPTATIONS: A Visit to William Blake's Inn was adapted as a filmstrip by Random House, *The Nightgown of the Sullen Moon* was adapted as a filmstrip with a cassette, read by Zoe Caldwell, and as a videocassette, both by Random House, and the Anatole trilogy and *Things Invisible to See* were adapted as audiocassettes by Recorded Books.

SIDELIGHTS: Known for both her poetry and her fiction, Nancy Willard is a versatile writer whose poetic gifts for observation, imagination, and expression win praise in many genres. Her books have also received numerous awards, including the first Newbery Medal ever to honor a poetry volume. A wife and mother, Willard celebrates even the ordinary parts of domestic life with wonder and insight in her poetry, and vivid flights of imagination carry her fiction into magical realms. According to *Dictionary of Literary Biography* contributors E. Charles Vousden and Laura Ingram, "Everything she writes affirms her belief in the 'magic view of life'; that is, a view of life that incorporates the imagination and stresses the appropriateness of things meant to be taken metaphorically."

Imagination and creativity were part of Willard's life from childhood, and she learned early to translate ideas into words and pictures. As a three-year-old she had a dream she wanted to remember; when she later learned to read and write she committed it to paper in the first of many dream notes. Art developed her visual creativity. Willard sketched her childhood friends, illustrated her own stories, and painted angels, mermaids, and other figures over cracks in her home's plaster walls. During summers near a Michigan lake, Willard and her sister printed their own newspaper, interviewing neighbors for news. In a *Publishers Weekly* interview with Sybil Steinberg, Willard remarked that this experience "taught me a lot about listening. These people could not have *written* the stories they told me, but they could *tell* them. So listening—hearing the story—has always been as important to me as reading."

A enchanted candy moon causes problems for a priest in Willard's *The Marzipan Moon.* (Illustration by Marcia Sewall.)

In addition to listening to the tales of neighbors and relatives, Willard read widely. Her family's books included classics such as Lewis Carroll's "Alice in Wonderland" stories, George MacDonald's fantasies, and the "Oz" series by L. Frank Baum, which became lasting favorites, as well as a previous resident's etiquette guides, staid Victorian novels, and a children's physiology book that said magic dwarves controlled the functions of the human body. "To me," she commented in *Writer,* "these books were as exotic as the descriptions of court life in 'The Sleeping Beauty' or 'Cinderella.'"

Willard's extensive reading of fantasy, her heritage as the daughter of a prominent chemist, and her acquaintance with people who believed in psychic experiences all helped her recognize that there was more than one way to view life. "I grew up aware of two ways of looking at the world that are opposed to each other and yet can exist side by side in the same person," she explained in *Writer.* "One is the scientific view. The other is the magic view. Most of us grow up and put magic away with our other childish things. But I think we can all remember a time when magic was as real to us as science, and the things we couldn't see were as important as the things we could. I call this belief in the power of the invisible, the magic view of life. And I believe that all small children and some adults hold this view together with the scientific one. I also believe that the great books for children come from those writers who hold both."

The magic worldview fills Willard's writing. In her well-known stories about Anatole, a character named after her son, a boy makes mystical journeys to fantastic lands, meets wizards and various intelligent animal characters, and takes part in struggles between good and evil. *The Marzipan Moon* shows how a wish magically—or miraculously—comes true, only to be ruined by human greed. And Willard's first adult novel, *Things Invisible to See,* begins with a bargain made between twins before their birth and includes a cosmic baseball game between the forces of life and death. Critics also found magic in her children's poetry volume *A Visit to William Blake's Inn: Poems for Innocent and Experienced Travelers,* which discusses events at an enchanted inn in both lyrical poems and nonsense verse.

In a career spanning more than twenty-five years, Willard has distinguished herself with her "effortless meshing of the concrete and metaphysical," wrote Steinberg in *Publishers Weekly.* Taking details from her own life, she transforms them in poetry and prose into glimpses of other worlds. Never condescending to her readers, she includes complex concepts and allusions even though they may be beyond the reach of many children. Willard believes that "children's books should be big enough for children to grow into," as she stated in a *Horn Book* essay. Indeed, reviewers assert that Willard's books for children also hold rewards for adults. In a *New York Times* review of *Things Invisible to See,* Michiko Kakutani noted a quality of her work that helps explain such broad appeal, observing that Willard crosses "the gap between the real and the fantastic ... nimbly and without the slightest trace of self-con-

sciousness or guile." As Willard herself commented in her *Publishers Weekly* interview: "I'm simply writing another kind of truth. I think for most questions there are two kinds of answers, the scientific and the mythic. My writing comes out of the second kind."

WORKS CITED:

Kakutani, Michiko, "The Real and Fantastic," *New York Times,* January 12, 1985, p. 13.
Steinberg, Sybil, "PW Interviews: Nancy Willard," *Publishers Weekly,* December 14, 1984, pp. 58-59.
Vousden, E. Charles, and Laura Ingram, "Nancy Willard," *Dictionary of Literary Biography,* Volume 52: *American Writers for Children since 1960: Fiction,* Gale, 1986, pp. 386-92.
Willard, Nancy, "The Spinning Room: Symbols and Storytellers," *Horn Book,* October, 1980, pp. 555-64.
Willard, Nancy, "Magic, Craft, and the Making of Children's Books," *Writer,* April, 1981, pp. 17-19.

FOR MORE INFORMATION SEE:

BOOKS

Children's Literature Review, Volume 5, Gale, 1983, pp. 243-50.
Contemporary Literary Criticism, Gale, Volume 12, 1977, Volume 37, 1986, pp. 461-66.
Dictionary of Literary Biography, Volume 5: *American Poets since World War II,* Gale, 1980, pp. 396-402.
Twentieth-Century Children's Writers, 3rd edition, St. James Press, 1989, pp. 1048-50.

PERIODICALS

Horn Book, August, 1982, pp. 369-79.
Los Angeles Times, November 29, 1981.
Los Angeles Times Book Review, January 20, 1985.
New Yorker, December 7, 1981.
New York Times Book Review, September 25, 1977; May 21, 1978; May 27, 1979; July 12, 1981; November 15, 1981; October 23, 1983; February 3, 1985; July 12, 1987; November 8, 1987, p. 50; September 25, 1988; July 9, 1989.
Publishers Weekly, February 26, 1988, p. 117.
Times Literary Supplement, March 26, 1982.
Voice Literary Supplement, December, 1989.
Washington Post, January 9, 1984.
Washington Post Book World, December 2, 1990, p. 3.

OTHER

Meet the Newbery Author: Nancy Willard (filmstrip and audiocassette), Random House, c. 1984.

—Sketch by Polly A. Vedder

*   *   *

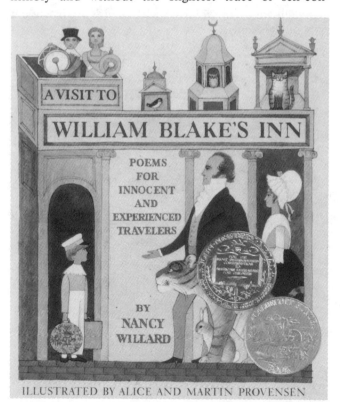

Willard's Newbery Award-winning poetry collection features William Blake as the proprietor of an inn where bewitched plants and animals mingle with guests. (Cover illustration by Alice and Martin Provensen.)

WILLHOITE, Michael A. 1946-

PERSONAL: Born July 3, 1946, in Hobart, OK; son of Ray Thomas and Shirley Elizabeth (Banks) Willhoite. *Education:* Oklahoma State University, B.F.A., 1968. *Politics:* Liberal Democrat. *Religion:* Secular Humanist.

MICHAEL A. WILLHOITE

ADDRESSES: Agent—c/o Publicity Director, Alyson Publications, 40 Plimpton St., Boston, MA 02118.

CAREER: Free-lance illustrator. United States Navy, Bethesda, MD, medical and general illustrator, 1973-81; Natick Research and Development Center, Natick, MA, audio visual specialist, 1981—. Member of Vokes Players (theater group).

AWARDS, HONORS: Lambda Literary Award, 1991, for *Daddy's Roommate.*

WRITINGS:

SELF-ILLUSTRATED

Now for My Next Trick (cartoons), Alyson, 1986.
Daddy's Roommate, Alyson, 1990.
Families: A Coloring Book, Alyson, 1991.
The Entertainer, Alyson, 1992.

Also author and illustrator of the *1990 Gay Desk Calendar.*

ILLUSTRATOR

Terry Boughner, *Out of All Time,* Independent School Press, 1988.
Leslea Newman, *Belinda's Bouquet,* Alyson Publications, 1991.

Also illustrator of *Painting with Words,* Independent School Press.

Willhoite recreates the excitement of big city living in his self-illustrated *The Entertainer.*

WORK IN PROGRESS: Three children's books with topics ranging from uncles to music.

SIDELIGHTS: Michael A. Willhoite told *SATA:* "All I ever wanted to be was an artist, almost before I could walk.... My earliest drawings were cartoons— or were taken from cartoons—and so my course was set." Willhoite was raised by his grandparents; from an early age, he was encouraged to draw by his grandfather. "As I showed a very early talent for drawing, [my grandfather] brought home reams, stacks, *bundles* of outdated forms, the backs, blessedly, blank," Willhoite recalled. "Perhaps this boon was the major spur to my creativity. Or perhaps my natural aptitude would have found another outlet."

The adults in Willhoite's family were staunch believers in reading to children. As a result, Willhoite became a "full-throttle devourer of books." He wrote his first story at age six. Willhoite remembered that the tale "consisted of a single sentence: 'Once there was a egg.' I proudly showed my grandmother my beginning sentence. She calmly explained the use of *an* before a word beginning with a vowel. I was so impressed by this early lesson in grammar that I didn't finish the tale."

As he grew up, Willhoite became more and more interested in caricature. "I practiced ... and strove to evolve my own style," he commented. By the 1970s, Willhoite had found an outlet for his creativity. "After years of denial I had finally come to realize that I was irrevocably gay," he noted. "I submitted cartoons and caricatures to a weekly gay newspaper, the *Washington Blade.* To this day, my work still appears there regularly." Eventually, Willhoite's cartoons became the basis for his first book entitled *Now for My Next Trick.*

Over time, Willhoite turned his attention to writing children's books, including *Daddy's Roommate,* and *Families,* and illustrating the work of others, such as Leslea Newman's *Belinda's Bouquet. Daddy's Roommate* depicted a father's divorce and subsequent cohabitation with another man. The author observed: "This book, virtually the first of its kind, was received with much media attention, overwhelmingly positive." In his work for both *Families* and *Belinda's Bouquet,* Willhoite presented other types of families—"nuclear and non-, ... gay and lesbian, interracial, and generally multicultural." "I'm pleased that my books so far have addressed 'issues,'" Willhoite related, "but I don't want to become known as merely a didactic writer. In illustration I can move from style to style with ease, so I feel there is no limit to what I may yet lay pen and brush to, in my own writings or those of others."

*   *   *

WILLIAMS, (Marcia) Dorothy 1945-

PERSONAL: Born August 8, 1945, in England; daughter of Martin Innes Gregson (an army officer) and Joan Alexander Carnwath (a writer); married Tudor Williams, February 21, 1976 (separated); children: Aramin-

DOROTHY WILLIAMS

ta Scarfe, Rufus Williams. *Education:* Educated in England and Switzerland.

ADDRESSES: Office—Walker Books, Ltd., 87 Vauxhall Walk, London SE11 5HJ, England.

CAREER: Free-lance writer and illustrator of children's books, 1986— .

WRITINGS:

SELF-ILLUSTRATED

The First Christmas, Walker Books, 1987.
The Amazing Story of Noah's Ark, Walker Books, 1988.
When I Was Little, Walker Books, 1989.
Jonah and the Whale, Walker Books, 1989.
Not a Worry in the World, Walker Books, 1990.
Joseph and His Magnificent Coat of Many Colors, Walker Books, 1990.
Greek Myths for Young Children, Walker Books, 1991.

WORK IN PROGRESS: The Adventures of Don Quixote, 1993; *Tales from the Thousand and One Nights.*

SIDELIGHTS: Dorothy Williams told *SATA:* "When I was a child, my parents lived abroad and I was sent to boarding school. Instead of the mandatory Sunday letter, I used to send home illustrated diaries and poems of the week's events; this is where my career began." Williams's mother was a writer with a passion for books who would often read to her daughter, mostly classics and mythology. "I found Proust and the Greek myths a little hard going," Williams remarked. "I was delighted, therefore, to discover later that many of these stories were exciting and amusing. I think this is why I enjoy making classic tales accessible to young children."

Williams's stories are usually based on something that she has seen or overheard. She related: "*When I Was*

Little, for example, was written after a visit to a Beatrix Potter exhibition. It was there that I heard a grandmother saying to her grandchildren, just as mine had said to me, 'When I was little....' I get enormous pleasure from the work involved in producing the stories and pictures for one of my books; I hope that some of it will be passed on to the reader!"

* * *

WILLIAMS, Suzanne (Bullock) 1953-

PERSONAL: Born April 28, 1953, in Eugene, OR; daughter of Charles James (a nurseryman and mail carrier) and Vivienne Hannah (a grade school teacher) Bullock; married Mark Williams, August 17, 1974; children: Ward, Emily. *Education:* University of Oregon, B.S., 1975, M.L.S., 1976; additional study at Seattle Pacific University and the University of Washington.

ADDRESSES: Agent—c/o Publicity Director, Houghton Mifflin Company, One Beacon St., Boston, MA 02108.

CAREER: Writer. Elementary school librarian in Washington state, 1976—.

MEMBER: Society of Children's Book Writers, Washington Education Association, Washington Library Media Association.

SUZANNE WILLIAMS

WRITINGS:

Mommy Doesn't Know My Name, Houghton Mifflin, 1990.
Library Lil, Bantam, 1993.

WORK IN PROGRESS: Picture books; a realistic young adult novel; a cookbook.

SIDELIGHTS: Suzanne Williams told *SATA:* "I didn't grow up knowing that I wanted to be a writer. I enjoyed the writing I did in school, but I didn't write for the school newspaper and I wasn't on the yearbook staff or anything like that. I came to want to write through reading. I was (and still am) a voracious reader. My parents read to me at an early age, and we visited the public library often." Williams's reading tastes covered many genres and authors. She enjoyed reading so much that it was often difficult for her parents to get her attention once she began a new book.

After graduating from high school, Williams went to college and studied sociology; unfortunately, her degree did not really prepare her for a career. At her father's suggestion, Williams took up library science. After getting married, moving to Washington state, and working as an elementary school librarian, Williams's thoughts again turned to writing. She began to keep a journal, chronicling everything from trips to Europe and China to the birth of her children.

Williams eventually enrolled in a writing course to refine her skills. "I learned the basics," she noted, "how to develop characters, write description and dialogue, and how to submit work to publishers." Williams's newfound skills came in handy when she began work on *Mommy Doesn't Know My Name,* which was based on the experience of her daughter Emily. Williams plans to keep on writing and getting her inspiration from things around her. She remarked: "I believe all writing is autobiographical, in some sense of the word.... No one writes out of a vacuum."

* * *

WOYCHUK, Denis 1953-

PERSONAL: Born July 16, 1953, in Brooklyn, NY; son of Ignatz and Ruth (an economist; maiden name, Entes) Woychuk. *Education:* State University of New York at Stony Brook, B.A., 1974; Brooklyn College, M.F.A., 1976; Fordham University School of Law, J.D., 1984.

ADDRESSES: Office—33 West 63rd St., New York, NY 10023. *Agent*—Kendra Marcus, Bookstop, 67 Meadow View Rd., Orinda, CA 94563.

CAREER: Writer. British Open School, Bristol, England, elementary school teacher, 1974; writing instructor at numerous colleges in New York City, 1976-84; art dealer and theatrical producer, New York City, 1984-88; attorney, New York City, 1988—.

DENIS WOYCHUK

WRITINGS:

The Other Side of the Wall, Lothrop, 1991.
Pirates, Lothrup, 1991.

Also contributor to periodicals, including the *New York Times, Penthouse,* and *Fordham International Law Journal.*

WORK IN PROGRESS: Mousey's Cat, Kitty, an adventure tale; *Friends of the Feast,* a woodland rhyme; *Borzoi Boy* and *Tommy's Tummy Goes Boom, Boom, Boom;* also researching psychiatric law, the insanity plea, and "issues of responsibility to and within society."

SIDELIGHTS: Denis Woychuk tells *SATA:* "I have always wanted to write books. I made my first serious attempt at age eight, a non-fiction interpretation of my father's childhood in war-ravaged Europe. It ran ten or so pages. I was very proud. But it wasn't until I was much older, practically eighteen, that I decided I wanted to write picture books. They had a tremendous appeal to me because they were ... so short, so exciting. In eight hundred words or a thousand words, the writer must convey not only the beginning, but the middle *and* the end."

As a child, Woychuk was more concerned with having fun than studying. He spent a lot of time making books from cut-up magazines and creating science projects. By the time he had finished college, Woychuk had written several manuscripts for children's books; unfortunately, it was years before any of these works were published. In the interim, Woychuk became a lawyer, an art dealer, a producer, and a businessman. His advice to other aspiring writers is simple. "Remember," he advises, "life has many secrets to tell, so listen closely."

Cumulative Indexes

Illustrations Index

(In the following index, the number of the volume in which an illustrator's work appears is given *before* the colon, and the page number on which it appears is given *after* the colon. For example, a drawing by Adams, Adrienne appears in Volume 2 on page 6, another drawing by her appears in Volume 3 on page 80, another drawing in Volume 8 on page 1, and another drawing in Volume 15 on page 107.)

YABC

Index citations including this abbreviation refer to listings appearing in *Yesterday's Authors of Books for Children,* also published by Gale Research Inc., which covers authors who died prior to 1960.

Author Index

The following index gives the number of the volume in which an author's biographical sketch, Brief Entry, or Obituary appears.

This index includes references to all entries in the following series, which are also published by Gale Research Inc.

YABC—*Yesterday's Authors of Books for Children: Facts and Pictures about Authors and Illustrators of Books for Young People from Early Times to 1960*

CLR—*Children's Literature Review: Excerpts from Reviews, Criticism, and Commentary on Books for Children*

SAAS—*Something about the Author Autobiography Series*

Ruzicka, Rudolph 1883-1978
  Obituary *24*
Ryan, Betsy
  See Ryan, Elizabeth (Anne)
Ryan, Cheli Durán *20*
Ryan, Elizabeth (Anne) 1943- *30*
Ryan, Jeanette Mines
  See Mines, Jeanette (Marie)
Ryan, John (Gerald Christopher)
  1921- *22*
Ryan, Mary E(lizabeth) 1953- *61*
Ryan, Peter (Charles) 1939- *15*
Rybolt, Thomas R(oy) 1954- *62*
Rydberg, Ernest E(mil) 1901- *21*
Rydberg, Lou(isa Hampton) 1908- *27*
Rydell, Wendell
  See Rydell, Wendy
Rydell, Wendy *4*
Ryden, Hope *8*
Ryder, Joanne (Rose) 1946- *65*
  Brief Entry *34*
Rye, Anthony
  See Youd, (Christopher) Samuel
Rylant, Cynthia 1954- *50*
  Brief Entry *44*
  See also CLR *15*
  See also SAAS *13*
Rymer, Alta May 1925- *34*

S

S., Svend Otto
  See Soerensen, Svend Otto
Saal, Jocelyn
  See Sachs, Judith
Saberhagen, Fred (Thomas) 1930- *37*
Sabin, Edwin Legrand 1870-1952
  See YABC *2*
Sabin, Francene *27*
Sabin, Louis 1930- *27*
Sabre, Dirk
  See Laffin, John (Alfred Charles)
Sabuso
  See Phillips, Irving W.
Sachar, Louis 1954- *63*
  Brief Entry *50*
  See also CLR *28*
Sachs, Elizabeth-Ann 1946- *48*
Sachs, Judith 1947- *52*
  Brief Entry *51*
Sachs, Marilyn 1927- *52*
  Earlier sketch in SATA *3*
  See also CLR *2*
  See also SAAS *2*
Sachs, Marilyn (Stickle) 1927- *68*
Sackett, S(amuel) J(ohn) 1928- *12*
Sackson, Sid 1920- *16*
Saddler, Allen
  See Richards, R(onald) C(harles)
  W(illiam)
Saddler, K. Allen
  See Richards, R(onald) C(harles)
  W(illiam)
Sadie, Stanley (John) 1930- *14*
Sadler, Catherine Edwards 1952- *60*
  Brief Entry *45*
Sadler, Mark
  See Lynds, Dennis
Sagan, Carl 1934- *58*
Sage, Juniper [Joint pseudonym]
  See Brown, Margaret Wise and Hurd,
  Edith
Sagsoorian, Paul 1923- *12*
Saida
  See LeMair, H(enriette) Willebeek
Saint, Dora Jessie 1913- *10*
St. Briavels, James
  See Wood, James Playsted
St. Clair, Byrd Hooper 1905-1976
  Obituary *28*
Saint Exupéry, Antoine de 1900-1944 ...*20*
  See also CLR *10*
St. George, Judith 1931- *13*
  See also SAAS *12*

St. John, Nicole
  See Johnston, Norma
  See also SAAS *7*
St. John, Philip
  See Del Rey, Lester
St. John, Wylly Folk 1908-1985 ....*10*
  Obituary *45*
St. Meyer, Ned
  See Stratemeyer, Edward L.
St. Tamara
  See Kolba, Tamara
Saito, Michiko
  See Fujiwara, Michiko
Sakharnov, S.
  See Sakharnov, Svyatoslav
  (Vladimirovich)
Sakharnov, Svyatoslav (Vladimirovich)
  1923- *65*
Salassi, Otto R(ussell) 1939- *38*
Saldutti, Denise 1953- *39*
Salinger, J(erome) D(avid) 1919- *67*
  See also CLR *18*
Salkey, (Felix) Andrew (Alexander)
  1928- *35*
Sallis, Susan (Diana) 1929- *55*
Salmon, Annie Elizabeth 1899- *13*
Salten, Felix
  See Salzmann, Siegmund
Salter, Cedric
  See Knight, Francis Edgar
Saltman, Judith 1947- *64*
Salvadori, Mario (George) 1907- *40*
Salzer, L. E.
  See Wilson, Lionel
Salzman, Yuri
  Brief Entry *42*
Salzmann, Siegmund 1869-1945 ....*25*
Samachson, Dorothy 1914- *3*
Samachson, Joseph 1906-1980 ....*3*
  Obituary *52*
Sammis, John 1942- *4*
Sampson, Emma (Keats) Speed
  1868-1947 ....*68*
Sampson, Fay (Elizabeth) 1935- *42*
  Brief Entry *40*
Samson, Anne S(tringer) 1933- *2*
Samson, Joan 1937-1976 ....*13*
Samuels, Charles 1902- *12*
Samuels, Gertrude *17*
Sanborn, Duane 1914- *38*
Sancha, Sheila 1924- *38*
Sanchez, Sonia 1934- *22*
  See also CLR *18*
Sanchez Alzada, Juan
  See Joseph, James (Herz)
Sánchez-Silva, José María 1911- *16*
  See also CLR *12*
Sand, George X. *45*
Sandak, Cass R(obert) 1950- *51*
  Brief Entry *37*
Sandberg, (Karin) Inger 1930- *15*
Sandberg, Karl C. 1931- *35*
Sandberg, Lasse (E. M.) 1924- *15*
Sandburg, Carl (August) 1878-1967 ....*8*
Sandburg, Charles A.
  See Sandburg, Carl (August)
Sandburg, Helga 1918- *3*
  See also SAAS *10*
Sanderlin, George 1915- *4*
Sanderlin, Owenita (Harrah) 1916- *11*
Sanders, Scott R(ussell) 1945- *56*
Sanders, Winston P.
  See Anderson, Poul (William)
Sanderson, Irma 1912- *66*
Sanderson, Ivan T. 1911-1973 ....*6*
Sanderson, Margaret Love
  See Sampson, Emma (Keats) Speed
Sanderson, Ruth (L.) 1951- *41*
Sandin, Joan 1942- *12*
Sandison, Janet
  See Cameron, Elizabeth Jane
Sandoz, Mari (Susette) 1901-1966 ....*5*
Sanford, Agnes (White) 1897-1976 ....*61*
Sanford, Doris 1937- *69*
Sanger, Marjory Bartlett 1920- *8*
Sankey, Alice (Ann-Susan) 1910- *27*
San Souci, Robert D. 1946- *40*

Santesson, Hans Stefan 1914(?)-1975
  Obituary *30*
Sapieyevski, Anne Lindbergh 1940- *35*
Sarac, Roger
  See Caras, Roger A(ndrew)
Sarah, DUCHESS OF YORK
  See Ferguson, Sarah (Margaret)
Sarasin, Jennifer
  See Sachs, Judith
Sarg, Anthony Fredrick
  See Sarg, Tony
Sarg, Tony 1880-1942
  See YABC *1*
Sargent, Pamela *29*
Sargent, Robert 1933- *2*
Sargent, Sarah 1937- *44*
  Brief Entry *41*
Sargent, Shirley 1927- *11*
Sari
  See Fleur, Anne
Sarnoff, Jane 1937- *10*
Saroyan, William 1908-1981 ....*23*
  Obituary *24*
Sarton, Eleanore Marie
  See Sarton, (Eleanor) May
Sarton, (Eleanor) May 1912- *36*
Saseen, Sharon (Dillon) 1949- *59*
Sasek, Miroslav 1916-1980 ....*16*
  Obituary *23*
  See also CLR *4*
Satchwell, John
  Brief Entry *49*
Sattler, Helen Roney 1921- *4*
  See also CLR *24*
Sauer, Julia (Lina) 1891-1983 ....*32*
  Obituary *36*
Saul, (E.) Wendy 1946- *42*
Saunders, Caleb
  See Heinlein, Robert A.
Saunders, Keith 1910- *12*
Saunders, Rubie (Agnes) 1929- *21*
Saunders, Susan 1945- *46*
  Brief Entry *41*
Savage, Blake
  See Goodwin, Harold L(eland)
Savage, Katharine James 1905-1989
  Obituary *61*
Savery, Constance (Winifred) 1897- *1*
Saville, (Leonard) Malcolm
  1901-1982 ....*23*
  Obituary *31*
Saviozzi, Adriana
  See Mazza, Adriana
Savitt, Sam *8*
Savitz, Harriet May 1933- *5*
  See also SAAS *9*
Sawyer, Ruth 1880-1970 ....*17*
Saxby, H. M.
  See Saxby, (Henry) Maurice
Saxby, (Henry) Maurice 1924- *71*
Saxon, Antonia
  See Sachs, Judith
Say, Allen 1937- *69*
  Earlier sketch in SATA *28*
  See also CLR *22*
Sayers, Frances Clarke 1897-1989 ....*3*
  Obituary *62*
Sazer, Nina 1949- *13*
Scabrini, Janet 1953- *13*
Scagnetti, Jack 1924- *7*
Scanlon, Marion Stephany *11*
Scannell, Vernon 1922- *59*
Scarf, Maggi
  See Scarf, Maggie
Scarf, Maggie 1932- *5*
Scarlett, Susan
  See Streatfeild, (Mary) Noel
Scarry, Huck
  See Scarry, Richard, Jr.
Scarry, Patricia (Murphy) 1924- *2*
Scarry, Patsy
  See Scarry, Patricia
Scarry, Richard, Jr. 1953- *35*
Scarry, Richard (McClure) 1919- *35*
  Earlier sketch in SATA *2*
  See also CLR *3*
Schachtel, Roger (Bernard) 1949- *38*